Intranet Working

George Eckel

William Steen

New Riders Publishing, Indianapolis, Indiana

Intranet Working

By George Eckel and William Steen

Published by:
New Riders Publishing
201 West 103rd Street
Indianapolis, IN 46290 USA

Printed in the United States of America 1 2 3 4 5 6 7 8 9 0

CIP data available upon request

Warning and Disclaimer

Publisher   *Don Fowley*

Publishing Manager   *Emmett Dulaney*

Marketing Manager   *Mary Foote*

Managing Editor   *Carla Hall*

Acquisitions Editor
Kristin Evan

Development Editor
Karen Scott

Project Editor
Jeff Durham

Copy Editor
Danica Matthew

Technical Editor
John Matthew

Associate Marketing Manager
Tamara Apple

Acquisitions Coordinator
Stacia Mellinger

Publisher's Assistant
Karen Opal

Cover Designer
Karen Ruggles

Book Designer
Sandra Schroeder

Production Manager
Kelly Dobbs

Production Team Supervisor
Laurie Casey

Graphics Image Specialists
Steve Adams
Brad Dixon
Sonja Hart
Todd Wente

Production Analysts
Jason Hand
Bobbi Satterfield

Production Team
Angela Calvert, Kim Cofer, Tricia Flodder, David Garratt, Erika Millen, Erich J. Richter, Christine Tyner

Indexer
Brad Herriman

About the Authors

William Steen is the author and co-author of a number of books from New Riders including *NetWare Security, Internet Security Professional Reference*, and *Managing the NetWare 3.x Server.*

He works as a Senior Customer Support Representative for BI, Inc., and also operates a consulting firm that specializes in providing networking solutions to city and county government offices. He is allergic to dogs and gets quite upset when people presumptuously bring their pets to visit.

George Eckel has worked on a number of books for Macmillan Publishing, including *Building a Linux Internet Server, Inside Windows NT Workstation,* and *Memory Management for All of Us.* As a professional writer, George has worked as a consultant for Hewlett-Packard, Sun Microsystems, Informix, AT&T, Time-Warner, and Silicon Graphics. Presently, he is part of the core team that developed and demonstrates the world's first interactive television system. George is now working on the Japanese (NTT) implementation of interactive television, and running a consulting business for companies setting up services on the Internet. You can reach him at geckel@warp.engr.sgi.com, or 510-820-5243.

George is the father of three children—Madeline, Nathalie, and Genevieve—and happy husband of Shirlee, whose patience and support helped make this book possible.

Trademark Acknowledgments

All terms mentioned in this book that are known to be trademarks or service marks have been appropriately capitalized. New Riders Publishing cannot attest to the accuracy of this information. Use of a term in this book should not be regarded as affecting the validity of any trademark or service mark.

Dedication

From George Eckel

In memorium for Nancy M. Eckel...

For all the lovely memories...

All the lovely times...

Until we are together again...

From William Steen

For my parents....thank you.

Acknowledgments

William Steen would like to thank all the people at New Riders who worked so diligently to make this book what it is. A special thanks to Emmett Dulaney for giving me a chance, and another, and another. Your guidance and encouragement, as always, were greatly appreciated.

About New Riders

New Riders is an imprint of Macmillan Computer Publishing USA (MCP), which includes QUE, Sams Publishing, Hayden Books, BradyGAMES, Sams.net, Ziff-Davis Press and Que Education and Training. MCP is a unit of Macmillan Publishing USA, a division of Simon and Schuster, the publishing operation of Viacom, Inc.

New Riders has emerged as the premier publisher of computer books for the serious, experienced computer user. The imprint is the world's leading NetWare publisher, and continues to provide professionals with expert advice on a variety of high-end topics and software. We concentrate on staying current and delivering the necessary depth and breadth of information our customers need. Whatever the task, New Riders provides the most authoritative, user-friendly tutorials and references to help its readers stay ahead of the dynamic marketplace. For mor e information on New Riders, explore our online resources. Our Internet site offers a listing of our most recent titles and a limited edition CNE Endeavor (a pracitical test engine aimed at measuring your knowledge). Vist our site at http://www.mcp.com/newriders (World Wide Web), gopher.mcp.com (Gopher), and ftp.mcp.com (FTP).

Contents at a Glance

Table of Contents

Part II: Services

7 Setting Up a WWW Service 165

8 Managing a WWW Service 189

12 Managing a freeWAIS Service   291

13 Setting Up a Gopher Service   311

Part III: Concerns

Introduction

To say that Intranets have become a "hot" topic is an understatement. It has bubbled out of the confines of computer user groups and become the common fare of individuals and workers in many corporations that use networked computers. The Intranet concept is showing up outside of computer sections in bookstores, magazines, and newspapers; it is appearing on the front pages of newspapers.

The Intranet has grown up with computer professionals and the wide spread adoption of the Internet. Its origins are in research and educational institutions, and its advocates and creative contributors, by and large, have been software engineers.

Businesses link to the Internet—the "Information Superhighway"—and see how easy it is to use and access information. They then ask why information on their own network cannot be that simple. The answer is that it can. All the server services available across the Internet are also available locally—on an Intranet—the subject of this book.

The use of Intranets and the Internet is exploding—the number of users is increasing at roughly five percent per month and businesses and the general public are awakening to the excitement and profit potential of the Information Superhighway. This growth can be attributed to lower costs, increased use of home computers, and the new Internet browsers capable of providing compelling presentations that enable users to navigate and retrieve information quickly and easily.

Pacific Bell
WWW site.

marketplace
MCI WWW
site.

Doneckers in marketplaceMCI.

How This Book Is Organized

As a business owner, it is important to understand the basic mechanics and the business applications of Intranets. As a system administrator, it is important to understand the tasks you need to complete to create Intranet services. This book is divided into three parts.

Part One: Overview

These chapters introduce you to Intranet technologies and describe how businesses can take advantage of them.

Part Two: Services

These chapters describe in detail how to offer and manage a variety of services, including an FTP service, a freeWAIS service, a Gopher service, or a World Wide Web service.

Part Three: Concerns

These two chapters discuss clients and security. Business owners and administrators should read these chapters.

All of the information in this book is, of course, time-stamped. Writing about moving targets is never easy. You might get frustrated if you find that software discussed in this book has been revised, or that some Internet addresses given no longer exist; such are the vagaries of Intranets or anything related to the Internet, and the hazards of writing about it.

New Riders Publishing

The staff of New Riders Publishing is committed to bringing you the very best in computer reference material. Each New Riders book is the result of months of work by authors and staff who research and refine the information contained within its covers.

As part of this commitment to you, the NRP reader, New Riders invites your input. Please let us know if you enjoy this book, if you have trouble with the information and examples presented, or if you have a suggestion for the next edition.

If you have a question or comment about any New Riders book, there are several ways to contact New Riders Publishing. We will respond to as many readers as we can. Your name, address, or phone number will never become part of a mailing list or be used for any purpose other than to help us continue to bring you the best books possible. You can write us at the following address:

> New Riders Publishing
> Attn: Associate Publisher
> 201 W. 103rd Street
> Indianapolis, IN 46290

If you prefer, you can fax New Riders Publishing at (317) 581-4670.

To send mail from the Internet, use the following address format:

    edulaney@newriders.mcp.com

NRP is an imprint of Macmillan Computer Publishing. To obtain a catalog or information, or to purchase any Macmillan Computer Publishing book, call (800)428-5331.

Thank you for selecting *Intranet Working*!

Part I

Overview

What Is an Intranet?

The following chapter barely scratches the surface of the technical sophistication of an Intranet. To offer an Intranet service, you do not need to know system architecture in detail, but you do need to know the basics of TCP/IP to have some idea how different connections work, and which type of connection your company should have.

Simply put, an Intranet is a combination of two technologies. The first is an area network—one that is confined to a company or companies, versus the whole world. The second is the ease of use found in the Internet, and predominately in the World Wide Web.

Local Area Networks and Wide Area Networks have been around for years. LANs and WANs allow PCs, minitowers, workstations, and mainframes to talk to one another. Rather than having to carry files around on floppy disks and transfer them from one place to another, instead, through the use of area networks, files on a server can be accessed by anyone at anytime. The drawback to area networks has always been that they are not the easiest things to install, administer, and use.

A few years ago, the Internet, which had been in existence for decades, came to the forefront of many minds. Suddenly, the number of users on it exponentially doubled every few months. Coupled with this came the invention of graphical browsers—front ends that allowed a user to avoid the command line and easily find what they sought by following a graphical route. Links lead a user from one location, or set of information, to another in an easy to follow pattern.

It did not take much thought for administrators to see the value in combining the ease of use of the Internet (mainly the Web) with the files and services available on their own area network. By making the information on the network easier to access and find, you eliminate a number of user problems and increase efficiency. Such marriages of graphical technology and networks is dubbed an Intranet.

To illustrate the value of such, imagine a large corporation. The large corporation has an employee manual defining how employees are to conduct business. The corporation wants to make the manual available to all employees electronically. Under the scenario of a wide area network, the corporation places it on the Human Resources server. Now, an employee logs on to their own server, attaches to the HR server, and maps a drive to the HR server. Next, the employee switches to that drive, runs File Manager, DIR, or some other utility to find a filename resembling the manual and brings it up in their word processor. After finding it, and reading it or printing it, the employee unmaps from the drive and cancels the attach.

With an Intranet, the employee brings up their browser, sets their URL to HR, and can see a list of contents available. Then by clicking on the manual, it is graphically displayed for them. The savings in time, frustration, and efficiency is immeasurable.

Because much of this technology is a result of the Internet, you will see Intranet and Internet often used interchangeably. The thing to know is that the only major difference between them is that an Intranet does not leave the company while the Internet does.

A Brief Introduction to TCP/IP

This discussion of TCP/IP barely scratches the surface of the topic, leaving the majority of the material for a later chapter. You do need to know the basics at this point, though, if you want to understand what is going on.

Actually, TCP/IP is a *suite* of protocols, the most important of which are Internet Protocol (IP) and Transfer Control Protocol (TCP). The following sections talk about each of these and one more, User Datagram Protocol (UDP).

IP

IP chops up a message (the data stream) into packages, called packets (usually around 200 bytes each), wraps each packet up to make it easy to carry, and then labels its contents and destination, as shown in figure 1.1.

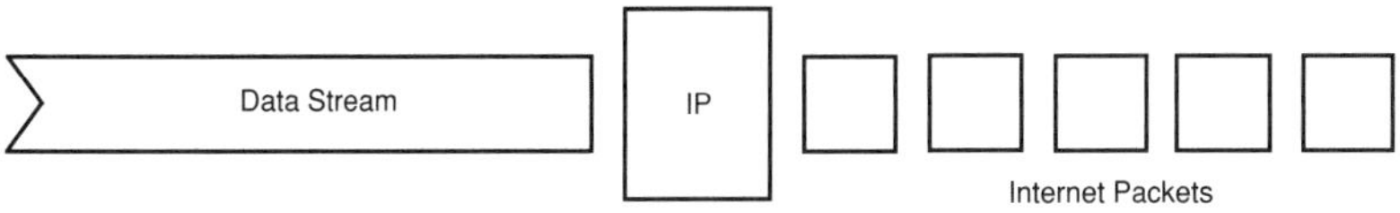

| Data Stream | IP | | | | | |

Internet Packets

Figure 1.1

IP makes packets.

Suppose, for example, that you want to look at a document that is on a remote server. After you request the letter be sent to you, IP chops the document into pieces, wraps up each piece, and sends the pieces. Strangely enough, IP is not very reliable. It does not guarantee that all of the pieces of a message will reach their destination, nor does IP make sure that all of the packets will line up in the correct sequential order.

Pathways lead from one router to another. The shortest route, however, is not always the fastest. Network load and network failures help determine the path that a message takes as it routes from the server to the client. As the remote server transmits the document over the wire one packet at a time, the second packet might find a quicker path to reach your computer than the first packet. Consequently, the second packet arrives before the first packet.

 Note A client is an application that sends requests, such as performing a function. A service is an application that (sometimes) runs on a different computer that fulfills the request. If the client and service are on different machines, as they are in the case of the Internet, then the connection between the two is carried out by stub files and the network.

The client address is one of the things IP puts on the packet. Computer addresses are 32-bit numbers. To make things simpler, these 32-bit addresses are split into four groups of eight binary numbers, separated by periods. The following is an example of a 32-bit address:

```
10101010.10101010.10101010.10101010
```

Each group translates into a decimal number between 0 and 256. A full address looks like the following:

```
12.24.132.112
```

The address is called a *dotted octet*, because each decimal number represents an 8-bit binary number.

Each computer has an address (one 32-bit binary number represents roughly 4.3 billion addresses). Your company, for example, might have an address that begins with 12. If, for some reason, the Internet reserved 12 for only your company, any message sent by any computer in the world that had an address that began with 12 would be routed to your site. If you are only going to use the Intranet within your corporation and do not foresee ever connecting to the Internet, then the only rule you must follow is that each server must have a unique address within the network. If you foresee the possibility of connecting to the outside world (the Internet), then the numbers need to be unique not only within your corporation, but throughout the world.

Suppose you had two subnetworks on your local network. Each would be given a different subnet address (the middle two three-digit, decimal numbers), for example, 12.123.234 and 12.123.235. We have come from the entire Internet to your network with the first number, 12, and now to the specific subnet in your company's local network, either 12,123.234 or 12.123.235. Each computer on each subnet is identified by the last of the four decimal numbers. (If you have more computers on a subnet than numbers (256), you need to make a new subnet.) At last, the packets, with IP packages, find the intended recipient.

The addressing scheme is hierarchical, which makes it easy to use. Routers only have to have a table of all the networks on the Internet, that is, they only have to use the first of the four numbers to send a message. The local router has to figure out which computer on the local network should receive the Internet message. If routers had to keep track of every computer on the Internet, they would have to use a pretty big table.

Note   The route a packet takes from the server to the target computer can be updated dynamically. During its transmission, a packet might travel through 30 routers before finding its way to the target computer, and at each router the message can take one of many courses. This is called *connectionless routing*.

Some packet-switching networks, however, are connection-oriented (X.25 networks, for example). Before a transmission begins, a fixed route is defined between the server and target; the route is not dynamically updated.

A connection-oriented network taxes router memory and requires routing calculations. Connectionless networks do not tax router memory, however—routing calculations are performed by every router along the transmission path.

TCP

Because of network peculiarities, all of the packets might come to the target computer totally out of sequence. Here is where TCP comes in. TCP puts the packets in their correct order and determines whether all of the packets arrived. How can TCP do this?

Hidden in the address information of each packet is a sequence number. IP simply increments it as each packet is mailed out. TCP uses these sequence numbers to put the packets into sequence and determine if any are missing. If one packet is detoured to Timbuktu for some reason, TCP sends a message to the remote computer to resend the missing packet. TCP keeps asking for packets until they arrive. Once all of the packets arrive, they are merged back into the steady stream of data they began as on the remote server.

TCP adds one additional layer of organization to the incoming messages: it sorts messages by port numbers. IP numbers identify specific computers; port numbers identify specific services running on the same computer. Port numbers are 16-bit, which range roughly from 0 to 65,000, with port numbers less than 1024 reserved for services. Because you might have more than one service running on your computer, the port number makes sure the message goes to the right one. On the same server, for example, you might have such multiple services running as Gopher, WAIS, WWW, Telnet, and so on.

A de facto standard exists for some port numbers. Port number 20 is used for FTP services, for example; port 70 is used for Gopher; and port 80 is used for HTTP (WWW) services.

UDP

The IP and TCP protocols facilitate communications. At times, you can get away without using the TCP protocol. If the message to be sent can fit in a single packet (200 bytes), there is no need to reorder anything. In this case, you can dispense with TCP and use the UDP protocol.

The UDP protocol sorts things by port number so that messages can reach the correct service on the server. UDP port numbers, however, are not equal to TCP port numbers. TCP 50, for example, does not go to the same service, necessarily, as UDP 50, unless you set up a server to specifically go to a particular service.

UDP performs one other optional service: it checks to see if the data in the packet was somehow changed in transit. This checking is called *checksumming*. The problem is, however, that this service slows down performance—so people often turn it off.

Naming Addresses

Dotted octet numbers make 32-bit addresses a lot easier to handle. Still, remembering dotted octet numbers is not exactly easy. When you want to e-mail someone, it can be a problem if you have to remember that Bob's address is 12.123.234.111. The Domain Name Service (DNS) solves the recall problem by allowing you to use, for example, Bob's name as the address.

DNS maintains a table that maps Intranet or Internet addresses, such as 12.123.234.111, to names, such as warp.engr.sgi.com. Such names can be longer or shorter, but the order of the parts of the name, separated by periods, follows a common logic. The name parts proceed from most specific to least specific, as you move from the first to last parts of the name. The first name is often the name of the computer. The next part is generally the subnet the computer is on. The second-to-last name part is often the company's name, and the last name part describes the kind of company it is, as shown in figure 1.2.

Figure 1.2

Parts of a name.

Extension	Description
.edu	Educational institutions
.com	Commercial sites
.mil	Military installations
.net	Service providers

Occasionally, you will see a final two-letter code that identifies the country the server is in. Country codes are standardized in the International Standards Organization's document ISO 3166.

A server that can tell you an IP address if you give it a domain name is called a *domain name server*. DNS clients ask these servers to return IP addresses for specified domain names. In completing its tasks, one DNS may ask another DNS for help, and so on, until an answer is found and a reply is sent to the DNS client.

You can also make an alias for a domain name. If, for example, you want to make a service on a server, serverName, available to FTP and WWW servers, you could create the aliases ftp.some.machine and www.some.machine, both of which point to the same server, serverName.some.machine.

Big Brother: inetd

It is great that you can put 65,000 (or even 10) services on the same server. Each service, however, eats up a chunk of memory. What works best is to start a service only when it has a pending request, and to terminate it when a reply is sent to the client making the request. The problem is, how does a service know when to wake up?

The wake up call is inetd's job—it is the big brother of services that run on most Unix hosts. *inetd* is a daemon that constantly monitors the hosts port to see if other services should start up. inetd monitors the port numbers of all service requests that come to a server. When a request comes in, inetd looks in /etc/services for the name of the service. After it has the name of the service to start, it looks in its configuration file, inetd.config, to get setup information. The configuration information in the file is similar in form to the following example:

```
gopher    stream tcp    nowait    guest /usr/sbin/gopherd  -l
```

The first field, gopher, is the name of the service. This name must match exactly the name of the service as it is found in /etc/services. The second field, stream tcp, describes the kind of connection the service will make. In this case, tcp will handle the packet ordering so that the downloaded information appears to be a steady stream of data. The other option for second field, dgram udp, specifies that UDP, not TCP, will handle the packet ordering.

The third field, nowait, tells the service to spawn itself for each service request that comes to the server. The other option for the third field, wait, tells the service to handle the service requests sequentially, starting a new request only after finishing the current one.

The fourth field, guest, specifies the user ID used to run the service. The fifth field, /usr/sbin/gopherd, specifies the name and path of the service. The last field, -l, is the equivalent of a command-line option that influences the execution of the service; for example, whether or not to enable logging.

You can keep track of inetd's actions by looking in the log file, syslog (unless you turn off inetd's logging).

Using Daemons

In cases in which services are started infrequently, inetd does a great job. A problem arises, however, when service requests come in every other second. In such cases, inetd starts and stops the service unnecessarily. Each stop and start takes a finite amount of time and degrades system performance.

To correct this problem, you can run a service continuously. This option increases system performance because the service only reads configuration information once, but it also permanently consumes system resources. It is the job of the service, then, to monitor incoming requests. When multiple, concurrent requests of the same service are made, the service spawns itself, one for each request.

How Service Requests and Replies Happen

Now that you know that the Internet and Intranets use a client/service architecture, let us look at a complete communication sequence to get a feeling for how everything works.

To illustrate a simple example of a WWW client requesting information from a WWW service, the sequence of events would transpire something like the following:

1. The user decides to look at a document offered in a company's home page. He requests the document by clicking on an icon.

2. The WWW client interprets the user's action and constructs an appropriate request IP packet.

3. The WWW client looks in /etc/services to find the correct port number for a WWW server. In this case, it finds the number 80.

4. The client finishes addressing the IP packet, or series of packets, with the TCP port number 80, and sends it to the WWW server across the Internet.

5. Inetd sees a service request come in with a port number of 80. It looks in /etc/ services to see what the name of the service is that it should wake up. It finds that 80 corresponds to WWW.

6. Inetd uses the information in the configuration file, inetd.config, to start the WWW service with the correct options.

7. Inetd backs out of the transaction to let the WWW client communicate directly to the WWW service.

8. The service processes the request by opening and reading the document file.

9. IP chops up the document and puts it in a series of packets and addresses each packet.

10. The document goes to the WWW client over the network.

 Note If the WWW document contains an image, a second TCP/IP connection is created between the WWW client and server to facilitate the download of the image.

11. The IP packets are cached on the WWW client machine. When they all arrive, TCP puts them in the correct sequence and presents them to the WWW client.

12. After the download is complete, the TCP connection is terminated and the WWW service terminates on the server.

13. The WWW client decides what, of the series of packets, to display. Some clients spawn external viewers in which the document is displayed.

Communication between Gopher clients and servers work in the same way as the WWW. Because Gopher documents cannot include graphic images, however, a second TCP/IP connection is never made.

File Transfer Protocol (FTP) works in a different way altogether. Two TCP/IP connections are always created between FTP clients and servers. One handles the data download; the other manages the communication. The data TCP/IP connection comes and goes, as needed. The managing TCP/IP connection, however, runs as long as the client is logged in to the service.

C H A P T E R

2

Understanding the Basics of Data Communications

A distributed environment is comprised of various system resources (data, computing power, programs, and so on) that are spread across multiple locations. These resources utilize a communication system to interact with one another. In this scenario, the communication system is the apparatus that provides the distribution mechanism to exchange control information and data. The communication systems that are essential for information distribution can be made totally transparent to end users, or they may be visible enough for the end users to be aware of the network that provides actual resource interconnection. In either case, communication between nodes is indispensable, requiring a physical network to connect all interacting nodes.

Communication and Distribution

Client/server architecture is a subset of cooperative processing, which in turn is a subset of distributed processing. The distributed processing environment is not designed for just the client/server computing model. The factors that are currently contributing to interest in distributed systems are as follows:

◆ Technological advances in microelectronics are changing the price-performance ratio in favor of multiple low-cost, high-performance systems.

◆ Interconnections and communication costs are falling dramatically.

◆ Users are demanding more economical, rapid, sophisticated, and reliable facilities.

An objective and benefit of distribution is resource sharing. A number of resources (such as computers, peripherals, special-purpose processors, programs, data, and so on), are interconnected by the communications system to allow the sharing of these resources. The interconnected systems form a network that can switch messages, or information *packets,* between different sites, systems, terminals, and programs.

The following definitions are useful to know when you discuss networks and communications:

◆ A *communication system* is the collection of hardware and software that supports intersystem and interprocess communication between software components in distributed nodes. The nodes are interconnected by a network that provides a physical path between nodes. The direct connection between two or more systems is sometimes referred to as a *link.*

◆ A system that performs main application functions and controls the communication system is sometimes called a *host* (or *server*).

◆ In a distributed system, the *name* of an object indicates a system, a process, or a node. An *address* indicates where the named object is, and a *route* tells how to get there.

Data is the most common shared resource in a distributed system. Most applications require that data be shared among diverse users with different computing facilities. By distributing data through replication, reliability may be improved. Local copies of replicated and partitioned data can reduce access time. The communication system is used to transmit both data and data requests between different sites, systems, and programs. Although interconnected systems may or may not form a distributed processing system, the data communication system used for message and data interchange can be considered as a distributed system.

Communication System Functions

The following functions are some of the most important functions of a communication system:

◆ Naming and addressing

◆ Segmenting

◆ Flow Control

◆ Synchronization

◆ Priority

◆ Error Control

Naming and Addressing

A communication system manipulates names for objects. These objects can be such items as processes, ports, mailboxes, systems, and sessions between users. Users typically supply names in symbolic form (such as Filename@DepartmentName@CompanyName) and then the communication system restates this form into a network address. The communication system must maintain translation tables (enterprise directories) to convert logical names into physical names.

Segmenting

If a user message or file to be transmitted is larger than a network packet, the communication system must fragment a single message into multiple segments and reassemble it before delivery to the end user.

Specific reasons for message segmentation include the following:

◆ Long messages extend access delays for other users because long messages could hold exclusive control over shared network resources for longer periods of time.

◆ Shorter messages improve efficiency and reduce transmission error rates.

◆ Internal buffers used by the communication system can optimize the transmitted message size.

◆ The networks that comprise a particular transmission route can have different packet sizes.

◆ Parallel data links and transmissions are possible in some networks. Breaking long messages into small segments may allow their use, thus reducing overall delays.

Flow Control

Many networks are designed to share limited resources among users on the assumption that not all users demand those services simultaneously. When the resulting traffic exceeds the network throughput capacity, network flow control is designed to optimize network performance by regulating the flow of information between a pair of communicating entities.

Synchronization

Before entities can communicate, their interactions must be synchronized. If the receiver is faster than the transmitter, it may possibly acquire and subsequently misinterpret extra information. Conversely, if it is slower than the transmitter it may lose information.

Because the client/server architecture typically subdivides major processes into component subprocesses, each of which executes on a different host, a mechanism must be in place to ensure that the various subprocesses remain syncronized. Similarly, when data resources are shared or distributed, it is necessary to coordinate all of the distributed resources to ensure that they remain synchronized. IBM Advanced Program to Program Communication (APPC) protocol is an example of such a multilevel synchronization protocol.

Priority

A communication system can apply priority to messages to allow preferential handling when competing for resources. High-priority messages (alarms, alerts, interrupts) have shorter delays. The communications system can apply priority statically or dynamically (such as according to message content or based on a message source or destination).

Error Control

Reliable, error-free communication is one of the prime objectives of communication system functionality. Error control functions include error detection, correction, and recovery. Error detection can be performed in three ways:

◆ By including redundant information. Redundant data can be compared to determine a possible error in the case of mismatch.

◆ By using control information that allows determination of information corruption. Control information can use various algorithms to calculate a check digit or a check sum of all information bits. By comparing calculated results with the ones received, errors can be detected.

◆ By assigning sequence numbers to messages and detecting sequence errors. Sequencing is used to determine lost, duplicated, or out-of-sequence messages.

Error correction and recovery are generally implemented by automatic retransmission or error-correction code.

Layers, Protocols, and Interfaces

The communication system is responsible for providing communication between nodes in a distributed system. This system allows any network node to transmit information to any other node connected to the communication network. Computer network architectures facilitate interconnectivity among homogeneous and (especially in an open systems arena) heterogeneous systems.

Because communication systems are complex, it is common to divide them into layers. Some layer structures represent formal models.

A Layered Model of Communication

To illustrate the concepts of layered communication models, it is possible to develop a three-layered model that generally describes communication. Consider the following three layers in terms of standard, person-to-person communication:

◆ The Cognitive layer includes concepts, such as understanding, knowledge, and existence of shared, mutually agreed upon symbols. This is the level at which the information becomes available for human use. Computer user interfaces work at this level.

◆ The Language layer is used to put concepts and ideas into words. Examples for humans are words or mathematics. Computers might use ASCII or EBCDIC characters.

◆ The Physical transmission layer provides the medium for the actual communication. This layer may be exemplified in several forms, such as sound vibrations in the air, written words on paper, or visual signs. Data communication may use electrical, radio, or light signals on a variety of media.

This example illustrates the nature of layered models. The three layers are independent of each other. The "upper" layers require the support of the "lower" ones. To communicate ideas, the language and conveyance are required, but the opposite may not be true.

The goals of a layered architecture mirror the goals of structured programming: to define functional modules with clearly defined interfaces. Modules are conceptually simplified and easier to maintain. Provided that the interfaces for a module remain stable, the internals of the module may be freely modified.

A Layered Model of Client/Server Computing

All major network architectures share the same high-level objectives:

◆ Connectivity permits various hardware and software to be interconnected into a uniform, single system image, networking system.

◆ Modularity allows building of diverse networking systems from a relatively small number of general-purpose components.

◆ Reliability supports error-free communications via error detection and correction availability.

◆ Ease of implementation, use, and modification provides generalized, widely acceptable solutions for network installation, modification, and management, and by supplying end users with network-transparent communication facilities.

To achieve these high-level objectives, network architectures support modular design. Each module's functions are organized into functional, hierarchical, architected layers.

A layered approach is especially useful when analyzing client/server computing. Communication between distributed processors takes place on numerous levels, from signals on wires to applications that exchange control information or data. At each level, the nature of the communication is somewhat different. Network hardware works in terms of pulses of electrical voltages and currents. Applications communicate through a number of mechanisms with names such as *Named Pipes* or *Advanced Peer-to-Peer Communication*; between are numerous other mechanisms.

Client/server uses features at all of these layers to facilitate a tight integration of processes running on different computers. Some understanding of the layers involved is necessary in order to understand how client/server computing works.

In data communication models, the layers are composed of entities, which can be hardware components and software processes. Entities of the same layer but in different network nodes are called *peer entities*. Layers at the same level in different nodes are *peer layers*.

The typical distributed system architecture consists of the following functional layers:

◆ **Application Layer.** This is the topmost layer of the architecture. Typically, it performs management of application processes, distribution of data, inter-process communication, and decomposition of application functions into distributable processes. Application layer functionality is supported by lower-level layers.

◆ **Distributed Operating System Layer.** This layer provides the system-wide distributed services required by the application layer. It supports global naming, directory, addressing, sharing of local resources, protection and synchronization, intercommunication and recovery. The distributed operating system unifies the distributed functions into a single logical entity and is responsible for creating the Single System Image (SSI).

◆ **Local Management and Kernel Layer.** This layer supports the distributed operating system in the individual nodes. It supports local interprocess communications, memory and I/O access, protection, and multitasking. This layer supports the higher-level layers by providing these services and by communicating with its peer layer in other nodes.

◆ **Communication System Layer.** This layer supports communications required by the application, distributed operating system, and local management layers.

The layered architecture provides several important benefits:

◆ **Layer Independence.** Each layer is only aware of the services provided by the layer immediately below it.

◆ **Flexibility.** An implementation change in one layer does not affect the layers above and below it.

◆ **Simplified Implementation and Maintenance.** The support of a modular-layered design and architected decomposition of overall system functionality into simpler, smaller units.

◆ **Standardization.** Encapsulation of layer functionality, services, and interfaces into carefully architected entities permits standards to be developed more easily.

Communication over different communications links is a complex task. Aside from its use in computer technology, the term *protocol* is possibly most familiar in diplomatic settings, in which a protocol is an agreement between parties that specifies precise rules of behavior.

Society requires adherance to protocols every day in the use of language. The grammar of any language defines a set of rules that governs interpersonal communication. If two people converse in the same language and dialect they will probably exchange information smoothly and without error. If a German and a Japanese diplomat endeavor to engage in an error-free discussion, they employ translators who understand the language-specific protocols and can perform the necessary translations.

Communication between layers is governed by protocols. Protocols include, but are not limited to, formats and order of the information exchange, and any actions to be taken on the information transmission and receipt. The rules and formats for the information exchange across the boundary between two adjacent layers comprise an interface between layers.

Data communications can easily be compared to the United Nations. Translation between communication protocols is a necessary and exacting process. In both cases, many protocols must be comprehended and carefully translated for information to be exchanged readily and without error.

To make the task of conceptualizing and organizing network communication protocols more manageable, the early designers of networking systems standards divided the process into several discrete parts.

The Seven Layers of the OSI Communications Model

The Open System Interconnection (OSI) model breaks up the job of moving data from one point to another into seven different tasks. The tasks are arranged hierarchically. Each layer contributes to the assembly/disassembly of a packet.

Data moves through the communications network in discrete bundles of bits known as *packets*. Each packet, in turn, is divided into four distinct parts:

◆ The starting characters alert receiving boards that a packet is on the way

◆ A packet header explains where the packet is going where it came from, and what kind of packet it is (either a data or a network controlling packet)

◆ The data the packet is carrying

◆ The final error-checking bits and the end-of-packet characters

The OSI model is concerned primarily with the contents of the header section of the packet, which is the part the packet which tells it where to go. In the header section, the layers built up on outbound packets and conversely stripped off on inbound packets. The layers are arranged in a hierarchical fashion. Each layer sends information only to the layers immediately above and below it. Figure 2.1 shows the building of a packet.

Each layer sends packets to the layers above it and below it, but each layer only understands and works with information that comes from the same layer on another stack. The network layer (layer three), for example, sends an inbound packet to layer four only after it strips off any layer three information. This same layer three sends an outbound packet to layer two only after it adds layer three information to the packet. On inbound packets, it examines the layer three information to see if it needs to take any action. If the layer three information says that this packet is bound for address 04 and the receiving board is address 90, it discards the packet and does not pass it on to layer seven.

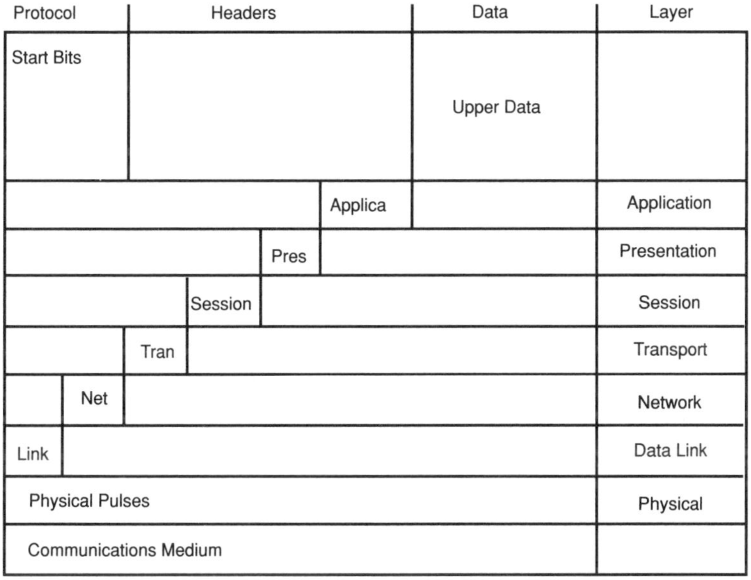

Protocol	Headers	Data	Layer
Start Bits		Upper Data	
	Applica		Application
	Pres		Presentation
	Session		Session
	Tran		Transport
	Net		Network
Link			Data Link
Physical Pulses			Physical
Communications Medium			

Figure 2.1

Building an OSI packet.

On outbound packets, layer three adds the source and destination addresses to the packet and passes this enlarged packet to layer two for further processing. Layer three on the receiving board responds only to what layer three on the sending board adds to the packet. Each layer on the stack communicates with the same layer on another stack, and is unconcerned with what other layers do.

Physical Layer

The physical layer generates the physical pulses, electrical currents, and optical pulses involved in moving data from the Network Interface Card (NIC) to the communications system. RS-232 is an example of physical-layer standard. The units managed at the physical layer are bits.

This layer does not include the communications system, but it does include the connection to it. It handles rise times and pulse durations. The physical layer does not manage the details of connectors and cabling, which are sometimes unofficially nicknamed the "level 0" layer of the model.

Datalink Layer

The datalink layer is the first level that collects bits and handles data as packets. This level does the final assembly on departing packets and performs first inspection on arriving packets. It adds error correction to leaving packets and performs the checksum on arriving packets. Incomplete and defective packets are discarded. If the link layer can determine where the defective packet came from, it returns an error packet. SDLC and HDLC are examples of protocols operating at this level.

Network Layer

When local area networks (LANs) exceed a certain size or geographic area, they must be divided into smaller logical LANs. Devices named routers, bridges, and gateways are used to divide the LAN and create the smaller sub-networks. The network layer routes packets through multiple devices to ensure that a packet arrives at the correct device on the correct sub-LAN.

This level maintains routing tables and determines which route is the fastest available and when alternative routes should be used. This is the first layer at which a device begins filtering out packets that are not going from one network to another so that overall network traffic is reduced. Internet protocol, the IP of TCP/IP, operates at this level, as does NetWare's Internetwork Packet Exchange (IPX). This network layer is the level at which "connectionless" or "datagram" services operate. These terms are defined later.

Transport Layer

Transfer Control Protocol (the TCP of TCP/IP) operates at the transport layer. This is a transition level (that is, the last of the levels that manages routing packets and error recovery). It accomodates any deficiencies that cannot be covered at the network level. If packets are received reliably at the network level, this level is a very simple one. If the communications system cannot provide reliable packet transmission, this level compensates by becoming more complex.

Session Layer

In many network settings it is desirable to establish a formal connection between communicating entities. This connection assures that messages are sent and received with a high level of reliability. Such precautions are often necessary when the reliability of a network is in question, as is almost always the case when telecommunications are employed. Therefore, session orientation is the norm in most mainframe communications. LANs are generally regarded as highly reliable, and session control is less common in LAN communication.

The session layer is the level that maintains "connection-oriented" transmissions. The process of making and breaking a connection at this level is one of "binding" and "unbinding" sessions. At this level, packets are presumed to be reliable. Error checking is not part of this level's function. The TCP component of TCP/IP, IBM's NetBIOS, and Netware's SPX operate at this level.

Presentation Layer

This level is not yet fully defined or widely used. Processing at this level performs any conversion that may be required to render the data usable by the application layer. Data compression/decompression and data encryption/decryption processes might be implemented at the presentation level. Data encryption and compression, however, can be performed by user applications that run above the OSI application layer.

Translations of data formats also can be performed at this layer. An example is the translation between the ASCII and EBCDIC encoding schemes. This function, however, is most frequently performed by the end-user's application.

The presentation layer is frequently misunderstood as presenting data to the user. The presentation layer is a network communication layer. It does not interface directly with end-user display devices. Production of screen displays is the responsibility of the application program executing on the user's workstation.

Application Layer

The application layer also is in the process of being defined. This layer deals with security issues and the availability of resources. The application layer is likely to deal with file transfer, job transfer, and virtual terminal protocols.

Extra Layers

The OSI model was developed when hierarchy was the norm and before the common LAN protocols (ARCnet, Ethernet, and Token Ring) were widely used. Since its inception, its layer definitions have evolved to make it fit in a world filled with LANs, as well as with minicomputers and mainframes. One of the adaptations is the informal addition of new layers and sublayers to the original seven layers. An example is the informal addition of level 0 to cover hardware details such as cable connectors and fiber optics.

Client/Server Connectivity Components

In a client/server architecture, client and server systems are constructed from a number of interconnected components. Each component provides an interface through which it communicates with other components. Communication between clients and servers can be viewed as the communication between relevant components. The two distinct classes of components are process components and resource components. *Process components* are software components that actively perform some functions. *Resource components* provide the services requested by process components.

From the point of view of client/server interactions, an active resource component acts as a *server*, and the users of the resource component and process components act as *clients*.

Process and resource components, in addition to clients and servers, enter into an association with each other for the purpose of communication. This association is the connection between a sender of information and a receiver of that information. The client/server connections can be static or dynamic. Static connections are set up at compile, load, or at system initialization time and cannot be changed. Dynamic connection can be changed "in-flight" at runtime.

Communication and Synchronization

In a client/server environment, coordination and cooperation between components is provided by the communication system's communication and synchronization actions. Communication functions involve the exchange of information. They are supported by flow control, error control, naming and addressing, and blocking and segmenting. Synchronization functions involve the coordination of actions between two or more components.

Communication and synchronization are closely related. When communication is performed in shared memory, closely coupled systems, such as Symmetric Multiprocessing systems, and software components, such as semaphores or monitors, are used for synchronization. In more traditional loosely coupled systems that are interconnected by communication networks, mechanisms such as message passing must be used for communication and synchronization.

In either case, the communication service provided by a communication system can be connectionless or connection-oriented. Connectionless services are those where each message transaction is independent of previous or subsequent ones. These are low-overhead services that are relatively simple to implement. An example is called *datagram* service, in which the user is not provided with any form of response to a transaction. Typically, datagram services are used for broadcast or multidestination message transmission.

A connection-oriented service provides a relationship between the sequence of units of information transmitted by a particular communication layer. This is similar to the process of establishing a connection between two telephones on the public telephone system. Switches at the telephone central offices establish a route through the telephone system that connects the two telephones. This route will probably be different each time. After the route is established, a *circuit* is established, and the telephones can communicate as if a continuous piece of wire connected them. In the early days of telephone communication, this circuit was literally a continuous set of wires, and it was possible to physically trace the connection between the conversing telephones. Such a connection is a *physical circuit.*

Modern communications systems rarely establish physical circuits. Instead they take advantage of new, high-capacity communication channels, such as optical fiber, microwaves, and satellites, that can carry hundreds or thousands of distinct messages. Devices seeking to establish a connection will be routed through an intermediate path. Individual parts of a message may even be disassembled and transmitted through different paths to be reassembled at the receiving end. Such flexible techniques ensure that messages will be handled efficiently, taking maximum advantage of available capacity.

This switching is invisible to the end devices, however, and after a data connection is established between two computer devices, the connection appears to be a continuous wire run between the computers. A connection that appears physical but in fact uses multiple routes is a *virtual circuit.*

The activity to maintain a virtual circuit between two devices is more complex than a connectionless communication service. Most connection-oriented services have three phases of operation:

1. Establishment. An establishment phase can be used to negotiate connection or session options and quality of service.

2. Data.

3. Termination.

A terminal session to a remote computer or X.25 packet-switched network protocols accepted by the CCITT are examples of connection-oriented services.

A connection-oriented system requires a lot of overhead to control session establishment and termination. This effort may be needed to ensure reliable communication over questionable media. However, when the media can be assumed to be reliable, as most LANs are, the virtual connection can be dispensed with. Messages may just be sent with confidence that they will be received by the intended device. The overhead associated with connectionless communication is low, and performance is consequently higher. Therefore, most LANs use connectionless (also called datagram) communication modes.

Connection-oriented communication is often termed *reliable*, not because every message is guaranteed to arrive, but because devices are guaranteed to be informed if a message is not delivered as required.

Connectionless communication is often termed unreliable because the network does not detect the failure to deliver a message. This makes it the responsibility of upper-level software, perhaps the application itself, to determine that an expected reply has not been received in a reasonable time. This approach works well on LANs.

With respect to connections in general, the flow of information can be uni- or bidirectional. The latter involves a return message and synchronization in response to the initial request.

Bidirectional communications are an essential form of communication for the client/server architecture. The client component requests some service from its possibly remote server. It then waits until the results of its request are returned. Bidirectional client/server interactions can be provided by a message-oriented communication implemented in such request-reply protocols as IBM's Logical Unit 6.2 (LU6.2) or by a procedure-oriented communication such as remote procedure calls (RPC).

Procedure-Oriented Communication

Procedure-oriented communication allows applications in a distributed computing environment, such as Open Software Foundation's Distributed Computing Environment (DCE), to run over a heterogeneous network. The basic technology that enables this functionality is the remote procedure call (RPC).

The RPC model is based on the need to run individual process components of an application on a system elsewhere in a network. RPCs use a traditional programming construct, the procedure call, which is, in this case, extended from a single system to a network of systems. In the context of a communication system role in a client/server environment, an RPC requesting a particular service from a resource server is issued by a process component (client). The location of the resource component is hidden from the client. RPCs are highly suitable for client/server applications. They usually provide developers with a number of powerful tools that are necessary to build such applications. These tools include two major components: a language and a compiler and a run-time facility. A *language and a compiler* simplify the development of distributed client/server applications by producing portable source code. A *run-time facility* enables distributed applications to run over multiple, heterogeneous nodes. They make the system architectures and the underlying network protocols transparent to the application procedures.

The DCE RPC standard appears to be one of the strongest candidates for RPC implementation and deserves close examination.

To develop a distributed, DCE-compliant client/server application, a developer creates an interface definition using the Interface Definition Language (IDL). IDL syntax is similar to ANSI C language with the addition of several language constructs appropriate for a network environment. After the definitions are created, the IDL compiler translates them into stubs that are bound with the client and the server (see fig. 2.2). The stub on a client system acts as a substitute for the required server procedure. Similarly, the server stub substitutes for a client. The stubs are needed to automate otherwise manual operations-copying arguments to and from RPC headers, converting data as necessary, and calling the RPC runtime.

RPC runtimes should have the following features:

◆ Transparency and independence from the underlying networking protocols

◆ Support for reliable transmission, error detection, and recovery from network failures

◆ Support for a common method of network naming, addressing, and directory services, while at the same time being independent of network directory services

◆ Multithreading support for parallel and concurrent processing, and the capability to handle multiple requests simultaneously, thus reducing the time required to complete an application

◆ Portability and interoperability with various system environments

◆ Support for resources integrity and application security

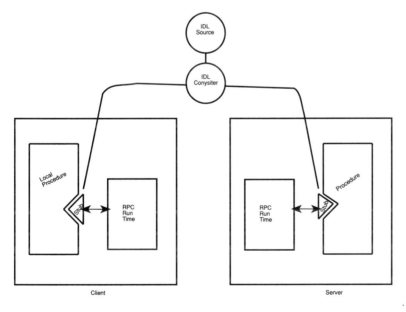

Figure 2.2

An RPC implementation.

The DCE implementation of the remote procedure calls includes specific semantics for both network transport independence and transparency. DCE RPC includes a pipe facility to eliminate such resource limitations as inadequate main memory. The ISO X.500 standard is used to provide global directory services. DCE RPC utilizes

Kerberos authentication and authorization to support security service and asynchronous threads to support concurrent and parallel processing.

Defining Local and Wide Area Networks

Under the client/server model, applications are closely allied with network services. It is, therefore, useful to have a general sense of how local area networks work even if your primary focus will be on programming at the application level.

The proliferation of personal computers throughout organizations has resulted in an increase in the number of PCs used for a wide variety of business functions. It also has resulted in an ever-increasing need for personal computers to communicate. The communication needs include intercommunications among personal computers as well as communication with centralized data processing facilities and the sources of corporate data. Several networking technologies have been developed to support this intercommunication. Among them are wide area networking and local area networking.

Intelligent workstations, such as personal computers or Unix-based technical workstations, can be used as stand-alone systems to support local applications. As workgroup environments become more and more popular, the reasons for interconnecting these intelligent workstations in a network are readily becoming more apparent. Among them are the following:

◆ The need to access data stored in another (not local) system

◆ The need for the members of the workgroup to share devices that are too expensive (such as a duplex PostScript laser printer) to be used only by a single user

◆ The need for the workgroup members to exchange information electronically

The distance between network users is one of the factors that determines the required network type and the underlying technology. One situation includes user requirements for access processing and data storage capabilities typically available from mainframes. Similarly, interconnectivity may be required by geographically widely separated users. In this case, the networking solutions may involve public telecommunication facilities for rapid data interchange. The networks that tie all these users together are called wide area networks (WANs).

It is sometimes useful to distinguish between WANs that can span remote locations at very large distances, measured in hundreds and thousands of miles (for example, users in Atlanta, Chicago, and Tokyo), and networks that link users within a particular metropolitan area. Networks that operate within a city or those that can use physical telecommunications facilities typically associated with the city infrastructure (for example, underground cabling system), are sometimes called metropolitan area networks (MANs). A typical MAN provides voice data and video communications at speeds of 45–600 Mbps (million bits per second) at distances ranging from 1 to 50 miles.

Relatively short-distance communications between intelligent workstations are supported by a networking technology known as local area networks (LANs). The Institute of Electrical and Electronics Engineers (IEEE) defines a LAN as a data communication system that allows a number of independent devices to communicate directly with each other, within a moderately sized geographic area over a physical communication channel of moderate data rates.

LANs can be used for shared data, application and device access, electronic mail, process monitoring in a factory environment, and even for alarm and security systems. The most interesting feature of a LAN is its capability to support cooperative applications in which an application runs partly on LAN stations and partly on a LAN server or possibly a mainframe host. The range of LAN applications can be significantly extended by interconnecting several networks. LAN interconnection can be implemented over WANs, thus extending the communication capabilities of LANs far beyond the traditional distance limitations of a typical LAN.

LAN Characteristics and Components

The IEEE definition of a LAN provides characteristics that distinguish local area networks from other networking technologies. This definition is as follows:

◆ By allowing independent devices to communicate directly with each other, the LAN supports peer communication between its nodes. This is in contrast with centrally controlled hierarchical systems such as IBM's Systems Network Architecture (SNA).

◆ By emphasizing a moderately sized geographic area, IEEE separates the LAN from wide area networks. Typically, it does not exceed a distance of about 5 to 7 miles, and often is limited to a single building or a group of buildings placed in close geographic proximity.

◆ By defining a physical communication channel with moderate data rates, IEEE contrasts LANs with wide area networks, which often use public-switched communication facilities.

Moderate data rates are used to imply that LAN data rates are slower than those of the direct mainframe links and channel-to-channel communication, which are measured in several million bits per second. Advances in physical transmission technology, especially fiber-optic communications, allow LANs to support data rates up to 100 Mbps.

A typical LAN that corresponds to the IEEE LAN definition consists of two general types of components: *nodes* and *links* between nodes. In LAN terminology, nodes, which can be any device attached to a network, are generally known as stations. All LAN stations are linked, or interconnected via a cabling system, which includes the physical communication channels and any devices necessary to attach the stations to the network.

To avoid the loss of a signal over the length of the wire, signal regenerators, or repeaters, are sometimes inserted into a LAN. Each station must possess adequate intelligence to handle the communication control functions. With this requirement in mind, peripheral devices, such as printers and hard disk drives, do not qualify as stations themselves, but rather are attached to some of the intelligent stations.

Networks, including local area networks, are characterized by the shape the cabling system takes, that is, the network topology. In addition, different local area networks are characterized by the following:

◆ **The Transmission Medium.** The type of cable that is used in a given LAN.

◆ **The Transmission Technique.** The technique that determines how the transmission medium is used for communication.

◆ **The Access Control Method.** The method by which LAN stations control their access to the transmission medium.

Network Topologies

A communication system has previously been described as the collection of hardware and software that supports intersystem and interprocess communication between software components in distributed nodes.

The actual links between nodes comprise a network. These represent an ordered collection of physical layers between interconnected nodes. This section presents the "basics" of networking-topology and technologies.

Network Switching Techniques

For many network topologies, not all nodes have direct physical links between them. A network must provide a relay function that switches the data between links to provide a point-to-point path between some nodes.

There are two main switching techniques used in modern networks: circuit switching and packet switching.

A *circuit-switching* network operates by forming a dedicated connection between two nodes. While the circuit is in place, the sender is guaranteed that the message will be delivered to the destination. Such a connection is dedicated to the participating nodes until they release it. The dedication of a communication path, however, means that the capacity of the path is reserved whether the communicating nodes are using the full capacity or not.

Packet-switched networks take a different approach. All traffic is divided into small segments (known as packets) that are mapped (or multiplexed) into a high-capacity intersystem connection for transmission from one node to another. The same media path may be shared among a wide variety of communicating nodes, and communication capacity will not be monopolized for any one purpose. To implement packet-switching, packets carry identification that allows network operating system (NOS) software to send them to their destinations, where the packets are reassembled by the network software.

The main disadvantage of the packet-switching technique is that as the activity increases, a given pair of communicating partners receives less resource capacity from the network. Opposed to the circuit switching, the available capacity is not guaranteed. New generations of low-cost, high-speed networking hardware are providing for high performance and wide acceptance of the packet-switching networking technique.

Sometimes the *message-switching* technique is described as an alternative to both circuit and packet switching. It involves storing messages (including files) in the switching node's storage. Messages can be stored until the destination node wants to receive the message. This type of packet-switching technique is often implemented in electronic mail applications.

Physical Topologies

A physical topology is the actual way that the wiring is strung between network nodes. Each of these network types is described in greater detail. Of these five types of networks, point-to-point and multi-point networks can be quickly dismissed as special-purpose approaches.

A point-to-point connection is a dedicated connection between two devices. These connections are generally used when performance is the overriding concern. They might be used to implement a high-speed connection between two network servers or multiuser hosts. Point-to-point connections are seldom utilized for normal traffic levels or to service workstations.

Multi-point connections implement a point-to-point connection between each pair of stations that needs to communicate. Cost of such a network escalates astronomically when more than a handful of stations are involved.

The principal idea behind a local or wide area network is that logical point-to-point connections can be established between any two stations on the network while sharing a common, inexpensive medium. A logical connection enables nodes to exchange data as if they were directly connected. These nodes share a common network on which various node-to-node messages are carefully routed and efficiently controlled. By combining a high performance cabling system with efficient protocols, stations can behave as though they are directly connected to each other even though they are "time-sharing" a common network.

The following sections discuss the three LAN physical topologies that support efficient use of network resources: the bus, star, and ring topologies. Keep in mind that a network also has a logical topology that defines the way the network functions beneath the surface. A network frequently has a logical topology that is different from its physical topology.

Bus Topology

A *bus* is the simplest form of multinode network. In a bus topology, all network nodes connect directly to the same piece of cable. Each network node has an address assigned to it, a number that uniquely identifies the node. This address allows nodes to identify messages intended for them and to direct messages to other specific nodes.

A segment of a network that uses a bus topology is a length of wire, generally *coaxial* cable, capped at each end with a *terminator*. It does not wrap back on itself. When a station on the network transmits a message, the electrical signal travels in both directions from the origination point until it reaches the end of the cable, where it is absorbed by the terminators. As the signal propagates down the cable, each station on the cable can examine the data. By adhering to the rules of a network protocol, each station retrieves only those messages that are intended for it.

The primary appeal of the bus topology is its extreme simplicity. Stations in close proximity can be networked simply by stringing a cable from station to station and tapping the station into the cable. A bus is also efficient to install.

The Ethernet networking protocols typically run over a bus topology, but not all buses are required to run Ethernet. Other protocols, such as ARCnet, also can be used for a bus physical topology.

Due to the electrical characteristics of a bus, every component on a bus network is capable of affecting the entire network. If a cable is broken at some point, the problem will be more severe than simply losing contact with stations on opposite sides of the break. The break actually causes each section of the cable to lose its termination, and signals reflect back from the break causing interference on the entire cable. One bad station sending out noise can bring down the entire bus. Under these circumstances it can be difficult to isolate the cause of the problem.

Bus topologies are limited in the number of nodes that can occupy a segment. As each new node is added to the cable, it absorbs a part of the signal on the cable. At a certain level, the signal strength falls to a point so low that it can no longer be relied on without the aid of a repeater. An Ethernet segment can generally only support 30 nodes. Beyond that, repeaters must be added to support additional workstations.

The advantages of a bus topology include that it uses a minimal amount of wire and that it requires inexpensive network hardware.

A single cable break or malfunctioning node, however, can bring down the whole LAN.

Star Topology

In a star cabling topology, a central system, which can be a server or a wiring hub, connects PCs or workstations. Each node is connected to the central system by an individual cable. Because each computer on a network requires its own wire to connect to the network hub, the star topology generally uses much more cable than either bus or ring topologies. The central wiring concentrators also represent a cost that is not required for a bus network. In general, a star network represents the highest-cost physical topology. A simple star network is shown in figure 2.3.

Despite this high cost, the benefits are drawing most network designers toward star topologies. Because each machine in a star network is individually wired, a cable break affects only one workstation. Concentrators can be excellent places to place network diagnostic devices. Because all signals are routed through the concentrator, they can be monitored from a central location. The higher cost of a star network is generally justified by the greater reliability that it provides.

Star topologies are employed for ARCnet, Token-Ring, and a version of Ethernet labeled 10BASE-T.

The advantages of a star topology include greater node autonomy—a cable break affects only the machine connected by that cable—and centralized locations for network diagnostic equipment.

The primary disadvantages are that a star topology requires both a large amount of cable and central concentrator components, which add to network cost.

Ring Topology

The foundation of a ring network is a loop of cable. Unlike a bus, in which a signal is broadcast throughout the network cable, ring networks operate by passing signals from node-to-node around the ring. Terminal servers, PCs, and workstations connect to the ring, as shown in figure 2.4. Each node receives a message that is passed to it, and, if the message is intended for another node, repeats the signal to the next node. Because this repeating action amplifies and reconditions each message to pass it on, ring networks are less sensitive to signal loss to increasing numbers of nodes on the network.

Local area networks are not generally implemented with ring physical topologies. Token-Ring, despite the "ring" in its name, is actually wired as a star because the star configuration offers advantages in terms of centralization and troubleshooting. Ring topologies also do not offer a central point for network management.

More frequently, rings are implemented over large geographic areas in which a star would be inefficient. A ring can be run to connect several sites within a city or even several cities across a multistate area. Rings also are implemented for fault-tolerant backbone technologies.

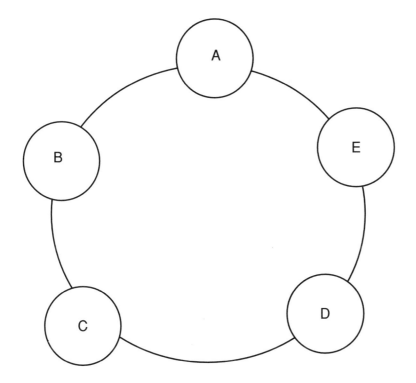

Figure 2.4

A simple ring network.

Most ring networks provide fault tolerance by implementing a backup signal path. If a break affects one of the ring segments the signal can often be routed back through the ring's backup unit. When a cable break failure occurs in a ring network, it causes the network to reroute the messages through the backup path, which usually runs in the direction opposite to the mainpath. This doubles the ring distance (and slows the network), but it keeps the network running. Network-management software can monitor the network and notify operators that the backup path has been switched on.

Advantages of a ring topology are that redundant media paths can reroute messages when a cable break occurs; and a ring topology uses cables efficiently when covering a large geographic area.

Disadvantages of a ring topology include no central place to monitor the network and generally lower throughput.

Structured Wiring

Structured wiring is increasingly used as networks become more complicated. Structured wiring systems consist of concentrators that accept plug-in modules. Some of these modules are wiring hubs, which support network connections between stations and the concentrator. Most hub modules support between 8 and 12 connections. Many concentrator types can service several types of logical networks, as well as bridges, routers, repeaters, and terminal servers. Concentrators also may contain component spares or redundant components to make networks fault-resistant or fault-tolerant. Structured wiring is considerably easier to manage than the nonstructured types of bus or star topologies.

Structured wiring distinguishes between a network's physical and logical topologies. All hubs use physical star topologies, but the logical topology can be ring, bus, or star. Also, several different networks with the same or different logical topologies can exist at once in a single hub. The concentrator conserves cabling by putting the cable backbones in a box.

Some structured cabling systems support stand-alone hubs, which can operate outside of a concentrator. Stand-alone hubs are small units that cannot be expanded. Because each hub is the center of a star topology, the connections from node to hub are star connections. The connections between hubs are a distributed network and can be another hub or a bus, ring, or star. Hub and concentrator architectures are highly modular. Hundreds of nodes can all be connected to one physical star topology.

Hubs can contain bridges, routers, and terminal servers as well as various logical networks. Hubs also may contain network management cards and support Simple Network-Management Protocol (SNMP).

Many hubs are sold as segmented products. These can be purchased as a base product with one LAN module that supports 12 nodes on an Ethernet, for example, and with add-in modules to add more nodes, such as a token-ring LAN, router, terminal server, or bridge.

As a general rule, the bigger the network, the lower the hub cost per node. Hubs are more costly than simple networks but offer several savings. The hub's high-performance backplanes allow for better throughput than other networking schemes. Additionally, hubs allow for more flexibility than traditional networks.

Because a hub's logical setup is different from the physical network, changes can be made without changing cables.

Because a hub uses a physical star topology, locating cable faults is easier because only one node is affected by a fault.

Although hubs are extremely flexible and can grow with a network, they generally require a larger initial investment than that needed for more traditional wiring schemes. But the concentration of network components and the separation of physical and logical topologies makes hub-network management simpler and less expensive than other methods.

Advantages of structured wiring systems include the following:

◆ Isolation of cabling for each node, which makes it easy to locate cable faults

◆ Plug-in modules, which make it efficient to move, add nodes, and change the network configuration

◆ Availability of integral network-management support

Disadvantages include the following:

◆ High start-up costs

◆ Higher per-node costs due to the high use of active components

Transmission and Access Control Methods

The physical transmission of information over a local area network can be described by two main categories: the actual medium used for the transmission and the way this medium is used.

Transmission Media

Current LANs are generally implemented with one of three media types: twisted pairs, coaxial cable, and fiber-optic links. Although they will not be discussed further, radio and microwave links also are occasionally employed.

Twisted pairs consist of two individually insulated and braided strands of copper wire. Usually, such pairs form a cable by grouping pairs together and enclosing them in a common protective jacket. The typical intrabuilding telephone wiring is an example of such a cable. Relatively low cost and high availability of such a cabling system have resulted in the popularity of the twisted-pair wire for LAN implementation. Un-shielded twisted-pair wire (UTP) can support transmission speeds of up to 10 MB/ second. Figure 2.5 illustrates UTP cable along with the RJ-45 connector usually employed.

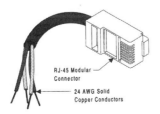

RJ-45 Modular
Connector

24 AWG Solid
Copper Conductors

Figure 2.5

Unshielded twisted-pair (UTP) cable.

To eliminate possible electrical interference, a twisted-pair cable can be enclosed in a special, high-quality protective sheath. Such cable is known as shielded twisted-pair cable (STP). Although it is slightly more expensive, it can be used where higher reliability and higher transmission rates over longer distances are required. The IBM Cabling System Type 1 and 2 cables are examples of twisted-pair cables.

Coaxial cable is familiar to television viewers, especially those with cable TV. Coaxial cable contains a central conducting core (generally copper), that is surrounded by the insulating material, another conductor (braided wire mesh or a solid sleeve), and yet another insulated protective and flexible jacket. Although more expensive, coaxial cable is better isolated from electrical interference than a twisted pair. Coaxial cable can support transmission rates of up to 100 Mbps. DECconnect Communication System's Thin and Standard Ethernet cables are examples of the coaxial cable used in LAN implementations. Figure 2.6 shows an example of coaxial cable along with a typical connector.

Figure 2.6

Coaxial cable with a typical connector.

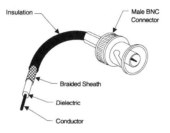

Insulation

Male BNC Connector

Braided Sheath

Dielectric

Conductor

Fiber-optic links are the newest transmission medium available for commercial LAN implementations. Optical fiber contains a core of an extremely thin glass thread, surrounded by a concentric layer of light insulator, called *cladding*. Optical signals take the form of modified light beams that traverse the length of the fiber-optic link. The cladding is made of a material whose refractive index is lower than that of the core. The light signals traveling along the core are reflected from the cladding back into the core. A number of these optical fibers are bound together into one fiber-optic cable, surrounded by a protective sheath. Fiber-optic cables are characterized by lighter weight than coaxial cables and significantly higher costs. The light signals transmitted over a fiber-optic cable are not subject to electrical interference. Optical transmission medium can support extremely high transmission rates. Rates of up to 565 Mbps can be found in commercially available systems, and experiments have demonstrated data rates of up to 200,000 Mbps. IBM Cabling System's Type 5 cable is an example of fiber-optic cables used for computer network. Figure 2.7 shows how fiber-optic cable and connectors are constructed.

Various implementations of these physical links can be found in a large number of commercially available cabling systems offered by general-purpose communication vendors as well as vendors of various computer networks.

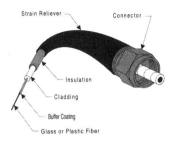

Figure 2.7

Fiber-optic cable with a typical connector.

Transmission Techniques

Whichever transmission medium is used in a given LAN environment, the LAN designer must select a technique that the LAN will use to transmit signals over a physical communication link. In general, there are two available transmission techniques for transmission over a physical communication channel: baseband and broadband.

Baseband transmission uses discrete signals (pulses of electricity or light that represent a binary 0 and 1) to carry information over a physical transmission medium. This signaling technique is called *digital signaling*. Baseband transmission uses the entire communication channel capacity to transmit a single data signal. LANs typically employ digital, baseband signaling.

By dividing the available transmission time into time slots, multiple stations attached to a network can share a common communication channel. This technique is known as time-division multiplexing (TDM). TDM frequently is used to combine several LAN baseband signals for transmission through a high-speed network such as a fiber-optic backbone, which can be used to interconnect various buildings or departments in large installations.

Broadband transmission typically employs analog (continuously varying) signals. Digital information is encoded into analog waves by using amplitude, frequency, or phase modulation of the base (carrier) signal. This technique is comparable to the practice of combining multiple television signals so that they may be transmitted over a single cable in a CATV system. A tuner can select the frequency for any individual signal and isolate it from the many signals that are being carried on the cable. Because the signals are each identified with a different frequency on the cable, this technique is known as frequency-division multiplexing (FDM).

In general, the higher the frequency of the carrier signal, the higher the volume of information that can be carried by this signal. The difference between the highest and lowest frequencies that are carried over the channel reflects that channel's information-carrying capacity and is referred to as the channel bandwidth. The bandwidth is directly related to another measurement of channel capacity the number of bits per second that can be carried over the channel, known as the *data rate.*

Typical baseband LANs operate at data rates of 10–20 Mbps. When networks grow to "campus" size, 10–20 Mbps of performance may be inadequate to connect large numbers of workstations in multiple departments or buildings. A common strategy is to interconnect local baseband networks via broadband networks (frequently designated as backbones), which simultaneously transport multiple signals.

Transmission Control

Technologies covered in this section are frequently referred to as "media access control" methods in that they are used to ensure that nodes on the network access and share the nework media in an organized fashion. In general, various transmission control methods can be classified as follows:

◆ **Centralized control.** One station controls the entire network and gives other stations permissions to transmit.

◆ **Random control.** Enables any station to transmit without being given specific permission.

◆ **Distributed control.** Gives the right to transmit to only one station at a time. The right to transmit is passed from one station to all the stations cooperating to control access to the network.

Each of these transmission control methods offers its own advantages and disadvantages and has access control methods specifically designed to work best with that particular transmission control.

Centralized Access Control

Centralized transmission control provides for easier network coordination and management and requires simple station-to-network interfaces. At the same time, centralized transmission control, by definition, provides a single point of failure and a potential network bottleneck. Centralized control may employ the following access control methods:

◆ **Polling.** A master station sends a notification to all other (secondary) stations indicating that a given station is allowed to transmit. Media access conflicts are eliminated since only the polled station may transmit.

◆ **Circuit Switching.** This can be used successfully in a centralized control LAN implemented by using a star topology. Here, a central station receives requests for a transmission from a secondary station and establishes a connection between the sender and its intended receiver. Circuit switching is widely used in telephony, especially in private branch exchanges (PBX).

◆ **Time-Division Multiple Access (TDMA).** This provides a specific time slot for each station on a network. The station is allowed to transmit only during this time slot. The time cycle is started and synchronized by a master station. TDMA can be successfully used on a bus topology.

Random Access Control

One of the best-known access control techniques for random transmission control is Carrier Sense Multiple Access with Collision Detection (CSMA/CD). Using this method, stations listen politely to determine whether the network is in use. If not, a station will attempt to transmit. The mechanisms are discussed later in this chapter when Ethernet is described in greater detail.

Carrier Sense Multiple Access with Collision Avoidance (CSMA/CA), used in Apple's LocalTalk networks, is very similar to the CSMA/CD access methods. However, stations utilize a variety of timing strategies to reduce the likelihood that collisions will occur.

The performance of both CSMA schemes is random since it cannot be predicted when stations will attempt to transmit. CSMA is an extremely simple access control mechanism, and there is little work associated with managing network traffic. However, the random element can cause problems when network traffic demands are high, and CSMA network performance can deteriorate rapidly as demand approaches capacity limits.

Distributed Access Control

Token ring passing is the most widely used method of distributed access control and is most frequently used in ring topology networks (for example, IBM's Token Ring). A token is a small message that is constantly circulating around the ring. Token passing can be used in a bus, star, or ring topology. Token bus methods are similar to a token ring, emulating the token ring method on a logical topology level. IBM Token Ring is the most commonly cited example of the use of token passing to control media access and is described in detail later.

Token passing is a more complicated mechanism than the CSMA schemes just discussed. It is, therefore, more expensive to implement and the network must have more controls in place to ensure proper operation. When network traffic is high, however, token passing becomes an effective means of ensuring that all network stations are allowed equal network access.

When designing local area networks, many interdependent factors should be taken into consideration: the transmission medium, transmission control and access methods, network topology, bandwidth, and data rates. All these factors affect network performance and cost. Decisions regarding network topology, transmission control, and access control methods should be made based on the processing and cost requirements of a particular LAN.

IEEE Local Area Network Standards

The IEEE undertook Project 802 in February of 1980 to identify and formalize LAN standards for data rates not exceeding 20 Mbps. Standardization efforts resulted in the IEEE 802 LAN standards.

The IEEE standards divide the OSI data link layer into two sublayers: the Media Access Control (MAC) layer and the Logical Link Control (LLC) layer. The MAC layer deals with media-access techniques to access shared physical medium. Token ring and Ethernet have different implementations of the MAC layer because their methods of sharing the physical media are different.

All IEEE LANs have the same LLC layer, as defined by standard 802.2. The advantage of a common sublayer, such as the LLC, is that upper layer mechanisms can be the same, regardless of the type of networking hardware.

The 802.3 and 802.5 standards define both the physical and AC components of Ethernet and Token Ring.

Major network vendors, including IBM, recognize that Ethernet and Token Ring will coexist for the foreseeable future and are rushing tools to market for integrating the standards. Network planners are free to match the cabling system to the application, with the understanding that future network-integration issues can be successfully dealt with.

Ethernet LANs

Ethernet was developed at Xerox Corporation and is the prototype for networks based on CSMA/CD media access control. The system was called Ethernet in honor of that elusive substance called *ether*, through which electromagnetic radiation was once thought to propagate.

Ethernet was proposed as a standard by Digital Equipment Corporation (DEC), Intel, and Xerox. The Ethernet proposal became known as the IEEE 802.3.

Before an Ethernet station can transmit, it listens for activity on the transmission channel. Ethernet frequently is described as a "listen before talking" protocol. Activity is defined as any transmission caused by other Ethernet station. The presence of a transmission is called a *carrier*, which can be sensed by the network interface card.

If an Ethernet station detects a busy channel, it refrains from transmitting. After the last bit of the passing frame, the Ethernet data link layer continues to wait for a minimum of 9.6 microseconds to provide proper interframe spacing. Following that gap, if a data frame is waiting for transmission, the station initiates the transmission.

If the station has no data to transmit, it resumes the carrier sense (listening for a carrier) operation. The interframe gap provides recovery time for other Ethernet stations.

If a station tries to transmit when the channel is busy, it results in a garbled transmission, known as a *collision*. If the channel is free (no carrier is detected), the station can transmit. Because multiple stations attached to the Ethernet channel use the carrier-sense mechanism, it is called carrier sense with multiple access (CSMA).

Collisions occur during the normal operation of Ethernet LANs because stations do not transmit based only on one fact: the presence of a carrier on the channel. They do not know whether packets are queued for transmission on other stations. Furthermore, the CSMA operation is complicated by propagation delay in LANs. In Ethernet, for example, signals propagate at 0.77 times the speed of light on standard (thick) cables and at 0.65 times the speed of light on thin Ethernet cables. A delay occurs before a transmission is heard by all stations, and a station may transmit because it has yet to hear another station's transmission.

Collisions are a fact of life in Ethernet LANs. Ethernet stations minimize the effects of collisions by detecting them as they occur. The stations involved in the collision abort their transmissions. The first station to detect the collision sends out a special jamming pulse to alert all stations that a collision has taken place. After a collision is detected, all stations set up a random interval timer. Transmission takes place only after this interval timer expires. Introducing a delay before transmission lessens the probability of collision.

When successive collisions occur, the average random time-out value is doubled. This doubling takes place up to 10 consecutive collisions. Beyond that, doubling the average random time-out value does not significantly improve the performance of the network.

Under the worst-case scenario, a station may wait indefinitely for an opportunity to transmit. Because this scenario is not acceptable for real-time applications, Ethernet is not well suited for real-time applications. Although this potential problem is frequently mentioned when comparing Ethernet to other LAN standards (such as token ring), problems with truly excessive collisions are seldom encountered on real-world Ethernet LANs.

At moderate traffic levels, Ethernet is an extremely efficient protocol. The next section will show that token ring requires a wide variety of control mechanisms that generate network traffic. Apart from collisions, however, most of the network traffic on an Ethernet is related to network transmission. As a result, Ethernet offers very high performance at most data rates. A 10M Ethernet often provides comparable performance to a 16M token ring until high traffic levels are reached.

Token Ring LANs

Ring-based logical networks have existed for many years. Ring LANs are a sequence of point-to-point links. They may be considered to be sequential broadcast LANs, with the point-to-point links forming a circle. Unlike that of Ethernet LANs, in which the carrier-sense mechanism may be analog, the technology of ring LANs is digital. An attractive feature of ring-based LANs is the deterministic response time, even under heavy load conditions.

The token ring LAN encountered most often is the IEEE 802.5. This LAN is often referred to as the IBM Token-Ring because IBM was the prime mover behind the IEEE 802.5 standard.

A special group of bits, called the token, is used to arbitrate access to the ring. The token circulates from station to station around the ring. If a station wants to transmit a frame, it must wait and seize the token. While in possession of the token, it can transmit a frame. At the end of the transmission, it must release the token so that other stations can access the ring.

For proper operation of the ring, the token must circulate continuously, even if there is no activity on the ring. There are 24 bits (three octets) in the token, and the ring must have enough latency or delay to hold 24 bits. If the bit rate on the ring is 4Mbps, the ring must have a latency of 24/4Mbps = six microseconds. While six microseconds may seem like a very short delay, consider a twisted-pair medium in which the propagation velocity is 0.59 times the speed of light. The minimum size then of the ring with these parameters is 1 kilometer. To bring the ring to a realistic physical size, a special station designated as the active monitor adds a 24-bit delay buffer to the ring. This buffer also compensates for any accumulated phase jitter on the ring. The active monitor is important for maintaining normal operation of the ring.

A token ring station operates in one of the following three modes:

◆ Transmit mode

◆ Listen mode

◆ Bypass mode

Protocols

Data communications protocols are used to coordinate the exchange of information between different network devices. They establish the mechanism whereby each device recognizes meaningful information from another device. In the communications world today, there are a number of protocols in use, along with several basic structures that handle different aspects of data communication.

While this book is about the TCP/IP protocol, it is important to understand the alternatives available to it. This section looks at four non-TCP/IP protocols that are most widely implemented in the context of the OSI Reference Model and the ways that protocols communicate over a network.

Once the domain of the small workgroup or office department, local area networks are becoming the major integration platform for enterprise-wide computing. The simple twenty-user network has now expanded to the 3,000–5,000 user enterprise internetwork, spanning time zones almost as easily as it used to span office cubicles. To match these new demands, LAN protocols have become increasingly powerful and flexible. The following four major LAN protocols support the workgroup and the enterprise model to varying degrees:

◆ Xerox Network Systems (XNS)

◆ Novell IPX/SPX

◆ NetBIOS

◆ AppleTalk

IPX/SPX

The Novell NetWare protocols are based on the Xerox Network Systems (XNS) protocols developed at Xerox Corporation's Palo Alto Research Center (PARC). The layer structure, protocol interaction, and network addressing closely correspond to XNS.

Novell's primary protocols are the Internetwork Packet Exchange (IPX) and Sequenced Packet Exchange (SPX). SPX is a reliable, connection-oriented protocol, while IPX is the unreliable datagram protocol.

NetWare uses a slightly modified version of the routing information protocol (RIP) originally developed as part of the TCP/IP Internet protocol suite to query and maintain routing-information tables on workstations and servers.

Network packets must be directed not only to a particular device but to a particular process running on the device. Devices are identified in the form of addresses, which are associated with a particular subnetwork on a LAN. The target process on the device is identified by a socket number. Novell adopted the internetwork-addressing structure of XNS in which a complete address is given by the network number, the host number, and the socket number on the host. The network number is 32 bits long, the host number is 48 bits long, and the socket is 16 bits long.

IPX

The Internetwork Packet Exchange (IPX) is Novell's network layer protocol. IPX provides a connectionless, unreliable, datagram service to workstations and servers.

IPX makes a best-effort attempt to deliver a packet to the destination but requests no acknowledgment to verify if the packet has indeed reached its destination. IPX relies on high-layer protocols, such as SPX, to provide a reliable, sequenced datastream service.

An IPX packet consists of a header (30 bytes) and data section. Because IPX does not provide any facilities for packet fragmentation, IPX implementations must ensure that the packets they send are small enough to be transmitted on any physical networks they want to cross. IPX requires that all physical links be able to handle IPX packets that are 576 bytes long. (Therefore, the safest approach is to send no packet larger than 576 bytes.) Many implementations refine this process slightly by detecting when they are sending packets directly to the destination over a single physical link. If this physical link can handle packets larger that 576 bytes, larger packets are used.

SPX

The Sequenced Packet Exchange (SPX) is the Novell transport layer protocol. It was derived from the Xerox Sequenced Packet Protocol (SPP).

SPX provides a reliable, connection-oriented, virtual circuit service between network stations. SPX makes use of the IPX datagram service to provide a sequenced data stream. This is accomplished by implementing a system that requires each packet sent to be acknowledged. It also provides flow control between the network stations and ensures that no duplicates are delivered to the remote process.

SPX reduces the number of times that an unneeded retransmission occurs to decrease the congestion on the network. Retransmissions normally occur after the sending station has timed-out waiting for an acknowledgment of a packet that is lost or damaged or dropped. SPX uses a heuristically enhanced timing algorithm to estimate accurate retransmission times. It also uses historic information to determine the initial time, and it then increases the time by 50 percent if a timeout occurs. The process continues until a maximum time-out value is reached or until acknowledgments return in time and retransmissions are no longer required. In the second case, the time-out stabilizes at a value that is accurate for the network conditions.

SPX adds 12 bytes to the IPX packet header, mostly to carry connection control information. Added to the 30 bytes of the IPX header, this results in a combined header of 42 bytes. The maximum size of an SPX packet is the same as the maximum for an IPX packet.

NetBIOS

The Network Basic Input/Output System (NetBIOS) is a high-level application program interface (API) that was designed to enable programmers to build network applications by using a network of IBM type PCs. It was developed by Sytek, and was originally implemented on an IBM PC Network Adapter card. NetBIOS was introduced by IBM in 1984 and adopted by Microsoft for use with its MS-Net network product. Later, IBM provided an emulator that enabled NetBIOS to work with network interface cards used with its Token-Ring networks.

NetBIOS is not really a protocol; it is an interface that provides network applications with a set of commands to establish communications sessions, send and receive data, and name network objects.

Today, all major networking companies, including IBM, Novell, Microsoft, and Banyan, support the NetBIOS interface either directly or through the use of emulators over their respective protocol stacks. Novell implemented NetBIOS support using the IPX protocol stack. Regardless of the implementation, the NetBIOS interface presented to the distributed application on the network remains consistent.

Many network applications are written using the NetBIOS interface. Because of its ubiquitous character, it continues to be a popular vehicle for developing distributed applications.

As seen from the perspective of the OSI Reference Model, NetBIOS provides a session-layer interface. At this level, NetBIOS is capable of providing a reliable, connection-oriented data-transfer stream, along with a naming system for identifying stations on the network. While NetBIOS can provide an unreliable connectionless datagram service, it does not provide a routing service, making the construction of internetworks very difficult.

AppleTalk

Apple Computer began to design a set of communication protocols, called AppleTalk, in late 1983 and early 1984. The goal was to connect Macintosh personal computers, along with printers, print servers, file servers, routers, and gateways, to computer systems built by other manufacturers. The most common first use of AppleTalk was to connect the graphical computer to an Apple LaserWriter laser printer.

Each Macintosh and Apple LaserWriter includes native hardware support for the AppleTalk networking architecture. Additionlly, the system software includes comprehensive network support. This combination of bundled hardware and software helps make AppleTalk one of the most common networking solutions for personal computers in use today.

AppleTalk was designed from the ground up, to be an open, extensible network architecture to support new physical network technologies and new protocol stacks. It provides for the connection of large numbers of computers and peripherals over a potentially large geographic area by linking local networks into internets.

AppleTalk is designed to support peer-to-peer networking (where there is no need for a separate name server to control the assignment and use of network names). The overall (workstation-centric) design philosophy of the Macintosh computer also extended to the network design. The user's model of interaction with the network had to be as transparent as possible so that the standard operations and paradigms are extended in accessing resources across the internetwork. This means that users can mount remote volumes on their desktop and make use of the files and folders by using the standard select and click operations.

The installation of the network nodes was designed to support a "plug-and-play" model, in which the user attaches the physical link. Most of the configuration is then automatically managed by the system software.

AppleTalk Phase 2 was introduced in June 1989 as an upwardly compatible extension to the existing AppleTalk (Phase 1). AppleTalk Phase 2 provides support for larger, enterprise-wide networks by enabling a greater number of nodes (workstations, printers, and servers) on the network. Although AppleTalk Phase 1 supported a maximum of 254 nodes on a single network, Phase 2 enables multiple network numbers to be associated with a single network, while enabling 253 nodes per network number. AppleTalk Phase 2 provides support for LocalTalk, EtherTalk, and TokenTalk. LocalTalk is the physical and data link specification for Apple's familiar shielded twisted-pair cabling scheme. EtherTalk and TokenTalk are Apple's implementation of Ethernet and Token Ring. The AppleTalk Internet Router also was modified to enable the connection of up to eight AppleTalk networks in any mix of LocalTalk, EtherTalk, and TokenTalk. (Each individual network must have only one type of physical link.)

Designers have used AppleTalk to provide a wide assortment of distributed applications such as supporting the Apple Macintosh, the IBM PS/2 and PC-compatible computers, workstations, and running Unix. These applications include file sharing, print spooling, printer sharing, and electronic messaging. In addition, gateways are available for linking AppleTalk networks with DEC mini- and mainframe computers.

Other LAN Implementations

While dozens of LAN implementations exist, this section covers the non-native TCP/IP choices currently popular for client/server LAN designers. It is important to note that they are not TCP/IP native, but most now offer additional packages allowing them to connect to TCP/IP.

Novell NetWare

Novell NetWare is one of the most pervasive LAN implementations, with direct support or a comprehensive protocol gateway on every major platform. NetWare can be used with Ethernet, CSMA/CD networks, as well as with token ring architectures. NetWare emulates NETBIOS, supports file and printer sharing, electronic mail, remote access, inter-LAN communication via a NetWare Bridge, and a gateway to IBM's SNA over a synchronous data link control (SDLC) line.

NetWare provides a number of utility and monitor programs that enable network administrators to add new users to the network, open/close files, and maintain system resources and security. NetWare provides for security down to a file level.

Both DOS and Unix vendors and developers offer direct support for Novell NetWare. Some Unix hardware vendors have released versions of Portable NetWare. To provide a more seamless link between standard NetWare and Unix hosts, Portable NetWare is implemented as "not native" to its host hardware platform. It runs as a guest under another operating system. As a result, high levels of Unix/NetWare connectivity can be achieved, along with the support of all traditional NetWare clients (DOS, Windows, OS/2, Macintosh) available for the Unix host.

Novell and various third-party vendors support NetWare on such client platforms as Apple, DOS (including Windows), OS/2, and Unix. NetWare servers can be hosted under Unix, IBM MVS, IBM VM, OS/400, and DEC VMS. Novell NetWare licensees include Data General, Hewlett-Packard, ICL, Interactive, Intergraph, MIPS, NCR, Prime, Pyramid, Unisys, and Wang.

Banyan VINES

Banyan Systems VINES is one of the most technically advanced distributed network operating systems (NOS) on the market today. VINES is designed to seamlessly support large PC networks and internetworks. Compaq, one of the Banyan Systems' largest customers, runs its internal network of approximately 11,000 geographically dispersed PCs using VINES.

VINES distributed architecture integrates directory, security, and network management services on interconnected servers, each of which supports one or more PCs. A VINES server, a version of Unix system V, can run on Intel 386 and 486 based PCs, and over a SCO-Unix–compliant version of Unix system V. Workstation clients include DOS, Windows, Macintosh, and OS/2.

The VINES architecture supports many types of network topologies, including Ethernet and Token Ring. VINES provides support for a variety of communication protocols, including 3270 Emulation, TCP/IP, and X.25 packet switching protocols. In addition, VINES can run over WAN server-to-server interconnections, providing a single, global view of an enterprise network.

VINES provides the user with a single, integrated view of the network. VINES uses an authorization mechanism to support network-wide security. Network administrators are provided with easily managed configuration and monitoring tools. VINES offers a set of services that include file and print services as well as VINES Network Mail.

SNA

The IBM Systems Network Architecture (SNA) was first introduced in 1977 and has dramatically changed since that time. It supports a wide diversity of applications over a large user base of approximately 40,000 SNA licenses. With the thousands of networks installed worldwide, SNA is one of the most accepted *de facto* network standards. SNA provides a consistent set of communication protocols, and the communication access method, known as Virtual Telecommunications Access Method (VTAM).

SNA is designed to satisfy large network user requirements for efficiency and cost-effectivity:

◆ SNA provides resource sharing. It eliminates the need to install separate communication links for different types of workstation applications, because networking enables access to an application of any host processor and from any workstation.

◆ SNA enhances network dependability. SNA protocols recognize data loss during the transmission, use data flow control procedures to prevent data overrun, avoid overload and congestion, recognize failures, and correct many errors. Network availability is high due to such SNA features as the extended recovery facility, alternate routing, backup host, and built-in control procedures in workstations, modems, and controllers.

◆ SNA helps users with network expansion and maintenance by providing open, documented interfaces, which are implemented in all SNA products. This reduces the amount of programming involved in system integration.

◆ SNA facilitates problem determination by providing network management services in each network component plus global management software, such as NetView.

◆ SNA maintains an open-ended architecture that helps to accommodate new facilities, such as digital networks, digitized voice, distributed systems, electronic document distribution, fiber optics, graphics, satellites, Token-Ring networks, Videotex, and Viewdata.

◆ SNA provides a network interconnection facility that enables the users in one SNA network to access information and programs in other SNA networks by using SNA gateways. These gateways make SNA network boundaries transparent to the network users.

◆ SNA provides network security through logon routines that prevent unauthorized users from accessing the network. SNA also provides encryption facilities.

SNA handles connections between users in a network so that the underlying physical aspects of network routing are transparent to the user. The end-points of a communication link are defined as logical units. The logical unit provides facilities that isolate the user from the physical characteristics of the network devices.

Historically, the application ran on a special network node, the host processor. The user used a terminal connected to the network's peripheral node, thereby supporting a host-to-terminal, master/slave hierarchical relationship.

One of SNA's objectives, especially in the framework of IBM's Systems Application Architecture (SAA), is to support distributed processing. SAA distributed processing implies a peer-to-peer relationship between applications, rather than the older master-slave type communication. In SNA, the necessity for peer-to-peer communications originated the creation of a new logical unit type (Logical Unit type 6.2), a new physical unit type (SNA Node type 2.1), and a new set of rules, called the LU6.2 protocol. This new protocol provides peer-to-peer communication capabilities and is marketed as Advanced Program-to-Program Communication (APPC).

SNA Components and Links

An SNA network consists of many hardware and software components connected via links. A link consists of a link connection and two or more link stations. A *link connection* is the physical transmission media connecting two or more nodes. Link stations use data link control protocols to transmit data over a link connection. The transmission media can be telephone lines, microwave beams, fiber optics, coaxial cables, etc.

Data link control protocols specify the rules interpreting the control data and providing the transmission across the link. In a LAN environment, SNA data link control protocols support IEEE 802.5-Token Ring.

SNA Compared to OSI

The structures of the OSI model and the SNA model are very similar. Both represent a hierarchical architecture consisting of seven layers. The layers of both models have the same properties. Each layer performs a specific model function (SNA function or OSI function); lower layers provide services for higher layers, and layers of the same level can communicate with each other as peers. Both models are built to formally describe how their respective communication networks should be implemented.

The purpose of the OSI model, however, is different from that of the SNA model. The goal of the OSI model is to bring "law and order" into the diverse world of network communication architectures to provide standard information exchange protocols for communication between autonomous, heterogeneous architectures.

Conversely, SNA is designed for the exchange of information between network nodes on the homogeneous architecture on which IBM builds its enterprise program offerings. This architecture allows IBM to tailor the network hardware and network components to achieve maximum efficiency and performance.

The functions of the SNA and OSI layers (compared in the following), are similar, even though there is no one-to-one correlation between SNA layers and OSI layers.

◆ Level 1SNA Physical Control Layer and OSI Physical Layers are functionally equivalent.

◆ Level 2SNA Data Link Control Layer can use SDLC and the OSI interface. SDLC is a subset of HDLC, which is used by OSI Date Link Layer.

◆ Level 3SNA Path Control Layer provides functions similar those defined for the OSI Transport and Session Layers.

◆ Levels 4 and 5SNA Data Flow Control and Transmission Control Layers provide functions similar to those defined for OSI Transport and Session Layers.

◆ Levels 6 and 7SNA Presentation Services and Transaction Services Layers provide functions similar to those defined for the OSI Presentation Layer and the Common Application Services in the OSI Application Layer.

◆ Level 7OSI Specific Application Services in the OSI Application Layer are considered to be end-user exchanges in SNA.

IBM recognizes the significance of the OSI model as the common standard for heterogeneous system interconnection. Various mixed-vendor networking organizations, such as the Department of Defense, plan to migrate to OSI by the mid-1990s, provided that the model is finalized and OSI-compliant products are available. SNA currently offers more and better functionality for IBM-based networks. As an interim solution, IBM has adopted the concept of the SNA/OSI Gateways and is pursuing the dual strategy of developing gateways from SNA to OSI, in addition to developing products based on the OSI architecture.

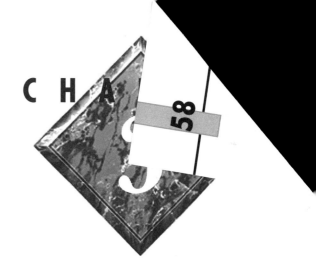

Introduction to TCP/IP

TCP/IP is a family of protocols used for computer communications. The letters stand for *Transmission Control Protocol/Internet Protocol,* but other than in the press, the full name rarely is used. TCP and IP are both individual protocols that can be discussed separately, but they are not the only two protocols used in the family. Often a TCP/IP user does not use the TCP protocol itself, but some other protocol from the family. To talk about using TCP/IP in this situation is still proper, however, because the name applies generically to the use of any protocol in the TCP/IP family. Because TCP/IP was developed by the Department of Defense, the protocol family is sometimes called *The DoD Suite,* but does not have a classical "marketing" name as does Apple's AppleTalk suite of protocols.

Protocols usually are grouped into "families" (sometimes called *suites* or *stacks*). Which protocols are grouped together is usually determined by the protocols' implementors. Many protocol families are developed by commercial organizations; for example, AppleTalk is a family of protocols developed by Apple Computers. Each protocol in a family supports a particular network capability. No protocol is of much use on its own and requires the use of other protocols in its family. In some ways, protocol families are like a set of golf clubs; each club is used for a particular purpose, and no one club can be used to play an entire game. Usually a golfer purchases all the clubs in a set from the same vendor. Just as each vendor might offer a slightly different set of clubs, network protocol families try to solve the same network problems with a slightly different set of protocols, but many are similar from family to family.

The TCP/IP protocol family includes protocols such as Internet Protocol (IP), Address Resolution Protocol (ARP), Internet Control Message Protocol (ICMP), User Datagram Protocol (UDP), Transport Control Protocol (TCP), Routing Information Protocol (RIP), Telnet, Simple Mail Transfer Protocol (SMTP), Domain Name System (DNS), and numerous others. Keeping all the acronyms straight can be difficult, especially because some are reused by other protocols (for example, the Novell, or IPX, family has a RIP protocol different from the TCP/IP family RIP protocol). An understanding of all the protocols in a particular family is not a prerequisite to knowing how a network basically works. This chapter concentrates on the IP and ARP protocols (mentioning the RIP and ICMP protocols briefly). This focus, coupled with a minimal discussion of a particular link protocol (Ethernet is used for the examples in this chapter), illustrates how a TCP/IP network causes data to flow smoothly across an internet.

Understanding TCP/IP: Six Questions

In TCP/IP, all protocols are transported across an IP internet, encapsulated in IP packets. IP is a *routable protocol*, which means that two nodes that communicate using IP do not need to be connected to the same physical wire. To have a basic understanding of how information travels across a routed network, it is only necessary to understand the answers to the following six questions:

1. What is the format of an address in this protocol?

2. How do devices get an address?

3. How is the address mapped onto a physical address?

4. How does an end node find a router?

5. How do routers learn the topology of the network?

6. How do users find services on the network?

The rest of this chapter answers these questions and illustrates by example how these answers tie together to explain how information flows across a TCP/IP-based network.

Understanding Basic Network Concepts

Before answering the preceding questions (or possibly even before understanding what they are asking), you must know the meanings of some terms and concepts discussed in this chapter.

Addressing

The central concept of networking is *addressing*. In networking, the *address* of a device is its unique identification. Network addresses are usually numerical and have a standard, well-defined format (each defined in its specification document). All devices on a network need to be given a unique identifier that conforms to a standard format. This identifier is the device's address. In routed networks, the address has at least two pieces: a *network* (or *area*) piece and a *node* (or *host*) piece.

In this chapter, *network* refers to a set of machines connected to the same physical wire (or set of wires connected only by bridges and repeaters). *Internet* means one or more networks connected by routers. The word *internet* (lowercase *i*) is not to be confused with the *Internet* (uppercase *I*). The Internet is a specific internet that connects millions of computers worldwide and is becoming predominant in the press and elsewhere.

If two devices on an internet have addresses with the same network number, they are located on the same network and thus on the same wire. Devices on the same wire can communicate directly with each other by using their datalink layer protocol (that is, Ethernet). The examples in this chapter use Ethernet as the medium connecting the devices. Although some particulars might differ, the concepts are the same if the networks are built on Token Ring, Fiber Distributed Data Interface (FDDI), or many other common physical media.

Correct addressing of devices on a network requires that every device connected to the same network (wire) be configured with the same network number. Also, every device with the same network number must have a different node (or host) number from every other device with the same network number. Finally, every network in an internet must have a unique network number. To rephrase, every network on an internet must have a unique network number, and every node on a network must have a unique node number within that network. This rule ensures that no two devices on an internet ever have the same network *and* node number and therefore have a unique address within the internet.

In addition to a unique address for every device on an internet, special addresses often are used to address multiple nodes simultaneously. These addresses are called *broadcast* or *multicast* addresses.

The following discussion references two different types of addresses—network layer addresses and Media Access Control (MAC) layer addresses. These two address types are completely independent of each other. The network layer addresses are all IP addresses. These addresses are used to communicate between nodes across an IP internetwork. The MAC addresses are used to communicate from node to node on the same wire and often are built right into the communications card (for example, the Ethernet card). MAC addresses are the lowest level addresses and are the means by which all information is ultimately transferred from device to device.

Packets

On most networks, such as TCP/IP networks, the information sent is broken down into pieces called *packets* (or *datagrams*) for two main reasons: resource sharing and error detection and correction. On networks that have more than two computers (for example, Ethernet or Token Ring), the medium connecting the devices is shared. If any two devices are communicating, no other devices can communicate at the same time. A network works like a party line in that respect. If two devices want to share a very large amount of information, it is unfair for them to become the sole users of the network for a long period of time; other devices might have urgent information to transfer to other parties. If the large block of information is broken into many small blocks, each of these can be sent individually, enabling other devices to interweave their own messages between the packets of the extended conversation. As long as each piece is individually addressed to the intended destination and contains enough information for the receiver to piece it back together, the fact that it is broken into pieces does not matter.

The other main use of packets is for error detection and correction. Networks are ultimately made up of wires (or radio waves or light beams) that are prone to interference, which can corrupt a signal sent across them. Dealing with corrupted messages is a big part of networking; in fact, most of the complexity in networking involves dealing with the what-if-something-gets-corrupted scenarios. Many error detection and correction techniques are based on *checksums*; when a sender transmits information (as bytes of data), a running total adding up all the bytes sent is kept and then transmitted at the end of the data transmission. The receiver computes the total of the data received and compares it to the total transmitted. If a difference exists between the total bytes received and the total bytes computed, then the data or the total is corrupted. The sender is asked to retransmit the data. This version is much simpler than what really happens, but is sufficient to illustrate the concept.

If the medium on which the transmission takes place has an average error rate of one bit in one million (that is, for every one million bits sent, one is corrupted on average), then there is a practical upper limit to the amount of data that can be sent in one transmission. Imagine that ten million bits are sent. Normally a transmission of this size contains ten errors, the checksum is wrong, and the sender is asked to retransmit. The retransmission size is the same as the original transmission, so it contains on average ten errors again. The only way to break out of this loop is to break the data into smaller pieces, each with its own checksum, that can be retransmitted individually.

Protocols

Each of these packets is a stream of bytes. For true communication to occur, these bytes must have meaning associated with them. This meaning is provided by the protocol specification. A *protocol* is a set of rules that defines two things—the format of the packets and the semantics of their use.

Most packets have a format that includes a header and a body. The *header* often includes information such as a source and destination address, the length of the packet, and some type indicator so that the receiver knows how to decode the body. The *body* can be raw data (for example, a piece of a file or an e-mail message), or it can contain another packet that has its own format defined by its own specification. Packet formats usually are depicted in a specification by a rectangular picture that gives the order, size, and names of the pieces of information that make up the packet. Figure 3.1 is an example of an Ethernet frame.

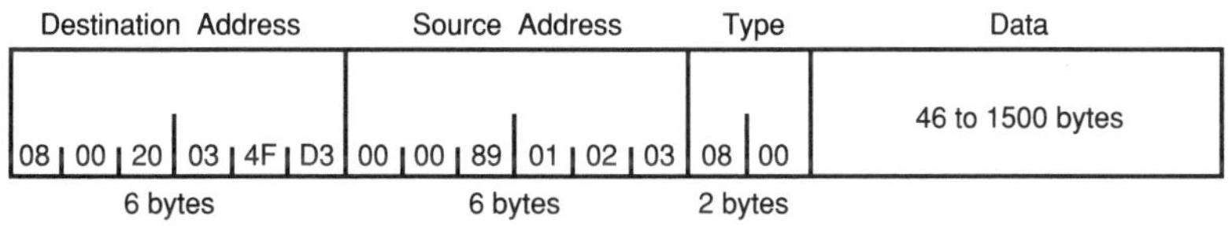

Destination Address	Source Address	Type	Data
08 | 00 | 20 | 03 | 4F | D3	00 | 00 | 89 | 01 | 02 | 03	08 | 00	46 to 1500 bytes
6 bytes	6 bytes	2 bytes	

Figure 3.1

An Ethernet frame.

You must know more than the format of a packet to understand the protocol. You also must know when to send which packets and what to do when they are received. Many protocols have very simple formats, but their use is very complicated. Imagine teaching a non-English speaker to behave as an English-speaking receptionist. The "packet formats" might be as follows:

> "Hello, this is company X."
>
> "How may I direct your call?"
>
> "Please hold."
>
> "Good bye."
>
> "That line is busy, may I take a message?"
>
> "That person does not work here."

The "protocol" for answering the phone needs to include when to say each of these phrases, how to look up an extension in the company phone book, what to say if the party being called is not in, how to take a message, what to do with the message after taking it, what to do with a wrong number, and so on.

A protocol specification specifies the format of the information exchanged (the packets) and the correct sequencing of that information as well as the additional actions (logging, mail delivery, table updates, and so on) that might be required. Just as the receptionist described earlier was only trained to direct incoming calls (and not answer tech support questions), each protocol has a specific set of functions with which it is designed to deal.

In the TCP/IP world, most protocol specifications are available online as Requests For Comment (RFCs). These specifications tend to be very technical in nature and are directed at engineers who intend to implement these protocols. One site (of many) on the Internet that makes the RFCs available for anonymous ftp is ftp.internic.net. An index is available at that site in the file /rfc/rfc-index.txt.

Routers and End Nodes

Routed networks have two classes of devices: end nodes and routers (see fig. 3.2). *End nodes* are the devices with which users interact—workstations and PCs, printers, file servers, and so on. *Routers* are devices that connect networks. Routers have the responsibility to know how the whole network is connected and how to move information from one part of the network to another. They shield end nodes from needing to know much about the network so that the end nodes can spend their time doing user tasks. Routers are connected to two or more networks. Every device on a particular network must have the same network number as every other device on that network, and every network must have a different network number. Thus routers must have a separate address for every network to which they are connected. Routers are very much the "post offices" of the network. End nodes send information they don't know how to deliver to the local router, and the router takes care of getting it to its final destination. Sometimes a device such as a file server also is a router, for example, when that end node is connected to more than one network and is running software that enables it to route information between those networks. Routing is often a CPU-intensive chore and can significantly impact the performance of a machine doing tasks other than routing. For this reason, most routers are dedicated machines.

Routers are introduced to networks for several reasons. Routers enable more devices to ultimately be interconnected because they extend the address space available by having multiple network numbers. Routers help overcome physical limitations of the medium by connecting multiple cables.

The most common reason for using a router is to maintain political isolation. Routers enable two groups of machines to communicate with each other while remaining physically isolated, which is especially important when the two groups are controlled by different organizations. Many routers have filtering functions that enable the network administrator to strictly control who uses and what is used on the network. Problems that occur on one network do not necessarily disrupt other networks.

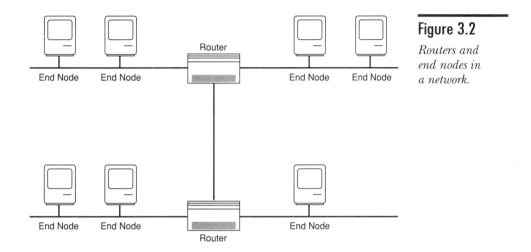

Figure 3.2

Routers and end nodes in a network.

End Node Network Send and Receive Behavior

When a node on a TCP/IP network has an IP packet to send to another node, it follows a simple algorithm to decide how to proceed. The sending node compares the network portion of the destination address with the network portion of its own address. If the two networks are the same, it implies that the two nodes are on the same wire—either directly connected to the same cable or on cables separated only by repeaters or bridges (see fig. 3.3). In this case, the two nodes can communicate directly using the datalink layer (for example, Ethernet). The sending node uses ARP to discover the destination node's MAC layer address and encapsulate the IP packet in a datalink layer frame to be delivered directly to the destination node.

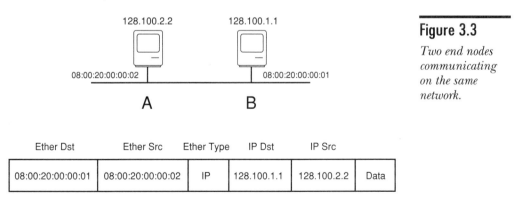

Figure 3.3

Two end nodes communicating on the same network.

If the network portions are different, the two nodes are separated by at least one router, which implies that the sending node cannot deliver the packet without using a router as an intermediary. The packet is encapsulated in a datalink layer frame

addressed to the MAC address of a router on the same wire (if no router is on the
wire, then that particular network is isolated and cannot send IP packets to other
networks). The router delivers the IP packet to the remote network.

When an end node receives an IP packet, it compares the destination address in the
IP packet to its own address and to the IP broadcast address with which it is configured. If the destination address matches either of these addresses, the end node
accepts the packet and processes it further. The way it is processed depends on which
subprotocol of IP it is. If the destination address does not match, the packet is
dropped (ignored), as shown in the following end-node algorithm:

```
Receive

if((dst addr == my addr) or (dst addr == broadcast)){
    process packet
}
else{
    drop (ignore) packet
}


Send
if(dst net = my net){
  deliver (may need to "ARP")
}
else{
    send to router
}
```

Router Send and Receive Behavior

When a node is functioning as a router and it receives an IP packet, it examines
the destination IP address in the packet and compares it to its own IP address. If the
addresses are the same or the destination IP address is the IP broadcast address,
the packet is processed as it would be for an end node. Unlike an end node, a router
does not automatically drop packets that are received but not addressed to it. These
are packets that end nodes on the network are sending to the router to be forwarded
to other networks (see fig. 3.4). All routers maintain routing tables that indicate how
to reach other networks. The router compares the network portion of the destination
address with each network in its routing table. If the router cannot find the destination network in its routing table, it checks for a default route (typically listed as a
route to 0.0.0.0). If it does not find a default route, the packet is dropped (and an
ICMP destination unreachable message is sent to the source IP address in the
dropped packet).

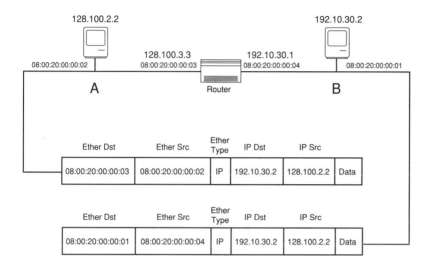

Figure 3.4

Two end nodes communicating on different networks.

When a matching route to a network is found (or a default route exists), the router checks the distance to the remote network. If the distance is listed as 0, the network is directly connected to the router. In this case, the router sends an ARP request for the destination IP address and encapsulates the IP packet in a datalink layer frame addressed to the MAC address of the destination returned in the ARP response. If the distance is greater than 0, the packet must travel through at least one more router. In this case, the router uses the next router field from this route and sends an ARP request for that router, encapsulating the IP packet in a datalink layer frame addressed to the MAC address of the next router. This way, an IP packet travels across an internet, maintaining the same source and destination IP addresses the entire time, but having the source and destination MAC addresses change for each hop. The algorithm a router uses when receiving a packet is as follows:

```
Receive
if((dst addr == my addr) or (dst addr == broadcast)){
   process packet
}
else if(dst net is directly connected){
   deliver (may need to "ARP")
}
else if(dst net in table){
   deliver to next router
}
else{
   drop (ignore) packet
}
```

Examining the Format of an IP Address

For any routable protocol to be efficiently routable, the address must have two parts. TCP/IP addresses have two components—a *network component* and a *host* (or *node*) component. Addresses used with TCP/IP are four-byte (32-bit) quantities called simply *IP addresses* (not TCP/IP addresses) (see fig. 3.5). These addresses are written in *standard dot notation*, which means that each byte is written as a decimal number separated by dots (the period character)—for example, 192.37.54.23 (pronounced "192 dot 37 dot 54 dot 23"). Because each piece of the IP address is 1 byte, its value must be between 0 and 255 inclusive—for example, the IP address 125.300.47.89 could not be a legal IP address because 300 is greater than 255 and would not fit in a single byte.

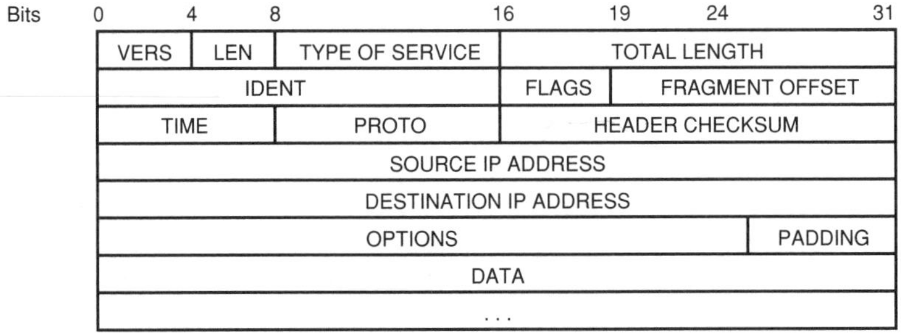

Figure 3.5

Format of an IP address.

Bits	0	4	8	16	19	24	31
	VERS	LEN	TYPE OF SERVICE	TOTAL LENGTH			
	IDENT			FLAGS	FRAGMENT OFFSET		
	TIME		PROTO	HEADER CHECKSUM			
	SOURCE IP ADDRESS						
	DESTINATION IP ADDRESS						
	OPTIONS					PADDING	
	DATA						
	. . .						

IP addresses are composed of a network portion and a host portion. The split is not as simple as the first two bytes being the network portion and the last two being the host portion. The designers of the TCP/IP protocols were concerned that they not limit the size of potential networks too severely, so they opted for a graduated method of network and host division. If the split was to be two bytes for each, no network could have more than 2^{16} hosts on it. Also, smaller networks would waste much of the address space by using only a fraction of the available nodes on any given network.

To provide for efficient address use, IP addresses are divided into *classes*. The three most important classes of networks are A, B, and C. IP addresses are split into these classes according to the first few bits of the address (or the value of the first byte, if you don't like working in binary), as in figure 3.6.

An IP network is customarily referred to as an IP address whose host portion consists of all zeroes—for example, 10.0.0.0 or 128.37.0.0 or 200.23.45.0. For example, 137.103.210.2 is a class B address that has a network portion of 137.103 and a host portion of 210.2. This network, the 137.103.0.0 network, can have up to two bytes worth (2^{16}) of hosts on it—all of which must share the exact same first two bytes 137.103 and must have unique host portions.

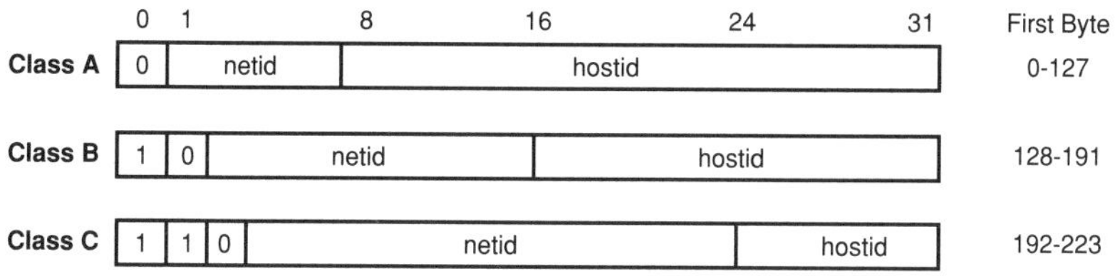

	0 1	8	16	24	31	First Byte
Class A	0	netid		hostid		0-127
Class B	1 0	netid		hostid		128-191
Class C	1 1 0	netid			hostid	192-223

Figure 3.6

The three classes of IP addresses.

Assigning IP Addresses to TCP/IP Devices

IP addresses can be assigned in a number of ways. If an organization wants to build a TCP/IP internetwork that never will be connected to any other TCP/IP network outside the organization, then it is acceptable to pick any class A, B, or C network number that allows an appropriate number of hosts on it. This method is rather short-sighted, as much of the benefit of having a TCP/IP network is the capability to connect to the outside world and share resources beyond those in the organization—for example, connecting to the Internet. A better strategy is to contact the InterNIC's registration services at Network Solutions, Inc. and request an officially assigned network number. The InterNIC ensures that the network number assigned to each applicant is globally unique. All the host ids on that network are free to be assigned as the assignee sees fit.

Sometimes when an organization connects to the Internet through another organization (for example, a commercial service provider or a university), that second organization provides the network number. In addition, many larger organizations have internal network administrators in charge of assigning IP addresses to individual users within the company.

When an IP network number has been acquired from an internal network administrator, service provider, or the InterNIC, it is possible to start assigning specific host IP addresses from that network to individual devices. Usually an organization keeps records of which IP addresses are assigned already and has some method of distributing the unused IP addresses to individuals who need to configure new IP devices. IP addresses must be configured into devices with the same network number as all other devices on the same wire but with a unique host portion. If two or more devices have the same IP address, they will not work reliably and will present a very difficult situation to debug.

Most IP devices require manual configuration. The person installing the device must obtain a unique and correct IP address and type it in to some configuration program or console, usually along with other information such as IP broadcast address, subnet mask, and default gateway address.

Some sites support dynamic configuration of IP devices. Protocols such as Boot Protocol (BOOTP) and Dynamic Host Configuration Protocol (DHCP) enable the use of centralized servers to hand out unique IP addresses and other configuration information on an as-needed basis. At the time of this writing, this sort of configuration is not a mature enough technology to find widespread use.

Mapping IP Addresses to MAC Addresses

Ultimately, all computer communication takes place by moving data from node to node over some form of link such as Ethernet, Token Ring, FDDI, and the Point-to-Point Protocol (PPP). Many links support attaching more than two nodes and therefore require that all data sent over them be addressed to a specific destination to be delivered correctly. These addresses have nothing to do with IP addresses; they are completely separate and in addition to IP addresses. These addresses are MAC addresses—sometimes called *physical*, *hardware*, or *link addresses*. Unlike IP addresses that are assigned, most MAC layer addresses are built into the hardware by the manufacturer of the device or network interface card (NIC).

On an Ethernet network, every device on the network has a built-in Ethernet address. This address is a six-byte quantity usually written using hexadecimal numbers with a colon separating the bytes—for example, 08:00:20:0A:8C:6D. Ethernet addresses are assigned by the Institute of Electrical and Electronics Engineers (IEEE) and are unique among all Ethernet devices. No two devices should ever have the same Ethernet address (manufacturing errors do occur on occasion). The Ethernet address is divided into two parts; the first three bytes constitute the *vendor code*. Each vendor of Ethernet equipment obtains a unique vendor code from the IEEE. Every piece of equipment supporting Ethernet made by that vendor is programmed with an Ethernet address that begins with that vendor code. In the preceding example, the vendor code 08:00:20 corresponds to Sun Microsystems; every Ethernet device manufactured by Sun begins with those three bytes (see fig. 3.7). The vendor is responsible for making sure that every Ethernet device it manufactures has the same first three bytes (vendor code) and a different remaining three bytes to guarantee that every Ethernet device in the world has a unique address built in.

If every Ethernet device already has a unique address, why are IP addresses necessary? First of all, not every device has Ethernet support; IP addresses enable devices that connect to fiber and Token Ring and serial lines to use IP without having to get an Ethernet address. Secondly, Ethernet addresses are organized by equipment vendor rather than by owner organization. To come up with an efficient routing scheme based on who made the equipment rather than on where it is located would be impossible. IP addresses are assigned based on a network topology, not on who manufactures the device. Finally, and most important, is that devices can be more easily moved or repaired when an extra level of addressing exists. If an Ethernet card breaks, it can be replaced without getting a new IP address. If an IP node is moved from one network to another, it can be given a new IP address without getting a new Ethernet card.

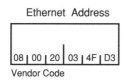

Figure 3.7

A typical Ethernet address including a vendor code.

Network hardware communicates only with other network hardware (for example, two Ethernet cards on two network devices). This network hardware often uses an addressing system that is not friendly to humans, but is convenient for the hardware itself. Users and services on networks communicate with other users and services. These services are easier to access if they are addressed in a way that makes sense to people. Addressing that is easy for humans to understand, however, is not always easy for hardware to manage. To solve this problem, a method of mapping user-level addresses to hardware is needed.

Ethernet addresses are long and cryptic and not meant to be regularly dealt with by users. To provide a mechanism for nodes to determine each other's hardware addresses without intervention from the user is possible. For TCP/IP, this mechanism is ARP. When an IP node wants to communicate with another node with the same network number, it assumes that having the same network number implies that the destination is on the same wire. On an Ethernet, for example, the source Ethernet card can directly communicate with the destination Ethernet card if it knows the Ethernet address. To determine the Ethernet address of a node on the same wire, the sending device sends an ARP request to the Ethernet broadcast address (see fig. 3.8). This address is a special address that all Ethernet cards are configured to listen to (it consists of six bytes of all ones, written in hex as FF:FF:FF:FF:FF:FF). Setting the destination Ethernet address to this value and sending an Ethernet packet causes every device on the Ethernet to accept the packet as if it were addressed specifically to it. It is the Ethernet equivalent of the U.S. postal address "Occupant."

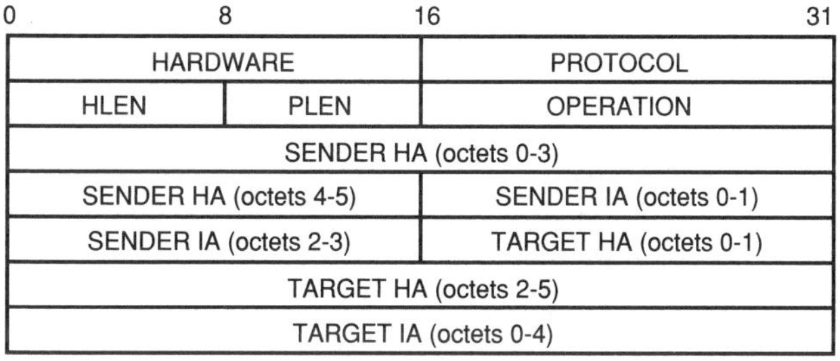

0	8	16	31
HARDWARE		PROTOCOL	
HLEN	PLEN	OPERATION	
SENDER HA (octets 0-3)			
SENDER HA (octets 4-5)		SENDER IA (octets 0-1)	
SENDER IA (octets 2-3)		TARGET HA (octets 0-1)	
TARGET HA (octets 2-5)			
TARGET IA (octets 0-4)			

Figure 3.8

The format of an ARP packet.

An ARP request asks every node on the wire what is the Ethernet address for a particular IP address. The ARP request contains (among other things) the sender's source IP address and Ethernet address as well as the IP address with which the sender wants to communicate. Every Ethernet device on the network accepts this packet and, if the receiving device supports IP, recognizes that it is an ARP request. The receiving device then compares its configured IP address to the IP address being looked for. If an exact match occurs, the receiving device sends an ARP response back to the sender (through the Ethernet address in the ARP request, not as a broadcast) containing its Ethernet address. The sender can then encapsulate the IP packet it wants to send in an Ethernet packet with a destination Ethernet address as specified in the ARP response.

Why doesn't the sending node simply broadcast every packet it sends? On a large or busy network, this would require every node to be interrupted to process every packet on the network to determine whether the packet was destined for it. This interruption would be very inefficient and would slow the network down considerably. To make sure that broadcasts are minimized, nodes on broadcast networks requiring the use of ARP maintain a list of IP addresses and the Ethernet addresses that correspond to them (determined by previous ARP requests). This list is called the *ARP cache* and is updated whenever an ARP response is received. A node needing to send many IP packets to the same destination sends an ARP request the first time it tries to contact the node and records the Ethernet address it receives in the ARP response. Subsequent IP packets use the Ethernet address in the cache instead of sending another ARP request. Each entry in the cache is kept for some amount of time decided by the implementor of the TCP/IP software in use. This timeout might be as little as 30 seconds or as much as several hours or even be configurable. The shorter the time, the more broadcast ARP requests there are. But if the time is too long, then a node that changes its Ethernet address (because the Ethernet card was replaced, for example) cannot be contacted until the entry is updated.

Examining How End Nodes Find a Router

To send a packet to a node on another network, an end node requires the aid of a router. If two nodes on the same network want to communicate, they can do so directly by encapsulating their IP datagrams in link level frames (for example, Ethernet frames) and sending them to each other. This procedure works because nodes on the same network are attached to the same wire (separated only by cable, repeaters, and bridges). When a destination is on another network, it is on another wire and can't be reached directly. The end node encapsulates the IP datagram in a link level frame destined for a router. The router then determines where to send the packet next. Because a router is needed to contact a node on another network, it is necessary for the router to be on the same network as the source node (otherwise the source node would need a router to reach the router!). Routers behave much like a post office for U.S. mail. If you want to deliver a message to someone very close (for example, next door), you would most likely deliver the message yourself. But if the destination is unfamiliar or is far away, you would deliver the message to the nearest post office. The post office would deliver the message for you if the message is for a local address serviced by that post office; otherwise it looks up which post office should deal with it next. The letter might pass through a number of post offices before being delivered.

To deliver a packet to a node on a different network, a source node sends the unmodified IP packet to the local router by encapsulating it in a link level packet addressed to the router's MAC address. If the link level is Ethernet, the source node needs to know the Ethernet address of the local router. For reasons given previously, nodes should not deal with Ethernet addresses directly; therefore, TCP/IP end nodes need to know how to obtain the Ethernet address of a router. By using the ARP protocol, an end node that knows the IP address of a router can obtain the Ethernet address. TCP/IP end nodes need to be manually configured with the address of at least one router (usually called a *default gateway*). Some TCP/IP implementations enable the router's address to be obtained dynamically by "eavesdropping" on the routers' conversations. In this case, the node is configured to "listen" to a particular routing protocol such as RIP.

How Routers Learn the Network Topology

For routers to fulfill their role as "post office" of the network, they need to know which networks are reachable and how to get to them. To accomplish this, routers store information about the topology of the network. This topology is usually stored as a *routing table* that lists each known network, tells how "far" away the network is, and indicates which router is the next one to send a packet to to reach a network not directly connected (see table 3.1 and fig. 3.9).

TABLE 3.1
A Routing Table for a Three-Router Network

Network	Distance	Next Router
Router 1		
1	0	—
2	0	—

continues

TABLE 3.1, CONTINUED
A Routing Table for a Three-Router Network

Network	Distance	Next Router
Router 1		
3	1	222.222.222.2
4	1	222.222.222.2
5	2	222.222.222.2
6	0	—
Router 2		
1	1	222.222.222.1
2	1	222.222.222.1
3	0	—
4	0	—
5	1	200.15.22.3
6	0	—
Router 3		
1	2	200.15.22.1
2	2	200.15.22.1
3	1	200.15.22.1
4	0	—
5	0	—
6	1	200.15.22.1

The *cost* of a network can be declared in many ways (depending on whose network you look at), but is most often simply a count of how many routers a packet must go through to reach a network. The cost to a network is often called the *distance* or *number of hops* to a network.

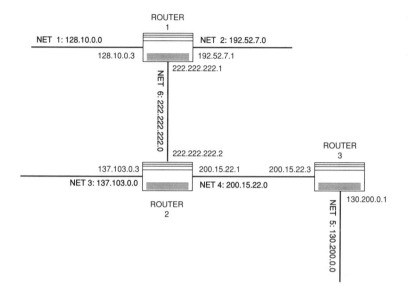

Figure 3.9

A network with three routers.

A cost of zero means that the specified network is directly connected to the router. Packets destined for such a network can be delivered from the router to the final destination by encapsulating the datagram in a datalink layer frame (for example, Ethernet) by sending an ARP request for the node. For this reason, the next router field for directly connected networks is meaningless.

When the cost is non-zero, the network in question is not directly connected and requires routing through at least one more router. In this case, the routing table indicates which router is the next one to send to. The router sends an ARP request for this "next hop" router and encapsulates the datagram in a datalink layer packet addressed to the MAC address of the next router. When this router receives the packet, it checks its routing table and determines if the packet can be delivered locally or needs to be routed to yet another router.

If the destination network (or default network) does not appear in the routing table, then the packet cannot be delivered and is dropped (ignored). This could happen for a variety of reasons, including the following:

◆ The sending node was mistaken or misconfigured

◆ The router was misconfigured and does not know about the network

◆ All routes to that network are no longer operating (a router farther along the path to the network went down)

Usually when a packet is dropped due to the lack of a route, the router sends an ICMP Destination Unreachable message to the source, which should cause the node to log a message informing the user that data is not getting through.

Routing tables are set up in routers by two means: manual configuration and dynamic acquisition. (Sometimes a combination of both methods is used.) Manual configuration is the most straightforward method, but the least robust in the face of a changing network, and also can be impossible to maintain in a very large network. When *manual configuration* is used, the person installing the router is responsible for typing in the various fields for the routing table—telling the router which networks are reachable, how far away they are, and which routers should be used to reach them.

Dynamic acquisition of routing tables is achieved by means of one or more routing protocols. In TCP/IP, the most commonly used routing protocol is RIP (not to be confused for the IPX routing protocol of the same name). *RIP* is a simple protocol that enables routers to tell each other what networks they know about and how far away they are. With this information, each router can assemble a table of every network on an internet, enabling packets to be sent from any network to any other network, which could mean excessively large routing tables if the network were attached to a worldwide network such as the Internet. Therefore, provisions are made to "clump" many networks together in a default route represented by the IP address 0.0.0.0. Routers advertising connectivity to network 0.0.0.0 are saying, "If you don't see the network number anywhere else, send the packet to me."

RIP updates are broadcast by every router on every network every 30 seconds. Because these updates can impact network performance considerably on very large or slow networks, more efficient (in bandwidth, at least) protocols are being developed. Open Shortest Path First (OSPF) is a routing protocol becoming popular. OSPF provides a number of benefits to large networks, such as less traffic and faster "flooding" of information regarding changes to the network, but at the expense of a more complex algorithm (implying the need for more memory) to implement. Other protocols are used by routers to learn dynamically the topology of the network and advertise changes in that topology. The mechanics of each one is different, but the general purpose of binding the network together is the same.

Finding and Using Services

In the end, the purpose of all this encapsulating and routing is to provide users access to services. Users are interested in terminal emulation, printing, file sharing, and e-mail; they're not concerned with how these services are created.

Services require support to make them easy to find and use. Most people are not very good at dealing with numbers even if they have sensible structures like IP addresses (never mind Ethernet addresses), for example. People like to deal with names that are like words (if not words themselves). The command Telnet server is far easier to remember than telnet 192.34.50.3, for example.

Most services in the TCP/IP world are found through well-known names. Such services are found published in books, in company documents, or by word-of-mouth from the system administrator to users. You can access services if you know the name of the device that provides the service and what program to use to access it. `FTP the file printers.txt from server.company.com` might be the directions to access the file that describes the names of all the printers you can use. A user would type **ftp server.company.com**; log in; and type **get printers.txt** to access the file.

IP packets cannot be addressed to a name; they require a four-byte IP address. Much like ARP is used to map an IP address to a hardware address, a service name can be mapped to an IP address in a number of ways. The simplest way is to maintain files that contain the name and IP addresses of devices of interest. This file is often called the *hosts file* because in Unix it is found in the file /etc/hosts, and many IP implementations for other platforms have maintained the convention of calling the file hosts. This solution is simple, but not efficient on large networks. To maintain an up-to-date file on every single IP device can be difficult.

Usually a network administrator configures one or more servers to maintain a network-accessible database of name-to-IP mappings. Two commonly used methods are the Domain Name System (DNS) and Sun's Network Information System (NIS). Maintaining such a database requires that one or more machines be designated as "keepers of the database," and all other machines send requests to these servers to have a name converted into an IP address or vice versa. A network-accessible database of name-to-IP mappings is easy to maintain on a large network and requires little per-device configuration (only needing to know which machine to go to for lookups).

Given the amount of information currently available on the Internet and the rate at which that amount is increasing, obviously, to have just the files and lists of where to find information is entirely inadequate. To ease the burden of locating services and information on a network of the scale of the Internet, many different applications are being built. Applications such as Mosaic, gopher, archie, and World Wide Web (WWW) are being worked on by many people, companies, and universities. These applications try to make wading through the vast amount of information available a little easier (or at least more fun). These applications usually have a graphical user interface or a simple text-based interface that makes sorting through some subset of everything out there much easier.

TCP and UDP

Transmission Control Protocol (TCP) and User Datagram Protocol (UDP) travel encapsulated in IP packets to provide access to particular programs (services) running on remote network devices.

Throughout this chapter the discussion of TCP/IP has revolved entirely around IP. IP addresses enable data to be addressed to a particular node on an internet. After the data arrives, some mechanism is needed to enable the proper service within the device to receive the data. The data might be e-mail or a file or part of a print job. To direct the data to the appropriate program, another level of addressing is needed. Each service available on a node is accessed through a unique address called a *port* (sometimes also referred to as a *socket*). Ports are identified by a simple decimal number. For example, port 25 is the SMTP address. These numbers are contained in the TCP and UDP headers of TCP and UDP packets, which are encapsulated within IP packets (see figs. 3.10 and 3.11).

Figure 3.10

Format of a UDP packet.

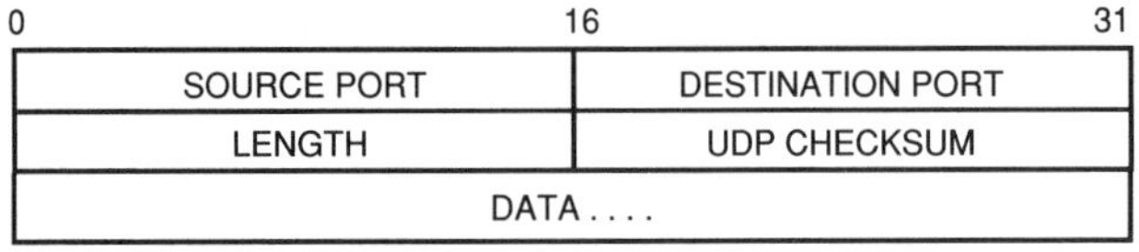

0	16	31
SOURCE PORT	DESTINATION PORT	
LENGTH	UDP CHECKSUM	
DATA		

Figure 3.11

Format of a TCP packet.

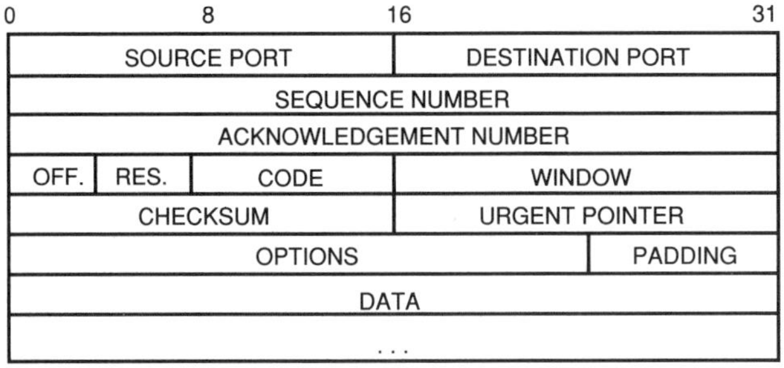

0	8	16	31
SOURCE PORT		DESTINATION PORT	
SEQUENCE NUMBER			
ACKNOWLEDGEMENT NUMBER			
OFF.	RES.	CODE	WINDOW
CHECKSUM		URGENT POINTER	
OPTIONS			PADDING
DATA . . .			

To understand the difference between UDP and TCP, you must know what is meant by datagram versus stream-oriented protocols, and what is meant by reliable versus unreliable protocols.

A *datagram-based protocol* is one that imposes a maximum size on the amount of data that can be sent in a single transmission. Ethernet, IP, and UDP are all datagram-based protocols. An upper limit to how much data can be sent in a single transmission exists. This type of protocol is analogous to sending a normal letter through the U.S. Postal Service. A single stamp limits the amount of "data" you can send at one time.

TCP is a *stream-oriented protocol.* A user of a TCP-based protocol does not need to worry about the maximum size of a transmission. TCP breaks the transmission into smaller sizes, retransmitting lost pieces, reordering data delivered out of order, and filtering out any extras that might occur due to faulty retransmissions. This type of transmission is analogous to a commercial freight carrier that can deliver as much "data" as the customer wants. The overhead necessary to support TCP is proportionally higher than that of UDP. An application that uses TCP requires more memory and more bandwidth to ensure that the transmission is completed properly.

The other factor that differentiates UDP from TCP is reliability. UDP is an *unreliable* or *best-effort* protocol. This definition does not mean that reliable data transfer cannot happen if based on UDP, but that the UDP protocol itself does not handle reliable data transfer. An application using UDP is responsible for implementing retransmissions, duplicate filtering, and so on, itself. If a UDP packet is lost or corrupted in transmission, it must be noticed by the application sending the data, which is again analogous to the U.S. Postal Service for normal mail. If the post office loses a letter, the letter is gone. They do not store a copy of it and "retransmit" it. Ethernet and IP also are best-effort protocols.

By pushing the overhead needed for reliability into an application, it is possible to make a reliable protocol or application that uses UDP. Sun Microsystems has implemented an entire file system—NFS—on top of UDP. NFS uses a less efficient set of algorithms than TCP to implement reliability, but the overhead is far less. UDP is appropriate for networks in which an application like NFS is used because the level of loss and corruption on a LAN is usually very low.

TCP is a *reliable protocol.* This definition does not mean that TCP guarantees delivery of the data it sends, but that TCP delivers the data if at all possible and reports back to the application if the data cannot be delivered (for example, if the destination node crashed). This reliability requires a great deal of overhead compared to UDP. Overhead is incurred to provide this service efficiently. TCP fragments and reassembles the data stream (so that the data can fit in datagram-based IP packets), retransmits lost packets, filters out duplicates caused by hasty retransmissions, handles flow control between computers of different speeds, and maintains *windows* (packets sent ahead that don't wait for an acknowledgment). If the network connectivity is preserved during the transmission, the data arrives in order and uncorrupted. If the connectivity is lost (the receiving program or machine crashed or an intermediate router went down), that fact is reported to the application using TCP.

Applications that invoke *sessions* usually use TCP to transfer data. These applications usually require the user to log in or connect before data can be moved. Applications that claim to be *stateless* are usually built on UDP, such as NFS.

Applications and protocols that use UDP include the following:

- ◆ NFS
- ◆ RIP
- ◆ Trivial File Transfer Protocol (TFTP)
- ◆ Simple Network Management Protocol (SNMP)

Applications and protocols that use TCP are as follows:

◆ FTP

◆ Telnet

◆ SMTP

TCP/IP Routing

J ust as stand-alone computers have readily become relics of the past, so too now are stand-alone networks. What was once simply a LAN must now become part of a WAN or MAN. Faced with the requirements to connect to wider geographical locations and more users, administrators have quickly had to embrace bridges, routers, and gateways.

This chapter examines routing on the TCP/IP protocol, how it is implemented, why it is implemented, and what you need to know to implement it.

Examining the OSI Model

Every technology has its own jargon; computer networks are no exception. No matter what the protocol is—TCP/IP or NetWare—the basic underlying concepts are the same. Today they all start with the Open Systems Interconnection model, more commonly referred to as the OSI model. Chapter 3, "Introduction to TCP/IP," discusses the OSI model in detail, so it is only briefly touched upon here as it relates to this chapter's topic.

Because of the existence of numerous types of computer operating systems, the OSI model was developed in 1977 by the International Standards Organization (ISO) to promote multivendor interoperability.

The OSI model itself does not specify any communication protocols. Instead it provides guidelines for communication tasks. It divides the complex communication process into smaller, more simple, subtasks. This way, the issues become more manageable, and each subtask can be optimized individually. The model is divided into seven layers as shown in figure 4.1. Note that the layers are numbered from the bottom up.

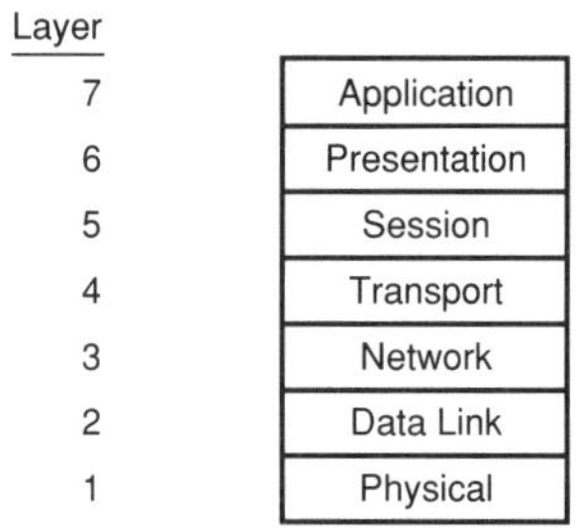

Figure 4.1

The OSI model.

Layer	
7	Application
6	Presentation
5	Session
4	Transport
3	Network
2	Data Link
1	Physical

Each layer is assigned a specific task. Also, each layer provides services to the layer above it and uses the services of the layer directly beneath it. For example, the network layer uses services from the datalink layer and provides services to the transport layer.

In the context of this chapter, it is important to explain the services provided by the first three layers of the OSI model:

◆ The *physical* layer (layer 1) provides the physical connection between a computer system and the network wiring. It specifies cable pin assignments, voltage on the wire, and so on. The data unit at this layer is called a *bit*.

◆ The *datalink* layer (layer 2) provides the packaging and unpackaging of data for transmission. The data unit at this layer is called a *frame*. A frame represents the data structure (much like a database record template).

◆ The *network* layer (layer 3) provides routing of data through the network. The data unit at this layer is called a *datagram.*

The TCP/IP protocol suite was developed before the OSI model was defined and is based mostly on the U. S. Department of Defense's own networking model, known as the *DoD model.* The DoD Model also is known as the *Internet model.* The DoD is discussed in the next section.

Examining the DoD Model

In the mid-60s, the U.S. Department of Defense defined its own networking model. The DoD model, which defines only four layers, is much simpler than the OSI model. Figure 4.2 compares the DoD model to the newer OSI model.

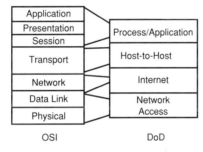

Figure 4.2

A comparison of the OSI and DoD models.

Although the DoD model predates the OSI model by some ten years, a comparison between the two can still be made:

◆ The *process/application* layer in the DoD model maps to the top three layers of the OSI model.

◆ The *host-to-host* layer in the DoD model maps to OSI's transport layer.

◆ The DoD *internet* layer corresponds to the network layer in OSI.

◆ The *network access* layer in the DoD model maps to the bottom two layers in the OSI model.

Associated with each layer is one or more protocols that specify how certain networking functions behave. The Internet/Network layer protocols for TCP/IP are discussed in a later section. The next section examines the internetworking devices associated with the first three layers of the OSI model (the first two layers in the DoD model)— physical, datalink, and network.

Internetworking Devices

The basis for all TCP/IP routing decisions is a table of routing information maintained by the stack and routing protocols. The routing table is one of the most frequently accessed structures in the TCP/IP stack; on a busy host this can be hundreds of accesses in a second. The TCP/IP netstat command can be used to view the contents of the routing table. The following table illustrates the output from the netstat -r command used to display information stored in the routing table.

destination	router	refcnt	use	flags	snmp metric	intrf
132.1.16.0	132.1.16.3	1	63	U	-1	lan0
132.1.16.5	132.1.16.4	0	22	U	-1	ppp0
127.0.0.1	127.0.0.1	1	0	UH	-1	lo0
default	132.1.16.1	2	1351	UG	1	lan0

Each entry in the table contains a destination and router (sometimes referred to as an IP gateway) address pair. For a given destination address, the router address indicates the host to which an IP datagram should be forwarded to reach that destination. The following minitable should help alleviate confusion about what a router does.

The flags in the table can have the following values:

Flag	Description
D	The route was created via a redirect message.
G	The route is to a gateway/router.
H	The route is to a host. If this flag is not set, the route is to a network or subnetwork.
M	The route has been changed by a redirect message.
U	The route is currently up.
<null>	If this flag is not set, then the destination can be reached directly.

A few comments are in order regarding the routing flags. If the G flag is not set, then the destination can be reached directly (i.e., the host has both the IP address and the physical or link layer address of the final destination workstation). The net result is that the IP datagram can be sent simply by encapsulating it in the physical network frame.

For indirect routes (G flag set), the IP address corresponds to that of the final destination workstation and the link layer address is the physical address of the gateway. The Address Resolution Protocol (ARP), an integral part of the TCP/IP stack, maintains a cache of local IP address and link layer address pairs to facilitate the translation of IP addresses to link layer addresses.

The Simple Network Management Protocol (SNMP) metric indicates the desirability of a given route; a positive metric indicates a more preferred route. The intrf field indicates the interface (transport type and unit number) that the route is associated with. Possible interfaces include lan<n> (Token Ring; IEEE 802.5), le<n> (Ethernet; IEEE 802.3), sl<n> (Serial Line Internet Protocol or SLIP), ppp<n> (Point-to-Point Protocol or PPP), and lo<n> (the Loopback interface). The terminal string <n> represents the interface unit number. Note that the actual name assigned to an interface is vendor specific and varies from system to system.

This section defines the terms *repeater*, *bridge*, *router*, *gateway*, and *brouter* and their functions. It is important to understand how each of these devices functions so that you can make an informed decision when it comes to time for you to either connect your network with another, or segment your existing network into smaller networks to improve performance.

Repeaters

When electrical signals traverse a medium, they attenuate (or fade) as a function of distance traveled. The longer the distance a signal travels, the lower the signal comes out at the other end. This shortcoming can be overcome with the use of a repeater. A *repeater* simply reconditions the incoming signal and retransmits it—in other words, it can be used to extend distance. Therefore, it works at the physical layer of the OSI model.

Because a repeater simply "passes on" the signals it receives, it performs no error checking. Therefore, any errors (such as CRC in Ethernet) are passed from one segment to another.

Note Repeaters cannot be used to connect segments of different topologies, such as Ethernet and Token Ring. However, repeaters can be used to connect segments of the same topology with different media, such as Ethernet fiber to coax Ethernet.

A repeater, such as an Ethernet multiport repeater, also can act as a signal splitter.

Tip A repeater does not slow down your network because it performs no filtering. A repeater is transparent to protocols; however, because a device is involved, you can expect minute delays (one to two seconds).

Bridges

A *bridge* is usually used to separate traffic on a busy network. A bridge keeps track of the hardware addresses of devices for each network to which it is directly connected. The bridge examines the hardware destination address of the frame and, based on its tables, decides if the frame should be forwarded or not. If the frame needs to be forwarded, a new frame is generated.

 Note A bridge is a *store-and-forward* device; it does not pass the original signal to the destination segment.

Consider figure 4.3. When Earth sends a frame to Jupiter, the bridge knows that (based on its internal tables) Jupiter is on the same segment (Segment A) as Earth; no frame is forwarded to the segment on the right (Segment B). However, if Earth sends a frame to Saturn, the bridge, knowing Saturn is not on the same segment as Earth, forwards the frame.

Figure 4.3

A bridged network.

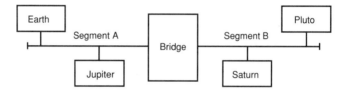

Because the bridge has access to information at the frame level, it "operates" at the datalink layer of the OSI model (see fig. 4.4).

Figure 4.4

A bridge in reference to the OSI model.

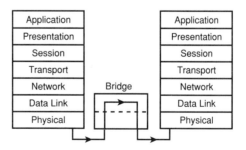

Like repeaters, bridges are transparent to protocols. Because the bridge "operates" at the datalink layer, it also can perform physical layer functions. Therefore, you can use a bridge to extend the distance of a segment.

 Note Unlike repeaters, bridges do not propagate errors from one segment to another.

The four types of bridges available today are as follows:

- ◆ **Transparent bridge.** The transparent bridge is the most common type of bridge. It does not care about the protocols on the wire. A transparent bridge also is known as the *learning bridge* because it "learns" about the hardware addresses of the devices to which it is directly attached. It also is referred to as *spanning tree bridge* because of the spanning tree algorithm (IEEE 802.1D) it uses to manage paths between segments with redundant bridges.

- ◆ **Source routing (SR).** The source routing bridge (SR) is popular in IBM Token-Ring environments. IBM uses source routing to determine whether a frame needs to cross a bridge based on ring number information within the frame.

- ◆ **Source route transparent (SRT).** The source route transparent bridge (SRT) is a combination of a transparent and a source routing bridge. It "source routes" if the data frame has the SR information, or "bridges transparently" it if does not.

- ◆ **Translational bridge.** Some manufacturers produce translational bridges that connect Ethernet to Token Ring. An example is IBM's 8209 bridge.

Note   In general, a bridge connects segments of similar topology such as Token Ring to Token Ring. They also can connect segments of the same topology with different media (much like a repeater).

If bridges are connected through a WAN link, they are known as *remote bridges*.

Some bridges have security features that you can define—by hardware address or protocol type—as to whether frames are passed to a certain destination address. This feature enables you to filter traffic that might be destined for a specific server.

Note   A workstation accessing resources across a bridge has slightly slower performance than a workstation accessing resources across a repeater because a bridge performs more functions than a repeater.

Routers

A *router* can determine the best route between two or more networks. A router has access to the network (software) address information, which means it operates at the network layer of the OSI model (see fig. 4.5). Because it needs to access the network address information, it is very protocol-specific. When a router encounters a datagram with a protocol it does not support, the datagram is dropped.

Figure 4.5

A router in reference to the OSI model.

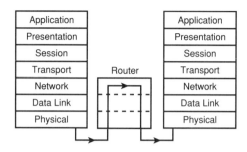

For example, if one of your networks has TCP/IP and NetWare traffic, and your router only supports TCP/IP (or only TCP/IP routing is switched on), no NetWare traffic will ever leave that segment. Therefore traffic is confined to a local segment.

A router is a much more intelligent device than a bridge; it can make decisions on selecting the best route for a datagram to reach its destination. This path can change depending on a number of factors, such as availability of links, traffic level, and others. A bridge, on the other hand, simply decides whether a frame needs to be passed on.

Note   Routers do not pass errors from one network to another.

Because a router works at the network layer, it has no information about the topology (the frame information is stripped off by the datalink layer). As a result, you can use a router to connect segments of different topologies.

Routers usually have some built-in filtering capability. The filtering is based on upper-layer protocols. For example, you can set up the filter table such that users cannot see certain servers across a given router. This type of filtering is much more powerful than filtering done with bridges.

Stop   A workstation accessing resources across a router has a slower performance than a workstation accessing resources across a bridge, which in turn is slower than when a repeater is involved. A router performs more complex functions than a bridge or repeater, resulting in slower workstation performance.

Traditionally in the IP world, routers were called *gateways* because they were the "gateway" to the outside world. However, with the accepted definition of the OSI model and standardization of internetworking terms within the industry, gateways are now called routers. Be careful, however, when reading some of the RFCs because the term "gateway" is still used liberally. Do not confuse that with the "OSI definition" of gateway as discussed in a following section.

A router connected to two or more physical networks has two or more IP addresses. In rare instances a TCP/IP host has two or more physical connections. Such a host is called a *multi-homed host*. If a multi-homed host's routing table is configured properly, it can function as a router.

Brouters

A *brouter* (bridging router) is a device that first routes the protocols it understands. Tailing that, it attempts to bridge the traffic.

Certain protocols (such as NetBIOS) cannot be routed because they have no network information. If you need to pass these protocols together with, for example, TCP/IP traffic, you need to use a brouter for your network.

In most cases, hardware-based routers, such as 3COM, Cisco, and Wellfleet are capable of being a brouter. Software-based ones, such as Novell's Multiprotocol Router, cannot (even though Novell's MPR 2.11+ supports Token Ring SR bridging).

 Note Check your router documentation; not all hardware routers can function as brouters.

Gateways

A *gateway* is a device that translates between two different protocols and sometimes topologies. For example, a gateway is needed to translate between TCP/IP over Ethernet to SNA over Token Ring.

 Note Gateways tend to be upper-layer-protocol specific, as is the e-mail protocol, for example. Therefore, if you need to exchange both e-mail and printing traffic between two hosts, two separate gateways may be needed.

Because a gateway translates most, if not all, protocol layers, it covers the entire seven layers of the OSI model.

Deciding Which Device to Use

Oftentimes, you need to modify your current network—expand, improve performance, or add new services, for example. How can the different internetworking devices discussed in the preceding sections help? What should you use when? Look at the following two simple case studies and apply what you learned in the preceding sections.

Case Study 1

You are given a task to extend the distance of your current Ethernet coax (10BASE-2) network to include another floor of the building. What device should you use?

Before you answer, ask yourself the following questions:

◆ How long is the existing network?

◆ Is traffic an issue right now? Will it be an issue with the additional distance?

◆ Is there more than one protocol on the wire? Do you need to separate them?

If the current network is within the distance specification of 10BASE-2 Ethernet, and the addition of the new segment does not exceed that, you can use a repeater to extend the distance. This is the lowest cost solution.

If the addition of the new segment exceeds the 10BASE-2 distance limitation, you need at least a bridge to extend the distance because the bridge has (at least) two network cards, and the other side of a bridge is considered a new network (as far as cabling goes, not protocol). Of course, you can use a router here, but it is more expensive.

Tip A router needs to look at the software address "buried" deep within a frame; therefore, it has to do more work to get at the information. A bridge only needs to look at the hardware address, which is near the beginning of the frame, requiring less work. Therefore, as a rule of thumb, a bridge can forward data much faster than a router. A repeater does not look at any "data"; therefore, it is faster than a bridge.

In reference to the second question, if traffic is a consideration, then a bridge should be used even if distance is not an issue. A bridge keeps traffic local and only passes frames to the other side when required.

Stop If (datalink layer) broadcast traffic (frames addressed to all devices on a network) is an issue, a bridge is not a good internetworking device to use. By definition, a broadcast address is not "local;" therefore, broadcast traffic always propagates across a bridge. In such case, use a router.

Use a router if multiple protocols are on the wire. A router helps you isolate the protocols, if desired. It also helps you reduce the amount of broadcast traffic as well as manage multiple paths.

Case Study 2

Today some sites do not want multiple protocols on the wire for various reasons. In such an instance a gateway serves as an ideal solution. Consider the sample network in figure 4.6.

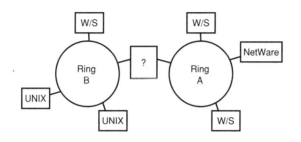

Figure 4.6

A sample network for Case Study 2.

This network contains two (Token) rings. The users on Ring A are Novell NetWare users with a NetWare server on the local ring. The Unix servers are located on Ring B; some Unix users also are on Ring B. Users on Ring A need to access a custom application on the Unix servers on Ring B, but the network management folks don't want NetWare traffic on Ring B or TCP/IP traffic on Ring A. What is the best solution?

If both TCP/IP and NetWare traffic are allowed on the rings, the solution is quite straightforward: load dual protocol stacks on the workstations on Ring A and put in either a bridge or a router to connect the two rings. Multiple protocols, however, are not permitted on the ring, which leaves only one solution: an IPX-TCP/IP gateway.

The workstations on Ring A will speak IPX (NetWare) to the gateway; the gateway will convert from IPX to TCP/IP and put them out on Ring B. Two examples of such a gateway are NOV*IX for NetWare (NLM-based) from Firefox, Inc. (408-321-8344; 800-230-6090) and Catapult (OS/2-based) from Ipswitch (617-246-1150).

Now that you know the difference between repeaters, bridges, routers, and gateways, take a look at the various routing protocols associated with TCP/IP.

IP Routing Protocols

Initially, a router only knows about the networks or subnets to which it is directly connected. It learns about other networks by two means: static routes and routing protocols.

A *static route* is a path in a router's routing table that is manually configured by a network administrator. For each network or host destination, the network administrator configures the next hop router and the cost associated with the route. This information is never changed, even if a portion of the path becomes unavailable. For example, in figure 4.7, a static route is configured for Router 1 so that to reach Network C, it must use Router 2.

Figure 4.7

A static route example.

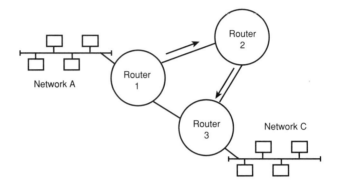

Should the path between Routers 1 and 2 or between Routers 2 and 3 go down, Router 1 cannot reach Router 3 through an alternate path until it is manually reconfigured.

This is not a problem if the connectivity between Network A and Network C is not critical, because it will take some time before Router 1 can be reconfigured. However, this option is not viable if the link is important or automated path reconfiguration is desired. In such a case, a *routing protocol* is required so that routers can exchange path information automatically and update any route changes dynamically.

A number of different routing protocols are used in the TCP/IP world. They are not compatible with each other, though. Therefore, to resolve IP routing problems it is essential that you understand them.

The four routing protocols discussed in some detail in later sections are as follows:

◆ Routing Information Protocol (RIP)

◆ Open Shortest Path First (OSPF)

◆ Interior Gateway Routing Protocol (IGRP)

◆ Internet Control Message Protocol (ICMP)

This chapter does not explain all the details of each of these protocols because you can easily refer to the Request For Comments (RFCs)—documents that detail the protocol—for such information. The information presented here, however, gives you a working understanding of each of the protocols.

Before learning about the individual routing protocols, however, you must understand the classification of routing protocols used today.

Classification of Routing Protocols

When dealing with internet routing, routing protocols are divided into different "classes"—*interior routing protocols* and *exterior routing protocols*.

Interior routing protocols, sometimes known as interior gateway protocols (IGPs), are generally used within an autonomous system to dynamically determine the best route to each network or subnet. An autonomous system (AS) is a group of routers that share information through the same routing protocol. Each autonomous system is assigned a unique identification number by the Network Information Center. The AS number is used by some routing protocols to control the exchange of routing information.

Exterior routing protocols, sometimes known as *interdomain routing protocols*, are used to exchange routing information between different autonomous systems.

Depending on the algorithm used to determine routes, cost of paths, and so on, routing protocols are further classified as either *distance-vector routing protocols* or *link state routing protocols*.

In *distance-vector routing protocols*, each router keeps a routing table of its perspective of the network. For example, as shown in figure 4.8, Router 1 sees that Networks A and B are one hop away (connected to directly), whereas Network C is two hops away. However, Router 2 sees Networks B and C as one hop away, and Network A as two hops away. The two routers "see" the network differently.

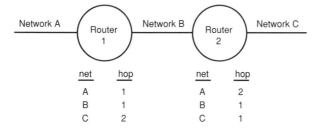

Figure 4.8

A sample network consisting of two routers and three network segments and its corresponding routing tables.

Note The distance-vector protocol is sometimes known as the *Ford-Fulkerson routing algorithm*, named after the inventors of the algorithm (L.R. Ford, Jr. and D.R. Fulkerson, *Flows in Networks*, Princeton University Press, 1962). The distance-vector protocol also is sometimes referred to as the *Bellman-Ford algorithm* because it was based on the Bellman Equation (R.E. Bellman, *Dynamic Programming*, Princeton University Press, 1957).

Each router takes the routing information passed to it, adds one hop to the route (to account for its own presence), and passes the updated information to the next router in line. In essence, distance-vector routing protocols use "secondhand" information from their neighbors.

Distance-vector routing protocols select the "best route" based on a *metric* ("some" unit of measurement). The metric used is different based on the actual protocol. One drawback of distance-vector routing protocols is that when routers send updates, they send entire routing tables. To keep the information up to date, the updates are *broadcast* at regular, fixed intervals.

The opposite of distance-vector routing protocols are link state routing protocols. With a link state routing protocol, a router calculates a "tree" of the entire network with itself as the root (see fig. 4.9).

Figure 4.9

Network layout as "seen" by Router 3 using link state protocols.

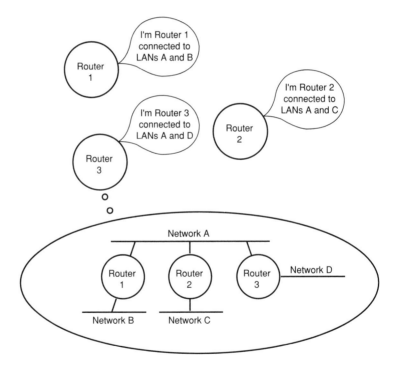

In this example, Router 3 constructs a network layout based on the route information received *directly* from the other routers. Under link state, each router distributes information about its directly connected networks and their associated metrics only.

The routers only include the best path derived by the metric to other nodes (routers). When a router detects changes in the state of its direct link (for example, a link comes up or goes down), the router distributes (broadcasts) the change to all other routers through a process called *flooding*. Flooding updates every router's database because it only sends state change information (hence the name link state).

In general, these flooding packets are very small and are sent infrequently. They contribute very little to the overall broadcast traffic unless routes change often.

The following sections examine the individual routing protocols.

Routing Information Protocol (RIP)

The Routing Information Protocol (RIP; RFC 1508/1388) was first introduced in 1988. RIP is a *distance-vector* routing protocol as discussed earlier.

Because distance-vector routing protocols have regular, fixed update intervals, RIP's update is sent every 30 seconds.

Stop For readers familiar with Novell's protocols, do not confuse this RIP with the RIP used by NetWare. Although they bear the same name and perform a similar function, NetWare RIPs are sent once every 60 seconds.

Therefore, in an environment in which you have both NetWare and TCP/IP, you will have RIP broadcasts from both protocols.

If a route is learned through RIP update messages, and then a subsequent update message does not refresh this route within 180 seconds (six update cycles), the route is assumed to be unreachable and is removed from the routing table.

RIP is probably the most common routing protocol used today because it is easy to implement. RIP has some serious limitations, however. For example, RIP data carry no subnet mask information, which limits RIP to advertise only network information (no subnet information), or requires RIP routers to make assumptions about the subnet mask. The latter makes it very vendor-implementation-specific and often causes interoperability problems.

Tip If you are experiencing routing problems, check the routing tables of the routers involved and see if RIP is enabled. Some network administrators who want to cut down on the amount of broadcast traffic on their network disable RIP on the routers and use static routes instead.

Some routers enable you to adjust the RIP update timer to reduce broadcasts. If you do this, check that all other routers are configured similarly. Otherwise, you might see routes "come and go" on certain routers, resulting in intermittent routing problems.

For RIP, hop count is used as the metric. In figure 4.8 Router 1 "sees" that Network C is farther away than Network A or B because Network C has a metric (hop count) of two, whereas the others have a metric of one. If Router 1 learns (from another router not shown in the figure) of another path to Network B with, say, two hops, it discards that new route because it has a higher metric.

Note   A RIP metric of 16 (hops) means that the destination is not reachable.

Recently some routers started supporting RIP II (RIP version 2; RFC 1388). RIP II is an enhancement over RIP that includes the subnet mask in its routes and variable length subnets, which enables subnet information to be passed on correctly. Also, authentication on routing update messages can be performed.

Stop   Not all RIP routers support RIP II. Make sure that your routers use the same protocol.

Some routers, such as Novell's Multiprotocol Router, can support RIP I and RIP II simultaneously.

The biggest disadvantage of distance-vector protocols such as RIP is the time it takes for the information to spread to all routers. This period is known as the *convergence* time. For a large network, the convergence time can indeed be long; and during this time, data frames have a much greater chance of getting misrouted and lost because of the "count-to-infinity" problem illustrated as follows.

Using the distance-vector algorithm, the distances between Network D and the various routers are as follows (see fig. 4.10):

◆ One hop from Router 3 (directly connected)

◆ Two hops from Router 2 (through Router 3)

◆ Three hops from Router 1 (through Routers 2 and 3)

If Router 3 fails or the link between Routers 2 and 3 is down, Router 2 removes Network D's route from its routing table by setting the metric for Network D to 16. However, Router 2 sends a RIP update to Router 3 indicating that it can reach Network D at a lower cost (two hops). Router 3 then adds one hop count to this route and updates its routing table with this new route (reach Network D through Router 2).

Router 2 thinks it can reach Network D through Router 3 (in two hops), and Router 3 thinks it can reach Network D through Router 2 (in three hops). You now have a routing loop! In this case, any data destined for Network D is routed back and forth between Routers 2 and 3 until its time-to-live counter expires.

However, over time as the routers continue to update among themselves, the hop count to Network D continually increases and eventually reaches 16 hops (infinity; unreachable), and the entry is removed from all routers. But as you can see, it can take a while, especially if you have a large network of routers.

RIP uses a technique called *split horizon* to prevent such routing loops—no routing information is passed back in the direction from which it was received. For example, Router 1 informs Router 2 that it is one hop away from Network A. Router 2 takes that information, adds one to the hop count for Network A, and passes that to Router 3 on Network C, but *not* back to Router 1 because that is the router from which it received the information.

Split horizon helps solve the count-to-infinity problem if you have a linear network. Most networks, however, contain redundant routes for fault-tolerant purposes, which reduces the effectiveness of split horizon. Figure 4.11 shows a network with multiple paths.

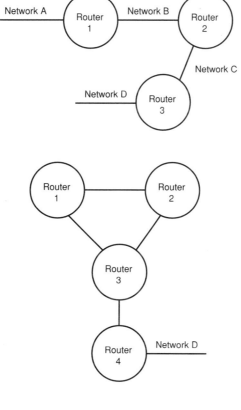

Figure 4.10

A simple count-to-infinity problem.

Figure 4.11

A complex count-to-infinity problem that involves multiple paths.

Router 3 informs Routers 1 and 2 that Network D is two hops away from it; thus the routing tables in Routers 1 and 2 list Network D as three hops away. If Router 4 fails or the link between Routers 3 and 4 goes down, Router 3 will know that Network D is no longer reachable and will inform Routers 1 and 2 of the fact. Through split horizon, Routers 1 and 2 cannot tell Router 3 about their routes to Network D right away. However, between Routers 1 and 2 a "valid" path still exists.

Router 1 learns from Router 2 that it is two hops away from Network D. Router 1 adds one hop to that route and passes the information (three hops to Network D) to Router 3, but not to Router 2 because of split horizon. Router 1 can pass information about Network D to Router 3 because Router 3 no longer advertises a route to Network D. Router 3 now thinks it is four hops away from Network D through Router 1. Router 3 passes that information to Router 2. Router 2 now thinks it is five hops away from Network D through Router 3. Router 2 propagates this to Router 1. Router 1 turns this into six hops, and passes this information to Router 3. Eventually, a hop count of 16 is reached, and split horizon didn't help much!

What can you do? You can use two more tricks: *poisoned reverse* and *triggered updates*, described in the following paragraphs.

With split horizon, routes are not advertised back onto the interface from which they were learned. With *poisoned reverse* enabled, however, such routes *are* advertised back to the same interface from which they are learned, but with a metric of 16. This immediately breaks the routing loop between any two routers. It helps to speed up the convergence time in the count-to-infinity problem, but does not necessarily eliminate it entirely.

Following are two packet captures taken using Novell's LANalyzer for Windows v2.1. This sample IP network has two routers. Router 1 is connected to IP networks 126.0.0.0 (with address 126.1.1.1) and 125.0.0.0 (with IP address 125.1.1.1). Router 2 is connected to IP networks 126.0.0.0 (IP address 126.2.2.2) and 120.0.0.0 (IP address 120.1.1.1). Router 2 has poisoned reverse enabled. Following is the RIP update from Router 126.1.1.1:

```
Station:126.1.1.1 ---->255.255.255.255
Protocol: UDP
    Version: 4
    Header Length (32 bit words): 5
    Precedence: Routine
          Normal Delay, Normal Throughput, Normal Reliability
    Total length:  52
    Identification:       802
    Fragmentation allowed, Last fragment
    Fragment Offset: 0
    Time to Live: 128 seconds
    Checksum: 0xB895(Valid)
```

```
udp: ================= User Datagram Protocol =================
        Source Port: ROUTER
        Destination Port: ROUTER
        Length = 32
        Checksum: 0x0000(checksum not used)
rip: ============== Routing Information Protocol ===============
        Command: Response
        Version: 1
        Family ID: IP
                IP Address: 125.0.0.0
                Distance: 1
```

The RIP update from Router 126.2.2.2 when poisoned reverse is used is as follows:

```
    Station:126.2.2.2 ---->255.255.255.255

    ...

    Precedence: Routine
                Normal Delay, Normal Throughput, Normal Reliability
    Total length: 92

    ...

 udp: =================== User Datagram Protocol ================
    Source Port: ROUTER
    Destination Port: ROUTER
    Length = 72
    Checksum: 0x0000(checksum not used)
rip: =============== Routing Information Protocol ==============
    Command: Response
    Version: 1
    Family ID: IP
        IP Address: 120.0.0.0
        Distance: 1
    Family ID: IP
        IP Address: 125.0.0.0
        Distance: Not Reachable
    Family ID: IP
        IP Address: 126.0.0.0
        Distance: Not Reachable
```

As you see in the first of the preceding two examples, Router 1 advertises to network 126.0.0.0 a route to network 125.0.0.0 with a hop count (distance) of one as expected. In the second example, Router 2 advertises a route to network 120.0.0.0 with a hop count of one, also as expected. Because it has poisoned reverse enabled, however, Router 2 also advertises network 125.0.0.0 (its local network) and network 126.0.0.0 (learned from Router 1) as not reachable.

A quick comparison between the RIP packets in the preceding examples shows that poisoned reverse generates more update traffic (larger update messages). On a large network, especially on a backbone, this level of traffic can cause traffic problems.

Consider the case of a building backbone connecting a number of different floors. On each floor, a router connects the backbone to a local network. Using split horizon, only the local network information is broadcast onto the backbone. But with poisoned reverse, the router's update message includes all the routes it learned from the backbone (with a metric of 16), as well as its own local network. For a large network, almost all the entries in the routing update message indicate unreachable networks.

 Tip   In many cases, network administrators choose simply to use split horizon *without* poisoned reverse to conserve bandwidth and accept the slower convergence time.

If your router supports triggered updates coupling it with poisoned reverse can greatly minimize convergence time. *Triggered updates* cause the router to send a RIP update when a route's metric is changed, even if it is not yet time for a regular update message.

 Stop   Be careful in the use of triggered updates because they can cause much broadcast traffic, similar to a broadcast storm.

 Tip   The count-to-infinity problem in using RIP can be avoided by designing your network without router loops.

If you must have multiple paths for redundancy, consider using a routing protocol other than RIP, such as OSPF as discussed later. Or simply keep in mind how RIP works, fix your downed link as soon as you can, or reset the routers to force a new routing table to be built.

Configuring Interface Routes

At boot time most hosts run a network configuration file, and each interface is configured. A routing table entry also is created for each interface. The interface is normally configured by the TCP/IP ifconfig command, as shown in the following example:

```
ifconfig lan0 9.67.111.214 netmask 255.255.240.0
```

This command configures the lan0 interface with an IP address of 9.67.111.214 and a netmask of 255.255.240.0. This IP address is on network 9.67.96.0 (obtained by performing a BITWISE AND between 9.67.111.214 and 255.255.240). The following routing table entry is created for the interface:

```
destination        router     flags intrf
   9.67.96.0    9.67.111.214    U      lan0
```

The H flag is not set because this is not a route to a host, and the G flag is not set because this is not a route to a router.

Assigning Static Routes

For simple networks, or networks whose configuration changes relatively infrequently, creating a static routing table using the TCP/IP route command is often efficient. This command provides a mechanism to manipulate the routing table by adding, modifying, and deleting table entries. For example, you can use the following command to create a default route to a network router whose IP address is 9.67.96.1:

```
route add default 9.67.96.1 1
```

The digit 1 following the IP address is referred to as the "hop count" and represents the distance (in number of routers) to the destination host or network.

Interior Gateway Routing Protocol (IGRP)

For a long time on the Internet, routers used the Interior Gateway Routing Protocol (IGRP) to exchange routing information. Although IGRP is a distance-vector routing protocol, it uses a number of variables to determine the metric, including the following:

◆ Bandwidth of the link

◆ Delay due to the link

◆ Load on the link

◆ Reliability of the link

By considering these variables, IGRP has a much better, and real-time, handle on the link status between routers. IGRP is much more flexible than RIP, which is based solely on hop count. IGRP can better reflect the type of link and choose a more appropriate path than RIP. In figure 4.11, the links between Router 1 and Router 3 and Router 1 and Router 2 are T1 links, whereas the link between Router 2 and Router 3 is a 56K line. RIP doesn't know the difference in line speed between the paths and sends traffic over the slower 56K line rather than the T1 lines simply because it has a lower hop count. IGRP uses the more efficient T1 lines.

The update interval for IGRP is every 90 seconds, as compared to every 30 seconds for RIP. However, like RIP, when an update is sent, the whole routing table is sent also.

Note   IGRP was developed by Cisco Systems, Inc., which is why for a long time when you acquired a link to the Internet, you were required to use a Cisco router. Now IGRP is supported by many other router vendors.

Open Shortest Path First (OSPF)

Open Shortest Path First (OSPF) is a link state routing protocol first introduced in 1989 (RFC 1131/1247/1583). More and more IP sites are converting to OSPF from RIP because of its much lower traffic overhead and because it completely eliminates the count-to-infinity problem.

Using "cost" as the metric, OSPF can support a much larger internet than RIP. Remember in a RIP-based internet, you cannot have more than 15 routers between any two networks, which sometimes results in having to implement more links for large networks.

Similar to RIP II, OSPF supports variable length subnetting, which enables the network administrator to use a different subnet mask for each segment of the network. Variable length subnetting greatly increases the flexibility and number of subnets and hosts possible for a single network address. OSPF also supports authentication on update messages.

Using cost, an OSPF metric can be as large as 65535.

Other than exchanging routing information within an autonomous system, OSPF also can exchange routing information with other routing protocols, such as RIP and Exterior Gateway Protocol (EGP). This exchange can be performed using an autonomous system border router.

Stop   If you are using multivendor routers in a mixed RIP and OSPF environment, make sure that routes are redistributed between routing protocols in a consistent manner. To create routing loops because a vendor does not increment the hop count when going from RIP to OSPF and back to RIP is possible.

To go into the details of OSPF concepts, OSPF areas, and other OSPF protocols (such as the OSPF Hello Protocol) is beyond the scope of this chapter. Refer to RFC 1583 for the latest definition of OSPF Version 2.

Internet Control Message Protocol (ICMP)

Sometimes even if you have not configured dynamic routing on an IP router, routes can be automatically added to your routing table by the Internet Control Message Protocol (ICMP).

ICMP was first introduced in 1980 (RFC 792/1256). Its function is to provide a dynamic means to ensure that your system has an up-to-date routing table. ICMP is part of any TCP/IP implementation and is enabled automatically. No configuration is necessary. ICMP messages provide many functions, including route redirection.

If your workstation forwards a packet to a router, for example, and that router is aware of a shorter path to your destination, the router sends your workstation a "redirection" message informing it of the shorter route.

The newer implementation of ICMP (RFC 1256) contains a *router discovery* feature. Strictly speaking, router discovery is not a routing protocol, but a way of finding neighboring routers. When a router starts up, it sends a router discovery request (multicast address 244.0.0.2; broadcast only if the interface does not support multicast) asking neighboring routers to identify themselves. Only routers directly attached to the network that the new router is on respond.

 Note   Router discovery is a rather new implementation for some routers and therefore is not supported by all routers.

Other Routing Protocols

The protocols discussed earlier are all interior gateway protocols (IGPs), and they are by far the most often encountered routing protocols in the field. However, at times you might encounter some exterior routing protocols. *Exterior routing protocols* are used to connect two or more autonomous systems (see fig. 4.12). Two exterior routing protocols—Exterior Gateway Protocol (EGP; RFC 827/904) and Border Gateway Protocol (BGP; RFC 1105/1163/1267)—are briefly discussed in this section so that you can become familiar with them.

Introduced in 1982, EGP is the earliest exterior routing protocol. Routers using EGP are called *exterior routers*. Exterior routers share only reachability information with their neighboring exterior routers. EGP provides no routing information—an EGP router simply advertises *a* route to a network; therefore no load-balancing is possible on an EGP network.

In 1989, BGP was introduced. BGP uses TCP as the transport layer connection to exchange messages. Full path information is exchanged between BGP routers, thus the best route is used between autonomous systems.

Autonomous System 1
Autonomous System 2
RIP
Router 1
Router 2
OSPF
Exterior routing protocol used

Figure 4.12
Linking two autonomous systems using an exterior routing protocol.

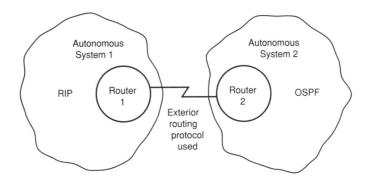

Default Routes

In general, to create a separate routing table entry for every remote network in your internetwork is not necessary. If a *default network* (sometimes called *default router* or simply *default route*) entry exists in your routing table, then packets destined for networks not specifically listed in the routing table are forwarded to that router.

A default router entry is simply an entry in the routing table whose destination is network 0.0.0.0. Figure 4.13 shows an example of such an entry for a NetWare server/router. In this setup, any packets for, say, network 120.1.1.15 are forwarded to router at 126.2.2.2 because the local router doesn't know how to handle it, and 126.2.2.2 is listed as the default router.

TCP/IP Console v1.01 (910801)
NetWare 386 Loadable Module
Host: 126.1.1.1 Uptime: 0 Days 1 Hour 32 Minutes 51 Seconds
Novell NetWare v3.11 (250 user) 2/20/91
ipReceives: 1,285
tcpReceives: 0
udpReceives: 1,246
ipTransmits: 1,524
tcpTransmits: 0
udpTransmits: 1,505
ipForwards: 0
tcpConnects: 0
TCP/IP Tables
Routing Table
Destination Next Hop Intf Cost Type
0.0.0.0 126.2.2.2 1 3 remote
125.0.0.0 125.1.1.1 3 1 direct
126.0.0.0 126.1.1.1 1 1 direct
<End of Table>

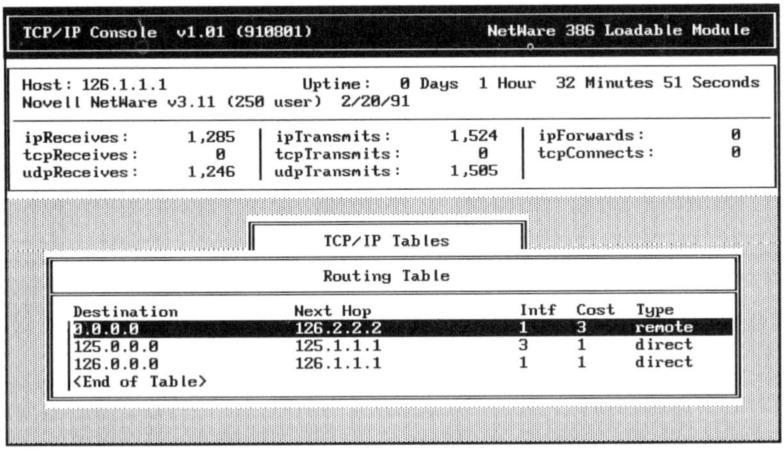

Figure 4.13
A default route entry on a NetWare server/router.

Tip   A default route entry is useful when you are not using any routing protocols on your network—for example, if you turned off RIP to save on the bandwidth, but your routers don't support other routing protocols such as OSPF. You do not need to create a static route for each router on your network or subnets on your internet. You can use a default router entry on most routers to "point" to a few central routers that have more complete routing tables.

Some Internet service providers do not use RIP for their connections. Therefore, if you are connected through such a service provider, you might need to use a default router entry to gain access to the Internet.

Path of an IP Packet

Now that you know how routes are determined between your networks and subnet, look at what happens to a frame when it is sent from a workstation to a host as it crosses bridges and routers. The sample network in figure 4.14 consists of two segments bridged together and a router connecting them to a third segment; the default network masks are used—255.0.0.0 for network 126.0.0.0 and 255.255.0.0 for network 133.7.0.0.

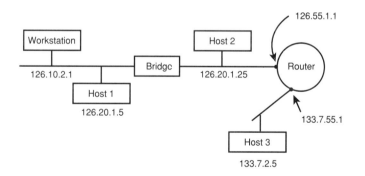

Figure 4.14

A sample network that consists of two bridged segments and one routed segment.

Local Segment

In figure 4.14, the workstation (126.10.2.1) wants to communicate with Host 1 (126.20.1.5). The TCP/IP software in the workstation determines that the destination is on the same network (126.0.0.0); therefore sending data between Workstation 1 and Host 1 does not need to involve a router.

To compose the frame at the datalink layer, the TCP/IP software needs the hardware address, also known as the Datalink Control (DLC) address or Media Access Control

(MAC) address, of Host 1. The TCP/IP software finds the hardware address using the Address Resolution Protocol (ARP). TCP/IP inserts the DLC address in the destination address field of the frame and its own DLC address (determined from the NIC installed) in the source address field. The frame is then transmitted onto the wire.

Both Host 1 and the bridge "see" this frame. The bridge, however, based on its learned table of addresses, knows Host 1 is on the same side as the workstation; therefore the bridge ignores the frame.

Host 1 sees its own address in the destination field, takes the frame, and processes it. Host 1 uses the DLC address in the source address field as the destination address in its reply messages. In this manner two devices learn about each other's DLC addresses.

Bridged Segment

The communication process in a bridged IP network environment is not much different than the local segment scenario discussed previously. Should the frame need to cross the bridge (to reach Host 2), the workstation uses ARP to obtain the DLC address for Host 2. The workstation then uses the DLC address in the destination field, puts its own address in the source field, and transmits the frame onto the wire.

In this case, the bridge notices that the destination address is listed on its other segment. Therefore, the bridge makes a copy of the frame and puts a copy on the other side—without changing anything, not even the DLC addresses.

Host 2 sees the frame and processes it, not knowing it actually came across a bridge. Remember, bridges are transparent to protocols.

Routed Segment

In a routed environment, the data frame addressing is a little more complicated than in the two cases previously covered. First, the workstation determines that the destination (Host 3) is *not* on its own network; therefore, it needs to use a router. However, which router is used if multiple routers are on the segment? When you install the TCP/IP software on a workstation, you are generally asked to specify a default router. This entry is not used if you are communicating locally. When you need to communicate outside your network, however, all frames are addressed to this default router.

Tip   Some workstation software (such as Novell's LAN WorkPlace for DOS v4.1 and higher) enables you to define multiple default routers, which give you some backup paths. Be careful, however, in load-balancing the specification so that no given router is overloaded.

The workstation finds the DLC address of the router by using ARP as in the preceding two cases. The TCP/IP network drive software puts the router's DLC address as the destination, rather than Host 3's address. This key concept is very important—in a bridged environment, the DLC address of the bridge is not involved in data frame addressing. In a routed environment, however, the router's DLC address (and IP address) is involved.

After the router receives the frame, it "unpacks" the frame by stripping off the DLC information. The router looks at the IP information (IP destination address) and checks with its routing table to see where the next stop is. If the destination is on a network directly connected to this router (as in the earlier simple example), the router uses the ARP protocol to determine the DLC address of Host 3 and creates a new *frame* using that information and its own DLC address. Host 3 knows the frame came from a router because the source IP network within the frame is different from its own network. The replies from Host 3 back to the workstation follow the reverse path.

If, however, the first router is not directly connected to the destination network, the router looks in its routing table to find where the next hop is, uses the ARP protocol to determine that router's DLC address, and sends a new frame with the new information. This process continues until the frame reaches a router directly connected to the destination network.

Now you can see why it is important to have the routing tables of *all* your routers up-to-date and consistent with each other. Any old routing information along the path of the frame results in lost data, causing retransmission in the best case and application crashes and incapability to communicate throughout your internet in the worst case.

CHAPTER

5

Using a Unix Backbone

Unix and TCP/IP have been interrelated for almost as long as networks have existed. Today, Unix workstations can be found in many corporate offices and virtually every college campus. With the affordability and powerful capabilities of Intel-based personal computers, public domain and commercial implementations of Unix are even finding their way into households and small businesses. So what's the attraction?—Unix's powerful networking connectivity featuring TCP/IP.

History of Unix

As with many technological advances, the creation of the Unix operating system would not have been possible without federal support. In the 1960s, the Department of Defense Advanced Research Projects Agency (DARPA) wanted an information system capable of handling the many echelons of governmental security clearances. They contracted a team consisting of researchers from AT&T's Bell Labs, Honeywell, and General Electric. In addition, the project known as Multiplexed Information and Computing Service (Multics) also included scientists from the Massachusetts Institute of Technology. Multics was designed to be a time-sharing system that would enable many users to work concurrently and share their work with selected colleagues while preventing others similar access.

Unfortunately, because of all the features promised with Multics, the development of the project quickly fell behind schedule. In 1969, Bell Labs decided to pull out of the project, which may have further hindered the work on Multics but, as it turned out, was beneficial to the creation of Unix. One of the former members of the Multics project, Ken Thompson, decided to try and implement some of the Multics concepts on a used Digital Equipment (DEC) PDP-7. He and another Multics project refugee, Dennis Ritchie, began work on a new system, Unix. Unix was designed to be a much simpler system capable of running on smaller computers. Soon others added their own contributions as Unix was adopted throughout Bell Labs. In 1973, Thompson decided to rewrite Unix, this time using a new language called C, created by Ritchie. The C language included many of the features expected in high-level programming languages and also incorporated the concept of portability. A *portable program* can be written on one machine, and then compiled and run on others. The concept of portability was later expanded to Unix itself, as Thompson and company began porting Unix to other computers.

While Unix was being developed at AT&T's Bell Labs, DARPA was involved in another project concerning communications. The results of this research led to the establishment of a network known as the Advanced Research Project Agency Network (ARPANET). The original goal of the network was to interconnect computers at research institutions as well as military installations. All information transmitted through this network was unclassified. The method by which information went from one computer to another was actually based on work done by Paul Baran of the Rand Corporation. Concerned by the potential breakdown in telephone communication resulting from a nuclear war, he worked on a concept that would disassemble electronic messages into small parts called *packets*. These packets could then be sent along the most efficient path to their destination, and when all the packets arrived, they could be reassembled into the original message.

As access to the ARPANET grew, so did the popularity of Unix. The University of California at Berkeley became the first institution to purchase Unix. Unlike many of today's operating systems, when Berkeley bought the operating system, they got everything, including source code. Several years later, *Berkeley Software Distribution* (BSD) Unix was born. Two graduate students, Bill Joy and Chuck Haley, began to add some of their own enhancements to the Unix code. This BSD flavor of Unix was then given to others. The modifications continued, supported by funding from DARPA.

DARPA recognized the popularity of Unix and, having already adopted TCP/IP as the communication protocol of the ARPANET network, decided that adding network support to Unix would encourage universities to accept TCP/IP. They accomplished this by first contracting Bolt, Beranek, and Newman, Inc., the creators of TCP/IP, to build TCP/IP for use with the Unix operating system. They then worked with Berkeley to make TCP/IP a part of the BSD Unix distribution. Berkeley did and, true to history, they added utilities to take advantage of the new connectivity. The electronic freedom to communicate and share information with others added to the general acceptance of Unix and led to the large-scale expansion of networks like ARPANET into the Internet of today.

Installing TCP/IP

Most BSD-based implementations of Unix already include TCP/IP networking support as part of the operating system. Usually, when you first boot a new Unix workstation, a program runs asking if the workstation is to be used on a network. If you answer yes, the program prompts you for information it needs to get all the networking features correctly configured. At times, however, your workstation may not initially be installed on a network, or you may need to change the configuration. This section describes the configuration files and programs that involve networking your Unix workstation.

Initial Planning

Before installing a network that includes Unix workstations, you must consider several things. Often, if you are adding a new workstation to a preexisting network, the network administrator can already provide you with most of the information you need.

IP Addresses and Host Names

Every machine on a TCP/IP network must have its own Internet Protocol (IP) address, and that address must be unique. Similarly, every machine should have its own name. This name is used to differentiate one machine from another within your network. Chapter 3, "Introduction to TCP/IP," covers these two topics in detail.

Making a New Kernel

The Unix *kernel*, or operating system, is a little different from most other operating systems. The kernel knows about every supported piece of hardware and how to use it. Fortunately, many types of hardware, such as hard disks or tape drives, conform to a standard already supported by the kernel, but sometimes this is not the case. If you were adding a new device to an MS-DOS personal computer, all you would need to do is run the supplied program or include the new device driver in the system's CONFIG.SYS file. Not so with Unix workstations. If you want to add a new device to a Unix workstation not already supported by the kernel, you have to create a new one. This is not as bad as it sounds and usually the documentation that accompanies the new device includes all the steps necessary to install it.

The steps for creating a new kernel depend on whether your version of Unix is based on Berkeley's BSD 4.3 (soon 4.4) or Novell's (formerly AT&T's) System V Release 4. If you are uncertain which type you have, check your documentation or contact the vendor from which you purchased your workstation. Typically, BSD versions already include support for TCP/IP networking, and most System V versions install the TCP/IP software as part of the initial boot-up installation program.

BSD Kernel Configuration

When you create a new kernel, what you are actually doing is compiling a series of C language programs. Normally, this requires that you edit a number of files, which could quickly become tedious. Fortunately, BSD versions of Unix include a program called /etc/config that makes the changes for you. To determine what changes are necessary, /etc/config reads a configuration file that is usually stored in the /usr/sys/conf directory.

If the kernel has never been modified, there is a basic configuration file called GENERIC. This file was used to create the kernel your workstation is currently running. Typically, when creating a new configuration file, give it the same name you selected for your machine.

The easiest thing to do when creating a new configuration file is to copy one that already exists, as in the following example:

```
# cd /usr/sys/conf
# cp GENERIC JUPITER
# chmod u+w JUPITER
```

A new kernel file, JUPITER, is created by copying one that already includes all the devices supported by the system.

Note It is best to copy the configuration file used to create the most recent version of the kernel. This ensures that all the changes made since the initial installation of the workstation are included.

Several statements need to be included in the kernel configuration file for the workstation to be networked. Most BSD Unix workstations come preconfigured for use in TCP/IP-based networks, so the configuration file may already include these options:

```
options                 INET

pseudo-device           loop
pseudo-device           ether
pseudo-device           pty

device                  qe0 at uba0 csr 0174440 vector qeintr
device                  le0 at SBus slot 0 csr 0xc00000 pri 5
```

INET is a mandatory entry. By including this option, the kernel supports networking protocols. Specific hardware requirements, however, are not required until later.

Pseudo devices are device drivers without corresponding pieces of hardware. The pseudo-device loop creates a loopback network device. The purpose of this device is covered later. The *ether pseudo-device* provides support for Ethernet connectivity. *Ethernet* is a low-level networking scheme through which most TCP/IP networks run. *Pty pseudo devices* enable users to connect through the network as if they had a direct terminal connected to the Unix workstation.

The last two lines in the preceding listing are the configuration information about the actual network device. Note there is some variance in the information. The first device is a Digital Q-Bus network adapter used in a MicroVAX II. The second entry is a LANCE Ethernet adapter commonly installed in most Sun Sparcstations. Documentation for newly installed network interfaces includes specific information on how to configure devices.

Note that these statements are not the only ones that appear in the configuration file. Entries for hard disk and tape controllers, keyboards, file system storage methods like Network File System (NFS) and Remote File System (RFS), and miscellaneous hardware devices also are included by the manufacturer.

After the configuration file is edited, the kernel files can be modified appropriately. The program that handles this is /etc/config. The following example shows the syntax for using /etc/config:

```
# /etc/config JUPITER
```

/etc/config reads the configuration file and creates a new directory (if it doesn't already exist) in /usr/sys. This directory uses the same name as the configuration file. C language files necessary for creating the kernel are then copied into this directory for compilation. The kernel is created using a program called /bin/make. /bin/ make reads its own configuration file (created by /etc/config) and begins compiling the code. Assuming that no errors occur, a new file, vmunix, is created. This is the new kernel program, as shown in the following example:

```
# cd /usr/sys/JUPITER
# make
  ... (Actual Compile Commands) ...
# ls vmunix
vmunix*
#
```

All that remains is to install it. BSD Unix expects the kernel file to be in the root directory. It's a good idea to back up the original kernel program first in case problems occur with the new kernel. After this is done, the new kernel can be copied to the root directory and is ready for testing:

```
# mv /vmunix /vmunix.old
# cp /usr/sys/JUPITER/vmunix /vmunix
```

System V Kernel Configuration

Unlike the BSD kernel that comes preconfigured for networking, System V kernels typically come configured with the bare minimum. When the system is first booted, a program is run that prompts you to enter information about which options you want to include. After this process is complete, a new kernel is created. This same program also is used later when devices are added or changed. The name of this configuration program varies among vendors; consult your documentation for details. As mentioned previously, before installing a new kernel, back up the old one first.

Configuring the Network Interface

Even though the device drivers needed for networking are loaded when the Unix workstation kernel is booted, the network interface still needs to be configured. The utility ifconfig provides this function. With ifconfig you can turn the interface on or off, assign an IP address to the interface, or define the network subnet mask and broadcast address.

The common usage of ifconfig is as follows:

```
ifconfig interface address netmask address broadcast address
```

The interface is the network device defined in the kernel. If you want to configure multiple network devices, you need to use ifconfig once for each interface. To apply a setting to every network interface, you can replace the interface name with the -a flag instead.

The address is the IP address of the workstation. You can either supply the numerical IP address or enter the host or machine name. If you choose the latter, ifconfig consults the /etc/hosts file to extract the machine's IP address. The /etc/hosts file is discussed later.

netmask refers to the subnet mask. Large networks are broken into smaller networks or subnetworks. The subnet mask is a 32-bit number that enables you to isolate only those machines on your subnet. If the bit is one, that bit corresponds to the network address. Otherwise, the bit is part of the host machine's address on the subnet. This entry can be entered in one of the following three ways:

◆ A hexadecimal number starting with 0x

◆ An IP address

◆ A network name corresponding to an entry in /etc/networks

The broadcast address is the address used to send messages to every machine on the subnet. Typically, the host portion of the broadcast address is 255.

In the following example, the Lance Ethernet adapter, le0, is being configured on a workstation named jupiter. This machine is on a Class C network with a domain IP address of 134.68.7. Broadcast messages are read if the message is sent to IP address 134.68.7.255.

```
ifconfig le0 jupiter netmask 255.255.255.0 broadcast 134.68.7.255
```

To see what the current setting of an interface is, use ifconfig *interface*:

```
# ifconfig le0
le0: flags=63<UP,BROADCAST,NOTRAILERS,RUNNING>
    inet 134.68.7.8 netmask ffffff00 broadcast 134.68.7.255
    ether 8:0:20:19:e3:bc
```

The last line displays the Ethernet address of interface le0. Unlike the IP address of the interface, the Ethernet address is set by the manufacturer of the interface and cannot be changed. The first three sets of numbers (8:0:20) indicate which manufacturer made the interface. In this case, it was Sun Microsystems. The remaining sets of numbers (19:e3:bc) form an internal number used by the manufacturer. The Ethernet address must be unique.

One of the first flags displayed is UP. With ifconfig, you can also enable or disable the interface:

```
# ifconfig interface down
# ifconfig interface up
```

Standard Networking Configuration Files

Several configuration files also provide networking information. Two have already been mentioned, /etc/hosts and /etc/networks. Others include /etc/ethers, /etc/services, and /etc/protocols. Each of these files consists of one entry per line. All text that follows the # is ignored as comments.

/etc/hosts

/etc/hosts is a database of networked machine names and their corresponding IP addresses. This file is consulted by a number of programs including ifconfig and ping, which are discussed later. An example of an /etc/hosts file follows:

```
#
# Host Configuration File
#
127.0.0.1          localhost
#
# New Riders Publishing Accounting Department Host Addresses
#
134.68.7.1      earth
134.68.7.2      venus
134.68.7.3      mercury
134.68.7.4      mars
134.68.7.5      saturn
134.68.7.6      neptune
134.68.7.7      uranus
134.68.7.8      jupiter
134.68.7.9      pluto
134.68.7.100        acct-gw
```

In addition to the machines found on the network, there is an entry for localhost. 127.0.0.1 is a special address referred to as a *loopback address*. This address can be used to test the network settings installed in the kernel.

/etc/ethers

Like /etc/hosts, /etc/ethers is a database of machine names and addresses. The difference is that this file includes Ethernet addresses. An example of an /etc/ethers file follows:

```
#
# New Riders Publishing Accounting Department Ethernet Addresses
#
8:0:20:23:3a:45      earth
8:0:20:78:36:19      venus
8:0:20:d4:62:7b      mercury
8:0:20:37:97:31      mars
8:0:20:40:e5:c9      saturn
8:0:20:1f:53:68      uranus
8:0:20:52:70:83      neptune
8:0:20:19:e3:bc      jupiter
8:0:20:81:88:3f      pluto
0:0:c:0:41:ba            acct-gw
```

/etc/networks

/etc/networks is an optional file that associates names with subnet mask values or domain network addresses. For larger networks with several subnets, using names makes it easier to remember which IP addresses and subnet masks are defined for which networks. An example of an /etc/networks file follows:

```
#
# New Riders Publishing Accounting Dept. Subnet Masks
#
acct.nrp.com     134.68.7
nrp-acct-mask    255.255.255.0
```

In this example, only one netmask for a Class C network is defined.

/etc/protocols

A number of protocols make up the TCP/IP suite. When a packet arrives, the host machine first checks to see if the packet is meant for it. If so, the machine next checks to see which upper level protocol can process it further. The machine determines this by extracting a protocol number from the packet and comparing it to the entries in /etc/protocols:

```
#
# Internet (IP) protocols
#
ip      0     IP        # internet protocol, pseudo protocol number
icmp    1     ICMP           # internet control message protocol
igmp    2     IGMP           # internet group multicast protocol
ggp     3     GGP            # gateway-gateway protocol
tcp     6     TCP            # transmission control protocol
pup     12    PUP            # PARC universal packet protocol
udp     17    UDP            # user datagram protocol
```

The first field is the official protocol name followed by the protocol number. The
third field is an alias for the protocol.

/etc/services

One of the popular networking features of Unix is the capability to run a program on
one machine and have information or services provided on another. This forms the
basis of client/server computing. The client machine informs the server of which
service it wants to access by including a port number within the packet requesting the
service. After processing the packet, the server routes the request to the process that
handles that port.

This assumes that the server uses the same port numbers as the client. That's the
purpose of /etc/services. This file includes the process name along with the port and
protocol associated with it:

```
#
# Network services, Internet style
#
tcpmux          1/tcp                  # rfc-1078
echo            7/tcp
echo            7/udp
systat          11/tcp                 users
daytime         13/tcp
daytime         13/udp
netstat         15/tcp
chargen         19/tcp                 ttytst source
chargen         19/udp                 ttytst source
ftp-data        20/tcp
ftp             21/tcp
telnet          23/tcp
smtp            25/tcp                 mail
time            37/tcp                 timserver
time            37/udp                 timserver
```

```
name          42/udp        nameserver
whois         43/tcp        nickname      # usually to sri-nic
domain        53/udp
domain        53/tcp
hostnames     101/tcp       hostname      # usually to sri-nic
#
# Host specific functions
#
tftp          69/udp
rje           77/tcp
finger        79/tcp
link          87/tcp        ttylink
supdup        95/tcp
iso-tsap      102/tcp
x400          103/tcp       # ISO Mail
x400-snd      104/tcp
csnet-ns      105/tcp
pop-2         109/tcp       # Post Office
uucp-path     117/tcp
nntp          119/tcp       usenet        # Network News Transfer
ntp           123/tcp                     # Network Time Protocol
NeWS          144/tcp       news          # Window System
#
# Unix specific services
#
# these are NOT officially assigned
#
exec          512/tcp
login         513/tcp
shell         514/tcp       cmd           # no passwords used
printer       515/tcp       spooler       # line printer spooler
courier       530/tcp       rpc           # experimental
uucp          540/tcp       uucpd         # uucp daemon
biff          512/udp       comsat
who           513/udp       whod
syslog        514/udp
talk          517/udp
route         520/udp     router routed
new-rwho      550/udp     new-who         # experimental
rmonitor      560/udp     rmonitord       # experimental
monitor       561/udp                     # experimental
pcserver      600/tcp                     # ECD Integrated PC board srvr
ingreslock    1524/tcp
```

As you can see, a large number of network resources are available. You may notice that some process names have several entries. This is because in some cases, different protocols can be used to request the same service. Sometimes ports are also referred to as sockets even though sockets typically include the IP address in addition to the port number.

Starting the Internet Daemon

A number of client/server applications are included in Unix. Some of these programs, called *daemons*, are running all the time, but most are not. If you were to continuously run every daemon, you would have little computer resources left to do anything else. So how do these daemons service requests?

A special daemon, known as the *internet daemon* or *inetd*, "listens" to many ports (mentioned earlier) for incoming service requests. If a request is received, inetd starts the appropriate daemon to handle it. After the service is provided, inetd shuts down the daemon. inetd knows which daemons it supports by reading /etc/inetd.conf when it is initially started, typically when the workstation boots.

/etc/inetd.conf contains a number of fields for each entry. Like the other files discussed, text following # is ignored as comments. The format is as follows:

```
service-name  socket-type  proto  wait-status  user  server-pathname args
```

`service-name` is the name of the service listed in /etc/services.

`socket-type` describes what sort of socket the service uses. Valid entries include stream, dgram (datagram), raw, and rdm (reliably delivered message).

 Note When installing a new service entry in /etc/inetd.conf, the documentation for the software includes the /etc/inetd.conf entry that needs to be added.

`proto` is the protocol used by this service. Valid protocols include those listed in /etc/protocols.

`wait-status` is kind of like a traffic cop for that service. If the status is set to *wait*, inetd must wait until the server releases the socket before listening for another request for that server. For *no-wait* status servers, inetd can continue to listen for more server requests without interruption. Usually, *stream* socket servers don't require inetd to wait, but many *dgram* servers do.

`user` is the name of the user who owns the server process when it runs. The effective permissions of the server are those assigned to that user.

server-pathname is the actual name of the server program to be run. To ensure that the correct program is selected, the full path is included with the name. Some entries have *internal* in the field instead. In these cases, inetd itself services the request because it would be more efficient than to start a separate daemon.

args include any command-line arguments needed to process the request correctly. At a minimum, the command name is entered in this field.

Unless you add a new service or disable a currently active one (putting # at the beginning of the entry), you shouldn't need to edit /etc/inetd.conf. If you do, you need to restart inetd to activate your changes. The following shows the commands needed to restart inetd. Note that the # character denotes the root command prompt.

```
# ps -acx ¦ grep inetd
  131 ? IW    0:04 inetd
# kill -HUP 131
```

A sample listing of /etc/inetd.conf follows. You may notice that some services have two entries. As noted when discussing /etc/services, some services can be requested through different protocols.

```
#
# inetd.conf - Configuration file of inetd
#
# Ftp and telnet are standard Internet services.
#
ftp     stream    tcp    nowait    root    /usr/etc/in.ftpd      in.ftpd -l
telnet  stream    tcp    nowait    root    /usr/etc/in.telnetd   in.telnetd
#
# Tnamed serves the obolete IEN-116 name server protocol.
#
name    dgram   udp   wait   root   /usr/etc/in.tnamed           in.tnamed
#
# Shell, login, exec, comsat and talk are BSD protocols.
#
shell   stream    tcp    nowait    root    /usr/etc/in.rshd      in.rshd
login   stream    tcp    nowait    root    /usr/etc/in.rlogind   in.rlogind
exec    stream    tcp    nowait    root    /usr/etc/in.rexecd    in.rexecd
comsat      dgram      udp       wait    root   /usr/etc/in.comsat in.comsast
talk    dgram   udp    wait    root       /usr/etc/in.talkd    in.talkd
#
# Run as user "uucp" if you don't want uucpd's wtmp entries.
#
uucp    stream    tcp    nowait    root    /usr/etc/in.uucpd    in.uucpd
```

```
#
# Tftp service is provided primarily for booting.  Most sites run this
# only on machines acting as "boot servers."
#
#tftp    dgram   udp     wait    root     /usr/etc/in.tftpd    in.tftpd -s /tftpboot
#
# Finger, systat? and netstat give out user information which may be
# valuable to potential "system crackers."  Many sites choose to disable
# some or all of these services to improve security.
#
finger     stream    tcp    nowait     nobody   /usr/etc/in.fingerd in.fingerd
#systat    stream    tcp    nowait     root     /usr/bin/ps         ps -auwwx
#netstat   stream    tcp    nowait     root     /usr/ucb/netstat    netstat -f
➥inet
#
# Time service is used for clock synchronization.
#
time    stream    tcp    nowait        root    internal
time    dgram     udp    wait          root    internal
#
# Echo, discard, daytime, and chargen are used primarily for testing.
#
echo    stream    tcp    nowait    root    internal
echo    dgram     udp    wait      root    internal
discard     stream    tcp    nowait    root    internal
discard     dgram     udp    wait      root    internal
daytime     stream    tcp    nowait    root    internal
daytime     dgram     udp    wait      root    internal
chargen     stream    tcp    nowait    root    internal
chargen     dgram     udp    wait      root    internal
#
#
# RPC services syntax:
#   <rpc_prog>/<vers> <socket_type> rpc/<proto> <flags> <user> <pathname> <args>
#
# The mount server is usually started in /etc/rc.local only on machines that
# are NFS servers.  It can be run by inetd as well.
#
#mountd/1    dgram    rpc/udp    wait root    /usr/etc/rpc.mountd    rpc.mountd
#
# The rexd server provides only minimal authentication and is often not run
# by sites concerned about security.
#
```

```
#rexd/1        stream     rpc/tcp     wait  root  /usr/etc/rpc.rexd    rpc.rexd
#
# Ypupdated is run by sites that support NIS updating.
#
#ypupdated/1    stream     rpc/tcp     wait  root  /usr/etc/rpc.ypupdated
rpc.ypupdated
#
# Rquotad serves UFS disk quotas to NFS clients.
#
rquotad/1     dgram      rpc/udp     wait  root   /usr/etc/rpc.rquotad  rpc.rquotad
#
# Rstatd is used by programs such as perfmeter.
#
rstatd/2-4    dgram      rpc/udp     wait  root   /usr/etc/rpc.rstatd   rpc.rstatd
#
# The rusers service gives out user information. Sites concerned
# with security may choose to disable it.
#
rusersd/1-2   dgram      rpc/udp     wait  root   /usr/etc/rpc.rusersd  rpc.rusersd
#
# The spray server is used primarily for testing.
#
sprayd/1      dgram      rpc/udp     wait  root   /usr/etc/rpc.sprayd   rpc.sprayd
#
# The rwall server lets anyone on the network bother everyone on your machine.
#
walld/1       dgram      rpc/udp     wait  root   /usr/etc/rpc.rwalld   rpc.rwalld
#
```

Connecting to Larger Networks

If your network is isolated, you should have no difficulty communicating with other hosts. But if your network is connected to a larger one like the Internet, you need to configure your workstation to communicate through a special machine known as a *gateway* to be able to access machines outside your local network.

/etc/routed, which is run during boot up, is a special program that handles communication to other machines through a gateway. routed learns about the gateway it should use by using /usr/etc/route to define it. The following example demonstrates the use of the /usr/etc/route commands. Note that # denotes the root command prompt.

```
# route -f add default acct-gw
```

In the preceding example, the routing table is erased through the -f option. A new default route, acct-gw, is then established. In large organizations, you can minimize confusion by selecting the same host number for every network interface used by the gateway. From the sample /etc/hosts file, acct-gw has an IP address of 134.68.7.100. If the gateway also connects to network 134.68.6, then the interface on that network should use 134.68.6.100.

To view the currently configured routes, you can use the netstat command, as follows:

```
# netstat -r
Routing tables
Destination          Gateway           Flags    Refcnt Use
Interface
localhost            localhost         UH       3      1332
lo0
default              acct-gw           UG       5      168358
le0
134.68.7.0           jupiter           U        11     42227
le0
```

Netstat is discussed again later in this chapter.

Advanced Networking Features

As Unix evolved, new features were added to further networking capabilities. By incorporating them, you can install workstations that can act as servers to provide access to shared disk storage, network configuration files, and domain name databases. Although some implementations of Unix may not include any or some of these enhancements, it's worth mentioning them here.

Network Information Services

One of the most difficult tasks that faces network administrators is keeping networking information consistent on every host machine on a network. For example, if you were to add a new host to your network, you would have to edit /etc/hosts on every machine already on the network. By using Network Information Services (NIS), this problem can be greatly minimized. Formerly known as *Yellow Pages*, NIS enables one machine to maintain configuration files such as /etc/passwd and /etc/hosts for all other machines on your network. Now, you only need to make changes on one machine, and those changes take effect almost immediately.

Domain Name Services

For networks not connected to larger ones such as the Internet, NIS is a good way to maintain a database of all reachable machines. However, with networks as large as the

Internet, thousands of machines are interconnected, and changes occur daily. There is no way you could keep track of all the changes. This is where Domain Name Service (DNS) servers help out. Typically, when you request a domain name from NIC, you create a DNS server. The purpose of this server is twofold. It maintains a database of all machines on your network as well as forwards queries for addresses of machines it does not know about. Client machines automatically connect to the name server through the resolve daemon when they need addresses. The whole process is transparent to the end user.

Network File System

Storage of user files can be another source of frustration for network administrators. With many machines on a network, a user can have files in numerous home directories. Backups become increasingly complex, not to mention inconsistent duplicates of information can quickly spread. A solution to this problem is to have a central server store all the users' files no matter to which network machine they connect. The Network File System (NFS) provides just that feature. To the client machines, the server's shared directories appear to be on the local machine. Only one machine needs to be backed up, and users have all their files available to them. For more information on NFS, see Chapter 3, "Introduction to TCP/IP."

Testing the Network Setup

Now that the kernel and all the network files have been configured, it's time to test the network. It's important to be systematic when doing this sort of troubleshooting. Otherwise, a simple problem can be confusing and difficult to isolate. Fortunately, Unix provides a couple of utilities for this purpose.

ping

Similar to the sonar "pings" used by naval vessels to determine the location of submarines, the Unix command *ping* checks to see if other machines on the network are reachable. The first goal is to check the networking capability of the kernel. This is accomplished by "pinging" the loopback interface, localhost:

```
# ping localhost
localhost is alive
```

Although no physical hardware corresponds to the loopback interface lo, when a request to localhost is sent, the kernel processes the request without sending anything out through the network. If the kernel is not properly configured for networking, you might see a message like this instead:

```
# ping localhost
No answer from localhost
```

Assuming that the network portion of the kernel works, you can now check to see if you can ping your machine by either its IP address or its host name as listed in /etc/ hosts, as in the following example:

```
# ping jupiter
jupiter is alive
```

If ping fails to reach your machine through the network, check to see that the interface is set up correctly. To do this, use the ifconfig command discussed earlier. Modify the interface configuration if it is incorrect and try again. If it continues to fail, check the machine's physical connection to the network.

When you can ping your machine, it's time to try reaching another one. As before, use the name of a machine found in /etc/hosts. Typically, if you can ping your machine, you should have no difficulty pinging another one. At this point, more detailed information also can be obtained. You can have ping attempt to reach another host once every second and display statistics. This is done by adding the -s option, as in the following example:

```
# ping -s saturn 64 5
PING saturn: 64 data bytes
72 bytes from saturn (134.68.7.5): icmp_seq=0. time=1. ms
72 bytes from saturn (134.68.7.5): icmp_seq=1. time=1. ms
72 bytes from saturn (134.68.7.5): icmp_seq=2. time=1. ms
72 bytes from saturn (134.68.7.5): icmp_seq=3. time=1. ms
72 bytes from saturn (134.68.7.5): icmp_seq=4. time=1. ms
----saturn PING Statistics----
5 packets transmitted, 5 packets received, 0% packet loss
round-trip (ms)  min/avg/max = 1/1/1
```

In this example, several arguments are entered after the hostname. 64 is the amount of data, in bytes, sent to saturn, and 5 is the number of times the data is sent to saturn. Without this last option, ping continues to transmit until Ctrl + C is pressed. For each attempt, ping displays the sequence number and amount of time in millisec- onds it took the packet to get to the destination and back. After all repetitions are completed, a summary is included.

 Note   On some versions of Unix, the default option for ping is equivalent to ping -s.

netstat

After you know that the workstation can communicate through the network, you need to know how well it is communicating. *netstat* is a utility designed to display statistics about each workstation's network interfaces. The amount of information displayed depends on what command-line options are included. To get a one-line entry per interface summary, you can use the -i option, as follows:

```
#netstat -i
Name  Mtu  Net/Dest      Address    Ipkts   Ierrs Opkts   Oerrs Collis Queue
le0   1500 acct.nrp.com  jupiter    695753  5     578323  0     1298   0
lo0   1536 loopback      localhost  68723   0     68723   0     0      0
```

Even though two interfaces are displayed, lo, the loopback interface, doesn't provide any useful information because no network traffic travels through it. The three fields you should be most concerned with are Queue, Ierrs, and Oerrs. If Queue is a nonzero number, then packets can't be transmitted out. This is symptomatic of a network cabling problem. Ierrs (Incoming packet errors) and Oerrs (Output packet errors) need not be zero, but the value should be very low. Values greater than 100 may indicate a problem such as numerous collisions of the network. Studying the percentage loss and round-trip time statistics generated by ping -s may assist in isolating this sort of problem.

On occasion, you may want to have detailed statistics on your workstation's network communication. This can be provided by using netstat -s, as the following code illustrates:

```
# netstat -s
udp:
     0 incomplete headers
     0 bad data length fields
     0 bad checksums
     0 socket overflows
tcp:
     345743 packets sent
         230978 data packets (24536791 bytes)
         1646 data packets (429969 bytes) retransmitted
         49946 ack-only packets (34452 delayed)
         25 URG only packets
         148 window probe packets
         50131 window update packets
         12869 control packets
     433439 packets received
         220994 acks (for 24541178 bytes)
```

```
            9023 duplicate acks
            0 acks for unsent data
            354661 packets (167477101 bytes) received in-sequence
            3248 completely duplicate packets (158506 bytes)
            6 packets with some dup. data (731 bytes duped)
            5289 out-of-order packets (74066 bytes)
            3 packets (1 byte) of data after window
            1 window probe
            1472 window update packets
            2 packets received after close
            0 discarded for bad checksums
            2 discarded for bad header offset fields
            0 discarded because packet too short
        5273 connection requests
        1580 connection accepts
        6138 connections established (including accepts)
        6878 connections closed (including 35 drops)
        732 embryonic connections dropped
        214259 segments updated rtt (of 220663 attempts)
        2886 retransmit timeouts
            0 connections dropped by rexmit timeout
        14 persist timeouts
        1393 keepalive timeouts
            119 keepalive probes sent
            420 connections dropped by keepalive
icmp:
        253 calls to icmp_error
        0 errors not generated 'cuz old message too short
        0 errors not generated 'cuz old message was icmp
        Output histogram:
            echo reply: 844
            destination unreachable: 253
            address mask reply: 8
        0 messages with bad code fields
        0 messages < minimum length
        0 bad checksums
        0 messages with bad length
        Input histogram:
            echo reply: 30107
            destination unreachable: 338
            source quench: 1
            echo: 844
```

```
        time exceeded: 7
        address mask request: 8
    852 message responses generated
ip:
    766386 total packets received
    0 bad header checksums
    0 with size smaller than minimum
    0 with data size < data length
    0 with header length < data size
    0 with data length < header length
    2119 fragments received
    0 fragments dropped (dup or out of space)
    0 fragments dropped after timeout
    0 packets forwarded
    1 packet not forwardable
    0 redirects sent
    0 ip input queue drops
```

Using the Network

When your workstation is networked and configured correctly, you can take advantage of a number of features. From your workstation, you can run programs on other workstations, transfer files among them, and even communicate directly with other users no matter how physically far away they are. This section briefly describes several of these utilities.

Remote Logins

In the early days of Unix, you had to have access to a terminal directly connected to the Unix machine to use it. The only remote computing possible required a modem and telephone access. Networks changed everything. Now, you connect to any network machine (assuming that you have an account on it) and can work on distant machines at a much faster rate. The program that provides this access is called *telnet*.

To connect to another machine, you simply include the address of the machine you want to use. If the machine is installed on your network, you can use the name of the machine as listed in /etc/hosts. Otherwise, you have to enter either the machine's fully qualified domain name or IP address:

```
% telnet saturn.acct.nrp.com
Trying 134.68.7.5 ...
```

```
Connected to saturn.acct.nrp.com
Escape character is '^]'.
SunOS Unix (saturn)
login: scott
password:
Last login: Mon Sep 12 10:34:24 from mars
SunOS Release 4.1.3 (SATURN) #1 Mon Aug 15 14:44:35 EST 1994
You have new mail
Mon Sep 12 11:55:40 EST 1994
%
```

The first thing telnet does is try and convert the entry on the command line to an IP address. /etc/hosts is checked for a match, and if it is not found there, telnet queries the DNS server, if available. Telnet discovers that 134.68.7.5 corresponds to saturn and attempts to connect to it. If telnet can connect to that address, telnet displays a message indicating success and prompts you to enter your login name and password. Notice that the password you type in is not displayed. This is to prevent someone from looking over your shoulder and stealing your password. Assuming that everything is correct, you are notified of when you last logged in and from where, and if mail has arrived since the last time you logged in. Now you can work on the remote machine.

Suppose that after you start telnet, you realize that you selected the wrong machine. If you have a valid account on that machine, you can log in then immediately log out, or you can wait for the login process to time out (60 seconds). Telnet provides better ways to end your login session.

When at the login prompt, you can press Ctrl+D. This is the control character Unix uses to mean End of File or <EOF>. When the login process encounters an <EOF>, it closes the session. This is demonstrated in the following code. Note that Ctrl+D is pressed at the login prompt.

```
% telnet mars
Trying 134.68.7.5 ...
Connected to mars.
Escape character is '^]'.
SunOS Unix (mars)
login: Connection closed by foreign host.
% telnet saturn
```

By entering Ctrl+D, the telnet session is immediately closed, and you can start another one from the Unix prompt. Another way to accomplish the same thing is to use the escape sequence to get to the telnet command prompt. Notice that telnet tells you what this sequence is as soon as you connect to the remote machine. By using Ctrl+], you can close the connection and start again. This is demonstrated in the following:

```
% telnet mars
Trying 134.68.7.4.
Escape character is '^]'.
SunOS Unix (mars)
login:
telnet> close
Connection closed.
% telnet saturn
```

Another time that this feature comes in handy is when the program you are running has locked your session. By using Ctrl+], you can close the session; then use telnet to reconnect to the remote machine. Only do this as a last resort.

Although used primarily for running remote login sessions, you also can use telnet to directly connect to other remote services. Standard port numbers are listed in /etc/ services. To connect to a specific port, enter the port number as a second argument to telnet, as shown in the following example:

```
% telnet saturn 23
Trying 134.68.7.5 ...
Connected to saturn.
Escape character is '^]'.
SunOS Unix (saturn)
login:
```

In the preceding example, telnet is used to connect to port 23 of saturn. By searching /etc/services, port 23 corresponds to telnet. This is the same port that the telnet program uses by default.

 Note   When using telnet to connect to other ports, you must know what information you need to supply to get the desired results. Some ports may provide online help, but many do not. It is best to use Unix utility programs to extract service information instead of trying to do it manually. The only time you should use telnet to connect to a port is if a special program uses its own port for remote user access. Multi User Dungeon (MUD) games often work this way.

Transferring Files

Files can be transferred from one machine to another through the File Transfer Protocol (ftp) program or anonymous ftp.

Using the Remote Commands

In addition to telnet and ftp, a common set of powerful networking utilities is included with virtually every implementation of Unix. These Unix-specific commands enable you to run programs to log in to remote machines, copy files back and forth through the network, and even provide information about which users are currently logged into a networked machine. These tools are commonly referred to as *remote* or *r commands* because each command starts with the letter *r*.

/etc/hosts.equiv and rhosts files

One of the most popular features of the r commands is that they can be configured so you do not need to enter your password when using them. This assumes a level of trust. All that is required is an entry in either /etc/hosts.equiv or a rhosts file in the user's home directory.

The entries in /etc/hosts.equiv are names of machines and users that are trusted. Trusted machines are typically on the same network and administered by the same group. In addition, these network administrators may have accounts on multiple machines and set them up so that they could log in from anywhere without needing to enter their passwords. A sample /etc/hosts.equiv file follows:

```
#
# hosts.equiv file for jupiter.acct.nrp.com
#
saturn
mars-jon
mercury+jon
-pluto
+ scott
```

Not only can you grant free access through /etc/hosts.equiv, but you also can deny it. The characters + and - provide this service, respectively. In the sample /etc/hosts.equiv file presented earlier, every user on saturn is granted free access; the same goes for mars, except for jon. However, only jon is granted free access from mercury. pluto is not a trusted host, so no one is granted free access. Finally, scott is granted free access to this machine, no matter which machine he is using remotely.

 Note   This free access extends beyond the local account bearing the same name. A user can gain access to any account, except for root. In the last entry, anyone with the username scott on any machine can gain free access to saturn.

In addition, users can define their own access list. By creating a file called rhosts in their home directories, they can grant access to their account to any or all users on a particular remote host. All that they need to include is the remote machine and user login name:

```
#
# User scott's .rhosts file
#
saturn
mercury
mars scott
mars -jon
venus orr
```

With this rhosts in scott's home directory, anyone can freely access scott's account from machines saturn and mercury. scott also can gain password-free access from mars, but jon is denied the same privilege. scott would also like to be granted free access from venus on which his username is orr.

When a user on a remote machine attempts to use an r command, the daemon that services that r command searches /etc/hosts.equiv to determine if the user of the remote machine is granted free access. Most of the r commands require that the username be the same on both the local and remote machine. If access cannot be granted through /etc/hosts.equiv, the user's home directory is checked for the existence of a rhosts file. This file also is searched to determine if free access should be granted.

In the early days of networking, security wasn't a major concern. Networking encouraged the sharing of information, and a level of trust was associated with users and machines on a local network. That was, of course, until some users took advantage of the laxity of security and compromised many systems. Probably the most significant event was the Internet Worm incident of 1988. In less than a day, this specialized program completely shut down much of the Internet. One of the security holes it exploited was the open access granted through use of /etc/hosts.equiv and user rhosts files.

Today, security is taken much more seriously. Many sites do not even allow /etc/hosts.equiv and rhosts files. Unfortunately, some of the popular r commands depend on the existence of at least one of these files to function.

Remote Login

The *rlogin* utility is very similar to telnet. Both enable you to log in to a remote machine. The only differences are in how access is granted. As mentioned earlier, telnet requires that you enter both your username and password before access is granted. However, when using rlogin, access can be granted without even including the username:

```
% rlogin jupiter
Last login: Mon Sep 12 19:30:56 from mercury
SunOS Release 4.1.3 (JUPITER) #1 Mon Aug 15 14:44:35 EST 1994
You have new mail.
Mon Sep 12 19:44:30 EST 1994
%
```

Because no username was supplied, rlogin used the same username as on the local machine. Sometimes, you may have different usernames on different machines. To specify a different username, include -l *remote_user_name* as an argument to rlogin:

```
% who am i
venus!orr      ttypb   Sep 12 19:23
% rlogin jupiter -l scott
Last login: Mon Sep 12 19:44:30 from saturn
SunOS Release 4.1.3 (JUPITER) #1 Mon Aug 15 14:44:35 EST 1994
You have new mail.
Mon Sep 12 19:53:17 EST 1994
%
```

Note Unlike most of the r commands, which display an error message and exit, if access cannot be granted through /etc/hosts.equiv or the user's rhosts file, you are prompted to enter your password before you can access the remote system.

Remote Shell

rsh (or remsh) is similar to rlogin, except that only one command is run on the remote machine and not an actual login session. In addition, rsh also includes the -l option. If free access cannot be granted, the command fails.

```
% rsh saturn date
Mon Sep 12 20:12:21 EST 1994
%
```

Remote Copy

rcp works exactly like its standard Unix counterpart, /bin/cp. You can copy one file, multiple files using wild cards, and even entire directory trees from one machine to another. One or both of the machines can be remote. The remote file is referenced as *hostname:file*. If the file does not include a full path, rcp uses the user's home directory. rcp doesn't support the -l option. Instead, you can switch between users by replacing the host name field with user@hostname. Like rsh, rcp must be granted free access or it will fail. An example of remotely copying a file from one machine to another is shown in the following:

```
% ls test
test not found
% rcp orr@venus:test .
% ls test
test
%
```

Remote Users

Unlike the previously discussed commands, rusers doesn't require any entries in either /etc/hosts.equiv or a user's rhosts. Its function is to list which users are currently logged into remote machines. If run without any command-line arguments, it queries every machine on your network and displays usernames in a space-separated list, one machine per line. By including a host name on the command line, only that host is queried:

```
% rusers jupiter
jupiter      scott scott jon damon scott damon debbie
%
```

If you want more information, include -l as a command-line argument, and rusers displays information similar to /usr/bin/who. You can see who is logged in, when and from where the user logged in, and how long it's been since he or she typed anything, as in the following example:

```
% rusers -l jupiter
scott     jupiter:console      Sep  3 18:33    0:02
scott     jupiter:ttyp0        Sep  3 18:34    0:02 (:0.0)
jon       jupiter:ttyp1        Sep  3 18:34    0:50 (:0.0)
damon     jupiter:ttyp2        Sep  3 18:34    8:06 (saturn)
scott     jupiter:ttyp3        Sep  3 18:34    2:23 (:0.0)
damon     jupiter:ttyp4        Sep  3 18:34    5:10 (mars)
debbie    jupiter:ttyp5        Sep  6 10:02    8:15 (mercury)
```

Note   The same functionality also can be provided through the *rwho* command. The rwho command is not discussed here because the rwho daemon server, rwhod, often utilizes a great deal of cpu time, and many sites choose to disable it.

Remote Up

rup is another remote query program. rup reports the amount of time remote machines have been operational. If you run rup without any command-line arguments, rup queries every machine on your network. In addition to the active time, rup also reports each machine's current cpu load. If you want this information for only one host, include the host name as a command-line argument. The following is an example of using rup:

```
% rup
 mercury    up 24 days,  7:29,    load average: 0.29, 0.27, 0.00
   venus    up 55 days, 13:58,    load average: 0.00, 0.00, 0.00
   earth    up 65 days, 10:04,    load average: 0.10, 0.02, 0.01
    mars    up  9 days,  5:53,    load average: 0.40, 0.37, 0.03
 jupiter    up 14 days, 10:17,    load average: 0.46, 0.39, 0.01
  saturn    up  3 days,  8:28,    load average: 0.00, 0.00, 0.01
  uranus    up 25 days, 14:37,    load average: 1.51, 1.41, 1.04
 neptune    up  4 days,  1:53,    load average: 0.25, 0.32, 0.00
   pluto    up 32 days, 14:06,    load average: 3.48, 3.66, 3.47
%
```

finger —The Network Phonebook

Although originally designed for use on a local machine, the vast amount of information finger can provide about the users on a system has made it very popular among network users as well. Suppose that you want to send some e-mail to a person you met at a conference. You forgot to ask for his e-mail address, but you do know his last name. With finger, you can query his system for the information you seek. An example of using finger to gain information about a user is shown in the following:

```
% finger orr@jupiter.acct.nrp.com
[jupiter]
Login name: scott                    In real life: Scott Orr
Directory: /home/users/scott         Shell: /bin/csh
Last login Mon Sep 12 11:37 on ttyp7 from saturn
Mail last read Mon Sep 12 15:27:35 1994
No Plan.
```

Notice that the last name *orr* was the only information provided to jupiter. Jupiter searches for orr in /etc/passwd and discovers that user scott's last name is Orr. scott's username, full name, home directory, and default shell are all extracted from his /etc/passwd entry. In addition, jupiter consults /etc/utmp to determine when scott last logged in and checks the permissions on scott's mail file to see when it was last read. All this information is then provided to the remote user.

Note Some users create files named .plan and .project in their home directories to give remote users additional information. If either file exists, finger also displays the contents of the file along with the other information.

Finger also can be used to provide much the same information that rusers -l does. You can see who is logged in, their full names, when and on which terminal they logged in, where they logged in from, and how long since they typed anything on the keyboard. Some people use this information to see if a coworker is logged in before trying to contact them. An example is shown in the following:

```
% finger @jupiter
[jupiter]
Login     Name            TTY Idle    When     Where
scott     Scott Orr        co 3:24 Sat 18:33
jon       Jon Burgoyne     p0    4d Sat 18:34   :0.0
scott     Scott Orr        p1    4d Sat 18:34   :0.0
scott     Scott Orr        p3 4:48 Sat 18:34   :0.0
jon       Jon Burgoyne     p4 2:45 Sat 18:34   :0.0
damon     Damon Beals      p5 5:10 Tue 10:02   mars
debbie    Debbie Smith     p6 5:12 Sat 12:50   mercury
```

Note Many security-conscious sites often choose to disable fingerd, the server daemon. With finger, a remote user can gain information about every account on a system, including those that have not been used for a while. People attempting to break into a system target these inactive users first.

E-Mail

No network system is complete without a method of sending messages from one user to another. Unix is no exception. E-mail has been part of the Unix operating system since the very beginning. Users all accessed the same machine, and mail messages were just files copied from one location to another. Then, with the inclusion of TCP/IP networking with BSD Unix, mail was revised to provide network support.

To send mail to a remote user, you include the user's name along with the fully qualified domain name of the machine on which the user has an account. The @ character separates the two, and together they form what's known as an e-mail address. A sample e-mail address is scott@jupiter.acct.nrp.com. When an e-mail address is used, the mail program copies the message to a special directory, such as /var/spool/mqueue, to await the e-mail delivery daemon to send it to the remote machine. The daemon that handles this transfer of mail is known as *sendmail* and is discussed further in forthcoming chapters.

C H A P T E R

6

Using a Windows NT Backbone

TCP/IP is a powerful transport protocol that gives you access to any number of network resources. Because most major computer platforms support TCP/IP, it should not surprise you that Microsoft has included TCP/IP support in Windows NT right out of the box. Windows NT includes many of the tools common in TCP/IP networks like ftp and telnet, but it also provides tools such as Dynamic Host Configuration Protocol (DHCP). The parts that are missing can be filled easily by third-party applications.

Exploring TCP/IP for Windows NT

Because the TCP/IP protocol is the most accepted and complete transport mechanism in the world, Microsoft decided to support it natively. For the user, this means that to use TCP/IP to communicate with other computers requires no additional software. Other products produced by third-party developers might enhance the functionality of TCP/IP on your Windows NT network, but with the tools provided, you can connect to systems using Windows NT, other Microsoft networking products, or with non-Microsoft systems such as Unix.

Windows NT includes many TCP/IP utilities such as telnet, ftp, finger, rcp, rexec, rsh, and tftp. These applications provide users access to resources on non-Microsoft hosts such as Unix. Windows NT also includes a suite of TCP/IP diagnostic tools such as arp, hostname, ipconfig, nbtstat, netstat, ping, and route.

You can use nbstat to check the state of NetBIOS over TCP/IP connections. To find out what name your server registered on the network, type **nbstat -n**. You also can use nbstat to update the LMHOSTS name cache.

tracert is another command you can use to troubleshoot your TCP/IP connections. tracert displays the route taken to a destination, including each router crossed. Type **tracert** *target_name*. The time taken to reach each router along the way also is displayed.

Windows NT also adds a few other utilities that you might not be as familiar with, such as DHCP and Windows Internet Name Service (WINS). You learn more about these utilities later in the chapter. All these tools and applications combine to make Windows NT a robust host on a TCP/IP network.

Tip   Some tools that Windows NT does not include, but for which third-party support is available, are X Windows, NFS, Gopher, and development tools, such as Xlib and ONC/RPC. If you feel the need to expand your TCP/IP support, check into these products. Luckily, you will find many companies interested in supporting TCP/IP on Windows NT.

Installing TCP/IP on Windows NT

You can install the TCP/IP components of Windows NT when you first set up your system or later as you expand your network. This section assumes that you already installed Windows NT on a machine and that you are adding TCP/IP functionality.

Note You must be logged in as Administrator or as a member of the Administrators group to install and configure all the elements of TCP/IP mentioned in this chapter.

Begin by opening the Control Panel and double-clicking on the Networks icon. The Network Settings dialog box appears (see fig. 6.1). Click on the Add **S**oftware button to open the Network Software Installation dialog box.

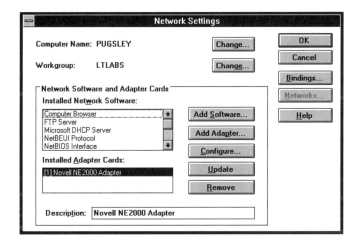

Figure 6.1

The Network Settings dialog box.

Scroll through the list of network software components until you see the option TCP/IP Protocol and Related Components. Choose this option, then click on the Continue button.

The Windows NT TCP/IP Installation Options dialog box that appears includes a number of different components (see fig. 6.2). You might want to install all of them eventually, but for now select TCP/IP Internetworking, **C**onnectivity Utilities, and S**i**mple TCP/IP Services.

The TCP/IP Internetworking component installs the TCP/IP protocols, NetBIOS, Windows Sockets, and the TCP/IP diagnostic utilities. The **C**onnectivity Utilities option installs the utilities like telnet, ftp, finger, and so on. S**i**mple TCP/IP Services installs utilities that enable your system to respond to requests from other machines. If you want more information about any of these items, read the hint bar at the bottom of each TCP/IP dialog box or choose the Help button to get more detailed information.

The dialog box shows how much space each component requires. Hopefully, you will have plenty of room for all the components you selected. To see the space required for all the components you selected and the space available on your hard drive, look at the values below the Components box. If you install all the components, you will need about 2 MB of free disk space.

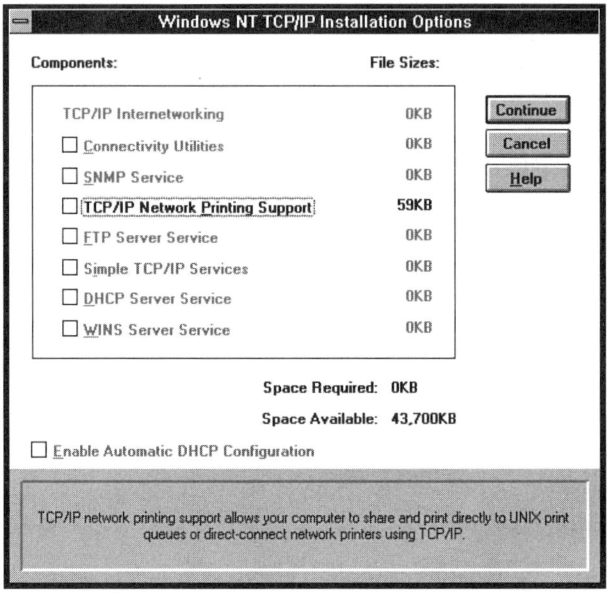

Figure 6.2

The Windows NT TCP/IP Installation Options dialog box.

Windows NT TCP/IP Installation Options		
Components:	**File Sizes:**	
TCP/IP Internetworking	0KB	**Continue**
☐ Connectivity Utilities	0KB	**Cancel**
☐ SNMP Service	0KB	**Help**
☐ TCP/IP Network Printing Support	**59KB**	
☐ FTP Server Service	0KB	
☐ Simple TCP/IP Services	0KB	
☐ DHCP Server Service	0KB	
☐ WINS Server Service	0KB	

Space Required: 0KB

Space Available: 43,700KB

☐ Enable Automatic DHCP Configuration

TCP/IP network printing support allows your computer to share and print directly to UNIX print queues or direct-connect network printers using TCP/IP.

Once you have selected all the components you want to install, click on OK, and Windows NT starts copying the necessary files.

After the TCP/IP software is installed on your Windows NT computer, you need to provide some configuration information. The first thing Windows NT asks you for is a valid IP address. The easiest way to get a valid address is to use a DHCP server. You learn how to install a DHCP server later in this chapter. For now, you need to insert the IP address information manually. In the TCP/IP Configuration dialog box, enter your machine's IP address, the subnet mask, and the default gateway (see fig. 6.3). The section of the box that deals with WINS is covered later in this chapter. Leave it blank for now.

Stop If your network is already running TCP/IP, make sure that you get a valid IP address from your network administrator. Otherwise, you might accidentally choose an address used elsewhere on the network, which causes all sorts of problems. For more information about IP addressing, see Chapter 3, "Introduction to TCP/IP."

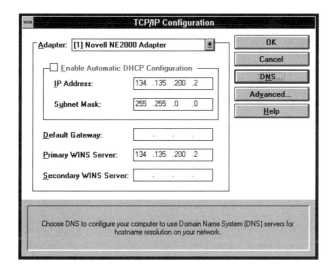

Figure 6.3

The TCP/IP Configuration dialog box.

If you are confused about any part of this dialog box, remember that components are explained in the hint bar. More detailed information is available if you click on the Help button.

Configuring TCP/IP to Use DNS

On the right side of the TCP/IP Configuration dialog box is a button labeled D**N**S (refer to fig. 6.3). DNS (or Domain Name Service) is a naming service popular in Unix networks that provides a means of resolving system names with IP addresses. If you have a DNS server on your network and want to use its naming services, Windows NT gives you the option.

The DNS Configuration dialog box is split into three sections (see fig. 6.4). In the uppermost section, you tell Windows NT which naming resources you want to search first. If you have a HOSTS file on your machine, it can use that in conjunction with the DNS server. You can configure TCP/IP to search either resource first.

In the middle section of the DNS Configuration dialog box, you insert the DNS server's IP address. You can include up to three IP addresses, but keep in mind that the order they are listed in this box is the order Windows NT uses to query the name servers. Therefore, you should list first the DNS server you use most often (if there is one). You can use the arrow buttons at the right of the box to change the order.

In the third section in the DNS Configuration dialog box, you can list domain suffixes. This list specifies the DNS domain suffixes to be appended to host names during name resolution. You can add up to six entries in this list. The domain suffixes are used with the host names to create a fully qualified domain name (FQDN). A FQDN consists of the host name, followed by a period, followed by the domain name. For example, if *editorial* is the host name and *lantimes.com* is the domain name, the FQDN is *editorial.lantimes.com*.

When you have filled in all the information necessary in the DNS Configuration dialog box, click on OK to return to the TCP/IP Configuration dialog box.

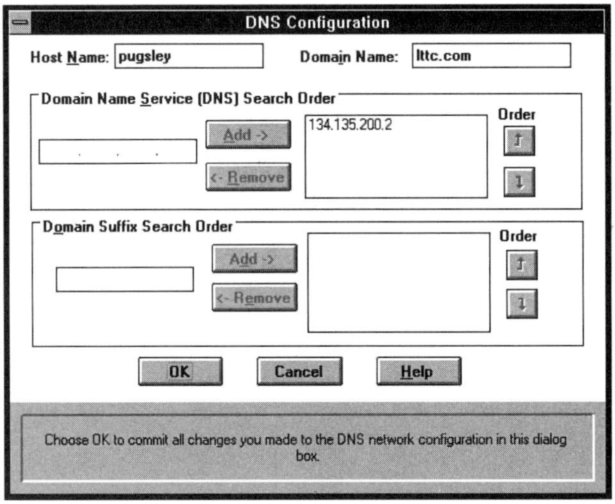

Figure 6.4

The DNS Configuration dialog box.

Configuring Advanced TCP/IP Options

Depending on the complexity of your TCP/IP network, you might want to configure the Advanced TCP/IP options of Windows NT. To do this, click on the Advanced button in the TCP/IP Configuration dialog box. The Advanced Microsoft TCP/IP Configuration dialog box appears (see fig. 6.5). At the top of the box, you can select the network adapter for which you want to configure specific options. If you only have one adapter, then this doesn't really matter to you; but if you have two or more adapters, some of the options in this dialog box are of special interest.

Below the Adapter setting is a section of the box in which you can add IP addresses and subnet masks to your machine. You can configure up to five IP addresses for each network adapter on your system. This feature comes in handy if you happen to run multiple IP networks on the same physical segment.

You also can define up to five default gateways for the selected adapter to use. As with the list of DNS servers, the order in which the gateways are listed is important. Windows NT searches the gateway at the top of the list first, and then on down the line.

Two other options deal specifically with Windows networking parameters. Normally, DNS servers are used in host-based TCP/IP environments like Unix. If you select the box next to the option Ena**b**le DNS for Windows Name Resolution, then you can use a DNS server to resolve naming requests for Windows networks also.

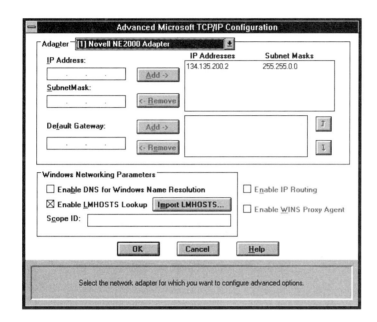

Figure 6.5

The Advanced Microsoft TCP/IP Configuration dialog box.

Another way to resolve naming requests on a Windows network is with an LMHOSTS file. If you aren't familiar with the function of LMHOSTS files, don't worry—you learn about it later in the chapter. The Advanced Microsoft TCP/IP Configuration dialog box also gives you the option of importing an LMHOSTS file.

The final option in this section of the dialog box is to enter a S**c**ope ID. A *scope ID* is a way to group a set of computers so that they only communicate with each other. If you enter a scope ID in this field, your computer will be able to communicate only with other computers on your network that have the exact same scope ID. Usually, you want to leave this value blank.

Finally, you have the option in the Advanced Microsoft TCP/IP Configuration dialog box to enable IP routing. This option is only available to you if you have two network adapters configured for the TCP/IP protocol with their own IP addresses. The WINS Proxy agent field applies only if you have a WINS server on your network.

Configure the options you want to change, then click on OK to return to the TCP/IP Configuration dialog box.

Configuring TCP/IP for Remote Access

Many Windows NT users install Remote Access Service (RAS) so that they can use their network from a remote site. Fortunately, this remote access is available for TCP/IP networks as well. Remote users can dial in to an RAS server and have complete remote access to the TCP/IP network as if they were physically connected to the network through a LAN adapter.

RAS has some special considerations in a TCP/IP network, however. For example, how do users resolve naming and address queries—through the RAS server on the LAN or through the remotely attached computer connected with a phone line?

To configure RAS for use on TCP/IP networks, you first need to run the RAS setup program. To get there, follow these steps:

1. Open the Networks icon from the Control Panel.

2. Select Add Software and choose Remote Access Service from the list.

3. In the Remote Access Setup dialog box, click on the Network button to open the Network Configuration dialog box (see fig. 6.6).

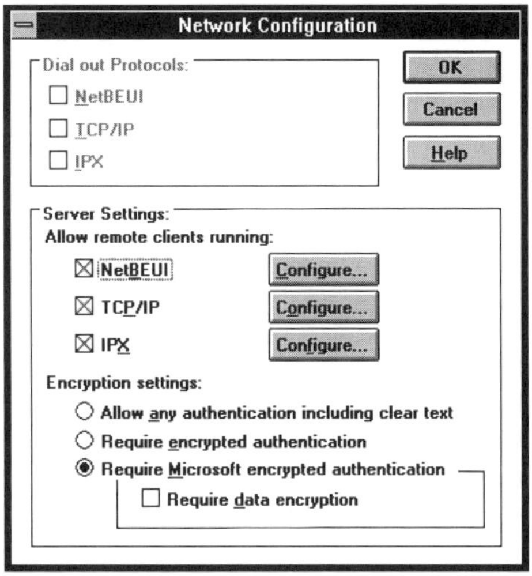

Figure 6.6

The Network Configuration dialog box.

4. From this dialog box, select TCP/IP and click on the Configure button next to it. (If TCP/IP is already installed on your system, that box is checked by default.)

The RAS Server TCP/IP Configuration dialog box appears (see fig. 6.7).

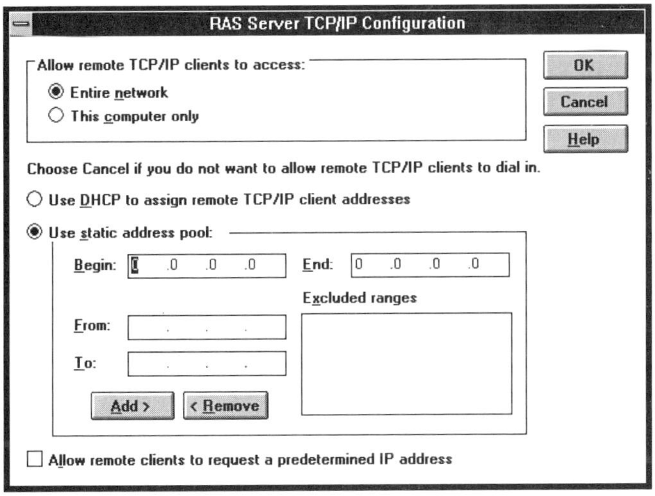

Figure 6.7

The RAS Server TCP/IP Configuration dialog box.

The RAS Server TCP/IP Configuration dialog box enables you to configure the IP address allocation for remote clients using RAS. You can configure remote users to get their IP addresses either from a DHCP server or from a static IP address pool. If you have a DHCP server on your network, it is preferable to use that option. But if you do not use such a server, select the Use static address pool option.

If you select the second option, you need to enter a valid range of IP addresses for remote users. If you want, you also can exclude a range of addresses that remote clients should not have. If your network uses a WINS server or a DNS server for machine name resolution, enter its address in the appropriate field in this dialog box.

All this assumes that the RAS server assigns the IP address. A RAS client can request its own specific address, however. To enable this option, select the check box at the bottom of the dialog box. If a remote client can request its own IP address, it also can request a specific DNS or WINS server for name resolution.

Using TCP/IP Utilities

By this point, you have read about DHCP servers and WINS servers, but you might not fully understand these terms. In this section, you learn about these TCP/IP features as well as HOSTS and LMHOSTS files and File Transfer Protocol (FTP) Server services of Windows NT.

Using DHCP

One of the biggest complaints in managing and maintaining a TCP/IP network is the difficulty keeping track of all the addresses and names. DNS servers help by giving clients a central location in which to look for names and addresses, but they still do not solve one problem.

As TCP/IP networking grows more prevalent, it becomes apparent to everyone that IP addresses are limited and sometimes hard to come by. Unfortunately, many of the IP addresses assigned to machines on your network might be used only sporadically, however the addresses are dedicated anyhow.

DHCP was designed to solve this problem while simplifying TCP/IP network adminis-tration. A DHCP server makes assigning addresses to machines a dynamic rather than static process. Normally, a new user on the network applies to the manager for a valid IP address. The manager then makes an entry in the HOSTS tables or DNS database. That user might only need that address sporadically or even temporarily; however, while the address is assigned to a machine, no one else can use it.

Another problem arises as users become mobile and take their machines with them. If you take your notebook from one network in your building to another, the old address might not work in the new local area network (LAN). To apply to the LAN manager for an address you will use for the afternoon doesn't make sense.

With DHCP, IP addresses are automatically assigned as needed and then released when no longer necessary. The process is quite simple. A DHCP server has a pool of valid addresses it can assign to clients. When a client's system starts, it sends a message on the network requesting an address.

Each DHCP server (several can exist) replies with an IP address and configuration information. The DHCP client collects the offers and selects a valid address, sending the confirmation back to the offering DHCP server. Each DHCP server receives the confirmation from the client. The DHCP server whose address the client selected sends an acknowledgment message back to the client. All the other DHCP servers rescind their earlier offers and put the offered address back into their pool. After the client receives the acknowledgment message from a DHCP server, it can participate in the TCP/IP network.

The DHCP server essentially leases the address to the client. That lease can have time limits so that unused leases are automatically returned to the address pool. If the lease expires, but the machine is still using the lease, the DHCP server can renew the lease so that the client can continue with the same address.

To install a DHCP server on a Windows NT machine, you need to go back to the TCP/IP Installation Options dialog box. If you need to, double-click on the Network icon in the Control Panel. Choose the Add **S**oftware button and select the TCP/IP Protocol and Related Components option in the software list.

Choose the DHCP Server Service from the list and click on OK. Windows NT begins copying the necessary files to your hard disk. That's all there is to the installation.

To configure the **D**HCP Server services, you must use the DHCP Administrator utility. This utility automatically installs when you install the DHCP services. Double-click on the DHCP Administrator icon in the Network Administration group.

The first thing you want to do is to create a DHCP administrative *scope.* A scope is equivalent to a subnet on your network. Highlight the Local Machine entry under the DHCP Servers list. Then select S**c**ope, **C**reate from the menu, and the Create Scope - (Local) dialog box appears (see fig. 6.8).

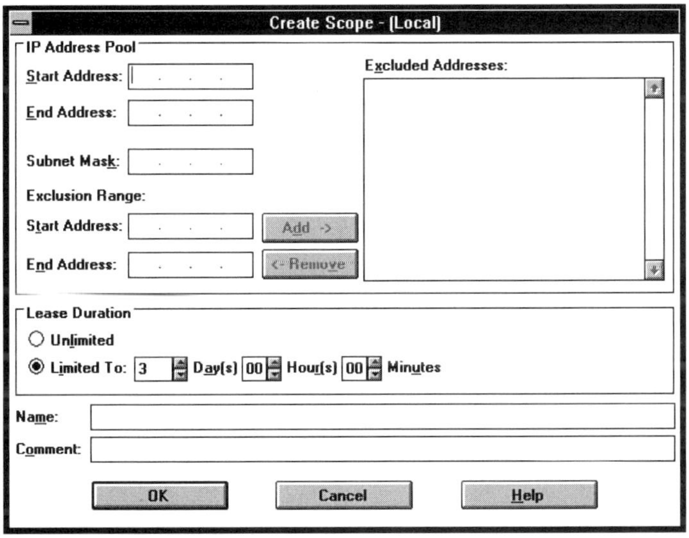

Figure 6.8

The Create Scope - (Local) dialog box.

In this dialog box, you define the pool of addresses DHCP dynamically makes available to DHCP clients. Enter the start and end addresses to define the range. If you want to exclude some addresses that are in that pool, you can either enter an excluded range or an excluded address. To insert an excluded range, enter values in the S**t**art Address and E**n**d Address fields. To exclude a single address, enter the address in the S**t**art Address field. The excluded ranges and addresses should include other DHCP servers, non-DHCP clients, diskless workstations, or RAS clients.

As you insert excluded ranges or addresses, click on the A**d**d button to add them to the list on the right. If you make a mistake or change your mind about an excluded address, highlight it and click on the Remo**v**e button.

The next part of the Create Scope dialog box, entitled Lease Duration, governs the length of time DHCP clients are allowed to keep their addresses. Remember that one of the main reasons for installing a DHCP server is so addresses can be assigned and released dynamically.

If you want your DHCP server to assign addresses as they are requested, but never release them, click on the Unlimited Lease Duration button. More likely, you want to define a duration of a few days or hours. If you specify a duration of three days (the default value), the DHCP server checks to see if the client is still using that address when the lease expires. If the client is still using the address, the lease can be renewed.

If you have a shortage of valid IP addresses on your network and machines go up and down quite frequently, three days might be too long for a lease. You might want to specify a few hours. The only problem with this is the added traffic of negotiating addresses between DHCP servers and DHCP clients so frequently.

If you have plenty of IP addresses for your network, but still want to free unused addresses after a while, it might be more appropriate to assign a longer lease duration (like 30 days).

The only other thing you need to enter in the Create Scope dialog box is a scope name and optional comment. The name can be up to 128 characters and can be any name you want to give the subnet. It can include letters, numbers, and hyphens. Any other information you want to include about the scope can be entered in the Comment field.

When you finish entering all the values in the dialog box, click on OK. Windows NT tells you the scope has been successfully created, but is not yet activated. You then have the option to activate the scope now. Click on **Y**es if you want to do so.

If you ever need to change the scope properties, you can do so quite easily. Highlight the scope on the left side of the DHCP Manager utility and select Scope, Properties.

Also from the Scope menu, you can select Active Leases to see which computers are using your DHCP server. The Active Leases dialog box appears (see fig. 6.9). If you highlight a client and click on the **P**roperties button, you can see the IP address, when the lease expired, the client name, and the Client Identifier, which is usually the media access control (MAC) address of the network adapter on that machine.

Choose the Add Reservations option to bring up the Add Reserved Clients dialog box, in which you can reserve a specific address for a specific client (see fig. 6.10). This option enables you to reserve a specific address for a specific client. You can specify any unused IP address from the address pool. In the **U**nique Identifier field, enter the MAC address of the network adapter on the client computer.

Next, fill in the computer name for the client to help you remember which client the address is reserved for. You do not have to enter the exact computer name for the client. Any other information you want to enter about the client can be put in the Client **C**omment field.

The DHCP Manager utility enables you to change the configuration parameters the server assigns to its clients. The options have been given default values based on standard parameters defined by the Internet Networking Group in RFC 1542. You can change these parameters to affect every client the DHCP server services or clients in a certain scope.

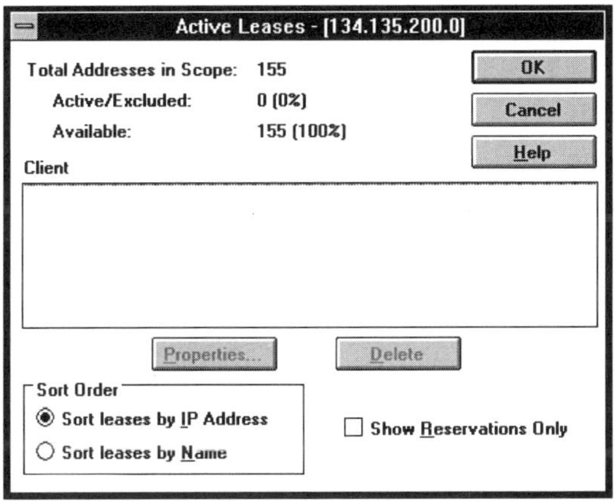

Figure 6.9

The Active Leases dialog box.

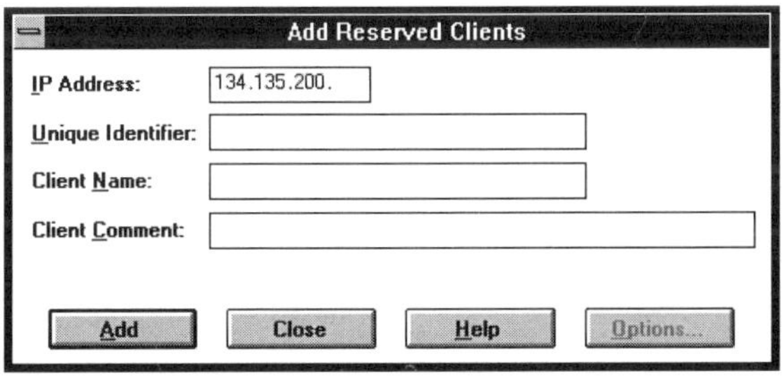

Figure 6.10

The Add Reserved Clients dialog box.

If you want to change the default values, you can do that as well. These TCP/IP networking options are advanced, and unless you know exactly what you are doing, you can degrade performance or make it unusable.

Using WINS

A Windows Internet Naming Service (WINS) server maintains a database of computers and their associated IP addresses. It provides dynamic name resolution support, and therefore is suited to work in conjunction with DHCP servers rather than the typical DNS server. In fact, when dynamic address changes are made through DHCP for computers that move between subnets, those changes are automatically made in the WINS database.

Like the DHCP software, WINS has server and client components. WINS name resolution is automatically installed and configured for you when you install DHCP. If you haven't enabled DHCP yet and want to check out WINS, you need to install it manually.

To install WINS, double-click on the Network icon in the Control Panel. After the Network Settings dialog box appears, click on the Add **S**oftware button to bring up the Network Software Installation dialog box. Select TCP/IP Protocol and Related Components from the list and then click on the Continue button.

The Windows NT TCP/IP Installation Options dialog box should be familiar to you by now. Click on the **S**NMP Service and **W**INS Server Service options, then click on Continue. Windows NT copies the necessary files to your hard disk.

When you install WINS, Windows NT adds a utility called WINS Manager in the Network Administration group. Use this tool to manage your WINS server.

On the left side of the WINS Manager application window is a list of WINS servers (see fig. 6.11).

Figure 6.11

The WINS Manager application window.

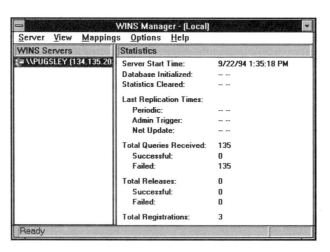

As you highlight a WINS server with a click of your mouse, statistics about that server appear on the right side of the window. Table 6.1 explains what these statistics mean.

TABLE 6.1
Statistics in WINS Manager

Statistic	Meaning
Total Queries Received	The number of name query request messages received by this WINS server
Total Releases	The number of messages received that indicate a NetBIOS application has shut itself down
Total Registrations	The number of name registration requests accepted by this WINS server

If you want to clear the statistics in this table, select **V**iew, Clear Statistics from the menu. Because the Statistics table does not dynamically update itself, you might want to refresh the numbers every so often while you have the WINS Manager open. To do so, select **V**iew, Re**f**resh Statistics, or press F5.

To add WINS servers to your WINS Manager list, select **S**erver, **A**dd WINS Server. Windows NT then prompts you to enter the IP address of the WINS server you want to add. To delete a server from the WINS Manager list, select **S**erver, **D**elete WINS Server.

To keep the WINS database on one server doesn't make sense. If that server goes down, someone else needs to handle name resolution on the network. For this reason, consider creating a replication partner for your WINS server. A replication partner helps ensure that the database is always available and also helps balance the job of keeping the database current between more machines.

To set up a replication partner, select **R**eplication Partners from the **S**erver menu, and the Replication Partners dialog box appears (see fig. 6.12). In the WINS server list, you should see your own local WINS server. To add other WINS servers to the list, click on the **A**dd button and enter the address of the WINS server you want to replicate. You can add several WINS servers and set up different relationships with each if you like.

The relationship that can exist between WINS servers is either a Pull or Push relationship. A *Pull Partner* is a WINS server that pulls replicas from its Push Partner. A *Push Partner* is a WINS server that sends replicas to its Pull Partner. Two WINS servers can be both Push and Pull partners with each other.

Because of the extra traffic, you probably do not want the database to replicate every time an entry is made. Click on the Configure buttons under Replication Options to define when and how often the WINS servers share data.

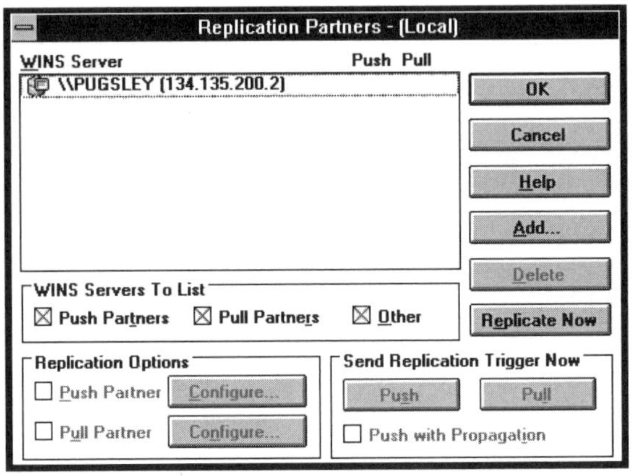

Figure 6.12

Setting up replication partners.

You can configure other aspects of your WINS server by selecting Configuration from the Server menu. You can adjust the parameters listed in table 6.2.

TABLE 6.2
WINS Server Configuration

Configuration Option	Meaning
Renewal Interval	Specifies how often a client reregisters its name. The default is 96 hours.
Extinction Interval	Specifies the interval between when an entry is marked *released* and when it is marked *extinct*. The default is 96 hours.
Extinction Timeout	Specifies the interval between when an entry is marked *extinct* and when the entry is finally scavenged from the database. The default is 96 hours.
Verify Interval	Specifies the interval after which the WINS server must verify that old names it does not own are still active. The default is 20 times the extinction interval.

You also can configure Push and Pull parameters of your WINS server. If you want your WINS server to Pull replication information when the server initializes, select the Initial Replication check box. If the servers do not respond immediately, you also can insert a Retry Count.

For Push partners, have your WINS server inform them of the database status when the system is initialized or when an address changes in a mapping record. When you are done configuring the options in this dialog box, click on OK.

To see a copy of the WINS database, select **M**appings, Show **D**atabase from the menu. The Show Database dialog box appears, in which you can see host names and the addresses to which they are mapped (see fig. 6.13). The database can be sorted however you like to make it easier to find information in the database.

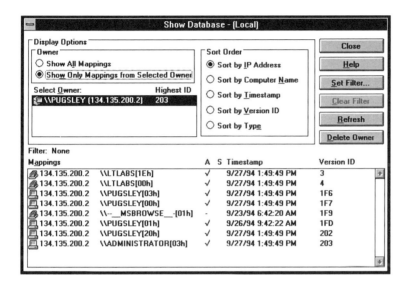

Figure 6.13

Local database mappings.

Additionally, you can configure this dialog box to show all the mappings in the database or only mappings that relate to a specific WINS server. If you want to view only mappings related to a specific host, you can use the **S**et Filter option to weed unwanted entries from the list.

Your local WINS database should periodically be cleared of unwanted entries. Sometimes entries are registered at another WINS server, but aren't cleared from the local database. The process of clearing unnecessary entries from the database is called *scavenging* and can be started by selecting In**i**tiate Scavenging from the **M**appings menu.

Using HOSTS and LMHOSTS Files

Although you probably want to use DHCP and WINS for name resolution on your TCP/IP Windows NT network, you also should be aware of a couple of other options Windows NT gives you to resolve host names.

TCP/IP for Windows NT uses two text files to resolve host names with their respective addresses. Both files are found in the \WINNT\SYSTEM32\DRIVERS\ETC directory. One is the HOSTS file; the other is the LMHOSTS file.

If you have any experience with TCP/IP networking on Unix or any other platform, you probably know what a HOSTS file is—a list of IP addresses and host names. If you attempt to use the TCP/IP utilities of Windows NT, you need to specify to which computer you want to attach or login. You can do this by providing either an IP address, which can be difficult to remember and a pain to type in, or a simple name. If you enabled TCP/IP for Windows NT to use the HOSTS file, it attempts to match the name you type in with an address in the HOSTS file. A HOSTS file is the easiest way to resolve names on a TCP/IP network.

The problem with HOSTS files is that they only work for the computer on which they reside. When your network expands, keeping a current HOSTS file on every computer can be time-consuming and problematic.

LMHOSTS files have many of the same problems as HOSTS files, but they are more flexible. Like HOSTS, LMHOSTS is a simple text file that contains mappings of IP addresses to Windows NT computer names (which are NetBIOS names). LMHOSTS has greater capabilities than the normal HOSTS file because it enables you to include *keywords* that tell the TCP/IP components of your Windows NT server how to handle name resolution.

The keywords that the LMHOSTS file uses are #PRE, #DOM:*domain*, #INCLUDE *filename*, #BEGIN_ALTERNATE, and #END_ALTERNATE. Normally in an LMHOSTS file, anything after the # sign is regarded as a remark statement and ignored. If the # sign is followed by one of the accepted keywords, however, LMHOSTS treats the statement as a command. Each of these keywords is explained in the following paragraphs.

#PRE following an entry in an LMHOSTS file tells Windows NT to load that entry into the name cache. Loading an entry into cache causes TCP/IP for Windows NT to resolve the name more quickly.

Adding #DOM:*domain* after an entry causes Windows NT to associate that entry with whatever domain you specify. It helps Windows NT resolve the names more efficiently because it does not have to search routing tables to find out to which domain the entry belongs.

An #INCLUDE *filename* entry tells your Windows NT machine where to look for other LMHOSTS files that reside on other servers. When entering the filename, you should use the Uniform Naming Convention (UNC)—that is, two \\ (backward slashes), the machine name, another \, and the filename including directory structure. If, for example, you want to include the LMHOSTS file on Windows NT server desdemona, you specify the filename as follows:

```
\\desdemona\winnt\system32\drivers\etc\lmhosts.
```

Before a group of multiple #INCLUDE statements, insert the line
#BEGIN_ALTERNATE. After you enter the statements, insert the line
#END_ALTERNATE.

The only other special keyword you can use in an LMHOSTS file is \0x*nn*, which is a
hexadecimal notation used to support nonprinting characters in NetBIOS names.
You probably do not need to use this keyword unless you have an application that
uses special names to function properly in routed topologies.

Tip   If you need help creating your HOSTS and LMHOSTS files, see the files themselves
in the winnt\system32\drivers\etc directory. The files that Windows NT creates
when you install TCP/IP connectivity functions contain sample entries and
explanations about their use.

Using FTP Server Services

One of the most commonly used applications in a TCP/IP environment is the File
Transfer Protocol (FTP). Windows NT includes an FTP client so that you can initiate
file transfers between your machine and another on the network. Windows NT also
provides an FTP server so that other machines on the network can initiate file
transfers.

One problem with using FTP Server services on your computer is that unencrypted
passwords can cross the network causing a severe breach in your security. Therefore,
you might want to think twice about turning your Windows NT computer into an FTP
server.

The security model of the FTP Server service is integrated with Windows NT's own
security model. Clients use the Windows NT user accounts and passwords to log into
the FTP server through TCP/IP. Access to directories and files on the server is
maintained by Windows NT's security structure as well. For this reason, Microsoft
recommends that the FTP Server service be installed on an NTFS partition so that the
files and directories made available through FTP can be secured.

To install FTP Server services, follow these steps:

1. Choose the Network icon in the Control Panel.

2. In the Network Settings dialog box, click on the Add **S**oftware button. The Add
   Network Software dialog box appears.

3. Select the TCP/IP Protocol and Related Components entry from the list to bring
   up the Windows NT TCP/IP Installation options dialog box.

4. Select the **F**TP Server Service option and click on OK.

A security warning similar to the one you read appears. If you still want to install FTP Server services, click on **Y**es. Windows NT copies the appropriate files.

After the FTP Server software is installed on your computer, the FTP Service dialog box appears on your screen (see fig. 6.14). Here you can configure such items as maximum connections and idle timeout periods. You also can specify the home directory FTP clients default to when they first connect.

Figure 6.14

The FTP Service dialog box.

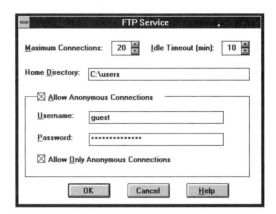

Another part of this configuration box enables you to configure anonymous connections. If you want, users can log into your FTP Server service with the username Anonymous. The password is their user account name. By default, the Anonymous FTP account has the same rights and privileges on the Windows NT system as user Guest, but you can change that if you want. You can create a user profile using the User Account Editor of Windows NT to create a default Anonymous user with whatever rights you choose and enter that username in the appropriate field.

Note If, for some reason, you have a username Anonymous on your Windows NT system and that user logs in to your FTP Server, she will receive permissions based on the Guest account, not the native Anonymous account.

You can set your FTP server to accept Anonymous connections only. If security is an important issue in your network, yet you still want to enable FTP Server services, then perhaps you should select this option. That way, the only passwords that need to travel the wire unencrypted are the usernames of the people logging in with the Anonymous account.

To complete the configuration process, click on OK to close the dialog box.

When FTP Server services start, you see a new icon for managing the server in the Control Panel. Double-click on that icon, and the FTP User Sessions dialog box appears. In this box is a list of users connected to your machine through FTP. You can see the usernames, IP addresses they are connecting from, and how long they have been connected. If they logged on using the Anonymous account, you can see the passwords they used. You can disconnect all of them if you need to by clicking on the Disconnect **A**ll button at the bottom of the dialog box.

While the box is open, click on the **S**ecurity button to see the level of security that FTP initiates on its own—independent of the Windows NT security architecture. The FTP Server Security dialog box appears (see fig. 6.15).

Figure 6.15

Setting up FTP server security.

The FTP Server Security dialog box enables you to configure each partition on your system for Read and Write access. One way to add an extra level of security to your system for FTP clients is to place all sensitive files on a separate partition and grant neither Read nor Write access to that partition. Or if you want to allow users to copy files from your server, but not copy files to your server, select the Allow **R**ead check box and leave the Allow **W**rite check box blank. After you configure the security options for each partition, click on OK.

Tip

If you have any questions about the FTP commands that Windows NT uses, select the Windows NT Help icon in the Program Manager Main group. In the Windows NT help window, click on the Command Reference Help button, then click the FTP commands entry in the Commands window. Click on each FTP command name to see a description of the command as well as valid parameters and syntax.

Printing with TCP/IP

With the TCP/IP utilities and resources installed on your Windows NT computer, you now have the ability to print to TCP/IP printers. TCP/IP printers can be connected directly into the network or attached to Unix computers. Furthermore, any Microsoft networking computer can use your machine as a gateway to access the TCP/IP printers—even if they do not have TCP/IP installed.

Follow these steps to configure your Windows NT computer for TCP/IP printing:

1. Double-click on the Network icon in the Control Panel.

2. Select the **A**dd Software button in the Network Settings dialog box.

3. When the Network Software Installation dialog box appears, select the TCP/IP and Related Components entry from the list and click on the Continue button.

4. In the TCP/IP Installation Options dialog box, select the TCP/IP Networking **P**rinting Support option and click on OK. Windows NT then copies the needed files to your hard disk.

With TCP/IP Printing Support installed, you can now use the Print Manager to connect to a TCP/IP printer the same way you connect to any other printer on the network. The only information you need is the DNS name or IP address of the printer, the printer name as it is identified on the host, and the TCP port ID on the host.

To create a printer to use on your Windows NT network, follow these steps:

1. Select Crea**t**e Printer from the **P**rinter menu in Print Manager.

2. Enter the appropriate information for Printer **N**ame, **D**river, and D**e**scription as you would with any printer.

3. Under the Print **T**o field, select Add Other Port from the list. The Print Destinations dialog box appears with a couple of options listed.

4. Select the LPR Monitor from the list, then click on OK. The Add LPR Compatible Printer dialog box appears.

5. Insert the information mentioned earlier to fill in the fields, then click on OK to return to the Create Printer dialog box.

6. If you want to share this printer with other users on the network—even if they don't have TCP/IP installed on their systems—click the check box to **S**hare this printer on the network. You can fill in the Sh**a**re **N**ame and **L**ocation fields to give others an indication of which printer they'll see in a Browse window and where the printer is located.

7. When you are finished, click on OK to close the dialog box.

Managing TCP/IP Computers with Windows NT

With TCP/IP installed on your Windows NT machine, you now have some additional tools available to help you manage the system. These two tools are the SNMP Agent and Performance Monitor. Although Performance Monitor itself is not new with the installation of TCP/IP software, several new monitoring options in that application are now available to you.

Using SNMP Management

Use the following steps to install the SNMP Service option:

1. Double-click on the Networks icon in the Control Panel.

2. In the Network Settings dialog box, click on the Add **S**oftware button. In the Network Software Installation dialog box, choose TCP/IP Protocol and Related Components from the Add Software list.

3. When the TCP/IP Installation Options dialog box appears, select the **S**NMP Service option and click on OK. Windows NT copies the necessary files to your hard disk.

When you return to the Network Settings dialog box, select SNMP Service from the Installed Network Software list box. Click on the **C**onfigure button to bring up the SNMP Service Configuration dialog box (see fig. 6.16).

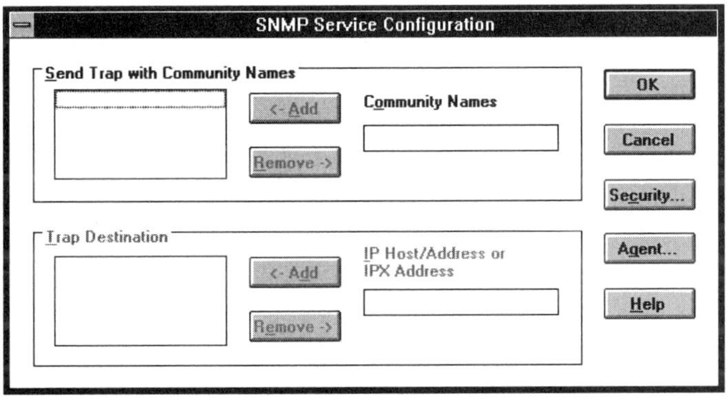

Figure 6.16

The SNMP Service Configuration dialog box.

From this dialog box, you can configure the communities to which you want your computer to send traps, and the hosts for each community to which you send traps. Type the community name or host ID in the field on the right of the box, then click on the **A**dd button.

If you are concerned about the security of your SNMP information, click on the Se**c**urity button to open the SNMP Security Configuration dialog box (see fig. 6.17). You can configure three things about SNMP security from this box.

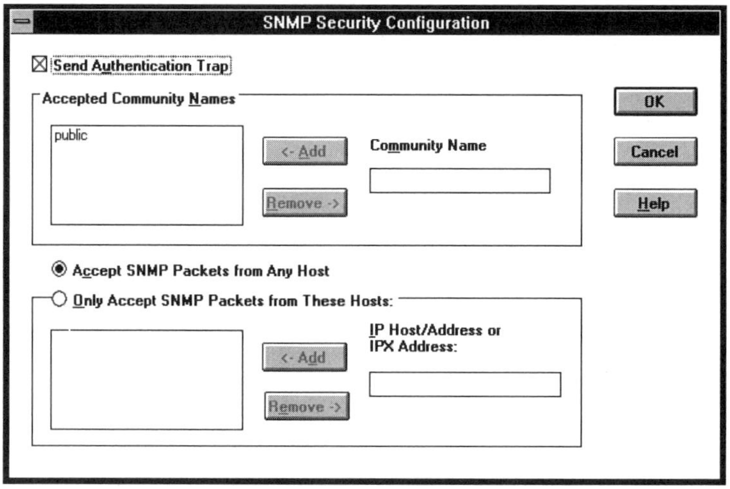

Figure 6.17

The SNMP Security Configuration dialog box.

The first item—Send A**u**thentication Trap—sends a trap for failed authentications. If you want this option, select the Send A**u**thentication Trap check box.

The next item—Accepted Community **N**ames—enables you to specify from which community names you accept requests. If the host is not on the list, the SNMP service does not accept the request. To add community names to the list, insert the name into the field on the right, then click on the **A**dd button.

The final SNMP security option enables you to specify from which hosts you accept SNMP packets. If you want to accept SNMP packets from any host, click on the A**c**cept SNMP Packets from Any Host radio button. If you want to create a list of valid hosts, select O**n**ly Accept SNMP Packets from These Hosts. To add to the list, insert the host name or address in the field to the right, then click on A**d**d.

When you finish configuring SNMP security, click on OK to return to the SNMP Service Configuration dialog box.

To configure the SNMP Agent, click on the A**g**ent button. The SNMP Agent dialog box appears, giving you the option to enter some specific data about your machine (see fig. 6.18). You can insert a contact name and location in the appropriate fields.

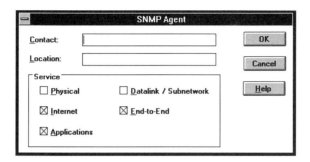

Figure 6.18

The SNMP Agent dialog box.

In the Service box, you can configure which services to report through SNMP. The services you select depend on the function of your Windows NT machine. Table 6.3 helps you to configure which services to report through SNMP.

TABLE 6.3
SNMP Agent Services

Option	Meaning
Physical	Select this option if your Windows NT computer manages any physical TCP/IP device, such as a repeater.
Datalink / Subnetwork	Select this option if your Windows NT computer manages a TCP/IP subnetwork or datalink, such as a bridge.
Internet	Select this option if your Windows NT computer acts as an IP gateway.
End-to-End	Select this option if your Windows NT computer acts as an IP host. This option should be selected for all Windows NT installations.
Applications	Select this option if your Windows NT computer includes any applications that use TCP/IP, such as e-mail. This option should be selected for all Windows NT installations.

When the agent is configured as you want, click on OK to return to the SNMP Service Configuration dialog box. Then click on OK again to close this box.

Using Performance Monitor

With TCP/IP components installed on your Windows NT computer, you now have a whole new batch of counters to watch from Performance Monitor.

 Note To use the TCP/IP performance counters, you should install the TCP/IP protocols and the SNMP Service.

Additional objects in Performance Monitor are IP performance counters, ICMP performance counters, TCP performance counters, UDP performance counters, FTP Server traffic, DHCP Server performance, and WINS Server performance.

To learn about each of these objects and counters, click on the **E**xplain button in the Add to Chart dialog box from within Performance Monitor. The information you gather here helps you realize when your server is becoming overloaded with process requests. If your machine is very busy as an FTP server, for example, you can move DHCP and WINS server support to another Windows NT machine on the network.

Part II

Services

Setting Up a WWW Service

All of the services discussed in this book are available for Intranet or Internet use. With the exception of WWW services, however, all the rest are command-line interfaces. As such, they are powerful and fast, but have a learning curve and are text based. You can make text look only so good. WWW services present a multimedia interface. If you work at all in a windowing environment, the GUI front end flattens out the curve for learning how to use a WWW browser. The color, sound, images, and video clips provide the flash and excitement that makes "surfing the Internet" so easy and fun.

The real tool that WWW services use to make interfacing so easy is *hyperlinks*. To look at a different document, just click on a highlighted word, button, or image. Rather than read the README files or look through reams of files that only might match your search criteria, WWW clients enable you to navigate the Internet with point-and-click ease (see fig 7.1).

Figure 7.1

A World Wide Web page.

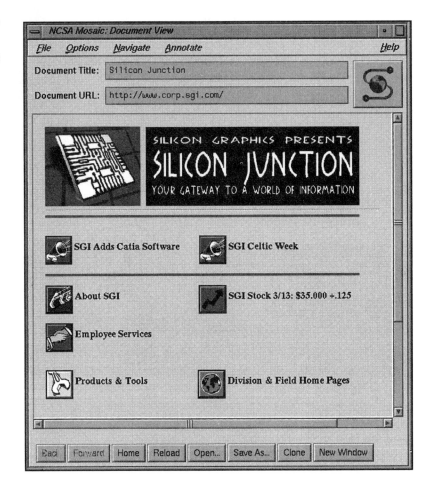

In addition to its graphical base, WWW clients can use many of the text-based services presented in later chapters—for example, a WWW client can access Gopher, FTP, and (for some clients) WAIS services, in addition to WWW services.

Getting the Client Software

The various WWW browsers all are free, and some will soon be reborn as commercial products. Table 7.1 describes the browsers and tells you where you can get them.

TABLE 7.1
WWW Browsers

Name	URL and Description
Lynx	`ftp://ftp2.cc.ukans.edu/pub/lynx/` A full-featured WWW browser developed at the University of Kansas that best displays character-based pages.
MidasWWW	`http://www-midas.slac.stanford.edu/midasv22/introduction.html` A full-featured WWW browser developed at Stanford Linear Accelerator Center (SLAC) for X Window systems. Similar to Mosaic, but provides better support for inline graphics, including .fig, .jpeg, and .tiff files, without having to spawn an external viewer.
Mosaic	`ftp://ftp.ncsa.uiuc.edu/Mosaic/` The most celebrated WWW browser, developed at the National Center for Supercomputer Applications (NCSA) at the University of Illinois, with versions for most Unix platforms, Apple Macintosh, and Microsoft Windows. MPEG movies, JPED images, and sound files automatically spawn external viewers, because Mosaic can only handle GIF or XBM image formats.
Netscape	`http://home.netscape.com` A full-featured, graphical browser created by Netscape Communications Corporation.
Emacs	`ftp://moose.cs.indiana.edu/pub/elisp/w3/` Compatible with Mosaic. Especially good for Mosaic users who also must dial in to the Internet, perhaps from home, on a slower line.
NeXT	`ftp://info.cern.ch/pub/www/bin/next/` Available for NeXT computers only.
perlWWW	`ftp://archive.cis.ohio-state.edu/pub/w3browser` A character-based WWW browser, written in PERL, developed at Ohio State University.

If you haven't already used a WWW browser, no description can substitute for getting your hands on and playing with a browser. Try it out first on the following URL:

`http://www.paramount.com`

Paramount's home page includes most of the tools you are likely to see in Web pages, including hypertext, buttons, and movie clips.

Getting Service Software

Three major WWW services have been written for the Unix platform. This book discusses installing the NCSA version of the Web service. Table 7.2, however, shows you where you can get the binaries for the other services, too.

TABLE 7.2
Binaries for other WWW Services

Service	URL and Description
CERN	`ftp://info.cern.ch/pub/www/bin`
	From the birthplace of the WWW, comes the public-domain CERN Web service, supporting clickable images, forms, and access authorization.
NCSA	`http://boohoo.ncsa.uiuc.edu` or `ftp.ncsa.edu`
	Like the CERN service, the NCSA service is in the public-domain and written in C. This small, fast service supports clickable images, searches, HTML forms, and access restrictions.
Plexus	`ftp://austin.bsdi.com/plexus/2.2.1/dist/Plexus.html`
	This service is written in PERL, so is easy to modify, but heavyweight.

This book discusses the NCSA Web service for the following reasons:

♦ It is small and fast.

♦ It can serve many documents simultaneously because the service draws so little on system resources.

♦ It can run as a stand-alone daemon, or under inetd.

♦ The service understands both the HTTP/1.0 and HTTP/0.9 protocols.

♦ You can limit user actions and connections and prevent users from specific hosts from connecting to your service. You can also require user authentication to gain access to your service, if the WWW client supports user authentication.

♦ If a browser supports user authentication, you can authenticate browsers with a user name and a password.

♦ It enables you to create HTML catalogs of your directories. Catalogs describe what is in the directories.

◆ You can write your own service scripts that generate documents on the fly.

◆ You can move document files to different directories and different servers without having to rewrite the HTML, and without having to advise users of the move.

◆ You can write scripts to handle form requests. Forms are documents that have one or more fill-in text fields that are often used for entering search criteria.

The NCSA Web service has a couple of features not found in the CERN service. Both services, however, are excellent.

Setting Up the NCSA WWW Service

To get the NCSA WWW service, you can either use a WWW client and point your URL at `http://boohoo.ncsa.uiuc.edu`, or use FTP to connect to `ftp.ncsa.uiuc.edu`.

After logging in as an anonymous user, change to the httpd_1.4 directory.

Note This book discusses the 1.4 version of the service. If a later version of the service exists when you connect to NCSA, you can choose to install it instead. If you do, make sure you check the README file and the installation documentation.

When you list the contents of the service directory, you find that there are two forms of the binary that you can download:

◆ Compiled

◆ Uncompiled

If your machine is on the following list, you're lucky: you can download a compiled version of the service. If not, you must download hpptd_1.4_source.tar.z and compile it after uncompressing and dearchiving it. NCSA offers the following compiled versions of their WWW service:

◆ httpd_1.4_aix3.2.5.Z

◆ httpd_1.4_aix3.2.5.tar.Z

◆ httpd_1.4_hpux9.0.5.Z

◆ httpd_1.4_hpux9.0.5.tar.Z

- httpd_1.4_irix5.2.Z

- httpd_1.4_irix5.2.tar.Z

- httpd_1.4_linux.Z

- httpd_1.4_linux.tar.Z

- httpd_1.4_osf3.0.Z

- httpd_1.4_osf3.0.tar.Z

- httpd_1.4_solaris2.4.Z

- httpd_1.4_solaris2.4.tar.Z

- httpd_1.4_sunos4.1.3.Z

- httpd_1.4_sunos4.1.3.tar.Z

All binaries come compressed, so you must uncompress and untar them—but first make sure you move yours to the directory in which you want it to reside, for example, /usr/bin/X11. Then use the following command:

```
% zcat httpd_1.4_operatingSystem.tar.Z ¦ tar xvf -
```

in which *operatingSystem* is one of the operating systems listed above, depending on your operating system, or source, if your operating system is not listed in the http_1.4 directory.

Executing the preceding command creates an httpd_1.4 directory, which contains a README file and the following subdirectories.

Subdirectory	Contains
cgi-bin	(Common gateway interface) Sample gateway binaries and scripts; where you put custom gateway binaries of your own
Makefile	Rules and dependencies that build the service
conf	Not surprisingly, service configuration files
icons	Icons for directory indexing
src	All of the .c executables
support	Applications that the password users need to access the service

Installation notes are included in a separate, compressed file, Install.txt.z. You must download it separately.

```
ftp> get Install.txt.z
```

To uncompress it, use zcat.

```
% zcat Install.txt.z ¦ more
```

The cgi-bin directory contains the following directories and files:

```
warp 188% cd cgi-bin
warp 189% ls
archie       date        fortune      nph-test-cgi
test-cgi.tcl uptime
calendar     finger      mail         test-cgi
test-env     wais.pl
```

These programs enable your service to connect to other Internet services.

The conf directory contains the following directories and files:

```
warp 243% cd support
warp 244% ls
Makefile              change-passwd.readme      inc2shtml.c
auth                  htpasswd.c                unescape.c
```

You use these programs to establish the passwords that users need to access the system.

Most likely, you will never have to work at all with the other directories, cgi-src, src, and icons.

Compiling the Generic WWW Service Binary

If you downloaded a precompiled binary, skip this section. If you downloaded the generic binary, httpd_1.4_source.tar.Z, this section is for you. You first have to configure the service and then compile it.

After you uncompress and untar the generic binary, you see that it contains all the subdirectories mentioned previously. You need to edit the Makefile, so make a copy of the original version.

To successfully compile the service, you must build and configure three things: the httpd service, the support programs, and the gateway application. The Makefile for these binaries is in src/. You need to edit it.

Editing src/Makefile

You need to edit the src/Makefile to customize the build for your platform. If your platform is listed in the httpd_1.4 directory, many of these variables are set for you in the Makefile. If your platform is not listed in the httpd_1.4 directory, you must set (or uncomment) each of the following variables:

◆ The CC variable is set to the name of your compiler. If you have an ANSI compiler, this variable is set to cc. If you use a non-ANSI compiler, such as those on Suns, set the variable to gcc. Make sure your gcc is 2.0 or later.

◆ Uncomment the AUX_CFLAGS variable associated with your platform. Entries for platforms look similar to the following

```
# For SGI IRIX. Use the EXTRA_LIBS line if you're using
# NIS and want user-supported directories
# AUX_CFLAGS= -DIRIX
# EXTRA_LIBS= -lsun
```

If you were working on an SGI workstation, you would uncomment the last two lines by removing the pound (#) sign. The EXTRA_LIBS variable specifies additional libraries your system needs.

If src/Makefile does not have an entry for your platform, you must edit the header file, httpd.h, to set the system flags. This is an important step.

◆ Add any flags to the LFLAGS variable that you need upon linking (for example, a flag that prevents dynamic linking).

◆ Add any library files you need to link to the EXTRA_LIBS variable. Usually, you do not need to add any libraries.

◆ Set the CFLAGS variable. This is done automatically if your platform is one of those listed in the httpd_1.4 directory. The following table describes the possible flags you can set for CFLAGS.

Flag	Description
DMAXIMUM_DNS	Creates a more secure host name resolution, but degrades service performance
DMINIMAL_DNS	Prevents reverse host name resolution
DNO_PASS	Precludes multiple child architecture
DPEM_AUTH	Enables PEM/PGP authentication
DSECURE_LOGS	Prevents cgi scripts from interfering with log files

Flag	Description
DXBITHACK	Makes service check the execute bit of an HTML file to see if it is a parsed file
g	Used when debugging the service
02	Used when optimizing the service

Most likely, you will not have to edit any other parts of src/Makefile.

After configuring src/Makefile, you can build the source files by changing to the src/ directory and issuing the following command:

```
% make
```

If you have problems, make sure you uncommented all of the lines in the Makefile that are relevant to your platform.

Editing support/Makefile and cgi-src/Makefile

The support/ and cgi-src/ directories also have Makefiles that configure the support and cgi programs. These Makefiles are shorter than src/Makefile, but they contain similar variables and should be set to the same values you used in src/Makefile. Normally, you only need to set the CC and CFLAGS variables.

After you edit the Makefiles, issue the make command again for each Makefile to build the gateway and support scripts.

Alternatively, if your platform is listed in the httpd_1.4 directory, you can run make on all three Makefiles at once by running make in the httpd_1.4 directory, as follows:

```
% Make sgi
```

If you look at the line in the httpd_1.4/Makefile associated with sgi, you can see how each of the three Makefiles are run.

```
sgi:
   cd src ; cd ../cgi-src ; make sgi ; cd
../support ; make sgi
```

Configuring the WWW Service

This section describes the minimal number of steps you must perform to configure your WWW service to your platform. The process involves editing three configuration files in the conf directory:

- httpd.conf-dist

- srm.conf-dist

- access.conf-dist

You should leave these configuration files as they are and make copies, perhaps saving without the -dist extension.

Note In all conf files, extra white space is ignored and only one directive can go on each line.

Whereas all of the basic configuration information is presented in the next several sections, advanced configuration administration is covered in the next chapter.

Setting Up httpd.conf-dist

The httpd.conf configuration file controls how the service, httpd, runs. Make a copy of httpd.conf-dist, call it httpd.conf, and use it to configure the service. Keep httpd.conf-dist as a reference copy.

Before you can edit the configuration file, you must decide whether you want the service to run under inetd or as a stand-alone daemon, and whether you want to restrict access to the service. In this section, you set the service to run as a stand-alone daemon that everyone can access. A later section discusses more involved configuration setups.

To set up httpd.conf, set the values of the directives in the following table.

Directive	Description
AccessConfig *fileName*	*fileName* is either an absolute pathname or a partial pathname relative to ServerRoot that specifies the location of the access.conf configuration file. The default is `AccessConfig conf/access.conf`.
AgentLog *file*	*file* is the file where you want to keep record of the client agent software. This directive is for statistical purposes and the tracing of protocol violations. You can only use this directive in stand-alone mode. The default is `AgentLog logs/agent_log`.

Directive	Description
ErrorLog fileName	*fileName* is either an absolute pathname or a partial pathname relative to ServerRoot that specifies the location of the error log file. httpd includes information such as segmentation violations, bus errors, bad scripts, timed-out clients, and .htaccess files that attempt to defeat access.conf directives. The default is `ErrorLog logs/error_log`.
Group [groupName | groupNumber]	Specifies the group ID that the copies of the service run as when answering client requests. This directive is only pertinent if the ServerType is set to stand-alone. The group ID can be either a name or user number. If you use a number, you must precede it with a pound sign (#). The default is `Group #-1`.
IdentityCheck [on | off]	Determines whether the remote user is logged in as themselves. This directive only works if the client application is running an RFC 931-compliant Identity daemon, such as identd. The default is `IdentityCheck off`.
MaxServers *number*	*number* is the maximum number of children for the hunt group.
PidFile *fileName*	*fileName* is a partial pathname relative to ServerRoot where you want httpd to record the process ID of each running copy of httpd. You can only use this directive in stand-alone mode. The default is `PidFile logs/ httpd.pid`.

continues

Directive	Description
Port *portNumber*	*portNumber* specifies the port number httpd listens to. Ports below 1024 are reserved by the system. Port numbers cannot be greater than 65536. Unless you do not want to make the service available to the Internet community, set the port number to 80. The default is `Port 80`.
ResourceConfig *fileName*	*fileName* is either an absolute pathname or a partial pathname relative to ServerRoot that specifies the location of the srm.conf configuration file. The default is `ResourceConfig conf/srm.conf`.
ServerAdmin emailAddress	emailAddress specifies the Internet System Administrator's address. It is a good idea to use an alias, for example, `ServerAdmin sysAdmin` so that you can change system administrators without changing the emailAddress. This directive does not have a default.
ServerName *hostName*	*hostName* specifies the the domain name of your server or a DNS alias, for example, `ServerName www.companyName.com`
ServerRoot *pathName*	*pathName* defines the absolute path of the root of your service above which users cannot trespass. The default is `ServerRoot /usr.local.etc.httpd`.
ServerType [inetd I standalone]	Specifies whether httpd is running under inetd or in stand-alone mode. The default is `ServerType standalone`.
StartServers *number*	*number* is the number of service processes you want to run concurrently.

Directive	Description
TimeOut *seconds*	*seconds* defines the maximum amount of time (in seconds) that the service waits for the client to submit a request once it has been connected, and the maximum amount of time the service should wait for the client to accept a request. The default is `TimeOut 1800.`
TransferLog *fileName*	*fileName* is either an absolute pathname or a partial pathname relative to ServerRoot that specifies the location of the log that records data, such as host, date, and file name, of service requests. These entries are described in greater detail following this table. The default is `TransferLog logs/access_log.`
TypesConfig *fileName*	*fileName* is either an absolute pathname or a partial pathname relative to ServerRoot that specifies the location of the MIME configuration file. The default is `TypesConfig conf/mime.types.`
User [userName I userNumber]	*userName* or *userNumber* defines the user ID the copies of the service run as when answering client requests. This directive is only pertinent if the ServerType is set to standalone. The user ID can either be a name or user number. If you use a number, you must precede it by a pound sign (#). By default, the copies run as user number one:

```
User #-1
```

Normally, you should run the service in standalone mode (ServerType standalone). If you run it under inetd, each time a service request comes in, inetd must fork off a new process, load the httpd binary, and load and parse all three configuration files. When running in standalone mode, httpd_1.4 just copies itself and the copy handles the new request. As you can see, system performance is improved using the standalone mode. The only exception to this rule is if the service is not often used. Then you have the CPU serving the httpd process even though there are not requests for it to do anything.

Entries in the access_log file, or the file specified by the TransferLog directive, have the following form:

```
host rfc931 authuser [DD/Mon/YYYY:hh:mm:ss] "request"
   ddd bbbb
```

The elements of the entry are explained in the following table.

Element	Description
host	Either the IP address or the DNS name of the client making the request
rfc931	Any information returned by identd for the client
authuser	The user name that was sent by the client for the purposes of authentication
DD/Mon/YYYY	The day, month, and year the request was received
hh:mm:ss	The hours, minutes, and seconds of when the request was made
request	First line of the request
ddd	Status code returned by the server
bbbb	The total number of bytes sent by the server

Setting Up srm.conf

The srm.conf-dist (server resource management) configuration file specifies the location in which the service finds your scripts and documents. Make a copy of srm.conf-dist, call it srm.conf, and use it to configure the service. Keep srm.conf-dist as a reference copy.

To set up the configuration file, set the values for the directives listed in the following table.

Directive	Description
AccessFileName *fileName*	*fileName* specifies the name of the file that you can include in any directory that specifies access permissions for that directory. The default is `AccessFileName .htacess`.

Directive	Description
AddDescription *text fileID*	Associates descriptive *text* with a type of file defined by extensions, a file name, an absolute path name, or a file name using wildcards (for example AddDescription "image file" *.gif).
AddEncoding *kind ext*	Specifies that files with *ext* are of type *kind* so that appropriate actions can be taken. For example, if the file is compressed, the browser can automatically uncompress it: `AddEncoding compress Z`.
AddIcon *path name1 name2 ...*	Specifies the icon to display with a kind of file; used when browsers display FTP menus.
AddIconbyEncoding *path name1 name2 ...*	Performs the same task as Icon except that the encoded information determines the icon used.
AddIconType *path type1 type2 ...*	Performs the same task as Icon except that the MIME type determines the icon used.
AddType *kind ext*	Supersedes MIME definitions for the specified extensions (*ext*) found in the mime.types file.
Alias *name path*	Substitutes *path* for *name* in path names. For example, if `Alias books /usr/resources` then books/apples is equivalent to /usr/resources/apples.
DefaultType *type*	Specifies the default MIME type. The default is `DefaultType text/ html`.
DefaultIcon *pathName*	*pathName* specifies the default icon to use when FancyIndexing is on. The default is `DefaultIcon /icons/ unknown.xbm`.

continues

Directive	Description
DirectoryIndex *fileName*	Specifies the *fileName* to return when the URL request is just your service, for example, `http://www.sgi.com`. The default is `DirectoryIndex index.html`.
DocumentRoot *path*	*path* specifies the absolute path to the directory from which httpd retrieves documents. The default is `DocumentRoot /usr/local/etc/httpd/htdocs`.
	If you have to serve documents outside this directory, you can provide symbolic links or an alias from this directory.
FancyIndexing [on | off]	Adds icons, filename data, headers, and footers to lists of files automatically indexed; necessary only for backward compatibility with HTTP V1.0. The default is `FancyIndexing on`.
HeaderName fileName	Specifies the filename to be used at the top of a list of files automatically indexed. The default is `HeaderName HEADER`.
IndexIgnore *kind1 kind2 ...*	Specifies kinds of files to be ignored during file processing. The default is `IndexIgnore */.??* *~ *# */HEADER* */README`.
IndexOptions *option1 option2 ...*	Specifies a variety of indexing parameters, including FancyIndexing, IconsAreLinks, ScanHTMLTitles, SuppressLastModified, SuppressSize, and SuppressDescription.
OldScriptAlias *name path*	Performs the same task as Alias, but provides for backward compatibility with HTTP V1.0.

Directive	Description
ReadmeName *fileName*	*fileName* specifies the footer information to attach to automatic directory indexes. The default is `ReadmeName README`.
Redirect *pathname URL*	Remaps *pathname* of document to new *URL*. There is no default for this directive.
ScriptAlias *name path*	Is similar to Alias, but used for scripts. This directive substitutes *path* for *name* in path names, for example, `Alias collection /usr/cgi-bin/` so that `collection/scripts` is equivalent to `/usr/cgi-bin/ scripts`. If you move `cgi-bin` from its default location, `/usr/local/ etc/httpd/cgi-bin`, you might provide an alias path to it with `ScriptAlias`.
UserDir [path | DISABLED]	Specifies the directory users can make available for httpd access. The default is `UserDir public_html`.

You set the UserDir directive to the partial path, relative to the user's home directory (as given in /etc/passwd), that leads httpd to personal files. The service adds this partial path to the requested path name to find the user's document, For example, if this directive were set to its default

```
UserDir public_html
```

httpd would translate a request for /~images/first.gif to ~images/public_html/ first.gif. You then define the path, public_html.

Because this directive can lead to security problems, you have the option of turning off this directive by using the keyword DISABLED:

```
UserDir DISABLED
```

Setting Up access.conf-dist

The access.conf-dist configuration file defines what service features are available to all WWW browsers. The default is to make everything available to all browsers. Make a copy of access.conf-dist, call it access.conf, and use it to configure the service. Keep access.conf-dist as a reference copy.

Note   The next chapter describes security measures you can take to protect your WWW service, so I put off an extensive discussion about security until then.

Many of the configuration directives in the access.conf-dist file are sectioning directives. They stand out because they use angle brackets.

Sectioning directives have a beginning and ending delimiter, for example:

```
<Directory>
...
(/Directory>
```

Any directives between the delimiters apply to the listing following the first delimiter. For example:

```
<Limit GET>
order allow, deny
allow from all
</Limit>
```

In this example, the sectioning directive, Limit, determines who can retrieve information from the service, which, in this case, is "allow from all."

To set up the access.conf file, perform the following tasks:

◆ Set the first Directory sectioning directive to the path of your cgi-bin directory. The default is

```
<Directory /usr/local/etc/httpd/cgi-bin>
```

◆ Remove the Indexes option from the Options directive (in the first Directory sectioning directive) so that users cannot browse through the httpd directory. The default is

```
Options Indexes FollowSymLinks
```

The possible values for the Options directive include the following:

  ◆ **All.** All features are enabled for the directory.

  ◆ **ExecCGI.** cgi scripts can be executed in this directory.

  ◆ **FollowSymLinks.** httpd follows symbolic links.

  ◆ **Includes.** Server side include files are enabled in this directory.

  ◆ **IncludesNoExec.** Enables server-side includes, but disables the exec option.

  ◆ **Indexes.** httpd allows users to retrieve service-generated indexes of this directory. Pre-compiled indexes in the directory are always available.

  ◆ **None.** No features are enabled for the directory.

  ◆ **SymLinksIfOwnerMatch.** httpd only follows symbolic links if the target file or directory is owned by the same user ID as the link.

◆ Set the second Directory sectioning directive to the path DocumentRoot defines in the srm.conf file. The default is

```
<Directory /usr/local/etc/httpd/htdocs>
```

In this case, allowing the Indexes option in the Option directive (within the second Directory sectioning directive) is fine, because you want users to browse your documents.

◆ Set the AllowOverride variable to None to prevent others from changing the settings in this file. This directive controls which access control directives can be overridden in a directory by the .htaccess file. The default is

```
AllowOverride All
```

Other values include the following:

  ◆ **All.** Access control files are unrestricted in this directory.

  ◆ **AuthConfig.** Enables the use of AuthName, AuthType, AuthUserFile, and AuthGroupFile directives.

  ◆ **FileInfo.** Enables the use of AddType and AddEncoding directives.

  ◆ **Limit.** Enables the use of the Limit sectioning directive.

  ◆ **None.** No access control files are allowed in this directory.

  ◆ **Options.** Enables the use of the Options directive.

The directives enabled by AuthConfig are defined as the following:

◆ **AuthName.** Sets the authorization name of the directory, for example,

```
AuthName CompProject
```

◆ **AuthType.** Sets the authorization type of this directory. Currently, there is only one type: Basic.

◆ **AuthUserFile.** Specifies the file to use that contains the list of users and passwords used in user authentication, for example,

```
AuthUserFile /usr/local/etc/httpd/conf/.htpasswd
```

◆ **AuthGroupFile.** Specifies the file that lists user groups for user authentication, for example,

```
AuthGroupFile /usr/local/etc/httpd/conf/.htgroup
```

◆ Set the Limit sectioning directive to the appropriate values. The directives that can come in Limit sectioning directive include the following:

◆ **allow hostName.** Enables specified hosts from accessing the service.

◆ **deny hostName.** Prevents specified hosts from accessing the service.

◆ **order ordering.** Determines the order in which the allow and deny directives are evaluated. Customary values are "deny,allow" and "allow,deny."

◆ **require entity1 entity2 ...** Entity values can be user, group, or valid-user. These are the authenticated users or groups that can access the system. Valid-user are users identified by AuthUserFile.

The only method that can currently follow the first Limit directive is GET, which allows clients to retrieve documents and execute scripts.

The default for the Limit sectioning directive is

```
<Limit GET>
order allow, deny
allow from all
</Limit>
```

In the default condition, the order directive defines the order in which allow and deny are evaluated, and everyone is allowed to retrieve documents.

Installing httpd

After you make basic changes to the configuration files, you can move httpd to the correct location in your file system. Use the mkdir command to create a directory—call it httpd—in a location specified by ServerRoot. Then copy httpd and all the subdirectories—conf, logs, icons, and cgi-bin to the new directory, httpd, using the following command line:

```
% cp -r httpd logs conf icons cgi-bin <pathName>/httpd
```

Use chown to make the logs directory writable by the user ID under which the service runs.

Starting Your WWW Service

Your service is ready to start! You now need to decide whether you want httpd to run under inetd or as a standalone daemon. If your service gets little use (I hope not!) or you are testing your service, you can minimize the impact of httpd on your system by starting your WWW service under inetd. However, if your service is accessed regularly, you should run httpd as a standalone daemon, because every time inetd starts up and shuts down the service (which it does for each service request) causes a delay.

The following three command-line options, however, are common to both run-time environments:

Option	Description
-d directoryName	Specifies the absolute path to the httpd binary if it's not in the default location; this path matches the path specified by ServerRoot in httpd.conf.
-f fileName	Specifies a configuration file to read instead of httpd.conf.
-v	Displays the version number of the service.

Running httpd Under inetd

inetd starts and stops services according to the requests the server receives: each service request starts an instance of the service, which terminates after sending a reply to the request. Each request specifies a port number; port numbers correspond to services running on the server. The standard port number for a WWW service is 80. You can change the Port variable in httpd.conf if you want the service to run on a different port. You would do that only to run a different version of the service for internal personnel, otherwise, all WWW services should run on port 80.

To make httpd run under inetd, complete the following tasks:

◆ Add a line to /etc/services similar to the following:

```
http portNumber/tcp
```

http is the name of the service and *portNumber* is normally 80.

◆ Add a line to /etc/inetd.conf similar to the following:

```
http stream tcp nowait nobody /pathName/httpd httpd
```

where *pathName* is the pathname to the httpd binary. You can add any necessary command-line options after httpd.

◆ Use the following command to restart inetd to make it read the configuration file, inetd.conf:

```
% kill -HUP <pid>
```

pid is the process ID of the service. The WWW service then starts whenever a request comes to port 80.

To stop the service, comment out the line you just added to inetd.conf.

Running httpd as a Daemon

The downside of running httpd as a standalone daemon is that it is always running. Of course, if your service is well liked, your service is going to run all the time anyway. The service runs faster in standalone mode because it does not need to repeatedly start, stop, and read the configuration files.

To start the service daemon using the defaults, type the following:

```
# httpd &
```

The ampersand (&) makes the service run in the background. You start the service as root so that the service can bind to port 80. After reading the configuration files, it changes the user ID and group ID to that specified in the httpd.conf configuration file.

Remember, if you have moved httpd from its default location, start the executable with options.

You probably do not want to do this every time you restart the server. To automatically start the service during server startup, edit the /etc/rc0 file, for example:

```
if [ -x /usr/bin/X11/httpd ]
```

then

```
/usr/bin/X11/httpd
fi
```

When you need to restart the service, find the pid of httpd. If httpd has more than one, which it probably does, be sure to kill the parent by finding the process that has the lowest ID and a parent process ID of 1.

You rest assured that the service is working well if the httpd server error log (logs/error_log, by default) says the following:

```
httpd: successful restart.
```

To restart httpd, execute the following on the command line:

```
# kill -1 'cat pidfile'
```

in which `pidfile` is the setting of PidFile for your service.

Alternatively, you can use the ps command to grep for httpd's process ID and send it a HUP signal.

To stop the service, execute the following on the command line:

```
# kill 'cat pidfile'
```

Testing httpd

Even if you have not yet populated your resources/ directory with data files, you at least can use a WWW browser to access the service adding the following to the URL field:

```
http://serverName
```

If you receive the contents of ServerRoot/index.html or a directory index, hooray!—your service works. If you don't, look at the access and error logs for some clues about what is wrong.

Another way to determine whether the service is running is telneting into it, as the following example demonstrates:

```
warp 106% telnet www.corp.sgi.com 80
Trying 192.26.51.29...
Connected to palladium.corp.sgi.com.
Escape character is '^]'.
HEAD / HTTP/1.0
HTTP/1.0 200 OK
Server: Netsite-Communications/1.0
Date: Saturday, 11-Mar-95 02:25:58 GMT
Content-type: text/html
Connection closed by foreign host.
warp 107%
```

The preceding display shows the name of the server and the version of the service software.

Managing a WWW Service

After you get your WWW service up and running, your job as System Administrator is far from done. You still have to do your common, everyday tasks, in addition to major tasks, such as revising the document tree.

Part of your managerial task involves maintaining your service's security. If you want your service to be open to everyone, the basic security measures presented in Chapter 7 might be enough for your company. If, however, your security requirements are more stringent, this chapter provides a little more octane for your service's security system.

Constructing URLs

Now you have a running service. Great! Let's make sure that people can find something to browse.

The search path for data files is called a URL (Uniform Resource Locator). To find your service, you only need the following URL:

```
http://serverName[:portNumber]
```

in which serverName is the name of your server and portNumber is specified only if you have your service running on a port other than 80.

If that's all the browser provides, httpd returns the contents of ServerRoot/ index.html, if it is defined. If it's not, it returns a directory index that looks like what you get when you do a ls -1.

When browsers want specific documents, they use an expanded URL of the following form:

```
http://serverName/[Alias \
       (or ScriptAlias)/][pathName/]fileName
```

Both Alias and ScriptAlias are pathnames defined in srm.conf. For example, to define WWW to represent /usr/resources/WWW, you would make the following entry in srm.conf:

```
Alias /www/ /usr/resources/WWW/
```

httpd substitutes the pathname defined in srm.conf for Alias or ScriptAlias. For example,

```
http://www.documentName
```

is resolved as

```
http://usr/resources/WWW/documentName
```

If httpd does not find an Alias (or ScriptAlias) in the URL, it checks to see if there is a prefix of the form

```
/~userName
```

If httpd finds this prefix, it substitutes for the prefix the user's public HTML subdirectory, public_html. httpd does not look for this prefix if, in srm.conf, you set UserDir to DISABLED.

If neither an Alias (or ScriptAlias) or user prefix is in the URL, httpd inserts the path defined by DocumentRoot in srm.conf.

Creating a Home Page

Your company does not need a home page, but it is nice to have one. Many users may never see your home page because they may go straight to one of the many data files in your source tree. If for no other reason, however, it is nice to have a point of entry for users who have decided that it would be interesting to learn more about your company. You might also provide a hyperlink in each Web page to the home page so that users can start over easily.

The standard name of the home page is home.html. You put it at the top of your source tree, for example: http://www.corp.sgi.com/home.html. It is also a good idea to copy home.html into index.html or to set DirectoryIndex in srm.conf to home.html. These provisions send out your company's home page with even the most minimal URL address.

You use the home page, first, to make people go, "Wow!," and second, to give people an index to what is going on at your company. You should take a look at a wide variety of home pages posted on the Internet beforc designing your own. Designing an Intranet home page is exactly the same as desiging an Internet home page. Your mission is still the same—to interest the user in the information you are presenting. For that reason, find several home pages you like and use the stylistic elements in them that you like most.

If your company has multiple divisions, each might like to maintain their own home page. You might like to have a company home page that points users to the home pages of each company division.

There are no conventions for home pages; however, users have come to expect several elements, as follows:

◆ "What's Hot" hyperlink, with the date it was last revised, publicizing your company's latest and greatest

◆ Hyperlink to the system administrator, often called the WebMaster, for user feedback

◆ Hyperlinks to major topics on the service, for easy navigation and an overview of your idea of what your company does best

◆ The date the home page was last updated

Writing Your Home Page

The file format for WWW pages is HTML. It is beyond the scope of this book to teach you HTML. After you see a Web page, you get a clear idea what HTML lets you do: hypertext links, interactive buttons (which are links), and clickable, inline pictures.

There are a number of free HTML editors available for X Windows, for example, htmltext, which you can learn about from URL:

```
http://web.cs.city.ac.uk/homes/njw/htmltext/htmltext.html
```

You also can embed HTML tags into documents using your favorite text editor. Learning the tags is easy, but there is some ramp up time involved.

Tip   Take a look at the HTML mode available for Emacs, URL:

```
ftp://ftp.ncsa.uiuc.edu/Web/html/elisp/html-mode.el
```

This extension to Emacs enables you to use keyboard commands to enter HTML tags easily.

Commercial HTML editors are emerging, such as HoTMetaL, URL:

```
ftp://ftp.ncsa.uiuc.edu/Web/html/hotmetal
```

or send email to

```
hotmetal@sq.com.
```

You also can use a variety of filters to convert files to HTML. Avalanche Development, makers of HoTMetaL, for example, has tools that convert WordPerfect and Microsoft Word documents to HTML.

The following gives you some other filters for documents you might like to convert:

FrameMaker to HTML	`http://info.cern.ch/hypertext/WWW/Frame/fminit2.0/www_and_frame.html`
	`http://ww1.cern.ch/WebMaker/WEBMAKER.html`
	`ftp://bang.nta.no/pub/`
	`ftp://ftp.alumni.caltech.edu/pub/mcbeath/web/miftran/`
	`http://www.seas.upenn.edu/~mengwong/txt2html.html`

BibTeX to HTML	`ftp://gaia.cs.umass.edu/pub/hgschulz/` `windex-1.2.tar.Z`
	`http://www.reasearch.att.com/` `biblio.html`
Interleaf to HTML	`http://info.cern.ch/hypertext/WWW/` `Tools/il2html.html`
	`http://info.cern.ch/hypertext/WWW/` `Tools/interleaf.html`
PostScript to HTML	`http://stasi.bradley.edu/ftp/pub/` `ps2html/ps2html-v2.html`
Troff to HTML	`http://cui_www.unige.ch/ftp/PUBLIC/` `oscar/scripts/ms2html`

For other conversion tools, look at URL

`http://info.cern.ch/hypertext/WWW/Tools/Fileters.html`

Managing Log Files

The WWW service has two log files: the *error log*, which contains error messages, and the *transfer log*, which contains information about who's using the service. You use the ErrorLog and TransferLog directives, respectively, to set the locations for these logs in the httpd.conf configuration file. The default locations of the files are /logs/ error_log and logs/access/log, respectively, relative to the directory in which the httpd binary resides. The ServerRoot directive in the http.conf configuration file specifies the binary's residence.

The transfer log contains entries that adhere to the following format:

`hostName  userCheck  authUser  dateTime  request  code  numBytes`

For example, the following:

`palladium.corp.sgi.com  -  -  [12/Mar/1995:09:12:18  -0900]  "GET/What's-`
`Hot.html  HTTP/1.0"  200  68742`

The following describes each field in the entry:

◆ **hostName.** The name of the host machine

◆ **userCheck.** If the IdentityCheck directive in httpd.conf is off, a dash appears in this field; if the IdentityCheck directive is on, httpd tries to connect to a RFC 931-compliant daemon on the machine running the WWW browser to get the user's name. If the browser machine has such a daemon, the user's name appears in the field; if the daemon is not running (usually the case), a dash (-) appears in the field

◆ **dateTime.** The time the request was made in the browser's local time including the number of hours difference from GMT, nine hours in this example

◆ **request.** The service request sent by the WWW browser

◆ **code.** Transaction's HTTP/1.0 status code (200 in this example)

◆ **numBytes.** The number of bytes sent to the WWW browser

Using Log Analysis Tools

Staring at log files might not give you the information you need. For example, the raw data in the log files might hide trends in the data that only programs that process the log data can elucidate. For example, it might not be clear, just from looking at the raw data, how the number of service users has varied over time.

Several log analysis tools are available for garnering more information from your log files, including getstats, wusage, and wwwstat.

Using getstats

getstats enables you to analyze your log files by various groupings; for example, you can analyze the data on a monthly basis, an hourly basis, by request, by domain, or by directory.

Kevin Hughes, kevinh@eit.com, wrote getstats (see fig. 8.1). It's available from the following URL:

```
http://www.eit.com/software/getstats/getstats.html
```

Using wusage

wusage creates statistics, graphs, and pie charts on a weekly basis and shows such things as the number of users that access the service and the location of users.

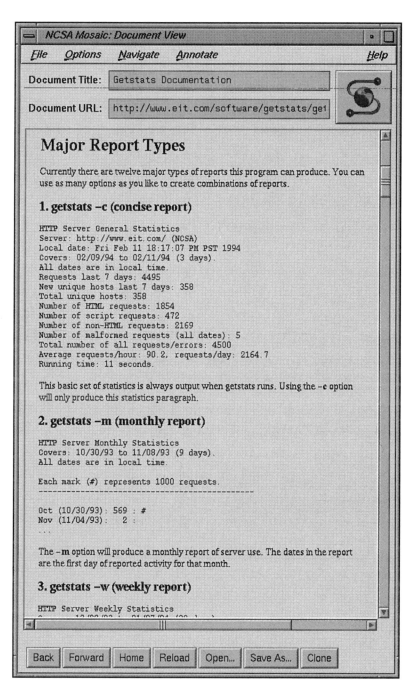

Figure 8.1

getstats.

Thomas Boutell, boutell@netcom.com, wrote wusage (see fig. 8.2). It's available from the following URL:

```
http://siva.cshl.org/wusage.html
```

Figure 8.2

wusage.

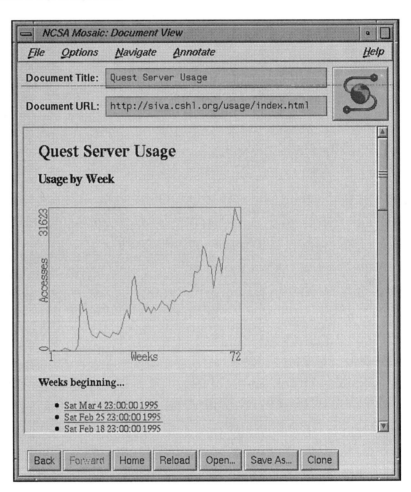

Using wwwstat

wwwstat, and its companion tool, gwstat, can provide graphical analysis of such things as the number of users accessing the service on an hourly basis.

Roy Fielding, fielding@ics.uci.edu, wrote wwwstat and gwstat (see fig. 8.3). They're available from the following URL:

```
http://www.ics.uci.edu/Admin/wwwstats.html
```

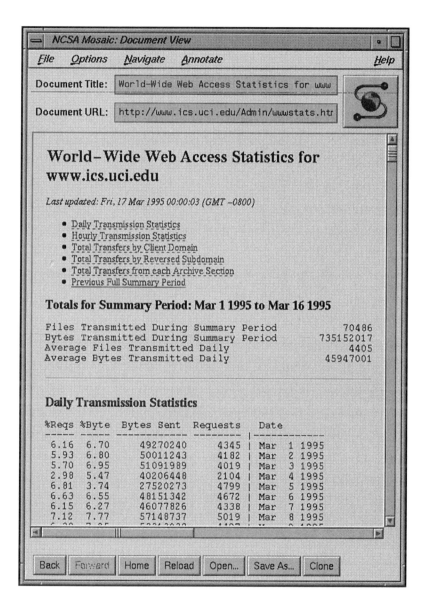

Figure 8.3

wwwstats.

Archiving Log Files

Log files grow forever. So, inevitably, you must archive, move, or delete them. Generally, you should write a cron job that does this task automatically. You can vary the parameters of the cron job according to the specifics of your service. For example, you might archive the log files to a separate directory at midnight every night, and delete the current files in the archive, or perhaps completing the same task on a weekly basis would be more appropriate. The problem you must solve is how to move the log files without disturbing the service. (You don't want to disturb the service every 24 hours.)

Running Under inetd

If httpd is running under inetd, you can just use the mv command to move the access_log files without affecting the overall service, owing to the fact that the next service request automatically starts a new access_log file.

Running httpd as a Standalone

When httpd runs in standalone mode, it keeps the log files open continuously (until it terminates). To move the log files to a new location, complete the following steps:

1. Use mv to move the log file to the archive file; httpd keeps writing to it anyway.

2. Restart httpd by issuing the following command, where *pid* stands for the process ID of the httpd service:

    ```
    kill -HUP pid
    ```

    When the service restarts, it opens a new log file as specified by the TransferLog directive in the http.conf configuration file.

Adding New Drives

Perhaps you're in the enviable position of having new Web documents from your company flooding onto the system to the extent that your disk space is filling up all too quickly. Now your problem is how to mount an additional drive without changing the pathname to the moved files.

Let's say your new drive is mounted as /anatomy/upper and your current file system looks like the following:

```
% ls /usr/resources/WWW/plastic_surgery
noses/
chins/
tummies/
```

You decide, since the noses directory has grown beyond expectations, to move it to the new drive. Follow these steps:

1. Use mkdir to create a noses/ directory on /anatomy/upper.

2. Use mv to move the files and directories under noses/ to the new drive under /anatomy/upper/noses.

3. Create an alias for the moved directory by using the Alias directive to construct an entry in srm.conf similar to the following:

```
Alias  /noses/  /anatomy/upper/noses/
```

When a user makes a request from the noses/ directory, httpd automatically substitutes a document from the /anatomy/upper/noses/ directory. Although the user is entering the same path for the desired document, the user is actually retrieving the information from the mounted drive.

4. Restart the httpd service using the following:

```
% kill -HUP pid
```

5. Use rmdir to remove the noses/ directory on the old drive.

Using the preceding procedure makes the new drive transparent to your service users.

Advanced Web Management

Although httpd can routinely handle about 30 different kinds if file types, others exist that it cannot handle. One set of types it cannot handle, for example, is called the MIME types. This section shows you how to handle MIME types.

One area in which WWW browsers are weak is in searching for documents. One way to help a browser is to put an index.html file (which you write) that describes the layout of the document tree, at the top of the tree. If you don't use such a file, httpd can automatically index the directories so the browser can see what is available.

The following section explores how to handle MIME types, and how to have httpd automatically index and present your document offerings.

Handling More File Types

As more and more file types get thrown into the pot of Web documents, it is very possible that your WWW service does not recognize some existing file types. For example, if you have a Word document that you want your WWW service to distribute, you must define the new type.

Version 1.0 of HTTP adds MIME (Multipurpose Internet Mail Extension) information to the header file of all documents sent between the service and the browser to define the file type being sent.

The syntax of the information sent by the service is as follows:

◆ First, the header information describing the file is sent.

◆ Second, a blank line is sent to delimit the file description information from the actual document.

◆ Third, the requested document is sent.

To send a .TIFF file, for example, the service first passes the MIME type "image" and the subtype "tiff" in the header information, as shown here:

```
image/tiff
```

Having this file description information up front lets the browser decide how to display the document the service sends. Many file types require the browser to spawn an external display. If the MIME types are text/html or text/plain, the browser displays the data file. If the service sends other MIME types, the browser spawns external viewers. For example, if the MIME type sent is image/tiff, an X browser would spawn an xv window.

 Note   When a WWW browser receives something other than an HTML or plain text file, it caches the document, and then looks in the .mailcap file for the correct type of viewer to spawn for the given document (MIME) type.

Every time a WWW browser makes a request, the browser passes to the service all of the MIME types it can use. The service makes sure it sends only one of those MIME types to the browser.

The configuration file, mime.types, defines the standard MIME types that browsers and services can use. This file contains a very complete set of standards. If, however, you find that you want to define a new MIME type, you can use three directives in srm.conf (server resource map) to do so (see the following minitable).

◆ **AddEncoding.** Adds MIME types that can be passed

◆ **AddType.** Defines a new file extension as representative of an existing MIME type

◆ **DefaultType.** Defines default MIME type

The AddEncoding directive has the following format, in which *fileType* is the type of file being passed, and *extension* is the extension to the filename that identifies the *fileType*:

```
AddEncoding  fileType  extension
```

If, for example, documents on your service use a new compressed-file format, you would add the following line to mime.types, so that any file with the .X extension would be identified as a "compress" file:

```
AddEncoding  compress  X
```

None of this works, of course, if the browser does not know what to do with an .X file, which is why it lets the service know beforehand what MIME types it can handle.

The AddType directive lets you add a new file extension to an existing MIME type. If, for example, you want to define type .tif to be the same as type .tiff (because a PC cannot use more than three characters in the extension), you would put the following line in srm.conf:

```
AddType  image/tiff  tif
```

The DefaultType directive defines the type of MIME type to send to the browser if the document has an extension that the service does not recognize. The default DefaultType is text/html.

Using these directives enables you to offer the latest file types to the your Intranet community.

Enabling Automatic Directory Indexing

When a user uses a URL that is a directory name rather than a filename, the WWW service automatically tries to return the index.html file for that directory. You are responsible for creating the index.html file. If you do not include one, you can use the Indexes option for the Option directive in access.conf to return an automatically generated directory index, or an error. To allow users to see an index of the file system, you would include the following line in access.conf:

```
Options Indexes
```

If, for some reason, perhaps pertaining to security, you do not want users to see the contents of a directory, use the NONE value for the Option directive:

```
Options NONE
```

Otherwise, leave the indexing option enabled.

The two styles of indexing are *fancy* and *drab*. (Actually, drab is not a value; FancyIndexing is turned on or off.) You control them using two directives in srm.conf: FancyIndexing and IndexOptions. FancyIndexing is a toggle switch used for backward compatibility for HTTP 1.0. The default is ON.

The IndexOptions directive has a FancyIndexing option, which, when included, turns on fancy indexing. The line in the access.conf file looks like the following:

```
IndexOptions FancyIndexing
```

Fancy indexing adds an icon before a filename and a file description after the filename.

You can use the following directives in srm.conf to customize the icons and descriptions associated with each filename:

◆ **Add Description.** Associates a brief file description with a file extension

◆ **AddIcon.** Defines the type of icon to display according to filename

◆ **AddIconType.** Defines the type of icon to display according to file type

◆ **DefaultIcon.** Default icon to display when FancyIndexing is on and an icon has not been associated with a file type

◆ **IndexOptions.** Controls fancy indexing display

The syntax of AddDescription is simple, as follows, where *description* is a brief description of the file type (note the quote marks), and *fileExtension* is the file extension to which the description pertains:

```
AddDescription  "description"  *.fileExtension
```

For example:

```
AddDescription  "TIFF image"  *.tiff
```

The description (must be in quotes) appears to the right of the filename in the directory listing for any files that have the .tiff extension.

Both AddIcon and AddIconType have the same syntax, where *pathName* is the pathname to the icon to be displayed, *fileName* is the name of a file, or kinds of listings (like the preceding *.tiff example), and *MIME_type* is a MIME type/subtype listing:

```
AddIcon  pathName  fileName
```

```
AddIconType pathName MIME_type
```

Rather than specify icons for specific directories, you can use wild cards with AddIcon to specify icons to use with different kinds of listings, including ^^DIRECTORY^^ for a directory, and ^^BLANKICON^^ for any blank lines.

You should make sure that you define an icon for every file type in your system. Mistakes do happen, of course, so it's a good idea to define a DefaultIcon, using the following syntax, where *pathName* is the pathname of an icon:

```
DefaultIcon pathName
```

For example:

```
DefaultIcon /usr/WWW/icons/whoKnows.rgb
```

The IndexOptions directive determines whether fancy indexing is turned on or off and what information is contained in the fancy indexing. The directive uses the following syntax:

```
IndexOptions option1  option2  option3
```

The possible *options* are as follows:

- ◆ **FancyIndexing.** Turns on fancy indexing

- ◆ **IconsAreLinks.** Makes the icons hyperlinks to their associated filenames

- ◆ **ScanHTMLTitles.** Displays, in the *description* field, the information between the <TITLE> HTML tags for HTML files without defined descriptions

- ◆ **SuppresslastModified.** Prevents the display of the last date the files were modified in the directory index

- ◆ **SuppressSize.** Prevents display of the file size in the directory index

- ◆ **SuppressDescription.** Prevents display of the description field for all files

Fancy indexing also lets you add header and footer information to an index. Header and footer information can be plain text or HTML. You specify the header information in the HEADER file. You can use the Headername directive in srm.conf to change the name of the file you want to be the header.

You define the footer information in the README file. You can use the ReadmeName directive in srm.conf to change the name of the file you want to be the footer file. For example, the following defines that the contents of the bottom file be used as footer information:

```
ReadmeName /usr/resources/bottom
```

You use the IndexIgnore directive in srm.conf to enable or disable displaying the header and footer. The default is not to display the header and footer in an automatic directory listing, as shown here:

```
IndexIgnore  */HEADER* */README*
```

You can eliminate that restriction for the entire service or for specific directories.

The following listing shows the defaults for directory listings:

```
AddIconType (TXT,/icons/text.xbm) text/*
AddIconType (IMG, /icons/image.xbm) image/*
AddIconType (SND,/icons/sound.xbm) audio/*
AddIcon /icons/movie.xbm .mpg .qt
AddIcon /icons/binary.xbm .bin
AddIcon /icons/back.xbm ..
AddIcon /icons/menu.xbm ^^DIRECTORY^^
AddIcon /icons/blank.xbm ^^BLANKICON^^
DefaultIcon /Icons/unknown.xbm
ReadmeName README
Geadername HEADER
IndexIgnore */.??* *~ *# */HEADER* */README*
```

The ".." indicates a partial filename.

Extending WWW Resources

You have seen that WWW browsers can access Gopher and FTP services, in addition to accessing WWW services. Other services, however, are not supported. Many WWW browsers, for example, cannot access WAIS services.

Not all information types are supported by WWW services either. Information can be derived from a table lookup in a database created dynamically at run time, for example. Most services expect information to remain dormant in source files.

The way to get around these restrictions is to use gateways. *Gateways* are programs or scripts written in a variety of programming languages—such as PERL, C, C++, C Shell, or the Bourne shell—that run external programs under the direction of a WWW service. The external program might pass user input to a WAIS service and return, to the WWW service, either HTML documentation, or a URL pointing to HTML documentation. The WWW service then passes that information onto the WWW client.

You can write your own gateways, use gateways written by others that are available either on the Internet or in your favorite software store, or use the gateways that come with your httpd service in the cgi-bin directory. Let's look at some of the included gateways.

Using Gateways in cgi-bin

What gateway software is in cgi-bin depends on the WWW service software that you installed. This discussion covers the software distributed in the NCSA version of httpd.

cgi-bin includes the following gateways:

◆ **archie.** Provides a gateway to Archie services using HTML <ISINDEX> tags

◆ **calendar.** Provides access to Unix's cal executable using HTML <ISINDEX> tags

◆ **date.** Displays today's date

◆ **finger.** Provides a gateway to Finger services using HTML <ISINDEX> tags

◆ **fortune.** Provides a connection to a fortune teller

Also included are some sample CGI test scripts, including the following:

◆ nph-test-cgi

◆ test-cgi

◆ test-cgi.tcl

The directory also includes miscellaneous HTML form examples, including jj, a submarine sandwich ordering form, and query, a generic form.

Service and CGI Script Interaction

There are two parts to the puzzle of service and CGI interaction:

◆ Getting input to the gateway script

◆ Getting information out of the gateway

Getting Input to the Gateway Script

Because you access a gateway script through a service, you might wonder how your gateway script can get any input. You cannot send your script information through switches on the command line. Instead, a gateway receives in formation in one of three ways:

- ◆ Environment variables

- ◆ Command line

- ◆ Standard input

Using Environment Variables

When a WWW service needs to pass a request made by a WWW client to a gateway, the service sets the following environment parameters as it executes the gateway program.

The following variables are set for all requests:

- ◆ **GATEWAY_INTERFACE.** The version number of the CGI specification supported by the WWW service

- ◆ **SERVER_NAME.** The name, IP address, or DNS alias of the WWW server

- ◆ **SERVER_SOFTWARE.** The name and version number of service

The following variables are set according to request:

- ◆ **AUTH_TYPE.** Used to authenticate the user ID, if the client host supports authentication

- ◆ **CONTENT_LENGTH.** The length of request as specified by WWW client

- ◆ **CONTENT_TYPE.** The type of data

- ◆ **PATH_INFO.** The input for the gateway script located at the end of the gateway's virtual pathname

- ◆ **PATH_TRANSLATED.** Provides the absolute pathname for PATH_INFO

- ◆ **QUERY_STRING.** The query information following the question mark (?) in the URL that specifies the gateway script

- ◆ **REMOTE_ADDR.** IP address of the client's host

◆ **REMOTE_HOST.** The name of the client's host

◆ **REMOTE_USER.** If the client host supports authentication, and the gateway script is protected, this is the user ID running the WWW client

◆ **REQUEST METHOD.** The method of the request, for example, GET, POST, and HEAD

◆ **SCRIPT_NAME.** The virtual path to gateway script

◆ **SERVER_PORT.** The port number of the client request

◆ **SERVER_PROTOCOL.** The name and version number of information protocol of the request

In addition to these variables, if the WWW client includes header lines in its request, the header names, with the prefix HTTP_ added, are set in the environment. The service, however, can ignore these variables if they have already been set, of if they conflict with other variables. Two such header names are ACCEPT and USER-AGENT. They become the following:

◆ **HTTP_ACCEPT.** Defines the MIME types the WWW client can handle

◆ **HTTP_USER_AGENT.** The name of the client's WWW browser

The two environment variables that mostly provide data for the gateway script are PATH_INFO and QUERY_STRING.

You can access a gateway script using its virtual pathnames. The PATH_INFO variable is set to any information beyond the virtual pathname of the gateway script.

The QUERY_STRING is any information beyond a question mark in your URL. The WWW client, for example, requests the following URL:

```
http://www.corp.company.com/pathName?ask+about+something
```

Notice that you use the plus sign (+) to fill in blank spaces between words in the query. When the WWW service starts the gateway script, it sets QUERY_STRING to "ask+about+something."

Passing data after question marks to gateway scripts is called the GET method of accessing a script. All gateway scripts using this method must read the QUERY_STRING variable and parse the request. Generally, you use the GET method when the gateway script requires only one argument. The meaning of the script depends on the gateway script.

You can check to see in what way your gateway script is being accessed by examining the REQUEST_METHOD environment variable.

Using Standard Input

If your gateway script requires more input, you can enter it using the standard input. This method of input is called the POST method. The POST method is generally used with HTML forms. An *HTML form* is a page with several fill-in-the-blank fields. Each field could be input data to pass to the gateway script. The length of the queries is contained in the CONTENT_LENGTH variable.

Using the Command Line

A third way to pass user input to the gateway script is by using an <ISINDEX> tag in an HTML document. When a browser finds such a tag, it displays the following message:

```
This is a searchable index. Enter search keywords:
```

The input is then sent to the gateway script using the GET method.

Using CGI Test Scripts

The cgi-bin directory contains a three test scripts you can use to see how the environment variables are set according to the information sent to the gateway script. The following URL:

```
http://hoohoo.ncsa.uiuc.edu/cgi-bin/test-cgi?  \
    ask+something+interesting
```

generates a test script report similar to the following:

```
CGI/1.0 test script report:

argc is 0. argv is .

SERVER_SOFTWARE = NCSA/1.4B
SERVER_NAME = hoohoo.ncsa.uiut.edu
GATEWAY_INTERFACE = CGI/1.1
SERVER_PROTOCOL = HTTP/1.0
SERVER_PORT = 80
REQUEST_METHOD = GET
```

```
HTTP_ACCEPT = text/plain, application/x-html,    \
     application/html, text/x-html, text/html
PATH_INFO =
PATH_TRANSLATED =
SCRIPT_NAME = /cgi-bin/test-cgi
QUERY_STRING = ask+something+interesting
REMOTE_HOST = companyGate.company.com
REMOTE_ADDR = 203.14.975.3
REMOTE_USER =
AUTH_TYPE =
CONTENT_TYPE =
CONTENT_LENGTH =
```

Getting Information from the Gateway Script

The only trick in getting documents returned properly to WWW browsers is adding a header to the returned document that defines the type of document that is returning. Documents can be almost any type, including audio clips, text, or images.

The first line of the header specifies the MIME type; for example, text/html or text/plain. The second line of the header is blank. The blank line tells the browser that the following lines are from the document that was retrieved.

Instead of returning documents, a gateway script can also return a pointer to another document on the same or different service. To return a pointer to another document, use the Location: directive. To point the WWW browser at a document in a different part of the service, for example, you return the virtual pathname to the file:

```
Location: /pathName/fileName.html
```

If the document your reply points to is on a different service, perhaps your Gopher service, you would use an absolute pathname, for example:

```
Location: gopher://furnace.engr.sgi.com/0
```

In each case, the WWW browser makes another request automatically to the file specified by the Location: directive.

Guidelines for Writing Gateway Scripts

This section contains only the broadest guidelines. For specific examples, look at the gateway scripts provided in the cgi-bin directory, or at the gateways available on the Internet listed in the following section.

It is a good idea to create a gateway script that can work both with and without information added to a URL. If the information is not added to the URL, your script must:

1. Get the input using the <ISINDEX> tag.

2. Send the request to stdout.

If the URL does have the query information following a question mark, your script must:

1. Retrieve the query from the QUERY_STRING environment variable.

2. Parse the query to rid it of the plus signs (+).

3. Carry out the query request.

4. Send the reply to stdout.

Gateway Security

Having your WWW service use gateways can open a Pandora's box of trouble. Receiving input from a WWW browser can waylay even the most innocent scripts. This section offers a simple checklist of areas of concern.

Consider the eval Statement

If the language that you write a gateway script in has an eval statement, such as PERL and the Bourne shell, be very careful how it can be misused. The eval statement allows the interpreter to execute a command, constructed using eval, outside of the gateway. Inputting metacharacters into eval statements can sometimes cause the execution of arbitrary commands on your service's server. PERL actually has a CGI library to detect the dangerous use of metacharacters at the following URL:

```
ftp://ftp.ncsa.uiuc.edu/Web/httpd/Unix/ncsa_httpd/cgi/cgi-lib.pl.Z
```

In short, do not trust the WWW client to behave responsibly.

Eliminate Server-Side Includes

Server-side includes should not be used at all on services. If they are on your service, however, at least disable them for the gateway script directories.

Avoid popen() and system()

Place backslashes in front of all characters if they have special meaning in the Bourne shell and if you can use WWW client data to create a command line that calls popen() or system().

Free Gateways on the Internet

There are a number of gateway scripts available on the Internet that are of terrific value for your WWW service. The following sections describe those offerings.

Genera

Stanley Letovsky (letovsky@cs.jhu.edu) wrote the Genera gateway to integrate the use of Sybase databases with WWW services. The script can use an existing Sybase database or create a new one, and use a WWW front end. For example, it can use HTML forms for querying the database.

You can retrieve the gateway at the following URL:

```
http://cgsc.biology.yale.edu/genera.html
```

Hytelnet

Earl Fogel (earl.fogel@usask.ca) wrote the Hytelnet gateway to provide WWW access to telnet sites accessible on the Internet.

You can retrieve the gateway at the following URL:

```
http://info.cern.ch/hypertext/WWW/HytelnetGate/Overview.html
```

man2html

Earl Hood (ehood@convex.com) wrote the man2html gateway to convert nroff manpages to HTML. The conversion is done on the fly. The advantage of this gateway is that you can be assured of receiving the latest version of the manpages. The disadvantage of converting documents on the fly is that they use CPU time.

You can retrieve the gateway at the following URL:

```
ftp://ftp.uci.edu/pub/dtd2html
```

Oracle

This gateway provides a WWW view of an Oracle database. The gateway turns the URL into a SQL SELECT directive and replies with an Oracle table.

You can retrieve the gateway at the following URL:

```
http://info.cern.ch/hypertext/WWW/RDBGate/    \
    Implementation.html
```

Making a WAIS Service Available to WWW Browsers

WAIS services are particularly powerful search engines. Searching for documents is one of a WWW browser's weakest aspects. One way around the problem is using a gateway to a WAIS service. This section describes how you can provide that.

You have the following options if you want to create a gateway to a WAIS service:

◆ Do nothing, because Mosaic can already access WAIS services

◆ Use a WAIS-to-WWW gateway available for free on the Internet

◆ Create your own WAIS-to-WWW gateway

◆ Buy a WAIS-to-WWW gateway

The Do Nothing Option

By "do nothing," I mean that all you provide the user through your WWW service is a hyperlink to a WAIS service. At the outset, this seems like an attractive solution. It costs nothing and it takes no time, and yet people with Mosaic can access a WAIS service.

Other WWW browsers may follow suit and also offer automatic access to WAIS services, but right now, that is not the case. All other WWW browsers receive that nasty message that says the WAIS service refuses to send its documents to you. This message makes your hyperlink look broken, which it is not, and it casts doubt on how well your WWW service is maintained. And if the WAIS service is valuable for one set of browsers, it must be valuable to all sets. Consequently, a "do nothing" solution is more of a step backward than forward.

Using WAIS-to-WWW Gateway Freeware

There are several sources on the Internet of free WAIS-to-WWW gateways. Use the following URLs to retrieve them:

```
http://www.ncsa.uiuc.edu:8001/WAISServerName:portNumber/databaseName?
```

```
http://info.cern.ch:8001/WAISServerName:portNumber/databaseName?
```

Actually, these services hide their true natures. They are really WWW services with WAIS gateways of their own. Your WWW service starts the gateway script that accesses one of these WWW services, that, in turn, use their WAIS gateway to carry out the WWW browser's request. When the WWW service receives the WAIS reply, it changes it into HTML, and hands it over to your WWW service, which, in turn, hands it over to the WWW browser. This seems like a roundabout way of conducting business; but it is free and it works—most of the time.

Creating Your Own Gateway

As you learned previously, gateways are programs or scripts that run external programs under the direction of a WWW service. The external program might pass user input to a WAIS service and return, to the WWW service, either HTML documentation or a URL pointing to HTML documentation. The WWW service then passes that information onto the WWW client. The Common Gateway Interface (CGI) provides a standard protocol for gateways that any WWW browser can use.

Gateway programs can be written in a variety of programming languages, including PERL, C, C++, and the Bourne and C Shell. The basic parts of the program include the following:

◆ User input

◆ CGI implementation

◆ A search engine

◆ HTML reply

To look at some gateway example code, look at the source files located at the URLs for the freeware WAIS-to-WWW gateways mentioned in the previous section, and look in the cgi-bin directory for wais.pl.

Buying Gateway Software

As the Intranet\Internet matures, more and more software for it will be for sale. Freeware may continue to be a major attraction, but it will become hard for programmers to resist selling people tools that they need.

WAISgate, a gateway software that you can buy, works with WWW browsers that support forms. WAISgate uses forms to create user queries.

You can get more information about WAISgate from the following URL:

```
http://www.wais.com/directory-of-servers.html
```

Choosing a Gateway

The most troublesome option is to create your own gateway software. Not only do you have to develop it, you have to maintain it. On the other hand, it probably offers you the best results. You can customize the interaction between the WWW and WAIS services.

WAISgate offers good results without having to develop the software. Its real downside, however, is that it does not support WWW browsers that cannot handle forms.

The freeware on the Internet is a good place to start while you are either buying or writing gateway software. The freeware, however, is not bulletproof.

Managing WWW Security

I know I don't have to make a case for being careful about what you let users touch. This section describes WWW-specific security measures you can take to restrict access to your service by virtue of the domain name of the browser's host, or the identification of the user.

Restricting Access by Domain Name

You can deny or allow a host to access your service across the entire service or on a per-directory basis. You specify global restrictions in the access.conf file; you place per-directory restriction specifications in each directory in a file called, by default, .htaccess. You can alter the AccessFileName directive in the srm.conf configuration file if you want to change the name from .htaccess.

The directives you use to accomplish this are defined in access.conf and are shown as follows.

- ◆ **allow.** Permits the specified host access to the service

- ◆ **AllowOverride.** Defines whether per-directory access overrides global access restrictions

- ◆ **deny.** Restricts specified hosts from access to the service

- ◆ **<Directory>.** Marker that has beginning and ending points within which all access directives apply to specified hosts

- ◆ **<Limit>.** Marker that has beginning and ending points within which the hosts are defined that can access a directory

- ◆ **order.** Describes the order in which the allow and deny directives are evaluated within a <Limit> section

The allow directive has the following syntax:

```
allow from host1  host2 ...
```

The *hosts* can define a host in one of the following ways:

all	Nobody gets in; all hosts are denied access
domain name	Only hosts from a domain name, for example, sgi.com, are granted service access
host name	Full name of the host, for example, warp.engr.sgi.com
IP address	Full IP address of the host, for example, 151.23.345.13
partial IP address	Up to the first three bytes of the IP address in case you want to make subnet access restrictions

The AllowOverride directive has the following syntax:

```
AllowOverride option1  option2 ...
```

The possible values for *option* include the following:

All	Everyone can override any global restrictions in this directory
AuthConfig	Enables use of AuthName, AuthType, TuthUserFile, and AuthGroupFile directives
FileInfo	Enables use of AddType and AddEncoding directives

Limit	Enables the use of the Limit directive
None	Prevents anyone from overriding any global restrictions in this directory
Options	Enables use of the Options directive

The default is AllowOverride All.

The deny directive uses the following syntax:

```
deny from hostName1 hostName2 ...
```

The possible values for *hostName* include the following:

domain name	Only hosts from a domain name, for example, sgi.com, are granted service access
host name	Full name of the host, for example, warp.engr.sgi.com
IP address	Full IP address of the host, for example, 151.23.345.13
partial IP address	Up to the first three bytes of the IP address in case you want to make subnet access restrictions
all	Nobody gets in; all hosts are denied access

The <Directory> directive specifies a directory, for example,

```
<Directory /usr/local/etc/hosts>
```

The directive also marks the beginning of a block of directives that all pertain to the specified directory. The </Directory> marks the end of the block of directives for the specified directory.

The <Limit> directive marks the beginning of a block of directives that define the users that have access to a directory, or at the global level, access to the service. The </Limit> directive marks the end of the block of directives that defines (limits) user access.

The <Limit> directive uses the following syntax:

```
<Limit option1 option2 ...>
```

The possible values for *option* include the following:

| GET | Enables browsers to run scripts and receive WWW documents |
| POST | Enables browsers to use POST scripts |

The only directives allowed between <Limit> directives are allow, deny, order, and require.

The order directive uses the following syntax:

order *ordering*

in which *ordering* has one of the following values:

| allow,deny | Considers allow directives before deny directives |
| deny,allow | Considers deny directives before allow directives |

Let's take a look at some examples.

Restricting Service Access to Internal Use

If you want to maintain a true Intranet—give employees, but not Internet users, access to your WWW service—you can put the following lines in the access.conf (at the highest level of your document tree):

```
<Directory  /usr/resources/WWW/rockets>
    AllowOverride None
    Options Indexes
    <Limit GET>
        order deny,allow
        deny from all
        allow from yourCompany.com
    </Limit>
</Directory>
```

In the preceding example, no one can override the global access restrictions (Override None). Within the <Limit> descriptors, the deny descriptor is read first (order deny,allow), which allows no one to use the service. The allow descriptor makes an exception for people in your company (*yourCompany.com*). If you want to allow access by people within a subdomain of your company, you would supply the subdomain, for example, engr.sgi.com, rather than the domain, sgi.com.

If you wanted to make the same restriction true for only one of the directories in your service, you would put the same <Limit> section in that directory's .htaccess file.

```
<Limit GET>
    order deny,allow
    deny from all
    allow from yourCompany.com
</Limit>
```

Look for directories in your service that require such protection.

Restricting Access to Several Companies

When your company works in concert with several others, you might want to create a common ground of documents available to each company but not to outside Internet users.

The implementation of this idea is parallel to the previous example, except that you need to name each company in the <Limit> directive:

```
<Directory /usr/resources/WWW/rockets>
    AllowOverride None
    Options Indexes
    <Limit GET>
        order deny,allow
        deny from all
        allow from yourCompany.com theirCompany.com
    </Limit>
</Directory>
```

You could limit only specified directories by putting the following lines in the .htaccess file:

```
<Limit GET>
    order deny,allow
    deny from all
    allow from yourCompany.com theirCompany.com
</Limit>
```

You cannot restrict access to specific files unless you put a file in a directory by itself, which makes for unwieldy file structures—but if necessary, however, is easy enough to implement.

Requiring Passwords

If you want to use password access to directories in your service, you need the program included in the support/ directory called htpasswd.c. This program is not included in the prebuilt versions of httpd. Consequently, if you want to use the program, you have to download the entire source code and build it according to the instructions in Chapter 17, in the section, "Compiling the Generic WWW Service Binary."

To add or edit a user's password, you use the htpasswd program with the following syntax:

```
% htpasswd [-c] .htpasswdUserName
```

UserName is the name of the user file that you want to edit or add. The -c option specifies that the file be created (not edited). If you create a new *UserName* file, and htpasswd does not find a duplicate name, it prompts you for the user's password. If htpasswd finds the name, it asks you to change the password. You simply type it twice (to make sure you make no mistake) and the user's password changes. These user names and passwords need not correspond to the system level user names and passwords.

The user name-password combination can provide individual access permissions to the entire service, or to specific directories. When users come upon WWW pages protected in this way, they are prompted for the correct user name and password. If correct, they can get the WWW page along with all protected pages in a similar manner; the user does not have to reenter the user name and password every time.

To give individuals permission to access the service and specified directories, you need to use, in addition to .htpasswd, the following four directives:

AuthGroupFile *path*	Specifies the absolute pathname to the file that lists user groups
AuthName *name*	Sets the authorization name for a directory; the name is descriptive and can contain whitespaces
AuthType *type*	Sets the type of permission a user has in the directory; currently, only Basic is implemented
AuthUserFile *path*	Specifies the absolute pathname, created using htpasswd, to the file that lists users and their passwords

All four directives work in concert; you cannot have one without the other three for the user authentication to work properly. They work at the service level and at the per-directory level.

Individual Permissions

Now, the idea is to put all these directives together so that only people who know a secret password can gain access to certain files.

In the access.conf file, add lines similar to the following:

```
<Directory /usr/resources/WWW/rockets>
    AllowOverride None
    Options Indexes
    AuthName secretPassword
    AuthType Basic
    AuthUserFile /usr/WWW/security/.htpasswd
    AuthGroupFile /usr/WWW/security/NULL
    <Limit GET>
        require user userName
    </Limit>
</Directory>
```

This all works, assuming you that you did use htpasswd to define passwords for users.

The NULL value in AuthGroupFile just means that the user does not have to belong to a System Administrator-defined group to gain access to the service.

If you want to accomplish the same task on a per-directory basis, put lines similar to the following in the .htaccess file in the directory:

```
AuthName secretPassword
AuthType Basic
AuthUserFile /usr/WWW/security/.htpasswd
AuthGroupFile /usr/WWW/security/.group1
<Limit GET>
    require user userName
</Limit>
```

Group Permissions

Rather than grant access to your service on a per person basis, you might just put people into groups and grant group access, which you might find easier.

The entries to access.conf are similar to the previous example, with one exception.

```
<Directory /usr/resources/WWW/rockets>
    AllowOverride None
    Options Indexes
    AuthName secretPassword
    AuthType Basic
    AuthUserFile /usr/WWW/security/.htpasswd
    AuthGroupFile /usr/WWW/security/.group1
    <Limit GET>
        require group groupName
```

```
    </Limit>
</Directory>
```

Now the requirement for access to the service is membership in .group1, as indicated by the require statement.

Now, you use your favorite text editor to create the file .group1. Place the file in the same directory as .htpasswd. The syntax of the entries are as follows, where *userName* is the user ID of each member of the group:

```
group1: userName1 userName2 userName3 ...
```

For every name you add to the group, you must use the htpasswd program to create a password for each one, for example:

```
% htpasswd /usr/people/.htpasswd userName1
```

Because you changed the access.conf configuration file, you have to reboot the system before the changes take effect. After you do so, only people who belong to the specified group can access your system.

Using Individual, Domain, and Group Permissions

Now that you've seen how to implement individual, domain, and group access, let's look at a combination of all three:

```
<Directory /usr/resources/WWW/rockets>
    AllowOverride None
    Options Indexes
    AuthName secretPassword
    AuthType Basic
    AuthUserFile /usr/WWW/security/.htpasswd
    AuthGroupFile /usr/WWW/security/groups
    <Limit GET>
        order deny,allow
        deny from all
        allow from company.com
        require group groupName
    </Limit>
</Directory>
```

The preceding example allows access to members of *company.com* that belong to *groupName*. If you wanted to allow access to only a subset of the people belonging to *groupName*, you would use the following within the <Limit> section:

```
require user userName
```

These restrictions, however, are more commonly used at the per directory level. You would put the same <Limit> section in that directory's .htaccess file.

Compromising Security

Restricting user access to only those who belong to a specific domain is trustworthy unless you cannot trust DNS (Domain Name Server).

Restricting user access using user IDs is only 90 percent safe. UserIDs and passwords are sent unencoded. Unscrupulous people who use sniffer programs sometimes can detect user names and passwords and use them to accomplish unscrupulous deeds.

A WWW browser can follow links from files in the resource tree to outside the tree, which poses a problem if, for example, one of the files in the directory is a symbolic link that takes the user to another directory. To prevent users from planting symbolic links that can take them all over, disable the followsymlink option in the Options directive (in access.conf).

Finally, use the None option with the AllowOverride directive whenever possible.

Misusing Personal HTML Directories

The Userdir directive in the srm.conf file permits users to make personal files available for public access. The default of the directive is as follows:

```
Userdir public_html
```

This means that under everyone's personal directory, they can access public_html. This all sounds fine, except for those people who plant their CGI (Common Gateway Interface) scripts and symbolic links to other parts of the file system. (Remember, HTTP does not protect against user access to the root directory with the chroot() function the way FTP and Gopher do.) To guard against possible misuse of these files, put the following entries in access.conf, where /home is the location of all users' home directories:

```
<Directory /home>
    AllowOverride None
    Options Indexes
</Directory>
```

If the users' home directories are more spread out, you need use wild cards creatively; for example, substitute the following (or whatever works in your file structure) for the first line above:

```
<Directory /*/public_html*>
```

Limiting the Options directive to only Indexes prevents the use of symbolic links and CGI scripts (because the ExecCGI option in the Options directive is not set).

If you have to compromise this position to give users the opportunity to create symbolic links, use the SymLinksIfOwnerMatch option in the Options directive. This directive allows the service to follow a symbolic link if the owner of the link matches the owner of the target file.

You might find CGI scripts in one of three places, as follows:

◆ cgi-bin

◆ cgi-bin subdirectories you use the ScriptAlias directive to create

◆ personal HTML subdirectories

All of these are potential problem spots. Make sure that in all of these places, the Options directive does not include the ExecCGI or FollowSymLinks options.

Server-Side Includes

Server-side includes are pieces of information automatically added to documents sent to browsers. Examples include the date, author, and other metacharacter variables.

I have not discussed server-side includes very much for two reasons:

◆ They degrade system performance

◆ They present a potential security breach

The problem is that you can write anything in a server-side includes. If someone were to write a bogus include, your server would infect all browsers that accessed it.

To prevent server-side includes, make sure not to use the All or Includes options in the Options directive. Or, if you find that you need to allow includes, use the IncludesNoExec option in the Options directive so that at least executable CGI scripts cannot be included in HTML documents.

CHAPTER

9

Setting Up an FTP Service

FTP is one of the most widely used services on the Internet, and is a tremendous benefit to Intranets, as well. Nearly every host has an FTP client or service—not too surprising when you consider that the FTP service, ftpd (or in.ftpd), comes with most standard flavors of Unix. You can usually find ftpd in the /usr/etc (or /etc) directory.

ftpd is great for services that do not require strict security and do not handle large archives. If either issue matters for you, however, you probably would benefit from implementing the WU version of ftpd. (WU stands for Washington University in St. Louis, MO.) The next chapter discusses this service. Read on, however, because many things in the standard implementation of ftpd are also true for the WU ftpd daemon.

You can offer two kinds of FTP service: *user-oriented* and *anonymous*. In the first case, users use their user IDs to log in to an FTP service; in the second case, they use the generic user ID, anonymous.

You really don't want to implement a user-oriented service because of the danger of security breaches. User IDs are broadcast over the network in plain text, which makes them vulnerable to mischievous hackers. If they can find a user's ID and password, they can use the system with the permissions of the user whose ID was detected.

You can restrict the permissions of specific users. There is, however, a significant administration task of establishing permissions for multiple user IDs. You might very well establish such permissions for people within your company, or even for people in a company working on a joint project with your company, but certainly not for people in the Internet community.

With anonymous FTP, you can restrict the kinds of actions users can take by defining the permissions of the anonymous user ID accordingly, and you can restrict users' access to your file system. Although you might give some of your employees user-oriented access to your FTP service, we will not even consider offering anything but an anonymous FTP service to the Internet community, should your Intranet extend that far.

Naming Your Service

There is a de facto standard for naming FTP services. By no means is it required, but it is the name users will try first and find easiest to remember. The format is

```
ftp.domain.type
```

in which *domain* and *type* are variables. Domain represents the alias domain name of your FTP server (often your company's name). Type represents the type of organization yours is; for example, edu is used for educational institutions, com is used for businesses. The following FTP service (of the company supporting the WAIS service) is a good example of an FTP name:

```
ftp.wais.com
```

Naming your FTP service www.domain.type, or abc.domain.type, or zzz.domain.type is not illegal, but it is not a good idea. You also do not want to use the real name of your host server in the name of your FTP service. If you change your FTP service from one server to another, you do not want to have to tell everyone accustomed to the old name to switch to the name of the new FTP server (which might change again in the future). You could easily lose your standard user base. Instead, you should use an alias for your server. To set up an alias for a server, edit the domain name services (DNS) database files by adding a line similar to the following:

```
ftp IN ftp.domain.type   real.domain.type.
```

Substitute your company's domain name for *domain*. Make sure that *real.domain.name* is the real domain name of the FTP server. Note the period that ends the line.

If you change your server, there is a lag time on the network determined by the time-to-live defined by your domain name service. The time-to-live variable is an expiration date for Internet servers. When it expires, other name servers must release data about your zone from their cache. If you plan to switch servers, reduce the time-to-live variable accordingly.

Configuring an FTP Service

inetd, the big brother of services, invokes ftpd. It watches port 21 for TCP packets. For every service request (TCP packet) that arrives at port 21, inetd creates a new copy of ftpd to service the request.

Note   For more information about inetd, refer to Chapter 5, "Using a Unix Backbone."

Many implementations of Unix already have an FTP service, ftpd, set up in inetd's configuration file, inetd.config. You often find inetd.config in the /etc directory. Some Unix implementations have a sample line in inetd.config (commented out) that sets up ftpd. If your configuration file has such a sample line, uncomment it. If you do not have any configuration information for ftpd in your inetd.config file, add a line in the file similar to the following:

```
ftp  stream tcp  nowait  root  /usr/etc/ftpd  ftpd -l
```

Chapter 5 includes a thorough explanation of the syntax of this line. (And soon we will look at the command-line options for ftpd.) Suffice it to say that this entry prescribes that TCP is responsible for reordering the FTP packets when they arrive at the client, that inetd should spawn a new service for each FTP request, that /usr/etc is the directory where ftpd lives, and that you want to start ftpd with the -l (logging) option. The entry in your inetd.config file might have a different location for ftpd, and might use different command-line options.

Depending on the computer platform, ftpd has several other options, as explained in the following table:

ftpd option	Description
-l	Turns on logging.
-d	Writes verbose debugging information in syslog.
-t *seconds*	Sets the timeout period in seconds. The default is 15 minutes; in other words, if the FTP session is inactive for 15 minutes, ftpd terminates it.

continues

ftpd option	Description
-T *seconds*	Sets the maximum timeout period in seconds that an FTP client can request. By default, the maximum timeout period an FTP client can request is 2 hours. If that is too long, use this option to shorten it.
-u *permission*	Sets the umask value, on some flavors of Unix, for files uploaded to a server using an FTP service. The default *permission* is 022: group- and world-readable. Clients can request a different mask.

The most common option is the logging option, -l. Having this option on is nice because it lets you monitor FTP connections and check for foul play. This option logs to syslog every failed and successful FTP session. If you specify the option twice, the get, put, append, delete, make directory, remove directory, and rename operations and their file-name arguments are also logged. If you specify this option three times, log entries for get and put include the number of bytes transferred.

The -d option logs all the commands and arguments sent by the client, except for arguments from the PASS command.

After you set the configuration file, the system must reread the file before it can take effect. The best way to do that is to use the kill command to pass a hang-up signal (SIGHUP):

```
% killall -HUP pid
```

in which `pid` is the process ID of inetd. But how do you get the pid? If you are using Unix System V, you use

```
% ps -ef ¦ grep inetd
```

The equivalent for the BSD distribution of Unix is

```
% ps ax ¦ grep inetd
```

The following example shows you the output of the ps command:

```
furnace 5% ps -ef ¦ grep inetd
      root   246     1  0  Apr 25 ?        0:45 /usr/etc/inetd
      geckel 6099  5796  2 10:19:19 pts/11   0:00 grep inetd
```

The second field in each line is the process ID.

Setting Up the Anonymous User

Now that you've configured the service, you must create a user that has the appropriate set of permissions and access to the file system. You set up the anonymous user in the server's /etc/passwd file. Before doing anything else, ftpd checks this file for whether a user exists. If you fail to create the anonymous user, ftpd prevents a user who logs in as anonymous from accessing any FTP archives.

You do not want to match any user or group IDs for the anonymous user to any system-level IDs. Hackers can use those IDs to access the entire file system through telnet or rlogin. You can prevent such a security breach by putting an asterisk (*) in the password field for all user IDs except anonymous. The asterisk prevents any entry from working in the password field. If there are utilities on your system that do not require a password to log in, you should set the login shell to /bin/false so that the asterisk safeguard is not overridden.

 Note Many man pages might suggest that ftpd ignores the login shell. Don't believe it; many versions of ftpd use it.

You might, for example, construct the anonymous user in the following way:

```
ftp:*:500:25:anonymous FTP  user:/usr/ftp:/bin/false
```

In this example, /usr/ftp is the user login directory, which is what you use as the root directory for anonymous FTP clients. If the login directory is the client's root, they do not have access to anything higher in the file system than /usr/ftp; they have access only to directories and files lower in the file system. These provisions give your system the level of security it needs by restricting the user's access to the file system.

The root of the anonymous user file system does not have to be under /usr. If you are offering a lot of data in your FTP service, you might allocate a separate disk, file system, or both for anonymous FTP use.

You restrict file access by using the change root command, chroot(). If ftpd calls this function and uses the anonymous user login directory as its argument, all absolute references begin at the login directory. For example, if a user were to change directory to root (cd /), they would only get to /usr/ftp. Or, for example, changing to /bin really moves the user to /usr/ftp/bin.

ftpd calls chroot() only if the FTP user is anonymous. Therefore, users who use user IDs to log in are not restricted to the file system specified by their login directory. So, not allowing user ID access to FTP archives confines FTP users to the restricted file system thereby protecting files outside that file system.

Reorganizing Your Files

One ramification of using chroot() to restrict users' access to your system is that you need to move all the files that ftpd needs into the restricted login directory. To do that, you need to set up a new directory structure that places several standard directories under the login directory. The following table shows the directories you need to copy.

Directory	Description
bin	Contains the program ls which supports the list commands.
dev	Use mknod to copy /dev/zero into ~ftp/dev with the same major and minor device numbers. Rld uses this file.
etc	Contains passwd and group. These files enable the ls command to display owner names instead of numbers. The password field in passwd is unused; it should not contain real passwords.
lib	Copy the files /lib/rld and /lib/libc.so.1 into lib. ls needs them in order to run.
pub	Contains the archive files available to FTP clients.

The important executable you want to copy to /usr/ftp/bin is ls.

 Stop   Do not copy the /etc/passwd or /etc/group files into /usr/ftp/etc, because it would allow anonymous FTP users to copy the files with encrypted passwords to their machines for their own devilish purposes. With this information, third parties might be able to crack the encryption. You should put a minimal amount of information into the passwd and group files. For example, if the FTP archive contains files created by ftp and bin, your password file should look similar to the following:

```
ftp:*:500:1:anonymous user:/users/ftp:/bin/false
bin:*:2:2:/:/bin/false
```

If FTP archives are given group access to *user* and *other*, your group file might look like the following:

```
user:*:1:
other:*:3:
```

Login Directory Permissions

So you don't want hackers to upload computer vermin into your service? Using the set of permissions listed in table 9.1 for the subdirectories under the login directory can help.

TABLE 9.1
Permissions for Subdirectories

Directory	Owner	Permission	Comments
/	root	555	Make the home directory unwritable
bin	root	555	Make this directory owned by the super-user and unwritable by anyone
dev	root	555	Make this directory owned by the super-user and unwritable
etc	root	555	Make this directory owned by the super-user and unwritable
lib	root	555	Make this directory owned by the super-user and unwritable
pub	root FTP administrator	555	Users can read and execute the archive files
upload	root other	777 733	Users can upload files, delete and replace existing files
dist	root FTP administrator	555	Users can read and execute the special archive files

All directories can be accessed by group *other*.

All users must to be able to read and execute (that is, search through) files in the login directory, or you don't have much of a service.

You make the /bin directory executable, because it contains only the ls binary, so users can use it, but unwritable so that nefarious users cannot replace your ls binary with one of their Trojan horses that suddenly brings your system to its knees.

The /etc directory contains valuable information about user permissions and group membership. The last thing you want is users resetting their system permissions and group memberships. Consequently, you need to make the directory unwritable.

The /pub directory contains your FTP archive files. These files must be readable and executable so users can search through and download interesting files. On the other hand, you do not want to give users write permission to the directory, because then users could replace or delete archive files that you strenuously maintain. Users cannot upload files in this directory.

Creating the /upload directory is optional. It gives users a place to upload files to the server running the FTP service. Separating these files into their own directory is a form of *damage control*. If someone wheels in a Trojan horse, hopefully its damage is confined to the /upload directory. If you see no reason to permit uploads, don't include the /upload directory.

The permission set for the /upload directory permits users to write and execute in the directory, but not read from it. This permission set is somewhat inconvenient because it prevents users from looking at files others upload to the server. On the other hand, it prevents users from perverting or deleting those same files.

Note   A byproduct of allowing users to read one another's uploaded files is that they can post files on your server completely unrelated to your service. These uploaded files can be bland or blasphemous. For the sake of your company's image, you don't want to inadvertently support the greatest porn or WaReZ (pirated software) archive in the country.

If you feel that protecting /upload files from in-house users of your system (not FTP users) who have access to this file is necessary, you can set the sticky bit on the permissions set by changing the permission to 1733.

The /dist directory also is optional; it's really nothing more than a regular FTP archive that you might find in /pub except that the files in /dist are documents or binaries that your company supports. They should not be programs that your company sells. They might be patches to programs, utility add-ons, driver updates, or tools that give added-value to your products. Because these binaries are not generic programs, you need not fear people copying, renaming, and publishing these programs under their name.

Again, you run into the same danger of someone uploading something into /dist somehow. You can combat such raiders by making the media that contains this directory read-only (by putting the files on a CD-ROM drive, for example). You might put as many of your files as you can on such media if the files and directories are not likely to change much.

Inside the /bin and /etc directories, you also must use chmod to set the permissions for the standard programs and files, as shown in table 9.2.

TABLE 9.2
Permissions for Programs and Files

File	Owner	Permissions	Comments
/bin/ls	root	111	Users can execute ls to search the FTP archive files
/etc/passwd	root	444	Users can only read file ownership
/etc/group	root	444	Users can only read about group membership

Naming the System Administrator

Everyone likes a helping hand. Part of the job of the system administrator is to provide that service to the user community. You should set up two mailboxes for yourself, one that handles your normal e-mail, and another that handles Intranet system administration requests. To make it easier for users to reach you, you should use a common alias rather than your e-mail address; for example, you might use ftp-system-admin.

You can point the ftp-system-admin alias at your user ID. This directs all FTP system administration concerns directly to your mailbox. Your aliases file is probably under /etc. To set up the alias, use the following syntax:

```
ftp-system-admin  real-user-ID@domain
```

Then again, you may choose not to make the ftp-system-admin user ID an alias for your ID because you might like to keep separate your Intranet FTP mail and your other mail.

If you set up an alias, it doesn't take effect until the system rereads the dbm-format database. You can make it take effect by executing newaliases.

Trying Out Your FTP Archive

Before you announce to the world that you have a great FTP service, you really should test it. If you can, let as many people as possible bang on the service to see if you can catch any bugs, inconsistencies, or anything that would frustrate real users to the point of not using the service. Also, you should try to break into restricted areas of the file system and compromise files that should not allow such nonsense. Write the hackers guide to your service—then fix it before anyone else does.

If you have problems, you can look at the entries in the syslog file—assuming you turn on logging (-l) for ftpd in the inetd.config file. If you did not start ftpd with logging enabled, change the inetd.config file by adding the -l option at the end of the FTP configuration line, then make inetd reread the configuration file by executing the following command, where *pid* is the process ID of the inetd service:

```
% killall -HUP pid
```

The /etc/syslog.conf file should specify the location of the log files, usually /var/log. Keep a window open with the syslog file in it. To watch the syslog file, use the tail command (tail -f) while you use an FTP client to interact with your FTP service. Change directories, list the files in the directories, and download several files to make sure all is working as planned.

Do a long listing of all the files and directories to make sure the permissions, owners, and groups are correct. Use the tables earlier in this chapter for guidance.

What Your Session Should Look Like

If everything is working okay, when you use your FTP client to ftp to your service, you should get a set of responses similar to the following (user input is in italics):

```
% ftp ftp.company.com

Connected to ftp.company.com
220 sizzle.asd.sgi.com FTP server (Version 4.2.321.2 Wed Feb 15 03:24:32 GMT
➥1995) ready.
Name (ftp.company.com:clinton): anonymous
331 Guest login ok. Use email address as password
Password: clinton@washington.com
230 Guest login ok, access restrictions apply.
ftp> cd /hot_topics
250 CWD successful
ftp> binary       — specify binary to download binary or non-ASCIIfiles
200 Type set to I.
ftp> get one_great_program.tar.Z
200 PORT command successful.
150 Opening BINARY mode data connection for one_great_program.tar.Z
226 Transfer complete.
ftp> quit
221 Goodbye.

%
```

To actually use the program, you would do the following:

```
% uncompress one_great_program.tar.Z
% tar xvf one_great_program.tar
```

The beginning of the syslog file should look similar to the following:

```
Feb 15 03:24:32 sizzle inetd[121]: ftp/tcp: Connection from sizzle (12.3.2.4)
➥at Wed Feb 15 03:24:32 1995

Feb 15 03:24:32 sizzle ftpd[121]: Connection from sizzle at Wed Feb 15 03:24:32
➥1995
```

What Might Go Wrong

If the path to the service in the inetd.config file is wrong, you might get a message in syslog similar to the following:

```
Feb 15 03:24:32 sizzle inetd[121]: ftp/tccp: Unknown service
```

If a directory should be executable but isn't, you get a message similar to the following:

```
ftp> ls
200 PORT command successful.
150 Opening ASCII mode data connection for /bin/ls.
. not found
226 Transfer complete.
ftp>
```

If ftpd is not on the host machine, you might get an error similar to the following:

```
ftp: connect: Connection refused
```

If you try to log in as anonymous, but have not set up the anonymous user correctly, you get a message similar to the following:

```
520 Guest login not permitted.
Login failed.
Remote system type is UNIX.
Using binary mode to transfer files.
ftp>
```

What files? It did not really transfer any files. You're not even logged in, which you can confirm by trying to ls.

When you try to download an archive file, it should be readable. If not, you get an error message similar to the following:

```
ftp> get download_file /tmp/mine
200 PORT command successful.
550 download_file: Permission denied.
ftp>
```

If you made a mistake with the permission set for a directory, and a directory that should be readable is not, you get a message similar to the following:

```
ftp> ls
200 PORT command successful.
150 Opening ASCII mode data connection for /bin/ls.
. unreadable
total 2
226 Transfer complete.
ftp>
```

If you cannot upload a file, make sure the /upload directory is writable.

If you cannot change to one of the directories under the login directory, check to see that they are executable.

This is hardly a complete list of what can go wrong. But it at least gives you a flavor of problems you might see and what you need to do about them. After banging away on your service for a good while, open it to the people in your company.

Setting Up a More Secure FTP Service

One of FTP's drawbacks is its lack of security features. It relies on firewall software to grant or deny access to users. What if there were a more secure version of FTP?

Actually, one does exist—the Washington University (WU) (in St. Louis) version of FTP. In addition to the FTP features previously described, the WU version includes the following:

◆ Control over user access based on group ID and class. A class is the combination of a user type and domain name (or IP address).

◆ Automatic compression (or decompression) and tar of files on the server just before they are downloaded.

◆ Sophisticated tracking of uploads and downloads in log files.

◆ Automated service shutdown.

The added security measures alone warrant consideration of the WU version of FTP. The other additions make this version even more attractive.

Getting the Source Code

You can get the source code for WU FTP from wuarchive.wustl.edu in the file /packages/wuarchive-ftpd/wu-ftpd-2.4.tar.Z, as follows.

```
ftp> ls
200 PORT command successful.
150 Opening ASCII mode data connection for /bin/ls.
total 201
-r--r--r-- 1 root archive 318 Apr 14 1994 CHECKSUMS
```

```
-r--r--r-- 1 root archive 7761 Apr 14 1994 patch_2.3-2.4.Z
-r--r--r-- 1 root archive 184907 Apr 14 1994 wu-ftpd-2.4.tar.Z
cd226 Transfer complete.
ftp> get wu-ftpd-2.4.tar.Z
local: wu-ftpd-2.4.tar.Z remote: wu-ftpd-2.4.tar.Z
200 PORT command successful.
150 Opening BINARY mode data connection for wu-ftpd-2.4.tar.Z (184907 bytes).
226 Transfer complete.
184907 bytes received in 56.97 seconds (3.17 Kbytes/s)
```

 Note   This chapter discusses version 2.4 of the software. If you find a later version, you might want to build that instead. If you do, check the NOTES file for differences between what is discussed in this chapter and the installation notes for the new version.

To uncompress and untar the source code, execute the following command:

```
% zcat wu-ftpd-2.4.tar.Z ¦ tar -xvf -
tar: blocksize = 16
x wu-ftpd-2.4/doc/examples/ftpaccess, 422 bytes, 1 block
x wu-ftpd-2.4/doc/examples/ftpconversions, 455 bytes, 1 block
x wu-ftpd-2.4/doc/examples/ftpgroups, 37 bytes, 1 block
x wu-ftpd-2.4/doc/examples/ftpusers, 83 bytes, 1 block
x wu-ftpd-2.4/doc/examples/ftphosts, 190 bytes, 1 block
```

After uncompressing and untaring, notice the new directory, wu-ftpd-2.4:

```
%ls
wu-ftpd-2.4
wu-ftpd-2.4.tar.Z
```

The new directory, wu-ftdp-2.4 contains the following directories and files:

```
warp 295% cd wu-ftpd-2.4
warp 296% ls
FIXES-2.4 Makefile    build      doc       support
INSTALL   README      config.h   src       util
```

Table 9.3 describes the contents of the directories.

TABLE 9.3
Description of Subdirectories in wu-ftdp-2.4

Subdirectory	Description
FIXES-2.4	Describes bug fixes and revisions from the previous software version
INSTALL	Describes how to install the service software
Makefile	Provides the Makefile instructions to run the make program
README	Describes the contents of the directories
build	Contains information necessary for the build
config.h	Contains the configuration variables
doc	Contains documentation on a variety of topics
src	Contains the source code for the service
support	Contains syslog and user authentication programs
util	Contains compression software and a log analysis package

Installing the Service

Building the service is a multistep process. This section explains each step in detail.

1. Edit src/pathnames.h to accurately reflect the pathnames in your system. The following table describes the pathnames in pathnames.h file.

Pathname	Description
_PATH_BSHELL	The absolute pathname of the file on the server that contains the executable for the Bourne shell; default is /bin/sh
_PATH_CVT	The absolute pathname of the file—ftpconversions—that contains the commands ftpd uses to compress, uncompress, and tar files; the default is /usr/local/etc/ftpconversions

continues

Pathname	Description
_PATH_DEVNULL	The absolute pathname of the file, on the server that contains device information; default is /dev/null
_PATH_EXECPATH	The pathname, relative to the chroot()'ed directory, of the directory of the executables users can use; default is /bin/ftp-exec
_PATH_FTPACCESS	The absolute pathname of the file—ftpaccess—that contains user-access information; default is /usr/local/etc/ftpaccess
_PATH_FTPUSERS	The absolute pathname of the file—ftpusers—that contains a list of users who may not access the service; default is /etc/ftpusers
_PATH_LASTLOG	The absolute pathname of the file on the server that contains the last logins of users and terminals; accessed by the list command on your server
_PATH_PIDNAMES	The absolute pathname of the PID files that store the PIDs of running ftpd's; the default is /usr/local/daemon/ftpd/ftp.pids-%s, where %s is replaced by the name of the class using the ftpd
_PATH_PRIVATE	The absolute pathname of the file that contains group membership and group password information; default is /etc/ftpgroups
_PATH_UTMP	The absolute pathname of the file—utmp—residing on your server, that contains user and accounting information for such commands as who, last, write, and login
_PATH_WTMP	The absolute pathname of the file—wtmp—residing on your server, that contains user information user and accounting information for such commands as who, last, write, and login
_PATH_XFERLOG	The absolute pathname of the file that logs file uploads and downloads; default is /usr/adm/xferlog

2. Edit the conf.h file.

Most likely, you do not have to modify the file at all. All the options in it are enabled by default. To disable any of the options, comment them out.

The following table offers a brief description of each variable.

Variable	Description
UPLOAD	Allows users to upload files to the server
OVERWRITE	Allows users to overwrite files as they upload them
HOST_ACCESS	Enables system administrator to allow or deny users access to the service based on their host name
LOG_FAILED	Logs failed attempts to log in to the service
NO_PRIVATE	Allows the use of private files
DNS_TRYAGAIN	Specifies that the service should try one more time if a DNS lookup fails

3. Build the service.

The build is different depending on the platform on which the service runs. The source code contains build scripts for the following platforms:

aix : IBM AIX

bsd : BSDI bsd/386

dgx : Data General Unix

dyn : Dynix

hpx : HP-UX

isc : ISC

lnx : Linux (tested on 0.99p8)

nx2 : NeXTstep 2.*x*

nx3 : NeXTstep 3.x

osf : OSF/1

sgi : SGI Irix 4.0.5a

sny : Sony NewsOS

sol : SunOS 5.x / Solaris 2.x

s41 : SunOS 4.1.x (requires acc or gcc 2.3.3 or better)

(if you must use gcc 1.4.2, mail me for a patch)

ult : Ultrix 4.x

If you are installing ftpd on a different platform, you have to create your own configuration file by copying and editing each of the following files:

```
% cp src/config/config.gen  src/config/config.Name
% cp src/makefiles/Makefile.gen  src/makefiles/Makefile.Name
% cp support/makefiles/Makefile.gen  support/makefiles/Makefile.Name
```

Name is the name of your computer platform.

Correcting the configuration information is specific to your platform, so it is not within the scope of this book. In general, the config.*Name* file contains information about system and library calls that the service needs to use. The Makefiles are general enough to support most platforms, but you should check the defines.

When you have set the Makefile and configuration files, build the service by executing the following command:

```
% build Name
```

Name is a three-letter abbreviation that describes your computer platform, such as aix or bsd.

 Note   Building ftpd requires an ANSI C compiler. You can FTP one from prep.ai.mit.edu in the file /pub/gnu.

If the compiler complains that strunames, typenames, modenames, or other variables are undefined, install support/ftp.h as /usr/include/arpa/ftp.h and do the build again. Replacing the old ftp.h is not a problem because the new ftp.h is a superset of the old file.

If the compiler complains that pid_t is undefined, add the following line to src/config.h:

```
typedef int pid_t;
```

4. Install the service by executing the following command:

   ```
   % build install
   ```

5. Edit the configuration file for inetd, inetd.conf, to start ftpd when receiving a FTP request.

6. Restart the system by sending the hang-up signal so that the new configuration specifications can take effect.

On BSD-ish systems, use the following command:

```
%kill -1 'ps -acx ¦ grep inetd ¦ cut -c-5'.
```

On SGI systems, use the following command:

```
% /etc/killall -HUP inetd
```

7. Install GNU tar and put a copy in the anonymous ftp hierarchy.

This software enables users to create .tar.Z files on the service host before receiving them over the Internet. You can download a copy of GNU tar from wuarchive.wustl.edu (IP address: 128.252.135.4) in the /gnu subdirectory.

8. Place a copy of compress in ~ftp/bin. This enables users to compress files before receiving them over the Internet.

9. From the doc/ directory, copy the ftpconversions, ftpusers, and ftpgroups files to the directories defined in pathnames.h.

10. Create at least one class in ftpaccess. For an example, look in doc/examples/ftpaccess.

11. Place any executables anonymous users can run in the directory specified by pathnames.h for _PATH_EXECPATH. The default is /bin/ftp-exec. Consider carefully what you put in this file.

12. Make sure the configuration files are set up correctly by running bin/ckconfig.

13. Hold your breath. Everything should now be working!

Installation Notes

Place into /etc/shells a list of all the valid shells in your system. If users do not have all the shells listed in this file, they cannot log in to the service.

Make sure the following files are in the chroot()'ed FTP subdirectory:

◆ All messages (deny, welcome, and so on)

◆ Shutdown

◆ The executables contained in the file defined by _PATH_EXECPATH

Read the INSTALL file for platform-specific build problems and corrections.

For additional help, you should subscribe to two mailing lists: wu-ftpd and wu-ftpd-announce. You can subscribe to both by sending e-mail to listserv@wunet.wustl.edu.

New Directories

Several new, important files have been added to the WU ftpd service; they include the following:

- ◆ ftpaccess

- ◆ ftphosts

- ◆ ftpconversions

These three files, not present in the standard ftpd service, reflect the added functionality of WU ftpd.

The ftpaccess file contains information that permits or denies user access to the service. Chapter 10, "Managing an FTP Service," discusses this file in greater detail.

The ftphost file contains information that permits or denies users from specified hosts access to the service. This file, too, is discussed in greater detail in the following chapter.

The ftpconversions file defines what programs should run as a filter, depending on the prefix/suffix of the file to be uploaded/downloaded. For example, a .Z indicates that uncompress is automatically run on a server file before sending it. The executables that perform these tasks reside in the directory specified by the _PATH EXEC PATH variable in the pathnames.h file:

ftpd uncompresses the file before downloading it. Conversely, if a file on the service is named *fileName*, you can make the following FTP request:

```
ftp> get fileName.Z
```

ftpd compresses the file before downloading it. You exercise these options depending on whether or not you have the uncompression software on your workstation. Always download the compressed version of the file if you have the uncompression software.

The ftpconversions file matches file extensions and executables. All files that have the extension .Z, for example, get compressed, if they are not compressed already.

The formal syntax of the entries in the ftpconversions files is as follows:

```
prefix:suffix:prefAdd:SuffAdd:command %s:  \
objType:option:errorText
```

Table 9.4 describes each of the fields.

TABLE 9.4
Formal Syntax of ftpconversions File Entries

Field	Description
prefix	The prefix to the retrieved filename that triggers the conversion
suffix	The suffix to the retrieved filename that triggers the conversion
prefAdd	The prefix added to the converted file
suffAdd	The suffix added to the converted file
command	The command to be executed (along with any options) according to the prefix or suffix added to (or subtracted from) the requested file name by the user; %s is replaced by the name of the requested file
objType	The kind of object specified by the file name, including T_ASCII for a text (ASCii) file, T_DIR for a directory, and T_REG for a non-text file
option	Works with the ftpaccess directory to define the kind of executed command, and to determine whether or not the user has permission to execute such a command; some users might not, for example, be able to untar files; or another example, a user who cannot uncompress a file (using Unix compress) might also be prevented from uncompressing a file with the extension .zip if the ftpaccess directory defines .zip and .Z as part of the same group
errorText	Used in error statements when the conversion fails; for example, errorText might be "untar" so that the error message "Cannot %s the file," reads appropriately

The section about ftpaccess in the next chapter discusses the option field in greater detail.

Let's look at a sample entry in the ftpconversions file:

```
: : :.Z:/pathName/compress -c %s:T_REG:O_COMPRESS:compress
```

In the preceding example, a regular file is compressed whenever the user adds the extension .Z to a filename.

The doc/examples directory in the software distribution provides the following example of ftpconversions:

```
warp 318% more ftpconversions
 :.Z: : :/bin/compress -d -c      %s:T_REG¦T_ASCII:O_UNCOMPRESS:UNCOMPRESS
 : : :.Z:/bin/compress -c %s:T_REG:O_COMPRESS:COMPRESS
 :.gz: : :/bin/gzip -cd     %s:T_REG¦T_ASCII:O_UNCOMPRESS:GUNZIP
 : : :.gz:/bin/gzip -9 -c %s:T_REG:O_COMPRESS:GZIP
 : : :.tar:/bin/tar -c -f - %s:T_REG¦T_DIR:O_TAR:TAR
 : : :.tar.Z:/bin/tar -c -Z -f -
%s:T_REG¦T_DIR:O_COMPRESS¦O_TAR:TAR+COMPRESS
 : : :.tar.gz:/bin/tar -c -z -f -     %s:T_REG¦T_DIR:O_COMPRESS¦O_TAR:TAR+GZIP
```

New Command-Line Options

The WU version of ftpd recognizes the following command-line options:

◆ **-A.** Disables the ftpaccess file.

◆ **-a.** Enables the ftpaccess file.

◆ **-d.** Enables debugging.

◆ **-i.** Enables logging (in xferlog) of all files uploaded.

◆ **-L.** Enables logging of any attempt to modify a user name.

◆ **-o.** Enables logging (in xferlog) of all files downloaded.

Using the ftpaccess file is enabled by default.

All the other command-line options available with the regular version of FTP, such as -l, -t, and -T, are also available with the WU version of FTP.

C H A P T E R

10

Managing an FTP Service

Now that you have created a wonderful FTP service, it is time to look at the tasks you need to accomplish to maintain and manage the service. This chapter discusses all the tasks related to managing the service. These tasks are described in terms of the job of the FTP system administrator.

The Intranet system operator is charged with the following tasks:

◆ Putting archive files into the system

◆ Creating and updating README files that describe the files in each directory

◆ Facilitating navigation between the files

◆ Linking one archive to another

◆ Updating files in the archive

◆ Removing old files

◆ Creating, renaming, and eliminating subdirectories

◆ Monitoring the files for security breaches and checking for computer viruses

◆ Answering user questions

◆ Reviewing files uploaded to the /upload directory for possible elimination or inclusion in /pub

◆ Interacting with company personnel to keep in touch with product and service revisions

◆ Understanding product and service revisions

◆ Keeping the FTP service up to date in terms of revisions to the service code and the availability of better service software

To perform these tasks, FTP system administrators do not need superuser access to the server host; they only need access to the directories they are going to change, such as the /pub and /dist directories.

If your company has many products, or your products and services are of such a difficult, technical nature that it is impossible for one person to keep up with all the revisions of all the products, some companies might choose to farm out some of the FTP system administrator jobs to appropriate company personnel. If one engineer in the company is responsible for one of the software products offered by the company, for example, you might put that person in charge of updating the FTP archive files relating to that engineer's product. In this case, you might consider changing the ownership of the directories to someone who is able to keep them current. You use the chown() command to change the ownership of the directories.

If you plan to distribute the job of the FTP system administrator among a variety of people in your company, it's best to set up a group, called something like ftpadmin, and add all the people administering the FTP service to that group. After you do that, you have to change the group ownership (to the ftpadmingroup) of all the files and directories on which these people need to work. Finally, you have to change the permission set on these files so that group members can write to the files.

Organizing Your Archive Files

In order to organize the archive files, the FTP system administrator needs to understand the contents of the files. At the highest level, it is easy to organize the files by subject matter; if your company has 30 products, you should create 30 subdirectories under /pub (or /dist). There might be lower levels of subdivision that make sense, but creating those subdivisions requires more specialized knowledge of the product. It is crucial, however, that subdivisions be accurate and descriptive of the product. If the FTP system administrator cannot break the subject matter into these smaller divisions, you might ask someone else to aid the FTP system administrator in making those divisions.

Nothing on the network has come down as written in stone. Administering your archives is no exception. However, it is worth paying attention to the *de facto* file extensions that give the user a clue as to the contents of the file. You should use the following typical file extensions when naming your archive files:

Extension	Description
bw	Image in black and white
c	C code
c++	C++ code
gif	Image in gif format
gz	Compressed file using gzip
idl	idl code
jpeg	Image in jpeg format
mpeg	Image in mpeg format
pit	Compressed file using PackIt
ps	PostScript
rgb	Image in rgb format
Sit	Compressed file using Stuffit
tif	Image in tif format
txt	Text
Z	Compressed file using Unix compress program
zip	Compressed file using PKZIP

Providing Navigational Aids

You can have some of the greatest archives in the world in your service, but if people cannot easily find them, they will remain buried treasures forever. FTP system administrators need to be vigilant in helping users effortlessly find appropriate FTP archive files. Because FTP is a text-based service, the tools you have to advertise files are limited. It is important, however, to use every tool at your disposal. These tools include the following:

- ◆ README files in each directory describing the files in the directory

- ◆ Aliases

- ◆ Search paths

- ◆ Symbolic links

- ◆ ls-lR files

- ◆ Archie

The following sections look at each of these tools.

Using README Files

In every directory, even at the login directory level, there should be a README file describing the files and subdirectories in the directory. Although this is a good principle, there are a few exceptions.

At the login directory level, the user's root, you should include (at least) the following information in a README file:

- ◆ The e-mail address (or alias—for example, FTP-administrator) of the FTP system administrator for users to use in case of problems

- ◆ General company information providing a list of available products and services and a corresponding list of directories where such archives reside

- ◆ Copyright information

- ◆ Aliases you use in administering the company's service

- ◆ Hot topics

- ◆ Disclaimer information renouncing your company's responsibility for any damage any archive files might cause to the user's machine

These topics get legal issues out of the way up front and provide navigation information.

 Note   The Washington University (WU) version of ftpd enables you to print this kind of information whenever a user accesses an FTP service. Messages longer than 24 lines scroll off the screen, so keep the messages short.

Just below the directory login level is the product or service level—one directory for each. In these README files, include (at least) the following information:

◆ Product or service description (assume that the user knows nothing about your product or service)

◆ Version number

◆ Information revision date

◆ Copyright information

◆ Disclaimer information

It's worth repeating the copyright and disclaimer information at this level so that there is no confusion about what is redistributable and what is not.

Using Aliases

Aliases give you the ability to call one file by more than one name. You generally use aliases to circumvent multiple layers of the file system—a necessary evil in hierarchical file systems. If a popular tool is buried under the directories /pub/productName/ debug/tools/toolName, for example, you can provide an alias so that users easily can use the cd command to move to the tools directory by adding the following entry to the ftpaccess file:

```
alias tool Name: /pub/productName/debug/tools
```

The only way you can use an alias is to use the cd command to move to the directory you want.

The only problem with using aliases is that you have to advertise them because they do not advertise themselves. You can do that by listing the aliases you use in your README files, and by asking the user to execute the following command:

```
quote site alias
```

The WU version of ftpd allows you to use aliases, not the vanilla version of ftpd.

The WU version of ftpd uses a file called ftpaccess to hold alias entries. The syntax of the entries follows:

```
alias  aliasName:  pathnameToRealFilesDirectory
```

For example,

```
alias FAQ:  /pub/productName/doc/troubleShooting
```

in which /troubleShooting is a directory that contains the FAQ file that the user wants to access. You can provide an absolute pathname (relative to the login directory) as shown, or use a relative pathname, depending on the location of the files.

For example,

```
alias FAQ: ../../doc/troubleShooting
```

Defining Paths

Another way of accomplishing what an alias does is to define search paths. Unfortunately, only services using the WU version of ftpd have this option.

Search paths are directories that are searched automatically when a user performs an operation on a file. If, for example, the user changes to a directory named distant,

```
ftp> cd distant
```

the current directory is searched first for the file (distant) and, if it is not found, the directories specified as paths are searched for the file.

To set up a search path, add a line to the ftpaccess file similar to the following:

```
cdpath   /pub/productName/tools
```

This line alleviates the need for the user to type the absolute pathname to get to a file in the /tools directory, that is, instead of typing

```
ftp> cd /pub/productName/tools
```

you can just type

```
ftp> cd tools
```

You easily might have more than one of these lines, one for each buried, but often requested, document.

The order in which the file system is searched for a file follows:

1. ftpd checks the current working directory for the requested subdirectory.

2. ftpaccess is checked to see whether an alias exists for the requested subdirectory.

3. The search paths listed in ftpaccess are used (in the order in which they are listed) to look for the requested subdirectory.

Using Symbolic Links

Symbolic links provide easy access to other parts of your file structure. A symbolic link file contains the name of another file to which it is linked. Symbolic links connect ideas as well as files. If one file describes a tool, for example, provide a symbolic link to the tool's file:

```
# ln -s /pub/productName/docs/tool  /pub/productName/tools/toolLibrary
```

This line links the file with the subdirectory—`toolLibrary`—where the tool resides. This approach maintains the logic of the file hierarchy that locates the documents under /docs and tools under /tools, while anticipating user interest by facilitating easy access between the different branches of the file hierarchy.

These absolute pathnames are relative to the login directory (the user's root), so /pub is, at the system level, really /usr/ftp/pub (or whatever the login directory is).

You also can use relative pathnames to set up links, as in the following example:

```
# ln -s tool  ../../tools/toolLibrary
```

Using relative or absolute pathnames is a matter of personal taste. Whenever the file system changes, you have to carefully review all links.

Stop   About the last thing you want to do is to provide a link from the user's work area into your general file system. Be careful when defining links not to defeat chroot().

Using ls-lR Files

A ls-lR file contains a list of all the files and directories within a branch of a tree. The file appears similar to the output of the ls command with the lR option, hence the customary name of the file. If you went to the top of the tree—perhaps to the /productName directory—and did a recursive listing in long format of the files below /productName, you would get the appropriate list of files for the ls-lR file.

You should create the ls-lR file in the following way:

```
# ls -lR > ls-lR
```

This line does a recursive listing in long format and redirects the output to a file called ls-lR.

Note   If your file system changes regularly, you might automate the creation of the ls-lR file by making its creation an automatic cron job. A *cron job* is an operation that executes at a specific time, perhaps the same time every night. The following example shows a line added to the roots crontab:

```
0 1 * * *  cd /usr/ftp ; su ftp -c  ls -lR > ls-lR
```

In this line, the ls-lR file is created only after changing to the /usr/ftp directory, changing the user to the ftp user (su -c), and then running ls. You really don't want to run ls as root, because there might be files in the directory accessible to root but not a user of the FTP service.

Examine the permission set of the ls-lR file. Make sure it is readable but not writable for FTP users.

If the file structure is large and creates a corresponding large ls-lR file, you can compress the ls-lR file using the standard compress utility, as in the following example:

```
0  1  *  *  *   cd /usr/ftp; su ftp -c  ls -lR  ¦  compress  > ls-lR.Z
```

Using Archie

Archie is a search tool that uses keywords or phrases to find related documents. You can make your FTP archive searchable to Archie by sending a message to archie-updates@bunyip.com saying that your FTP service is running and that the ls-lR file contains a recursive listing of files and directories in your FTP archive. In order to provide maximum exposure for your service, you must create the ls-lR file at the top of your hierarchical tree.

After your FTP service is registered, your ls-lR file is polled automatically at regular intervals. All the words and phrases in ls-lR then become the content matter searched when a user uses Archie to find all files relating to a keyword or phrase. For example, the command

```
% archie myProduct
```

might produce the following output:

```
Host  sizzle.asd.sgi.com
      Location: /dist/ship/2.1
         FILE  -rwxr-xr-x 2346  Feb  16  11:42   myProduct
```

It then is easy for users to take this information and ftp to the file, myProduct.

Note For more information about using Archie, send the following e-mail to mailserv@is.internic.net, leaving the subject field empty:

```
send  using-Internet/searches/archie/using-archie
```

Before you connect your FTP service to an Archie service, make sure that you do not have either of the following problems:

◆ Unresolvable symbolic links

◆ Permission problems using ls

Checking syslog Files

syslog files contain important information describing how much your FTP archive is used daily. The only problem is that the data is buried under anonymity. A program called xferstats, which is included with the WU version of ftpd, fleshes out this information and puts it in a readable form, as the following example shows.

TOTALS FOR SUMMARY PERIOD Fri Feb 17 1995 to Fri Feb 17 1995

```
Files Transmitted During Summary Period          8
Bytes Transmitted During Summary Period          92216
Systems Using Archives                           0

Average Files Transmitted Daily                  8
Average Bytes Transmitted Daily                  92216

Daily Transmission Statistics
                 Number of    Number of    Average     Percent Of   Percent of
Date Sent        Files Sent   Bytes Sent   Xmit Rate   Files Sent   Bytes Sent
--------         ----------   ----------   --------    ----------   ----------

Fri Feb 17 1995      8          92216      54.4 KB/s    100.00       100.00

Total Transfers from each Archive Section (By bytes)

                                            --- Percent of ---
```

```
Archive Section   Files Sent   Bytes Sent   Files Sent   Bytes Sent
---------------   ----------   ----------   ----------   ----------
/upload               4           46792        50.00        52.37
/pub                  3           42395        37.50        46.11
/Index/Info files     1            3029        37.50         1.62
```

Hourly Transmission Statistics

```
         Number of    Number of    Average       Percent Of   Percent Of
Time     Files Sent   Bytes        Xmit Rate     Files Sent   Bytes
----     ----------   --------     ---------     ----------   --------
00           8          92216      53.7 KB/s      100.00       100.00
```

This report shows that eight files were sent containing 92,216 bytes from three subdirectories.

You can change the duration of the report to look at weekly and monthly statistics. You can use this information to see whether parts of your FTP archive are used on a regular basis. If parts of your archive are not used regularly, you might reconsider the pertinence of the files or revise the navigational aids that direct users through those directories.

You also can use this information to monitor hardware needs. You initially might have set up your network service with a minimum of machinery. These statistics give you a good idea about pub load. If you plot the growth of your service over time with a simple usage versus time graph, you can anticipate when you will need additional disk storage.

Checking ftpadmin E-Mail

If you set up an alias for yourself, you have the daily chore of checking the ftpadmin e-mail. If you require that users send you e-mail when they upload files, the first thing you should do is match newly uploaded software in /upload with corresponding e-mail. If you find software without e-mail, consider the uploaded file suspicious. Actually, consider all uploaded files as potential threats to your system. Even though you took the trouble to isolate uploaded files in one directory, they still can do harm.

You also can direct other error messages to this address. If you use a cron job to create the ls-lR file, for example, send errors to ftpadmin.

The remainder of the mail is a combination of user complaints, questions, and requests. Remember that you are the first line of customer contact for your company.

Potential customers appreciate timely feedback, curious answers to questions, and references to additional information.

 Note   The remainder of this chapter discusses system administration of the WU version of ftpd.

Configuring the WU Version of ftpd

The WU version of ftpd uses the ftpaccess file as the holding place for configuration information. You can do any of the following things:

◆ Restrict user access to the FTP service by user type

◆ Restrict user access according to CPU load

◆ Restrict user access by group

◆ Automatically display information to users

◆ Log information about service usage

◆ Provide shortcuts for file access

◆ Control uploading of files

The following sections describe how to accomplish each of these tasks.

Restricting User Access

As an FTP system administrator, you need some ammunition to fight people who misuse your service. The WU version of ftpd enables you to deny access to your FTP service; the vanilla version of ftpd does not.

ftpd cannot single out specific users to deny access to; it can only deny access to the entire FTP client host. To deny access to host rusty.nail.com, for example, you create a file called ftphosts and put in it the following entry:

```
deny ftp rusty.nail.com
```

To deny access to the entire archive, you use the ftpaccess deny command:

```
deny   host.com    /etc/doc/refuse
```

in which host.com is the name of the host machine whose users you want to deny access, and refuse is a text file that prints when users from host.net try to ftp into the archive. Or, instead of domain names, you can use IP addresses to define hosts.

You even can deny access to entire domains by using wild cards, as in the following example:

```
deny ftp *.nail.com
```

You can restrict host access by allowing only specified hosts to access the FTP service. For example:

```
allow ftp *.nail.com
```

means that only users from nail.com can access the FTP service anonymously.

In the ftphosts file, if you have more than one deny or allow entry, make the order of the entries proceed from most to least specific. Otherwise, the general case, if read first, will obliterate a specific case, as in the following example:

```
deny *.nail.com
allow  forge.engr.nail.com
```

Although the second entry grants access to forge.engr.nail.com, the first entry overrides the second entry.

You also can deny users of a specific host access to specific parts of your archive by using the ftphosts deny command:

```
deny   ftp   host.com
deny   anonymous   host.com
```

in which ftp and anonymous are the accounts to which you want to deny access.

You can limit user access by defining classes in ftpaccess. A *class* is a combination of a user type and a domain name (or IP address). For ftpd, there are three types of users:

User Type	Description
Anonymous	Users restricted by chroot() to a subset of the file system
Guest	Users with IDs and passwords that have been restricted to a subset of the file system
Real	Users, usually company employees, who have full access to the file system

The class construct assigns users from specific hosts to a particular user type, using the following syntax:

```
class   className   userType   user.host.com
```

For example,

```
class   friend   guest   *.sgi.com
```

defines all users in sgi.com accesses as user type guest; the class of these users is friend. If a user is not defined as part of a class, he has no access to the system. If he is defined by more than one line in ftpaccess, his user type and class membership are defined by the first class whose specifications he satisfies. If a user is both class friend, user type guest, and class everyone, user type anonymous, for example, and if class friend is listed before class everyone in ftpaccess, his user type is defined as type guest. For this reason, you list the narrowly defined class definitions first, and the general class definitions last. If you were to put class everyone first whose domain name was all users (*), all users would be defined as class friend, regardless of what followed in the listing of classes.

To give anonymous FTP users access to the public archives, you have to define them in the following way:

```
class   everyone   anonymous   *
```

Restrict User Access Based on CPU Load

Whenever there is an ftp request, inetd spawns a new copy of ftpd to handle the request. As more and more requests come in, more and more ftpd processes are spawned. The more people using the FTP service, the greater the CPU load. At some point, depending on the speed of the computer, the CPU cannot handle the workload, and service to all FTP clients slows.

You can cure that problem automatically by restricting the number of users of a specific user type at any one time. You can do that by using the limit command with the following syntax:

```
limit   className   maxNumber   dayTime overloadMessage
```

For example,

```
limit   friend   150   SaSu700-1800   /usr/doc/overLoad
limit   friend   100   Any            /usr/doc/overLoad
```

limits the number of users of class friend to 150 on Saturday and Sunday between 7 a.m. and 6 p.m., or 100 users at any other time. All FTP clients that try to log on that exceed the number of maximum users receive the I'm sorry... message defined in /overLoad.

The format of the time field is that the day of the week is represented by the first two letters of the day (Su, Mo, Tu, and We, for example), and you use a 24-hour clock. You can use a series of times for the same limit specification by using the OR (|) operator. Mo800–1300 | Fr900–1400, for example, means Monday 8 a.m. to 1 p.m. or Friday 9 a.m. to 2 p.m.

Notice that you put your most restrictive limit clauses first and proceed to the least restrictive. If you put the Any limit statement before the SaSu700–1800, for example, the Saturday-Sunday statement would have no effect.

ftpd reads the limit information and denies FTP connections before doing the chroot().

Restricting Access for Security Reasons

An FTP client, by default, has five chances to log onto ftpd before getting a kind "See you later" message. You can change the number of login attempts by using the loginfails command in the ftpaccess file:

```
loginfails 3
```

This limits the number of failed attempts to three.

If it is important to you that you get an e-mail address as the password when a user logs in, the WU version of ftpd enables you to check the format of the entered password.

Remember, this version does not check the authentication of the password—just the format. To check the format, you use the passwd-check command in ftpaccess, as follows:

```
passwd-check   formatCheck   reaction
```

in which formatCheck can be one of three values:

none	Does not provide password format checking
trivial	Checks to see whether there is an at (@) sign in the entered password
rfc822	Checks to see whether the entered password has a domain part and a local part (meaning that it complies with RFC 822)

The reaction field can have one of two values:

warn   Sends a warning to use the correct format when entering passwords

enforce Terminates the FTP client's login if the password is formatted
        incorrectly

Restricting Users Actions

Not only can you keep people out of your system, you can keep users and groups of
users from taking specific actions.

Restricting the Use of tar and compress

The WU version of ftpd enables you to prevent specified user classes the right to tar
or compress files. You do that by adding one or both of the following lines to the
ftpaccess file:

```
compress  no  friend
tar       no  friend
```

The second field is yes or no, depending on whether you want the class, defined in
the third field, to compress or tar. The default is yes.

Restricting File Functions

You can restrict types—not classes—of users from performing a number of file
manipulations. The syntax of the command is similar to the compress and tar expressions—the second field is yes or no, and the third field names the type of user:

```
chmod      no      anonymous
delete     no      anonymous
overwrite  no      anonymous
rename     no      anonymous
umask      no      anonymous
```

These poor users can't do anything, but sometimes that is appropriate.

Creating and Managing Groups of Users

It is possible to restrict a group of users to a different part of the file structure than
that of anonymous users. The principle is the same as with anonymous users: you use
chroot() to restrict the group to the file system under the login directory, which

becomes their root directory. You might want to do that if your company is working jointly with another company. In that case, you want to give employees of the other company access to some of your file structure, but not the entire file structure!

To create a group called guests, you put an entry in /etc/group similar to the following:

```
guests:*:25:type1,type2,type3,type4
```

Then you enter encrypted passwords for each user type (type1, type2, and so on) in the /etc/passwd file. The entry is similar to the following:

```
guests:aTerriblePassword:200:25:guests FTP user: \
    /users/guests/./type1:/bin/false
```

This entry uses chroot() to restrict a type1 user under the login directory, /users /guests/, and makes her login directory /type1 (whatever follows the /.), which is a subdirectory of the login directory.

In ftpaccess, you then associate groups and guest users using the guestgroup command:

```
guestgroup guests
```

You can grant specified classes of anonymous users special access rights as well. You do that by making a class of anonymous users a group. If you have defined a class of anonymous users as allies, who are employees of corporation XYZ (XYZ.com), using the entry

```
class allies  anonymous  *.XYZ.com
```

you can create a group for them in /etc/group using an entry like the following:

```
XYZ::25:
```

To assign users of class allies to the group XYZ, you use the autogroup command in /etc/group:

```
autogroup XYZ  allies
```

Now that you have defined a group of users, you can make the files and directories under the login directory readable to the group XYZ only.

Changing Groups

You can allow FTP users to change their group ID using two commands:

```
site group groupName
site gpass groupPassword
```

in which *groupName* is the name of the group the FTP user wants to change to, and *groupPassword* is the password of the group. After logging in as anonymous, for example, the user uses the following commands:

```
ftp> site group engr
350 Request for access to grouop field accepted.
ftp> site gpass Wjsile23kl23jsic
350 Group access enabled.
ftp>
```

Notice that the password is not hidden in this case.

To allow FTP users to use the site group and site gpass commands, you must set the private option in ftpaccess as in this example:

```
private yes
```

Then you must create the directory, /ftpgroups, under the same directory that /group is under—usually ~ftp/etc. In /ftpgroups, you specify the group, defined in /group, that the site group maps to, and the gpass password, as in the following example:

```
engr:Wjsile23kl23jsic:XYZ
```

In this case, the site group is engr, the gpass password is Wjsile23kl23jsic, and the file access is the same as that granted to group XYZ.

Sending Messages to FTP Users

The WU version of ftpd provides four commands to display messages to logged in FTP users:

◆ banner

◆ message

◆ readme

◆ shutdown

Using the banner Command

The banner command displays a file at user login. You specify, in ftpaccess, the pathname to the display file using the banner command, as in the following example:

```
banner /usr/ftp/greetings/bannerMSG
```

This pathname is relative to the system root, not the login directory.

The banner message should contain any information you want the FTP users to know before logging in. You might want them to know that they must use their e-mail address as a password to log in or who to contact if there are problems, or you might want them to see a simple greeting. Your banner message can include macros to provide updated information. The following table shows the macros you can use with the banner and message commands.

Macro	Replaced by
%C	Current working directory name
%E	e-mail address (of FTP system administrator) defined by the e-mail entry in ftpaccess
%F	Number of free kilobytes in current working directory
%L	Host name where FTP archive files reside
%M	Maximum number of users of the users class allowed to log in
%N	Current number of users of the current user's class
%R	Current user's host name (name of FTP client)
%T	Time of day, in the format weekday month day hour:minute:seconds year. For example, Sunday Feb 24 8:30:30 1995
%U	User's name, as specified at login

You might use vi to create the following banner message:

```
%U logged in at %T from %R.

For system administration help, email %E.

Maximum number of users: %M
%U, you are number: %N

Welcome!
```

Using the message Command

The message command works much like the banner command; it even uses the same macros. The difference is that the message command controls when the message is displayed. There are two instances in which the message is displayed:

◆ At login

◆ When the user changes (using the cd command) to a specific directory

To display the message at user login, use an entry in ftpaccess similar to the following:

```
message /usr/ftp/greetings/messageMSG login
```

where /usr/ftp/greetings/messageMSG is the pathname and the file of the message to display.

To display a message when a user changes to a specific directory, use an entry in ftpaccess similar to the following:

```
message /usr/ftp/greetings/messageMSG cwd=dirName
```

where dirName is the name of the directory that triggers the display of messageMSG. Instead of a specific directory, you can use the asterisk wild card (*) to specify that any directory trigger the messageMSG.

To display the contents of a file in each directory, name the files the same in each directory (but make the content different). If the name of the file is README, for example, you could use the following entry:

```
message .README cwd=*
```

You might put in the README file a description of the contents of the current directory.

To display a message only to a specified class of users, put the name of the class at the end of the entry, as in the following example:

```
message /usr/ftp/greetings/friendMSG cwd=home friend
```

You can display the same message to more than one class by adding each class name to the end of the entry, separating each class name by a white space. If the messages are for anonymous or guest users, make sure that the messages are in files under the login directory.

Using the readme Command

You use the readme command to alert users that the README file has changed in a directory. The syntax of the entry is the same as that of the message command:

```
readme pathname (login ¦ cwd=dirName) [className ...]
```

where pathname is relative to the FTP login directory.

The command does not display the README file; it only alerts the user that there has been a change.

If you update all the README files, you can alert the user with the following entry:

```
readme README cwd=*
```

Using the shutdown Command

There are two ways of shutting down the FTP service:

◆ Using the shutdown command in ftpaccess

◆ Using the utility program ftpshut

The utility program, ftpshut, is discussed in a later section.

The shutdown command uses the following syntax:

```
shutdown   pathname
```

pathname is the name of a file that contains shutdown information. ftpd periodically checks for the existence of the file. If you create it, ftpd reads the file for shutdown information in the following format:

```
year month day hour minute denyTime disconnectTime
message
```

The first five fields specify the exact time of the shutdown. month is an integer in the range of 0 to 11, and hour is an integer between 0 and 23.

denyTime is the number of hours and minutes before shutdown time when users will be denied access to the FTP service. disconnectTime is the number of minutes before shutdown time when active users are disconnected from the FTP service. Both denyTime and disconnectTime use the following format:

```
HHMM
```

To deny FTP service access 1 hour and 15 minutes before shutdown, for example, denyTime would equal 0115.

The message in the shutdown file can include all the macros used by the banner and message commands, plus the following three:

Macro	Replaced By
%d	disconnectTime
%r	denyTime
%s	shutdown time

People denied access to the FTP service receive a standard shutdown, call later message. Current users receive the shutdown message specified in the shutdown file.

Logging User Events

The WU version of ftpd enables you to log user events, such as uploading and downloading files, by using the log commands command. You can do that only for specified user types—real, guest, or anonymous. To turn on logging, you put an entry in ftpaccess using the following syntax:

```
log commands userType [userType ...]
```

where userType is real, guest, or anonymous. You can specify more than one user type to log commands. Separate the user types with a white space. You have to have at least one user type to turn on logging.

The log entries appear in the syslog file as RETR and STOR commands for downloads and uploads, respectively.

If you want to log more information than that, you have to use the log transfer command. Like the log command, you can specify the user type that you want to monitor. You also can restrict the log events to downloads or uploads only.

The log transfer command has the following syntax:

```
log transfer userType [userType ...] flow [,flow]
```

where userType is the type of user whose actions you want to log, and flow is inbound or outbound. You can specify either flow or both inbound and outbound flows.

Instead of putting the logging information in syslog, log transfer puts the log information in the file defined in pathname.h; the default name is xferlog.

Understanding Log Transfer Logs

You used the log transfer command because you wanted more information than that given by the log command. The log data suffers the same fate as anything squeezed into as small a space as possible: the data is cryptic. Here's an example:

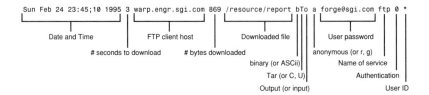

Descriptions of these fields follow.

Field	Description
1–5	The first five fields are date and time information in a customary format.
6	The number of seconds it took to download the file: 3.
7	The host of the FTP client: warp.engr.sgi.com.
8	The number of bytes downloaded: 869.
9	The name of the downloaded FTP archive: /pub/report.
10	The a tells you that the downloaded file was in ASCII. The other option, b, signifies that the downloaded file was binary.
11	The T tells you that the file was archived using Tar. The other options are C (compressed) and U (uncompressed).
12	The o stands for outbound, meaning that the file was downloaded. The other option, i, inbound, means that the file was uploaded to the FTP server.
13	The a specifies that the user type is anonymous. Other options include r (real) and g (guest) user types.
14	The user's e-mail address he used as a password when logging into the FTP service: forge@sgi.com.
15–16	The last two fields involve the authentication of the user. The second-to-last field, 0, means that there is no authentication involved; you simply believe the user is who he says he is in the password entry. The asterisk (*) means that the user ID can be anything.
	If the service authenticates the user, the second-to-last field is set to 1 and the last field is the user ID. Authenticating the user involves running an authentication service on the same server as the FTP service.

You can compile this log information into an interesting set of statistics using the PERL script, xferstats, included with the WU version of ftpd. You can tell from the statistics, for example, which files are downloaded most often, or the times when people access the service the most.

Restricting Uploading

As mentioned earlier, if you are going to allow people to upload files at all, you should restrict uploads to a single directory (for this example, suppose that the directory is called /upload). You restrict uploading privileges because you need to douse the glee in hackers' eyes who have specially formulated a Trojan horse virus designed to incapacitate your system.

To define uploading permissions, you can use the upload command in the ftpaccess file, using the following syntax:

```
upload pathName dirName yes¦no owner group mode      [dirs¦nodirs]
```

The yes¦no option gives you the opportunity to allow¦disallow, respectively, uploading to the directory, dirName, under the file hierarchy, pathName. If you allow uploading to a specified directory, you can define the owner, group, and mode of the file. The final field, dirs¦nodirs, specifies whether users can create subdirectories in /upload.

To block all uploads to all directories under the login directory, use an entry in ftpaccess similar to the following:

```
upload /usr/ftp * no
```

This entry says that users may not upload to any directory under /usr/ftp (the login directory). To allow uploading to the file /upload, use an entry similar to the following:

```
upload /usr/ftp upload yes root engr 0600
```

This entry allows users to upload files into the /upload directory. Those files become owned by root and group engr. The mode of the file is 0600, which gives the owner read and write permissions on the file, but no permissions to anyone else. Because other users cannot read or write to the file, they cannot view or change it. This prevents users from setting up the hottest porn Internet site on your server.

Restricting Uploading by Nonanonymous Users

The upload command applies only to anonymous users. To restrict the filenames that other users can upload, you use the path-filter command, which has the following syntax:

```
path-filter userType pathName expOK [expNotOK]
```

This command specifies that users of type `userType` may upload files consisting of filenames described by regular expressions, `expOK`, and may not upload files consisting of filenames described by the regular expressions, `expNotOK`.

If a filename does not contain any of the regular expressions, `expOK`, or it does contain disallowed regular expressions, `expNotOK`, ftpd does not permit the upload and, instead, displays the message in `pathName` to the user.

For example,

```
path-filter guest /usr/upload ^[-A-Za-z0-9] ^.
```

allows users of type guest to upload files with filenames consisting of alphanumeric characters only, and not, specifically, filenames containing periods.

Using the Administrative Tools

The WU version of ftpd provides three administrative tools. One tool, ftpshut, forewarns users of the service shutdown and then it shuts down the service. The other two tools, ftpwho and ftpcount, provide interesting statistics about who is using the service and how many are using it.

Using ftpshut

The ftpshut command warns users that a service is going to shut down, denies access to users because a service is shutting down, and performs the service shutdown. By default, new users are denied access to the FTP service 10 minutes before shutdown; active users are disconnected from the service, by default, five minutes before shutdown.

You can change these default values by using the –l option to set the number of minutes before shutdown that new users will be denied access to the service. You can use –d to set the number of minutes before shutdown that active users will be disconnected from the service.

The syntax of the ftpshut command follows:

```
ftpshut [-l minutes] [-d minutes] shutDownTime       [message]
```

where shutDownTime is the time the service will be shut down, and message is the message displayed to active users just as their connection to the service is terminated.

The message can contain any of the macros available to the shutdown command, as described previously in the section "Using the shutdown Command."

Using ftpwho

The ftpwho command tells you how many people of each user class currently are using the archive, how many are allowed per user class, and some additional information about the service running for each user.

The format for the output of ftpwho is identical to that of your system's ps command. The following is a sample output of ftpwho:

```
%ftpwho
Service class friend:
    0   S   0   634   58   0 198 18 209ebd90 62 23849723 ?
        0:00 ftpd
    -      1 users (2 maximum)
```

Actually, there is a line similar to this one for each defined user class. The meaning of these values varies by system, so you need to check your man pages for the definition of the fields in ps.

Using ftpcount

The ftpcount command tells you the number of users per user class that currently are accessing the FTP service. It also tells you the maximum number of such users allowed at any one time, as defined by the limit command in the ftpaccess file.

The following is an example of the output of ftpcount:

```
%ftpcount
Service class friend               -     5 users ( 25 maximum)
```

Again, there would be a line similar to this for each user class.

Setting Up a freeWAIS Service

I f your service includes an enormous database of information that you want to make available to others, you should offer a Wide Area Information Server (WAIS) service. A WAIS service allows WAIS clients and the latest version of WWW clients to search for keywords and key phrases throughout a database, and then to display the database matches. The database can contain text, binaries, and JPEG images.

WAIS was created as public domain software by Thinking Machines, a company that builds a massively parallel supercomputer called the Connection Machine. Thinking Machines developed WAIS in coordination with Apple Computer, Dow Jones, and KPMG Peat Marwick to prove that a networked information service could be created using TCP/IP (and also, what a great WAIS server a Connection Machine could be). WAIS quickly became the prototype database search engine. It became formally described as protocol Z39.50.

The popularity of WAIS grew so fast that Thinking Machines stopped supporting the public domain version of WAIS and spun off a separate company—called WAIS, Inc.—that provides and maintains a commercial version of the software. The freeware version of the software was picked up by CNIDR (Clearinghouse for Networked Information Discovery and Retrieval). CNIDR folded in enhancements from several versions of WAIS.

Currently, CNIDR maintains a version of WAIS called freeWAIS. This is the version of WAIS that is discussed in this chapter. For more information about the commercial version of WAIS, you can contact WAIS, Inc. at freeWAIS@cnidr.org.

This chapter describes the parts of freeWAIS (the indexer, the service, and the client), how those parts interact, how to compile the software, how to set up the service, and how to test the service.

Understanding the Parts of freeWAIS

freeWAIS is divided into three parts, as shown in figure 11.1:

◆ Indexer

◆ Service

◆ Client

Figure 11.1

The three parts of freeWAIS.

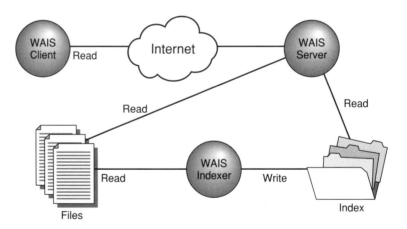

The freeWAIS indexer takes data stored in a database and creates an index from it. It creates, among other things, a list of words that occur in the database documents, and a table that shows where those words occur in the documents.

The freeWAIS service uses the index created by the freeWAIS indexer to match data in the database document with the search criteria defined by the user. The service also is responsible for splitting up a user's natural language search criteria, using each word as a keyword, finding documents in the database that contain those words, and keeping a score that suggests to users how pertinent a document might be per given search criteria. If the freeWAIS service finds 10 documents that contain (some or all of) the search criteria, for example, it lists each document and gives each a score between 0 and 1,000. The higher the number, the better the document matches the search criteria.

freeWAIS clients use the Z39.50 protocol to build search criteria in the appropriate form. Clients also display the list of matching documents found by the service, and allow a user to retrieve any of the matching documents. Document types include simple ASCII text, binaries, audio files, PostScript documents, HTML documents, JPEG files, and GIF files. Figure 11.2 shows a freeWAIS client.

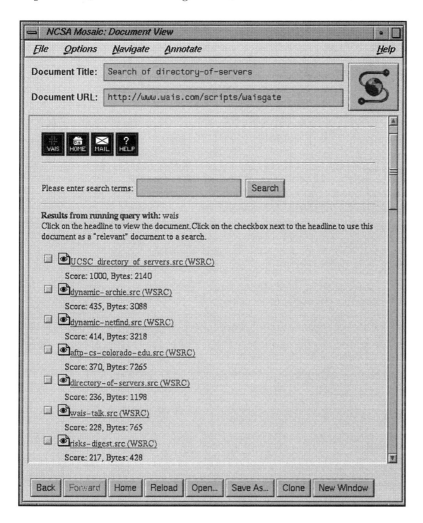

Figure 11.2

A freeWAIS client.

freeWAIS clients originally were available only for the Mac and text-based Unix. Today, you can find freeWAIS clients available for Microsoft Windows and graphical Unix front ends such as Motif. The latest version of WWW clients, such as Mosaic and Netscape, also act directly as a front end to freeWAIS services. The advantage of using a WWW client is that you can use it to find and graphically display information in the database. A freeWAIS client cannot display an HTML document. Assuming that people will use a WWW client, however, you can use it to populate your WAIS database with multimedia documents. In fact, you can include just about every file format you can think of in the index, including images, sounds, videos, x-rays, PostScript files, SGML-encoded text, e-mail, Usenet news, lexicon lists, and catalogs!

An Overview of freeWAIS

This section shows you how to perform a simple search so that you can get a feeling for how freeWAIS works. Although it might be putting the cart before the horse—you don't have your service running yet—this section offers you some understanding of what freeWAIS is and how it works. The section can help you make sense of some configuration options you will choose when setting up your service.

The following example shows the output of a text-based freeWAIS client searching for documents relating to cryogenics:

```
% waissearch -h warp.engr.sgi.com -d newSource -p       cryogenics


Search Response:
 NumberofRecordsReturned:3
     1:Score 666, lines:      6     `after death´
     2:Score 333, lines: 369     `absolute zero´
     3:Score 333, lines: 231     `outer space´
```

The search reveals three sources of information relating to cryogenics. The scores 666, 333, and 333 are called the relevancy feedback. The higher the number (1000 is the maximum), the more likely the document discusses the search criteria, cryogenics in this case. The last field identifies the document. At this point, you choose a document by entering **1**, **2**, or **3**.

```
View document number [type 0 or q to quit]:1
Headline: after death
Researchers now use the science of cryogenics to maintain body parts, even
entire cadavers, for weeks, months, and even years after the death of the
person. The Neptune Society maintains vaults of cryogenic environments in which
cadavers are maintained in the hope they can be revived in the future.
```

```
View document number [type 0 or q to quit]: q
Search for new words [type q to quit]: q
```

This abstract about the document is called a *headline*. You create one for each document in the index. The user now should know whether or not this document is the one he wants.

Following this general introduction to freeWAIS, read on to see how to build the service.

Getting the Software

You can ftp freeWAIS from ftp.cnidr.org in the following directory:

```
/pub/NIDR.tools/freewais/freeWAIS-0.4.tar.Z
```

When you look in the freeWAIS/ subdirectory, you see many versions of the freeWAIS binary. Each version is tailored to a specific platform, as illustrated in the following output:

```
ftp>cd/pub/NIDR.tools/freewais
250 CWD command successful.
ftp>ls
200 PORT command successful.
150 Opening ASCII mode data connection for /bin/ls.
total 21185
-rw-r--r--  1 root    system   5657033 May 26  1993 freeWAIS-0.1.tar.Z
-rw-r--r--  1 root    system   1580065 Oct 1   1993 freeWAIS-0.2.tar.Z
-rw-r--r--  1 root    system   1583161 Oct 3   1993 freeWAIS-0.201.tar.Z
-rw-r--r--  1 root    system   1580247 Oct 6   15.46 freeWAIS-0.202.tar.Z
-rw-r--r--  1 root    system   1956601 Jan 23  1993 freeWAIS-0.3.Solaris.tar.gz
-rw-r--r--  1 root    system   731597 Mar 21  1994 freeWAIS-0.3.tar.gz
-rw-r--r--  1 root    system   1501607 Jan 23  15.46 freeWAIS-0.4-Alpha.tar.gz
-rw-r--r--  1 root    system   632378 Jan 23  15.46 freeWAIS-0.4-Linux.tar.gz
-rw-r--r--  1 root    system    9183 Jan 23  15.46 freeWAIS-0.4-RELEASE-NOTES
-rw-r--r--  1 root    system   1428633 Jan 23  15.46 freeWAIS-0.4-SGI.tar.z
-rw-r--r--  1 root    system   732808 Jan 23  15.46 freeWAIS-0.4-Solaris.tar.gz
-rw-r--r--  1 root    system   849330 Jan 23  15.46 freeWAIS-0.4-SunOS.tar.gz
-rw-r--r--  1 root    system   1320332 Jan 23  15.46 freeWAIS-0.4-Ultrix.tar.gz
-rw-r--r--  1 root    system   1203170 Jan 23  15.46 freeWAIS-0.4.tar.Z
-rw-r--r--  1 root    system   756841 Jan 23  15.46 freeWAIS-0.4.tar.gz
226 Transfer complete.
```

Hopefully, your platform is in the preceding listing. If it is, be sure to download that version of freeWAIS. It contains the correct service configuration information in the binary. Because your service is preconfigured, you can skip most of the discussion of configuring the service.

If your platform is not represented in the preceding output, download the generic binary of the service—freeWAIS-0.4.tar.Z—or download freeWAIS-0.4.tar.gz if you want to use gzip rather than zcat to uncompress the file.

 Note Version 0.4 of freeWAIS is the last version supported and developed by CNIDR. The next version of the software is called ZDIST 1.0 and, as of this writing, it is in beta form. For more information about ZDIST, see Chapter 15, "Setting Up and Managing a ZDIST Service."

Before you go any further, you might want to check the condition of the source code. To see if there are new patches or known bugs, refer to the newsgroups comp.infosystems.wais, wais-talk@think.com, and zip@cnidr.org, each of which discusses freeWAIS.

The source code comes compressed. So, after ftping it, cd to the directory where you want the code to reside, and uncompress it using the zcat command, as shown here:

```
% zcat freeWAIS-0.4.tar.Z ¦ tar xvf -
```

As the file uncompresses, it creates a directory called freeWAIS-0.4 that includes a Makefile, documentation files (including INSTALLATION, many READMEs, and RELEASE-NOTES), and a number of other directories, as shown:

```
warp 106% cd freeWAIS-0.4
warp 107% ls
ANNOUNCEMENT             README-s              iubio-wais.readme
COPYRIGHT                README.gopher_and_v0.4    lib
DOCUMENTS                RELEASE-NOTES         man
INSTALLATION             bin                   sound.readme
INSTALLATION.auto        config.c              src
Makefile                 config.c.auto         wais-sources
Makefile.auto            doc                   wais-test
NEXT-RELEASE             include
README       iubio-wais.news
```

The following table describes the functions of the directories.

Directory	Description
bin	Contains the binaries you will build
config.c	Contains .c code that implements configuration information
doc	Contains helpful information, including a FAQ, written by Thinking Machines and CNIDR
include	Contains all the header files used by the service and clients
lib	Contains library functions used by freeWAIS
man	Contains man pages
src	Contains the source code for all of the executables, including waisserver, waisindex, waissearch, waisq, freeWAIS client-based on X11, and other freeWAIS clients
wais-sources	Contains the src file for the directory of servers that your WAIS clients can access
wais-test	Contains sample scripts for the indexer and service

Understanding Files in the src Directory

Many important files that you need to customize are in the src directory. The following table explains what these files are.

File	Description
src/indexer	waisindex source code
src/server	waisserver source code
src/ir/	The WAIS toolkit library
src/client/	Client programs source code tree
src/client/ui/	Example routines for user interfaces
src/client/emacs	GNU Emacs client interface
src/client/swais/	Character-based (VT-100 compatible) client
src/client/waisq/	Command-line client
src/client/waissearch/	Command-line client
src/client/x	An X-based (X11R5), Motif client

Now that you have the service software, you need to configure the service by editing the Makefile, config.h, and server.h (and, optionally, the included freeWAIS clients). After editing these files, you run % make default. But let's examine the configuration options first.

Editing the Makefile

The Makefile contains a large list of variables; you will need to set many of them. The first variables you set are standard programs and the locations of Unix commands. The following table describes these settings:

Standard programs	Description or commands
CC	Equals the name of your system's ANSI C compiler: gcc or standard cc.
RANLIB	Set this variable equal to the pathname to your system's ranlib command. On SGI and HP machines, because there is no ranlib command, uncomment the line, RANLIB=true.
RM	Set this equal to the absolute path to the rm Unix command on your system (for example, /bin/rm).
MV	Set to Unix move command, mv.
MAKE	Set to standard make program (for example, make).

freeWAIS supports ANSI C. freeWAIS can use GNU CC and non-ANSI C compilers because of the addition of many library routines. If you have a choice, however, set CC to the ANSI C compiler, CC.

Editing the Directory Paths

You must set the TOP variable equal to the absolute path of the freeWAIS source directory. The other subdirectories get positioned under the TOP directory. *Unless* you are working in SunOS, uncomment the following line in the Makefile:

```
#TOP;sh=pwd
```

The preceding instruction assumes that you build the service in the current directory. Then you should comment out the line marked comment me. If you are using SunOS, do not uncomment the TOP line, because the line following comment me sets TOP correctly. You can change the location of subdirectories, such as INCLUDE, BIN, AND LIB; however, not many good reasons exist for doing so.

Setting Library Variables

Most of the default settings in this part of the Makefile will probably suit your system. You should, however, look at least at the following variables:

◆ **RESOLVER.** Set equal to nothing unless your system uses a namespace resolver, in which case you set the variable equal to –lresolv.

◆ **CURSELIB.** Set the version of the curse library.

Setting Compiler Options

The CFLAGS (compiler flags) variable sets the default flags you use when you compile. Table 11.1 describes these options.

TABLE 11.1
Compiler Options

Flags	Set This Flag For
Architecture-Specific Flags	
–cckr	Irix version 4+ (SGI)
–DBSD	Pre-4.3 versions of BSD
–DBSD43	4.3+ versions of BSD
–DSYSV	System V Unix (AT&T)
–DUSG	Versions of Unix that include dirent routines in the C library
–M3e–Zi	XENIX
–DNeXT-posix	NEXTSTEP
–A_UX	A/UX
Indexer and Server Flags	
–DBIO	This flag adds indexing for biological symbols and terms. Unless you are in the same business as Darwin, you might pass on this flag.

continues

TABLE 11.1, CONTINUED
Compiler Options

Flags	Set This Flag For
–DBOOLEANS	When you search for a phrase such as `white night´, the default is to score a hit if `white´ OR `night´ is found. If you compile waisserver with –DBOOLEANS set, you also can use the Boolean operators AND and NOT. This is a good flag to set.
	Conventional freeWAIS clients store descriptions about your service options automatically in /wais-sources. Because users can read this file, tell them about the Boolean options available and other significant flags you have set.
–DDUMP_CORE	Setting this flag dumps the core when waisserver aborts. This is a good option to set when you are debugging the server. If your disk space is limited, however, you should recompile with this flag unset when you are done testing the service so that your disk space is not eaten up by core dumps.
–DEND_MERGE	Setting this flag makes waisserver wait until the end of its search to merge index files. This flag uses additional disk space compared to the default method, which merges indexes as the service is running. Unless you have a good reason, do not set this flag.
–DLIST_STEMS	Setting this flag instructs the indexer and service log to record the stem of words.
–DLITERAL	Setting this flag enables you to search for strings in a document. The strings must be enclosed in single or double quotation marks. The words `I hope I find this phrase´, for example, must exactly match a phrase in a document for a hit. If you use double quotation marks, you must use escapes with them—for example, \"I hope I find this phrase\". Make sure not to include extra white spaces at the beginning or ending of the phrase unintentionally.
	There are a couple of potential problems when using literals with waisserver. To register a hit, the first word in the phrase must be indexed and not be in the stoplist (described later). The other problem is that waisserver uses stemming, which often conflicts with literal. *Stemming* is the process of removing

Flags	Set This Flag For
	endings to words, such as *es, ing,* and *s.* Stemming is used to generalize a search so that `hoping to see you´ scores a hit when waisserver finds `hope to see you´. If waisserver stems `hoping´, however, to `hop´, it might not score a hit when literal is set and the document contains `hoping´. Ironically, `hoping to see you´ might not hit `hoping to see you´, because it is stemmed to `hop to see you´. You might think twice before setting this flag.
–DNEED_VSYSLOG	If you choose to set the –DUSE_SYSLOG flag and your system does not have the vsyslog() function, you must set this flag.
–DPARTIALWORD	Setting this flag enables users to search using the asterisk (*) wild card. The asterisk can represent zero or more alphanumeric characters, as in the following example: "lad*" matches "lad," "lady," "ladies," "ladel," "ladelling," "ladder," and "latent" (it scores a hit for misspelled words too!). This is a good flag to set.
–DRELEVANCE_FEEDBACK	Setting this flag to On allows freeWAIS clients to use documents found in previous freeWAIS searches as search criteria for a new freeWAIS search. This is a good flag to set.
–DSECURE_SERVER	This flag enables the system administrator to reset the uid under which the service runs using the –u argument after startup.
–DTELL_USER	Using this flag gives the service your user ID at connect time.
–DBIGINDER	Use this flag if you have to index many documents.
–DSTEM_WORDS	Here's that stemming option discussed earlier with –DLITERAL. When the flag is set, waisserver shaves standard endings off words, such as *s, ing, es,* and *ly,* to create, in effect, a wild-card search, so that `surely´ scores a hit when finding `sure´. This is a good flag to set.
–DUSE_SYSLOG	Setting this flag makes waisserver log events to syslog rather than using fprintf.

The Makefile has CFLAGS defined for many different platforms. If you find a CFLAG for your platform, uncomment it. Otherwise, set your own CFLAGS. An example follows:

```
CFLAGS=-I$ (INCLUDE) -DTELL_USER -DSECURE_SERVER -DRELEVANCE_FEEDBACK -DUSG
-DSOUND -DBOOLEANS
```

The Makefile has several other, highly specialized flags that are not of general interest. If you are curious (or work for NASA), look in the Makefile.

Building X and Motif Clients

The Makefile builds the following freeWAIS clients by default:

◆ swais

◆ waisq

If you want to build an X client—xwais—you must uncomment the following line in the Makefile:

```
#cd x; (env TOP=$(TOP) CC=$(CC) \
   CFLAGS="$(CFLAGS)" MAKE="$(MAKE)" ./makex
```

You can find the preceding under the following line:

```
xwais: libftw libs ui
```

You can use imake to build a Motif version of the freeWAIS client. Look in the Imakefile in /freeWAIS-0.4/src/client/x for the following line and uncomment it:

```
LOCAL_LIBRARIES = $(UI_LIB) -lXm $(XAWLIB) $(XTOOLLIB) $(XMULIB) $(XLIB)
```

The preceding line includes the Motif library (–lXm) in LIBS.

If your C compiler cannot use ANSI prototypes, you need to uncomment the following line in Imakefile:

```
CDEBUGFLAGS = -g -Bstatic -DUSE_ALTFONT -DMOTIF -D_NO_PROTO
```

Look in your C libraries to make sure all of the symbols are defined.

Building the Service

Now that you have finished customizing the build instructions in the Makefiles, make sure you are at the top directory and type the following:

```
% make default
```

If your build does not work, find out whether your operating system does not pass environment variables in Makefiles. If it does not, you have to edit the CFLAGS line in the Makefile.

Also, double-check the Makefile. Many platform-specific settings are commented out. An example follows:

```
# SGIs want this uncommented
# SHELL=/bin/sh
```

It is easy to overlook them. Do a search on your platform name. An example follows:

```
:/sgi
```

If you are reading this section out of frustration because nothing you do seems to make the build work, take solace in the fact that you are not the first to experience build problems. There are many, many specific errors you can get information about by reading the Internet newsgroup comp.infosystems.wais. See whether your problem already has been addressed by the newsgroup. If it has not, pour out your heart on the Internet. Hopefully, someone will come to your aid.

Testing Your freeWAIS Service

Before you open shop on your freeWAIS service, you need to test it. Complete the following two tasks:

1. Use the indexer to index some files.

2. See whether the freeWAIS clients you just built can use the indexes.

The following sections look at each of these steps.

Indexing Files

The first thing you want to do is create directories for the index files, as in the following example:

```
% mkdir /wsindex
```

Index files should be easy to find and manipulate, so locate the index directory at the root or in some logical place.

Also, make a directory for the freeWAIS server log files, as in the following example:

```
% mkdir /usr/local/logfiles
```

Now you need something to index. You need a directory with one or more files in it. You might use, for example, the files in a pubs directory. At this stage of the game, keep the size of the file(s) small—this is just a test, after all.

Run the indexer—waisindex—on your directory of files (to see whether the indexer works):

```
# waisindex -d test -t one_line /usr/resources
```

Use the -d option to define the name of the source test file, and the -t option to specify how you want the file indexed. /usr/resources is the location of sample files.

The –t option has two possible values: one_line and text. The one_line option indexes each line of a document. If waissearch finds a keyword match in a document, it can retrieve the specific line where the match occurred. With the text option, on the other hand, if waissearch finds a keyword match, it must retrieve the entire document. The default is text.

waisindex creates a source file—test—that waissearch can search through for matches with user-specified selection criteria. A freeWAIS source file is an indexed database consisting of a set of files. Chapter 12, "Managing a freeWAIS Service," discusses freeWAIS sources in greater detail.

Using freeWAIS Clients to Find Documents

Included in the software distribution is a directory called wais-test. In it is the script, test.waisindex, which creates the following four WAIS databases:

◆ **test-Bool.** An index of three small documents illustrating the Boolean capability and the use of synonyms. Use the Boolean condition, and, to search for "black and fox." Then, in the document called Bool.syn, search for synonyms; for example, "lazy dog" and "lazy mutt" return the same documents even though the word "mutt" is not in the documents.

◆ **test-Comp.** An index that demonstrates the indexer can handle compressed source files, a compressed mail folder, and document type "mail_or_rmail" in this example.

◆ **test-Docs.** An index of files in the /doc directory, showing the directory recurse switch and plain ASCii document indexing.

◆ **test-Multi.** An index of GIF images and text caption files demonstrating the multi-document-type capabilities of the indexer. Use the X-based freeWAIS client (or a graphical browser, such as Netscape or Mosaic) to search for "gumby." (The other freeWAIS clients do not support multiple document types.)

Starting and Checking Your Service

As with the other services, you have the option to start your service by itself or to have it started and terminated by inetd. The tradeoffs are the same: the consumption of CPU time (if the service runs constantly) versus the slow startup time (because the configuration files must be read) if triggered by inetd. If your service is not used often, let it run under inetd. If your service is contacted frequently, start the service yourself and let it run.

Starting waisserver with inetd

There are several reasons why you might want waisserver to run under inetd:

◆ Without inetd, you must have a waisserver running continuously so that it can listen to port 210.

◆ Some operating systems, like HP-UX, can limit access to services running under inetd.

To start waisserver with inetd, you must perform the following tasks:

1. Add an entry to the /etc/services file or the NIS database that looks similar to the following:

```
z3950    210/tcp    #freeWAIS service
```

This entry just says the service is running on TCP port 210.

2. Add an entry to the inetd.conf file similar to the following:

```
z3950 stream tcp nowait root /usr/local/bin/waisserver\
    waisserver.d -u peasant \
    -e /usr/local/log/logfile \
    -d /usr/local/index_location
```

waisserver is the name of the service, and the -u option designates the service to run as user peasant (with restricted permissions) after it starts. The -e option names the log file—logfile—to use, and the -d option names the default location of the indexes.

After the service is running, you do not want to run it as root, because a software bug might permit a mischievous user access to the system as root. The user peasant is someone who cannot log in; he has permission only to read document and index files, and to write all the log files.

To make the change in the configuration file take effect, first find the process ID (pid) of inetd, as follows:

```
# ps -ef ¦ grep inetd
```

Then, send a hang-up (HUP) signal to the inetd process, as in the following example:

```
# kill -HUP pid
```

pid is the process ID of inetd.

Check the syslog file to make sure that the service was added. The log file should contain an entry similar to the following:

```
inetd[111]: z3950/tcp: Added service, server
    /usr/local/etc/waisserver
```

Starting waisserver without inetd

You might choose to start waisserver from the command line to avoid the delay incurred by inetd as it starts the service.

To start the service from the command line, you use the same command syntax as you used with inetd, except that you have to include the –p option, as in the following example:

```
# waisserver -u peasant -p -l 10 \
    -e /usr/local/log/logfile \
    -d /usr/local/index_location
```

Use the -p option to tell waisserver to listen to a specific port: the one specified after -p, or the one defined in /etc/services (210) if no port number follows -p. Generally, you do not want to follow the option with a port number.

You need to leave the service on port 210 so the rest of the world can access it. You can, however, run different versions of the service on different ports. The software distribution even includes a file called start.myserver; it contains the startup commands for the service to run on port 1024.

All port numbers less than 1023 require root privileges to run. If you change the port to a number greater than 1023, you can let an engineer who is extending the functionality of the service start and stop the service without root access.

After testing your service (described in the next section), you might choose to start the service automatically at system startup.

Testing waisserver

Now that you have waisserver installed and running, it's time to test it. You can do that by creating a new source (src) file with waisindex with the export command, and then using waissearch to search the source. But first, remove the test.src file created earlier:

```
$ rm test.src
```

Create the index file using waisindex, as in the following example:

```
$ waisindex -d /etc/hosts -t one_line -export test
```

The export option adds the domain name and the IP address of the freeWAIS server, and the port number on which the freeWAIS service runs.

Now run waissearch on the file and test for the occurrence of a word—in this case, "found":

```
$ waissearch -p 210 -d test found

Search Response:
NumberOfRecordsReturned: 1
1: Score: 666, lines: 20 `23.43.241.32 found´

View document number [type 0 or q to quit]:
```

If you look at the syslog file, and if you are running the service under inetd, you should see an entry like the following:

```
Connection from warp (23.43.241.32) at Fri Mar 3 18:32:42      1995
```

This entry shows that your freeWAIS client—running on the machine, warp—is connected to your service.

If you do not see a message like this, make sure that you have defined the correct pathname to the service in inetd.conf. You also might try using telnet to connect to port 210. If you do not get a connection, the service is not starting.

After you confirm that the service is working, you are ready to move it to its permanent position in your file structure and let people in your company try it out.

Letting the World Know about Your Service

Once you are confident that your service is stable, you should let everyone know it is up and running. You do that by sending an entry to the Directory of Servers, at quake.think.com and cnidr.org. The following command indexes your service's files, yourFiles, and registers the index with the Directory of Servers.

```
# waisindex -export -register yourFiles
```

Before you make your service available, however, you might first read in the next chapter about making your service secure.

Altering the Service and Clients

The software distribution enables you to alter the service and the clients, should you want to. The file, ir.c, is a service toolkit. The file, ui.c, is a client toolkit. These files allow you to customize the service and clients to your needs.

C H A P T E R

12

Managing a freeWAIS Service

Now that you have freeWAIS up and running, you have some important tasks to perform:

◆ Make the service as secure as possible

◆ Provide content for indexing and distribution

This chapter describes all the waisindex options and all the document types that it can index.

Making waisserver Secure

Chapter 17, "Network Security," discusses security issues in greater detail and suggests industrial-strength security systems. There are several important things you can do with WAIS service directly, however, to increase its level of security.

Changing the User

Because waisserver runs on port 210, a Unix reserved port, you must start the service as root. All processes binding to waisserver must also run as root.

Because devious minds love to gain root access to a system, it is prudent to change the user of waisserver right after it starts. You can do that by using the –u option. You associate a user ID with the option, for example:

```
# waisserver -u engr -l 10 -e /usr/local/wais/server/server.log -d /usr/local/
wais
```

To change to the user ID specified by the –u option automatically after service start up, include the –DSECURE_SERVER option in your CFLAGS definition.

The user ID you use with the –u option should have very restricted permissions. If someone gains access to the system, you do not want them to have root permissions, only the permissions of the user ID. So, set the permissions with the worst-case scenario in mind.

Restricting Service Access

You can restrict the clients that use waisserver by domain name. You can specify the domain names of hosts you want to service by:

◆ Uncommenting the following line in ir.h:

```
#define SERVSECURITYFILE        "SERV_SEC"
```

◆ Including the domain names in the file whose name is defined by the SERVSECURITYFILE variable in ir.h; the default is SERV_SEC. You have to create the SERV_SEC file. If it does not exist, the service grants every client access.

Place the SERV_SEC file in the same directory as the index files. Make sure that it is readable by the user waisserver is running as, but modifiable only by root (or the freeWAIS system administrator).

Each entry in SERV_SEC must have the following format:

```
domainName     [IP address]
```

domainName is the domain name of a host. The domainName is required; the IP address is optional. If you provide an optional IP address, clients then can gain access to the service by virtue of their domain name *or* IP address. If, for some reason, the host name does not match the IP address, access is given to both the domain name and the IP address; freeWAIS does not treat this as an error.

To grant access to your service only by folks at Silicon Graphics and the host warp.engr.mit.edu, for example, your SERV_SEC would look like the following:

```
sgi.com          198.33.422.12 warp.engr.mit.edu
```

Notice that you have to use the entire domain name to identify a host.

If you use an IP address in SERV_SEC, you have to be careful not to inadvertently grant access to more networks than you intend. If you grant access to 198.33.233.1, for example, waisserver permits access to all addresses that have the same prefix, including 198.33.233.10 through 198.33.233.19. Be careful to provide the full address.

Likewise, you can inadvertently grant access to more than one network. If you define the network as 198.23, for example, networks 198.230 through 198.239 gain access to the system. To permit access to the entire network 198.23, but not 198.230 through 198.239, use a trailing period—198.23., for example.

Controlling Access to Sources

You can restrict the clients that use database by domain name. You can specify the domain names of hosts you want to service by:

◆ Uncommenting the following line in ir.h:

```
#define DATASECURITYFILE      "DATA_SEC"
```

◆ Including the domain names in the file whose name is defined by the DATASECURITYFILE variable in ir.h; the default is DATA_SEC. You have to create the DATA_SEC file. If the file does not exist, every host has access to every source. If the file does exist and a source is not named in the file, no one has access to the database.

Place the DATA_SEC file in the same directory as the index files. Make sure that it is readable by the user waisserver is running as, but modifiable only by root (or the freeWAIS system administrator).

The entries in the DATA_SEC file must have the following format:

```
dataBaseName     domainName     [IP address]
```

Only `domainName` and `[IP address]` have access to `dataBaseName`. The domain name is required; the IP address is optional.

waisserver enables you to use the wild card asterisk (*) to make your life easier. For example,

```
welcome     *     *
```

grants all hosts access to the database, `welcome`.

If you provide an optional IP address, clients then can gain access to the database source by virtue of their domain name *or* IP address. If, for some reason, the host name does not match the IP address, access is given to both the domain name and the IP address; freeWAIS does not treat this as an error.

To grant access to your database source only by folks at Silicon Graphics and the host warp.engr.mit.edu, for example, your DATA_SEC would look like the following:

```
welcome     sgi.com          198.33.422.12
welcome     warp.engr.mit.edu
```

Notice that you have to use the entire domain name to identify a host.

If you use an IP address in DATA_SEC, you have to be careful not to inadvertently grant access to more networks than you intend. If you grant access to 198.33.233.1, for example, freeWAIS permits access to all addresses that have the same prefix, including 198.33.233.10 through 198.33.233.19. Be careful to provide the full address.

Likewise, you can inadvertently grant access to more than one network. If you define the network as 198.23, for example, networks 198.230 through 198.239 gain access to the system. To permit access to the entire network 198.23, but not 198.230 through 198.239, use a trailing period—198.23., for example.

A Security Caveat

As mentioned before, the industrial-strength security comes from constructing a firewall that separates your local network or Intranet from the Internet. Firewalls prevent requests from reaching you directly. That means that returns from a freeWAIS service cannot reach your machine on the local network. (ftp requests fail for the same reason.)

To get around this problem, you have to set up the computer that functions as your company's gateway to the Internet (that contains the firewall) as a forwarding freeWAIS server. The following two steps enable you to do that:

◆ Change the ui/source.c code.

◆ Modify the source description files used by your freeWAIS clients.

In ui/source.c, there is a commented-out line that starts with

```
/* #define FORWARDER_SERVER
```

That is just what you want to define. Uncomment the line and follow it with the domain name of the gateway machine. Call it fire.bus.com, for example:

```
/* #define FORWARDER_SERVER "fire.bus.com"
```

The source description files for your freeWAIS client start something like the following:

```
(:source
    :version 3
    :ip-address "198.33.22.11"
    :ip-name "rocket.science.edu"
    :tcp-port 210
    :database-name "rockets"
    .
    .
    .
```

Change the `ip-address` and `ip-name` definitions to that of the gateway machine, and modify the entry for the `database-name`, as in the following example:

```
(:source
    :version 3
    :ip-address "198.55.44.33"
    :ip-name "fire.bus.com"
    :tcp-port 210
    :database-name "rockets@rocket.science.edu"
    .
    .
    .
```

After you make these changes, it appears that the freeWAIS client has direct access to the Internet when, in fact, it is using the Internet host as an intermediary.

Providing Content

Now that you have a running, secure service, it is a good idea to offer some content, at least a little more than the files generated by the waisindex.test script described in the preceding chapter. The job of populating the database with source material is an ongoing one. It requires an understanding of the subject matter and the means by which it might be searched.

The primary tool used to create free sources is *waisindex*. The terminology surrounding waisindex is a bit tricky. waisindex takes data files of all types and creates seven or more index files that contain, for example, a list of each unique word used in a document. These index files are combined into one database called *WAIS source*, or just *source*. The waisserver compares the WAIS source with search criteria supplied by the WAIS client requests to see whether there is a match.

Understanding What waisindex Does

waisindex extracts from the raw data files (that WAIS is indexing) all the pertinent data it needs to fill multiple index files used by waisserver to match search criteria to data files.

 Note In this chapter, data file is used as a generic term to represent all file types, such as text and GIF.

Parsing the data files before a WAIS client makes a request reduces the amount of time it takes waisserver to determine to what extent there is a match between search criteria and the data files. The only down side is that the WAIS sources consume a significant amount of disk space, often equaling the size of the raw data files.

The command-line options you can use with waisindex follow:

Command-Line Option	Description
-a	Appends to existing index
-contents	Indexes file contents
-d	Specifies the base filename for the index files
-e filename	Specifies log file for error information; default is stderr, or /dev/null if -s is selected

Command-Line Option	Description
-export	Adds host name and tcp port to the source description to enable Internet access
-l	Specifies log level
-M	Links data files of multiple types
-mem	Restricts memory usage during indexing; the higher the number, the faster the indexing
-nocontents	Prevents the indexing of file contents
-nopairs	Prevents adjacent, capitalized words from being indexed together
-nopos	Prevents proximity of keywords in data file from influencing relevance feedback
-pairs	Indexes adjacent, capitalized words together
-pos	Uses proximity of keywords in data file to influence relevance feedback
-r	Indexes subdirectories recursively
-register	Registers your sources with the Directory of Services
-stdin	Enables you to enter filenames from the keyboard (standard input)
-stop	Specifies a file that contains stopwords
-t	Specifies data file type
-T *type*	Sets the type of data file to *type*

You should use the -a option when you just want to update the index files. This saves the time it would take to regenerate all of the files. If a file that was indexed is changed, and the update contains the new index entries, however, the old index entries remain. These old entries both take up space and may lead to erroneous results. Periodically, you must reindex all of the files.

To save disk space, you can exclude the contents of files from being indexed by using the -nocontents option. Even with this option, the header and filename are still indexed. The default is -contents, include the contents of the file in the index.

The -d option specifies the base filename of the index files, for example, if you use

```
-d /usr/local/common
```

the index files are called /usr/local/common.dct, /usr/local/common.fn, and so on.

The only logging levels that have meaning are as follows:

0	do not log
1	log errors and warnings of very high priority
5	log medium-priority events, including indexing filename information
10	log every event

WAIS Index Files

Let's look in more detail at the seven index files that waisindex creates from raw data files. Six of the seven are not human readable. The Source Description (.src) file is meant to be read by people.

Inverted File (index.inv)

The Inverted file contains a table that associates the following elements:

◆ Every unique word found in all the data files.

◆ A pointer to all the data files a word is in.

◆ The importance of the word in the data file, based on how close the word is to the beginning of the data file, and the number of times the word occurs in the data file divided by the number of words in the data file. The higher the percentage, the more likely the word describes the subject matter of the data file.

Document File (index.doc)

The Document file contains a table associating the following elements:

◆ **filename_id.** Specifies which database file the data file is in (there can be more than one database file of data files)

◆ **headline_id.** A pointer to the associated headline for the data file

◆ **start_character.** The location of the start of a data file in the database file

- ◆ **end_character.** The location of the end of a data file in the database file

- ◆ **document_length.** The number of characters in a document

- ◆ **number_of_lines.** The number of lines in a document

- ◆ **time_t.** The date the document was created

Filename File (index.fn)

The Filename file contains a table that lists the filenames of the database along with their write-dates and the type of file it is.

Headline File (index.hl)

The Headline file is a table that contains a list of all the headlines of all the documents in the source. A *headline* is a short description of the data file that is returned to the WAIS client when the data file appears to satisfy the search criteria.

Dictionary File (index.dct)

The Dictionary file contains a list of every unique word in the data files. These words are arranged alphabetically. Each word is matched with a pointer to the Inverted file so that, when the search criteria matches one of the words in the Dictionary file, waisserver can tell which data file the word is part of.

Source Description File (index.src)

The Source Description file contains basic descriptions of the source information, including the following:

- ◆ The name and IP address of the host on which it runs

- ◆ The port the service monitors

- ◆ The source's name

- ◆ Cost information for using the source

- ◆ The e-mail address of the person maintaining the source

- ◆ The headline

- ◆ A description of the source

If a source description file already exists, waisindex does not create a new one unless you have edited it enough so that waisindex considers it significantly different than the original version. If you change basic information about the source, like the host it runs on, you can delete the file and rerun waisindex to make sure the changes are reflected in the source file. If you choose to add a description of the source, you must maintain that manually.

waisindex does not really supply much of a description of the source. Because this is a file designed to be read by others, you might want to beef up the source description. You also might specify a different e-mail address for people to consult if you know who is charged with maintaining the source.

Here's an example of a source file:

```
(:source
     :version 2
     :ip-address "198.32.121.3"
     :ip-name "kiln.asd.sgi.com
     :tcp-port 210
     :database-name "graphics libraries"
     :cost 0.00
     :cost-unit :free
     :maintainer "librarian@kiln.asd.sgi.com"
     :subjects "major graphics libraries"
     :description
"Server created with WAIS-8 on Mon Mar 5 04:45:32 by warp@sgi.com"
```

As you can see, the description section is a little wanting. It would be worth your while to add to it.

You also might supply an alias for a source maintainer to avoid the problem of trying to maintain in each source file who maintains the source.

Status File (index.status)

The Status file has a table that contains user-defined parameters.

Determining the Relevance Ranking

waisindex uses an algorithm to determine, as best as it can, how closely a source matches the search criteria supplied by the WAIS client. The algorithm returns a number between 0 and 1,000, with 1,000 being a perfect match, based on the following factors:

◆ **Word location.** waisindex uses the position of the word in the source to assign it a high, medium, or low value. If the word appears in the headline, the data file receives the highest value. If the word is capitalized in the data file, the data file receives a medium value. If the word simply occurs in the body of the data file, it receives the lowest value.

◆ **Word occurrence.** waisindex divides the number of times a word occurs by the number of words in a data file. The higher the fraction, the more likely the search criteria describes the subject matter of the data file, and the higher the relevance ranking.

◆ **Word commonalty.** If waisindex finds a word in many documents, the word is given less value in determining the relevance ranking than if the word had been found in only one document. The idea behind this calculation is that if 100 data files use a word, probably none of them are about the word; whereas, if only several data files contain a particular word, chances are higher that those data files actually are about the word. If waisindex finds the word "entomology" in 1,000 data files, for example, it's hard to know which, if any, of the data files really are about entomology. If, however, only two data files contain the word, chances are better that the main theme of one or both of the data files is entomology.

◆ **Word groupings.** If the selection criteria is a group of words, waisindex assigns a data file a higher relevance ranking if the words occur together than if they occur far apart in the data file. If the search criteria is "cost of living," for example, finding that phrase or "of living costs" is more likely to satisfy the search requirements than if the words were spread throughout a data file.

Stopwords are words that are too common to warrant indexing. Common stopwords are "and," "a," and "the." freeWAIS version 0.4 comes with 389 predefined stopwords in the src/ir/stoplist.c file. If you want to add more stopwords for all documents, simply add to the stoplist.c file.

If you want to add more stopwords for specific documents only, create your own stopword file that includes all the words in /stoplist.c plus your additions. To use this file, use the –stop <*filename*> option with waisindex, where *filename* is the name of the stopword file.

You must include in your file all the stopwords in /stoplist.c, because waisindex does not use /stoplist.c if another stop file is named on the command line with the –stop option.

Indexing Different Data File Types

You have to tell waisindex what kind of information is contained in a data file so that it can index it correctly. Currently, waisindex can handle more than 30 data file types. To see all of the supported types, execute the waisindex command with no arguments, as follows:

```
# waisindex
```

The types describe the following:

◆ The content of the data file

◆ What to use as the headline

◆ Whether to index the contents of a file

◆ How a data file is divided

If a data file consists of a TIFF image, for example, you probably do not want the binary code indexed. Usually, one document is in one data file. waisindex can index separately many documents in one file, however, if they are separated by at least 20 dashes.

To define a data type when indexing a data file, use the –t option, as in the following example:

```
% waisindex –d newSource –t text –r /usr/resources/*
```

This line indexes all the subdirectories under /usr/resources as type text.

The most common data file types follow:

Data File Type	Description
dash	Tells waisindex that more than one document is in each file, and that the documents are separated by 20 or more dashes. Each dash-delimited document is indexed separately, and the first line of each document is used as a headline.
dvi and ps	Indicate printer-oriented formats (device-independent TeX and PostScript). waisindex assumes that there is one document in each file, so it indexes each file separately, and uses the filename for the headline.

Data File Type	Description
filename	Handled identically to the text type, except that the filename, instead of the pathname, is used as the headline.
first_line	Handled identically to text, except that the first line of the data file, instead of the pathname, is used as the headline.
ftp	Contains FTP code so that the user can FTP from another server. waisindex indexes the README and INDEX files on remote servers. WAIS clients can search this index and then FTP the file automatically if there is a match. This is an uncommon file type, but a very powerful one.
GIF, PICT, and TIFF	Used with files of images in their respective formats. waisindex assumes that one image is in each file, but it does not index the contents of the file. It simply uses the filename as the headline so that users can search by image name (or, at least, by filename).
mail_digest	Takes standard mail and indexes them as individual messages. The subject field of each message is used as a headline.
mail_or_rmail	Takes standard Unix mailbox files (mbox) and indexes them as individual messages. The subject field of each mailbox file is used as a headline.
netnews	Enables waisindex to index each standard News file separately. For headlines, waisindex uses the subject field of each file.
one_line	Splits up a file into sentences; each sentence is indexed separately. The sentence is its own headline. Because this data file is indexed line by line, waissearch can be very specific about locating the search criteria in a document. This data file type, however, is memory intensive.
text	Indexes the entire file as though it were one document. The pathname is used as the headline. This type is the most common.

continues

Data File Type	Description
URL	Enables waisindex to use, as headlines for files, valid URLs by stripping off part of a pathname and replacing that part with another path-like description. For example,

```
% waisindex -d newSource -t URL /usr/
resources ftp://kiln.asd.sgi.com -r /usr/
resources/*
```

indexes the files in all the subdirectories under /usr/resources. It provides as a headline for each file its pathname, stripped of /usr/resources, and replaced by http://kiln.asd.sgi.com. So, if waissearch found that file /usr/resources/alpha/ beta matched the selection requirements, waissearch would display the headline as `http://kiln.asd.sgi.com/alpha/beta`. This format enables your WAIS service to support WWW browsers. The only down side to the URL data file type is that older WAIS clients also return URL-valid headlines. If users are unfamiliar with URLs, they might be confused by the pathname.

Be careful to use the correct data file format when indexing your files. Indexing files incorrectly can prevent them from being viewed. Some WAIS clients, such as xwais, use the data file format to determine what kind of viewer to use to display a data file. If you format a GIF file as PICT, for example, GIF viewers cannot view the GIF file because it is indexed as a PICT file.

Indexing Undefined Data File Types

waisindex can index just about every kind of file that exists. There are some file formats that it cannot index, however, such as MIME files. For such a condition, you use the –T option (instead of –t) to declare the format of the file. The default action is not to index the contents of the file and to use the filename as the headline. If you want the contents indexed, you add the –contents option (it has no argument) to the waisindex command. Even though waisindex does not understand the data file format, everything works fine as long as the WAIS client understands the format. waisserver sends the data file to the client as if it were a binary file.

If a data file type is indexed by default, and you do not want the content of the file to be indexed, use the –nocontent option.

Making Data Files Available to WWW Browsers

You can make your WAIS source files searchable by multimedia WWW browsers, such as Mosaic or Netscape. To do so, execute waisindex with the –T option, for example,

```
% waisindex -d WWW -T HTML -contents -export /usr/resources/*html
```

Now WAIS clients can do keyword searches on HTML documents.

Indexing Multiple Files for WWW Browsers

Sometimes it is nice to give users a little more than they asked for. If the user does a search on the words "Tasmanian Devil," for example, it might be nice to let the user know that not only does your source have a document about the devil, but it also has a video clip and still image of the devil. To associate each of these files with one another, you have to format the names of the files correctly.

To associate files, all the *base names* (the part of the name before the period and the extension) must be the same, and the extensions must be in all capitals. Your directory might look like the following:

```
% ls
Devil.TEXT
Devil.GIF
DeviL.MPEG
```

You use the –M option to associate the files, as in the following example:

```
% waisindex -d Tasmanian -M TEXT,GIF,MPEG  -export *
```

Now when one of the files is selected, the WWW browser displays buttons that lead to the other, associated files.

Linking Files

You also can use the –a option to append files—especially files of different types. When people get your file about rockets, for example, you also might want them to get a nifty image in a GIF file. Generally, sources contain one data file type specified by the –t option. So how do you link files of different types?

You cannot actually mix the data file types, but you can append one data file type to another. In this case, you might index the text files about rockets and then append the image files, using –a, as in the following example:

```
# waisindex -d rockets -t text -r /usr/resources/aerospace
# waisindex -d rockets -t gif -a -r /usr/resources/aerospace/images
```

Using the -a option in this way enables text to be displayed as text and images to be displayed as images; and the source, `rockets`, contains both text and images.

Using Synonyms

Another way to lead users to related files is by setting up synonyms. Synonyms alleviate several problems, such as when a user looks up "stars," but not "astronomy," or the user looks up "TV" when your documents only use the term "television." When a user specifies a keyword, waisserver automatically looks up the synonyms as well, as defined in SOURCE.syn, which is located in the same directory as the other source files, such as SOURCE.cat.

Each entry in the SOURCE.syn file has the following syntax:

```
reference_word synonym {synonym...]
```

For example, you might have the following entry:

```
work job occupation employment joke
```

As a conscientious system administrator, you want to take a look at the log files for waisserver. If you have the log setting at 10, you can see what words people are using as search criteria. If you see that the service did not return any documents for a keyword, you might consider whether there is a synonym that would have satisfied the search criteria.

Specifying Source Options

There are several things you can do with source files:

- ◆ Name them with the –d <*name*> option.

- ◆ Export them with the –export option.

- ◆ Register them with the –register option.

- ◆ Update them with the –a option.

Throughout this chapter, the examples have used –d to name the source file that is created by waisindex. The –export option adds the name of the host and the TCP port on which the service is running, to the source file. The clients use this information. If the –export option is not used, the service can only be used for local searches.

One service that everyone uses is called the *directory of services*. It lists all the source files (src) submitted to it. If anyone wants to find out what is new on the Internet, this is a logical place to look. The –register option automatically sends all your source files to the directory of services.

The system administrators of the directory of services reserve the right to delete your offering from the service if they find that your service often is down, or that it is not updated on a regular basis.

After you create source files, you need to update them when the files they represent change. You can update the source files in several ways, as follows:

◆ Reindex all the files using waisindex

◆ Reindex a subset of the files

◆ Append changes to the end of the source file using the –a option

Reindexing all the data files could be quite time consuming, depending on the number and size of the data files. Periodically, you have to bite the bullet and perform this function, but it is not something you want to do every time one of the data files changes a little.

If you put all your changes to the data files in one file, you can reindex just that file. Otherwise, you can add the changes to the end of the current source file by using the –a option with the waisindex command.

The larger your source, the larger the problem reindexing is. When you reindex, your service is unavailable to users. So, if your indexing takes an hour or more, you might want to consider alternatives to turning off your system. You have the following two options:

◆ Create the new source in a different directory and then move or rename the new source so that it replaces the old one

◆ Add on to the end of the file using the –a option

The first option is nice only if you have disk space to hold multiple copies of your source—a luxury that some cannot afford. You can create a simple cron job that executes waisindex in a directory other than your production directory. When it finishes, simply move the new source to the production directory and remove the source in the nonproduction directory.

To add source information to the current source for a new set of files, use the –a option, as in the following example:

```
# waisindex -d Cats -t URL -a -r /usr/resources/felines/newSpecies
```

Logging Messages During Indexing

waisindex can send status messages to a log file if you use the –e and –l options, where the argument of –e is the path and name of the logfile, and the –l option defines the logging level.

Logging levels range from 0 to 10. Following –l with 0 turns off logging. Level 1 logs only high-priority messages, level 5 also logs medium-priority messages, and level 10 logs all messages. The log messages just relate the status of the indexing process.

Indexing Controls

You might have directories that you do not want waisindex to index—for example, image files and files in the /tmp directory. To exclude the files in a directory from being indexed, include its name on the command line:

```
% waisindex -d presidents /tmp
```

If, on the other hand, you want waisindex to recursively index directories, use the –r *<directoryName>* option:

```
% waisindex -d Devils -r /usr/resources/Tasmanian
```

This line indexes all the files under /Tasmanian and creates a source file called Devils.

Relative Position of Words

When the search criteria contains more than one word, it is possible to take into account how close the words are in a document when computing the relevancy score. The default, however, is not to use that information in the relevancy score. To override the default value, use the –pos option. (The reverse option is –nopos.)

If two capitalized words are adjacent, waisindex adds them together to the dict file. If you know that this is inappropriate for your document, use the –nopairs option.

Freeing Memory and Disk Space

WAIS source files find a way to ravenously eat up disk space, and waisindex loves to consume CPU cycles. If you find that your disk space is low or your system performance is poor, you can use two options with waisindex to conserve disk space: –mem and –nocat.

The –mem <*numberMbytes*> option enables you to specify the maximum number of megabytes of memory you want waisindex to use. Of course, when you restrict the amount of memory waisindex can use, you slow down its execution. If you have to run waisindex in the background, consider using this option.

Setting Up a Gopher Service

I f you have ever run around a file system using simple Unix commands such as ls and cd, you are familiar with the model Gopher uses to display files and directories on Gopher services. When you log onto a Gopher service and do not specify a directory to look at, the Gopher service automatically sends you a directory listing (like ls) of the root directory of the Gopher service, as shown in the following.

```
          Internet Gopher Information Client v2.0.16


              Home Gopher server: corp.sgi.com
-->     1. Introduction
        2. Preface
        3. New Developments/
        4. Special Effects/
        5. Magic Carpet/


Press ? for Help, q to Quit            Page:1/1
```

The preceding shows a combination of files and directories, just like a Unix listing. If you want to retrieve a file or move to a different directory, you simply select the one you want.

Although there are similarities between Gopher and basic Unix directory navigation, there are important differences:

◆ The Gopher listing contains headers and footers and an arrow that shows the entry you select to retrieve. ls, on the other hand, only lists names of files and directories.

◆ The names of files and directories displayed by Gopher are long and descriptive, whereas Unix file and directory names are generally not as long.

◆ Files (and directories) in Gopher lists can reside on different machines, whereas files in a Unix directory are generally on the same machine.

◆ When you select a file on a Gopher service, it downloads to the (Gopher) client machine. On a Unix system, you never download from a directory listing.

◆ The commands you use to access files and directories often are displayed at the bottom of the screen (which eliminates the burden of remembering Gopher commands), whereas Unix commands go only on the current command line.

The descriptive file (and directory) names give users some indication of what they can expect to find in a file. This is a nice feature; however, the limitations on the length of the name often pose problems and create confusion. Gopher+ solved this problem.

Gopher provides a transparent interface between services residing on different machines, so the user appears to access files from only one machine when, in reality, each file listed might reside on a different machine. These files can be offered by other Gopher services or other services altogether, such as an FTP service. This transparency eliminates the mental baggage imposed by FTP that forces you to consider the machine a document resides on.

Gopher services take care of other details automatically. If you download a compressed text file, for example, Gopher uncompresses it. If the file is archived, Gopher can untar it. If you download an image, Gopher generates an external viewer to display the image.

Gopher provides other features that make it as different from ls and cd as a seed is from a full-grown plant. For example, Unix gopher can do the following:

◆ Search local WAIS indexes

◆ Send queries to remote WAIS services and return results to gopher clients

◆ Send queries to remote FTP services and return results to gopher clients

◆ Answer queries sent by WWW clients that use HTTP or built-in Gopher querying methods

Other software supports Gopher; here are some highlights of some of the more interesting products:

Program	Description
Fwgstat	Creates a usage report of the service.
Glass	Produces 22 different service reports.
GLOG	Analyzes Gopher log files.
gopherdist	Returns the contents of any directory or file in Gopherspace.
Gophreport	Generates reports based on a variety of factors.
jughead	Stands for *Jonzy's universal Gopher hierarchy excavation and display*. Retrieves menu information from Gopher services.
Linkmerge	Merges directories from a selected set of Gopher services to which you can add your own Gopher resources.
veronica	Stands for *very easy rodent-oriented net-wide index to computerized archives*. Provides the capability to search, by keyword, most gopher-service menu titles in all the Internet-connected Gopher services.

As you can see, Gopher is well supported.

Versions of Gopher

There are two versions of Gopher that you can use:

◆ Gopher

◆ Gopher+

Gopher is freeware; Gopher+ is not. This chapter discusses the installation of Gopher+, because its added functionality makes it worth the licensing fees. If you choose to install Gopher, however, because Gopher+ is a superset of Gopher functionality, many of the installation options are the same. When in doubt, look at the INSTALL file that comes with the source code.

The following section presents an overview of Gopher+. Because Gopher+ contains all the functionality of Gopher, those functions are not repeated in the Gopher+ section.

A section at the end of this chapter describes the future of Gopher: GopherVR. Yes, virtual reality! It's a 3D version of Gopher. GopherVR is in the alpha stage of development, so it is not quite ready to use as a service yet.

Introducing Gopher+

Even a good thing can get better; such is the case with Gopher. Gopher+ incorporates all of Gopher's features and enables you to perform additional tasks:

◆ Retrieve extended information, called *file attributes*, about a Gopher file

◆ Return several files when selecting just one menu item—for example, a plain text and PostScript version of the same text

◆ Retrieve a description of the file, called a *file abstract*

◆ Retrieve documents based on forms filled out by the user

These Gopher+ features only work with Gopher+ clients (and WWW browsers). Gopher clients can access Gopher+ services, but Gopher clients cannot use any of the advanced features. Likewise, Gopher+ clients can access Gopher services.

Understanding Gopher and Gopher+ File Attributes

File attributes provide valuable information about files. Gopher file attributes include the following:

Attribute	Description
Host	Name or IP address of the service host
Name	Name of the file as shown in the menu
Path	Path and name of the file—for example, top/intro
Port	Port number (usually 70) associated with the Gopher service
Type	Type of document file
URL	WWW URL pathname

The Type attribute identifies what a menu item is in a Gopher listing. Gopher recognizes a variety of menu item types, including the following:

Type Reference Number	Type of Document
0	File
1	Directory
2	CSO (qi) phone-book server
3	Error

Type Reference Number	Type of Document
4	BinHexed Macintosh file
5	DOS binary archive of some sort
6	Unix uuencoded file
7	Index-Search server
8	Points to a text-based telnet session
9	Binary file
g	GIF type
h	html type
I	Image type
I	Inline text type
M	MIME type; item contains MIME
P	Adobe Portable Document Format (PDF)
s	Sound type; data stream is a mulaw sound
T	TN3270 connection

Gopher+ adds the following attributes to the Gopher list:

Attribute	Description
Admin	Name and e-mail address of the system administrator responsible for the file or directory
Document Type	Description of the file type—for example, text/plain
Language	Language in which the document is written
ModDate	Date file or directory was updated last
Size	Size of file in bytes

In addition, the abstract of the file provides valuable information for people trying to find topics without having to download the file and read it. You can get this information by pressing the equal sign (=) when the Gopher arrow is pointing at a menu item. The following printout shows what you get with a Gopher client when you push the equals sign when "Introduction" is selected.

```
Link Info (ok)                                          100%
+-------------------------------------------------+
#
Type=1
Name=Introduction
Path=top/intro
Host=corp.sgi.com
Port=70
URL: gopher://corp.sgi.com:70/top/intro
A Gopher+ display looks more like the following:
Link Info (ok)                                          100%
```

The following is a display of a Gopher+ client for the same file, "Introduction."
Compare the Gopher and the Gopher+ displays to see the differences.

```
    -------------------------------------------------+
#
Type=1
Name=Introduction
Path=top/intro
Host=corp.sgi.com
Port=70
Admin=Rick <gopherAdmin@corp.sgi.com>
ModDate=Sat Apr 9 09:18:53 1995 <19950410091853>
URL: gopher://corp.sgi.com:70/top/intro

ABSTRACT
    -------------------------------------------------+


The introduction describes the layout of resources on this Gopher service. This
file can save you time in searching for documents.


Size            Language           Document Type
----            --------           ------------
8k              English (USA)      text/plain
14k             English (USA)      application/FrameMaker


+-------------------------------------------------+
[Help: ?]  [Exit: u]
```

The Gopher+ attribute listing shows that the Introduction comes in two formats:
one is in plain text, and the other is in the FrameMaker format. If you select the

Introduction, which version of the Introduction you get depends on the Gopher client. The simple Gopher client enables you to choose between the two versions.

Using Gopher+ Forms

In Gopher+ menu listings, menu items followed by <??> indicate that they display forms after you select them. The following shows an example of such a listing.

```
              Internet Gopher Information Client v2.0.16


                    Home Gopher server: corp.sgi.com


  -->       1. Introduction
            2. Newsletter Sign-up <??>
            3. New Developments/


Press ? for Help, q to Quit                      Page:1/1
```

If you select menu item 2, the Gopher service returns a form for the user to complete (see fig. 13.1).

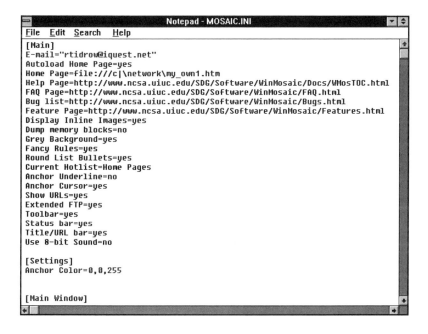

Figure 13.1

A Gopher+ form.

Choosing the Service Software

There are three major sources for Gopher service software:

◆ University of Minnesota (freeware version 1.3) Gopher

◆ University of Minnesota version 2.13 Gopher+

◆ GN Public License

The University of Minnesota is the major development site for Gopher service software. The earlier version of the service software, 1.13, is free to all. However, the University is no longer adding functionality to Gopher. Their effort is going into Gopher+.

The later version of the software, 2.13, is free if you are creating a Gopher service for an educational institution. There is a licensing fee for businesses using the service, however. The fee structure is described in the next section.

The GN version of Gopher is similar to the freeware version of the University of Minnesota's. This software doubles as a WWW service. It is a nice combination and deserves your attention.

Note GN's WWW service, at present, is not robust. It does not, for example, support the Common Gateway Interface (CGI).

Note Most of the installation and configuration information for Gopher is identical to that for Gopher+. When in doubt, refer to the INSTALL file that comes with the software.

Licensing Gopher+

The Gopher+ team at the University of Minnesota felt it necessary to start charging for the service software because of the exigencies of being a cost center at the university.

There are three general classes of Gopher+ service providers:

◆ Government and educational institutions

◆ Businesses that produce a gross income of less than $3.5 million per year

◆ All other businesses

All licenses expire one year after the effective date of the agreement.

Small Business Fee Structure

The Gopher+ license fee is $100 if the following conditions are met:

◆ The service does not offer products or services for sale.

◆ There is no charge for access to or information retrieved from the service.

The Gopher+ license fee is $500 if the following conditions are met:

◆ The service is accessible from the Internet.

◆ Products and services are offered for sale through the service.

◆ There is no charge for access to or information retrieved from the service.

The Gopher+ license fee is $500 or 2.5 percent of the total amount charged to Gopher service users (whichever is larger) if the following condition is met:

◆ There is no charge for access to or information retrieved from the service.

Standard Fee Structure

The Gopher+ license fee is $100 per service if the following conditions are met:

◆ The service does not offer products or services for sale.

◆ There is no charge for access to or information retrieved from the service.

The Gopher+ license fee is $2,500 per service if the following conditions are met:

◆ The service is accessible from the Internet.

◆ Products and services are offered for sale through the service.

◆ There is no charge for access to or information retrieved from the service.

The Gopher+ license fee is $2,500 or 2.5 percent of the total amount charged to Gopher service users (whichever is larger) if the following conditions are met:

◆ There is no charge for access to or information retrieved from the service.

◆ The business is not an educational or governmental institution, and it earns over $3.5 million per year.

Getting the Service Software

To get the software for Gopher+, use ftp to get the source from the following host:

```
% ftp boombox.micro.unm.edu /pub/gopher/Unix
```

I had trouble with this address, but the IP address worked fine:

```
% ftp 134.84.132.2
```

You also can point your WWW browser at URL:

```
ftp://boombox.micro.umn.edu/pub/gopher;
```

To contact the University of Minnesota, you can send e-mail to
gopher@boombox.micro.umn.edu. Or, send a letter to this address:

> Internet Gopher Developers
> 100 Union St. SE #190
> Minneapolis, MN 55455
> Fax: (612) 625-6817

After connecting and logging into boombox, which, because of its popularity, is no small feat, you should change to the correct directory (Unix), list the contents, and pick out the latest version of the software. The following shows what appears on-screen.

```
ftp> cd pub/gopher/Unix
250 CWD command successful.
ftp> ls
200 PORT command successful.
150 Opening ASCII mode data connection for /bin/ls.
total 10194
-rw-rw-r— 1 1147 bin 29865 Feb 26 08:32 2_1_2to2_1_3.patch
drwxr-xr-x 9 1147 bin 1536 Mar 24 08:22 GopherTools
-rw-r—r— 1 1147 bin 648 Aug 24 1994 MIRROR.LOG
-rw-r—r— 1 1147 bin 972547 Oct 7 1991 NeXTtext.tar.Z
drwxr-xr-x 2 root bin 512 Sep 2 1994 ask-examples
...
-rw-r—r— 1 1147 bin 306508 Mar 8 1994 gopher1.13.tar.Z
drwxr-xr-x 2 1147 bin 512 May 31 1994 gopher2.0-patches
-rw-r—r— 1 1147 bin 426337 Jun 30 1994 gopher2.016.tar.Z
-rw-rw-r— 1 1147 bin 579000 Feb 26 08:26 gopher2_1_3.tar.Z
...
226 Transfer complete.
```

Use the FTP get command to download the service software, as shown in the following.

```
ftp> get gopher2_1_3.tar.Z
local: gopher2_1_3.tar.Z remote: gopher2_1_3.tar.Z
200 PORT command successful.
150 Opening BINARY mode data connection for gopher2_1_3.tar.Z (579000 bytes).
226 Transfer complete.
579000 bytes received in 32.30 seconds (17.51 Kbytes/s)
```

You find the source code listed in your current directory as the following:

```
gopher2_1_3.tar.Z
```

You need to uncompress and tar this file by using the following command:

```
warp 149% zcat gopher2_1_3.tar.Z ¦ tar -xvf -
```

Your workstation then happily spits out gobs of updated information that you do not have to pay attention to unless you see error messages.

```
warp 149% zcat gopher2_1_3.tar.Z ¦ tar -xvf -
tar: blocksize = 16
x gopher2_1_3/doc/INSTALL, 4311 bytes, 9 blocks
x gopher2_1_3/doc/Makefile, 534 bytes, 2 blocks
x gopher2_1_3/doc/TODO, 686 bytes, 2 blocks
x gopher2_1_3/doc/admit1.setup, 759 bytes, 2 blocks
x gopher2_1_3/doc/client.changes, 38996 bytes, 77 blocks
x gopher2_1_3/doc/clientlogging.vms, 9612 bytes, 19 blocks
x gopher2_1_3/doc/gindexd.changes, 2819 bytes, 6 blocks
x gopher2_1_3/doc/gindexd.doc, 6666 bytes, 14 blocks
x gopher2_1_3/doc/gopher.1, 7440 bytes, 15 blocks
...
```

If you list your current directory, you see that a new directory was created:

```
%ls
gopher2_1_3
gopher2_1_3.tar.Z
```

When you change to the new directory, gopher2_1_3, and list the contents, you see the files and directories, shown as follows.

```
Copyright           Makefile.config.dist    doc         make.com
MANIFEST            README                  gopher      object
Makefile            conf.h                  gopherd     patchlevel.h
Makefile.config     copyright               gophfilt    test
```

The contents of these files follow:

Directory	Description
conf.h	A list of service and client configuration options.
doc	A directory that contains the documentation for all parts of the software distribution, including the Gopher service, the Gopher client, revision notes (*.changes), installation (INSTALL), and configuration notes.
gopher	A Gopher, text-based client application.
gopherd	The Gopher+ service application.
gophfilt	A Gopher filter program.
make.com	Some routines that make uses when running on a VMS machine.
Makefile	The Makefile you use to build the service and client applications.
Makefile.config	The list of compile-time variables you can configure before running Makefile. You should edit this file and conf.h, not the Makefile file, when specifying configuration options.
Makefile.config.dist	A reference copy of Makefile.config so that you always can revert to it.
MANIFEST	A list of all the files in all the directories in gopher2_1_3.
object	A directory of, among other things, libraries, sockets, and arrays used by the service and client applications.
patchlevel.h	#defines of the version numbers of the service and client applications.
README	The file that describes some of the directories in the distribution and recognizes individuals for their contributions.
test	A directory that contains, among other things, sample data.

Gazing into the Future of Gopher Services

The next release of Gopher will be a complete rewrite of the code, called GopherVR. It uses 3D scenes as a user interface for surfing the Internet and displaying relationships between documents. The alpha version of Unix GopherVR clients is available by using gopher and anonymous ftp from

```
boombox.micro.umn.edu
```

in /gopher/Unix/GopherVR. You can retrieve the code by using the following URLs:

```
GOPHER://boombox.micro.umn.edu/11/gopher/Unix/GopherVR
FTP://boombox.micro.umn.edu/pub/gopher/Unix/GopherVR/
```

GopherVR binaries (only) are currently available only for SUN Sparc, SGI, and IBM AIX RS-6000 platforms.

In this alpha-test release, you can do the following:

◆ Browse through Gopher directories by driving around Gopherspace

◆ Move between Gopher services by driving through 3D scenes

◆ Open objects by clicking them

◆ Retrieve information about the neighborhood you are in

◆ Retrieve descriptive information about objects

For the latest information about GopherVR, subscribe to gopher-news by e-mailing to this address:

```
gopher-news-request@boombox.micro.umn.edu
```

Major Gopher software releases are announced on gopher-announce. To subscribe to gopher-announce, send e-mail to this address:

```
gopher-announce-request@boombox.micro.umn.edu
```

The Future of GopherVR

Future versions of GopherVR will incorporate the following features:

◆ Definition of 3D icons for objects in Gopherspace

◆ Placement of objects in 3D scenes

◆ Additional navigation features that enable users to browse in the 3D scenes

Managing a Gopher Service

Managing a Gopher service is crucial to its success. As a system administrator, you are responsible for the architecture of the file system and the naming of files and directories. The choices you make, in this regard, determine the usability of the service interface—no small responsibility!

Your job also includes reviewing the log files to see how often your service is being used, and to see which files and directories are used. Also, you need to set a number of configuration variables.

Editing the gopherd.conf File

The gopherd.conf file sets configuration options for the Gopher service. The settings are straightforward. You might not need to change any settings from their default values. In this section, you examine all the options. Remember, changing the configuration can be as simple as uncommenting or commenting out a line in the configuration file. Don't delete lines; that action can come back to haunt you.

Creating an Alias for the Service

It is not a good idea to tie a specific machine to your Gopher service. There are times when you might replace the machine or split the Gopher service across machines. Instead, you should create an alias for the machine. Then, when you move your service to a new machine, you simply point the alias at it.

To create an alias, you use the hostalias keyword:

```
hostalias: host_alias
```

where `host_alias` is the alias for your server that is returned to Gopher/Gopher+ clients. Before a client can access a Gopher/Gopher+ service using the host_alias name, you must create an entry in your Domain Name Service (DNS).

Setting Cache Times

You can set the length of time a cache file remains valid by using the cachetime keyword:

```
Cachetime: time_seconds
```

where `time_seconds` is the duration in seconds of the cache file. To hold a file for 180 seconds, for example, use this entry:

```
Cachetime: 180
```

Checking File Decoders

When users request a file, they can add an extension to it, such as .Z or .gz. Gopher recognizes these extensions and, in this case, compresses the file using zcat before sending it to the client. The file decoder section of the configuration file links extensions to associated programs.

gopherd.conf, by default, has two file decoders enabled and two commented out (with the pound sign).

```
decoder: .Z /usr/ucb/zcat
decoder: .gz /usr/gnu/bin/zcat
#decoder: .adpcm /usr/openwin/bin/adpcm_dec
#decoder: .z /usr/gnu/bin/zcat
```

In this example, the .Z extension accesses the compression program, zcat, located in /usr/ucb. You might find other extensions to include in this section—for example, tar.

Limiting Concurrent Sessions

The PIDS_Directory variable identifies the location of the file that specifies the maximum number of concurrent service requests the service will handle. The more requests, the slower the performance. The fewer the requests the service accepts, the more frustrated users get who cannot access the service. You must find your own middle ground between system performance and satisfying user demand.

This part of the service, as of this writing, is still under major revision. You might want to ignore this variable until it becomes more stable.

The default in the configuration file is

```
#PIDS_Directory: /pids
```

As you can see, it is commented out by default. If you choose to uncomment it, make sure the file that contains the information, /pids in this example, is in part of the file system restricted by chroot().

Setting Maximum Number of Clients

You can use the MaxConnections keyword to define the maximum number of clients you want your service to handle. To have a maximum of 20 concurrent users, for example, use the entry:

```
MaxConnections: 20
```

Figuring Out File Contents

Gopher must know the correspondence between file extensions and gopher formats. The mapping, defined in gopherd.conf, establishes a standard notation so that

Gopher clients know whether they need to generate an external viewer to display Gopher information. The format for the mapping follows:

```
viewext: ext go-type pfx gopher+type ISO_language
```

in which `viewext` is the keyword that establishes the mapping. Explanations of this syntax follow:

Elements of viewext Entry	Description
ext	File extension
go-type	Gopher type number, as defined in the previous chapter
pfx	A prefix for the service's selector string
gopher+type	MIME document type
ISO_language	ISO abbreviation for the language of the document

For example,

```
viewext: .txt 0 0 Text/plain En_US
```

shows that the file extension, `.txt`, is equivalent to Gopher type 0, Text/plain, written in English.

The Gopher type number is one of the following:

Gopher type Number	Description
0	File
1	Directory
2	CSO (qi) phone-book server
3	Error
4	BinHexed Macintosh file
5	DOS binary archive of some sort
6	Unix uuencoded file
7	Index-Search server
8	Points to a text-based telnet session
9	Binary file
g	GIF type

Gopher type Number	Description
h	html type
I	Image type
i	inline text type
M	MIME type—item contains MIME data
P	Adobe Portable Document Format (PDF)
s	Sound type—data stream is a mulaw sound
T	TN3270 connection

The prefix used for the service's selector, pfx, is used as a quick way of parsing user requests. Generally, the value is set to 0, for text files, or 9, for binary files.

The Gopher+-type field is based on the definitions used for MIME. This information is important because it helps the Gopher client determine which application to begin so the document can be viewed. An image might start an xview window, for example.

The last field in the format is optional. It specifies the language the document is in. This field, of course, does not make much sense for image files. The convention is to use a two-letter (ISO-compliant) language code, followed by an underscore, followed by a two-letter country code (for example, Es_ES means Spanish from Spain).

There are many viewext definitions. The following is just a sample to give you a flavor:

```
# Different Languages
viewext: .txt.spanish 0 0 Text/plain Es_ES
viewext: .txt.portuguese 0 0 Text/plain Pt_PT

# Graphics file formats
viewext: .gif I 9 image/gif
viewext: .jpg I 9 image/JPEG
viewext: .tif I 9 image/tiff

# Sounds
viewext: .snd s s audio/basic
viewext: .wav s s audio/microsoft-wave

# Movies
viewext: .mov ; 9 video/quicktime
viewext: .mpg ; 9 video/mpeg

# Binary files..
viewext: .zip 5 9 application/zip
```

```
viewext: .tar 9 9 application/x-tar
viewext: .ps 0 9 application/postscript

# These are defined by IANA..
viewext: .rtf 0 0 application/rtf
viewext: .word 0 0 application/MSWord
```

There is also the promise that Gopher will recognize the file type automatically, as shown by the following definitions:

```
#magic 0 GIF 9 I Gif
#magic 0 snd s s audio/basic
```

Those definitions are not yet implemented, however.

You might find that you have document types not included in any viewext definition. You will have to define the new document type at that time. If you define a new document type, start the Gopher+ type field with an application. If you want to define a type for FrameMaker files, for example, you can use the following definition:

```
viewext: .frm 0 0 application/framemaker
```

Hiding Files Based on File Types

No doubt, there are files that you do not want visible to Gopher clients. You can use the keyword, ignore, to specify file extensions for such files. The extensions are not case-sensitive.

The following sample list shows you the file extensions included by default with the ignore keyword in gopherd.conf:

```
ignore: lost+found
ignore: lib
ignore: bin
ignore: etc
ignore: dev
ignore: ~
ignore: .cache
ignore: .cache+
ignore: .forward
ignore: .message
ignore: .hushlogin
ignore: .kermrc
ignore: .notar
ignore: .where
```

Many of these file extensions refer to system files that are not for general consumption.

You might add or subtract to this list according to the needs of your system. You should take care when adding to the list, however, that you do not currently have any filenames ending with the string you specify with the ignore keyword. If you add the following line, for example, any filename ending with that string (Making Money, for example) would be invisible to Gopher clients:

```
ignore: money
```

Using Character Patterns to Hide Files

The ignore keyword hides files from Gopher clients based on the ending of filenames. The ignore_patt keyword hides files whenever a pattern of letters occurs (anywhere) in a filename. The pattern of letters is case-sensitive.

Here are some sample patterns:

```
ignore_patt: ^core$
ignore_patt: ^usr$
ignore_patt: ^tmp$
```

Again, if you choose to add to this list, be careful not to hide files unintentionally.

Splitting Files into Multiple Parts

There might be times when you want to combine files and send them all at once to the Gopher client. This saves time and, perhaps, suggests an association between the group of files.

To distinguish separate documents that appear as one, you can use the filesep keyword to define characters that separate the documents. For example, you could use the following separator:

```
filesep: ^-------------------------------------------
```

Editing gopherdlocal.conf

There really are only a couple of lines that you must edit in the gopherdlocal.conf file. If you do not, however, it automatically publishes nasty little notes about your system administrator!

Identifying System Administrators

There are two keywords in gopherdlocal.conf that gopherd uses when it needs to identify system administrators:

◆ Admin

◆ AdminEmail

Follow the Admin keyword with the alias for the system administrator and any other contact information you want to include, such as a phone number or address.

Follow the AdminEmail keyword with the e-mail address of the system administrator alias.

The defaults follow:

```
Admin: blank
AdminEmail: blank
```

You therefore have little choice but to complete these lines, unless your system administrator's name is "blank," and their e-mail address is "blank."

Adding an Abstract

The keyword Abstract identifies a sentence as an abstract, or a concise description of what your service provides. The entire description needs to be on one line, so connect sentence fragments broken over a number of lines by using the backslash (\).

The default message follows:

```
Abstract: blank\
The server administrator has not set an abstract \
for this machine. Please ask them to do so!
```

Ouch! Better make sure not to skip this step.

Including Gopher Site Information

The next section of gopherdlocal.conf asks for general information about the Gopher site. By default, the following information headings are listed without content (except the last field):

```
Site: blank
Org: blank
Loc: blank
Geog: blank

Language: En_US
```

Descriptions of these headings follow:

Heading	Description
Site	Name of service
Org	Name of institution supporting service
Loc	City, state, and country where institution resides
Geog	Latitude and longitude of institution
Language	Language in which documents are written
TZ	Timezone in Greenwich Mean Time offset (the timezone field is not displayed by default)

Defining User Messages

The keyword BummerMsg specifies the reply that is dispatched automatically when users try to access the service inappropriately, or the service *load* (or number of users) is already at its maximum. Here is the default:

```
BummerMsg: We're sorry, we don't allow off-site access to this server
```

Defining Access Permission

The keyword access defines what users are allowed to do with Gopher data, and how many users can be working on the service at the same time.

The format of the keyword follows:

```
access:  hostName_IPAddress  permissions  #users
```

where hostName_IPAddress is the name of the host or its IP address, respectively; permissions specifies the permission set of service users; and #users specifies the maximum number of users that can be connected to the service at any one time.

The permissions follow:

- ◆ **Browse.** Denying someone the right to browse means that users cannot query directory contents; they can, however, access non-directory items.

- ◆ **Read.** Denying someone the right to read a file means that they receive the BummerMsg instead of the file when they ask to retrieve it.

- ◆ **Search.** Denying someone the right to search means that users cannot access indexes (Gopher type 7) that you have made available through Gopher+.

- ◆ **FTP.** Denying someone the right to FTP means that Gopher+ cannot act as a gateway to FTP services.

Consider this example:

```
access: sgi.corp.com  search !browse read !FTP  5
```

In this example, folks at sgi.corp.com can search and read files, but not browse and FTP them. Also, a maximum of five users at any time from sgi.corp.com can access the service.

You restrict a user from using these permissions by preceding the permission with an exclamation point (!). To deny someone the right to browse, for example, you can use this code:

```
access: 192.23.423.12 !browse
```

You also can use a partial IP address to limit everyone on a particular network to the defined access permissions:

```
access: 192.23. !browse
```

Be sure to include the period (.) after the 23. Otherwise, any IP address starting with 192.23 would have the same permissions—for example, 192.234.67.25 and everyone in 192.235 network.

Also, instead of an IP address or full host name, you can use the word default. The default access permissions pertain to all hosts accessing the service that do not have specific access permissions defined for them. For example, you might make the default permissions the following:

```
access: default !browse, read, search, !FTP, 15
```

These default permissions allow hosts to search and read Gopher directories, but not to browse or FTP them.

The default access permission set becomes the base from which you vary. Given the default definition, the following permission set allows up to 15 concurrent users at sgi.corp.com to FTP, read, and search Gopher directories:

```
access:   sgi.corp.com  FTP search !browse read !FTP 5
```

Likewise, the permission set

```
access:   sgi.corp.com !read, !search
```

prevents sgi.corp.com users from doing anything with Gopher directories, because this permission set cancels the only access allowed by the default access permissions.

Authenticating Users

It has been the goal of many service creators to identify who is accessing their service so that if the user is up to no good, a system administrator can put the finger on someone. This goal has not yet been reached for a variety of reasons. If Joe Schmo finds out a login name and password, or if a workstation is not password protected, Joe Schmo's identity is hidden behind the login name.

Still, there is the desire to make authentication a reality. The gopherd.conf file contains two keywords to that end:

◆ Authitem

◆ Serverpw

The Authitem keyword specifies a file or directory that requires a password and user authentication before it can be accessed. The format of Authitem is

```
Authitem:  authMethod  /file_dirName_regularExpression
```

where `authMethod` is the method of authentication, and `/file_dirName_regularExpression` identifies the file, directory, or regular expression that is to be protected. Currently, there are two methods of authentication:

◆ **Unix.** Uses the Unix passwd file.

◆ **Unixfile.** Uses a passwd file in the /etc directory under the dataRoot directory.

For example,

```
Authitem: unix /hippos
```

protects the directory, `hippos`, by requiring a password based on the Unix passwd file.

You also can specify a password to gain access to the service by defining the keyword Serverpw (server password), for example:

```
Serverpw: 0ver_the_ra1nb0w
```

You need to change these values from their default settings:

```
Authitem: unixfile /secure
Serverpw: super_secret_squirrel
```

Configuring the Compile-Time Options

The two files where you configure compile-time options are Makefile.config and conf.h. Some of the options are platform-specific. So, in addition to considering the tasks discussed in this section, look at the comments in the configuration files to see whether there are other configuration options you should edit.

Editing Makefile.config

The Makefile is the description file that helps build your service. The Makefile.config file provides configuration definitions that Makefile uses.

The Makefile.config file is quite long. This section only looks at those parts that are generic to all platforms.

About five pages into the configuration file, you see the following options:

```
# Where shall we install stuff?
#
PREFIX = /usr/local
CLIENTDIR = $(PREFIX)/bin
CLIENTLIB = $(PREFIX)/lib
SERVERDIR = $(PREFIX)/etc
# On SCO manuals are in /usr/man but its easiest to do a
# symbolic link from /usr/local/man to /usr/man for this and other packages
MAN1DIR = $(PREFIX)/man/man1
MAN5DIR = $(PREFIX)/man/man5
MAN8DIR = $(PREFIX)/man/man8
```

These options specify where all the Gopher files are installed. Descriptions of these options follow:

Option	Description
CLIENTDIR	Directory for the client application and gophfilt
CLIENTLIB	Directory of the client Help file, gopher.hlp
MAN1DIR	Directory of the man pages for the gopher client and gophfilt
MAN8DIR	Directory in which the man pages for gopherd are installed
PREFIX	Base pathname that defines where everything is installed
SERVERDIR	Directory of the service (gopherd) and the server configuration file (gopher.conf)

The locations of these files, as specified in the Makefile, are standard and do not require modification.

Configuring the Service

In addition to SERVERDIR, there are four other variables that configure the Gopher service: DOMAIN, SERVERPORT, SERVERDATA, and SERVEROPTS.

The DOMAIN variable sets the domain name of the service host:

```
DOMAIN = .micro.umn.edu
```

Note that the leading period is required.

If the hostname command returns a fully qualified domain name on your system, as in this example,

```
% hostname
engr.sgi.com
```

set DOMAIN to NULL:

```
DOMAIN =
```

Otherwise, set it to the part of the domain name that the hostname command does not return.

The SERVERPORT variable, as you might expect, defines the port to which the service listens. The default is 70. Change this port number only if you do not want to make the service available to Internet users. If you are modifying the service, for example, you might want to put the developmental version of the Gopher service on a high port number (between 1024 and 9999).

The SERVERDATA variable defines the starting location of the data provided by your Gopher service. You must change it from its default form:

```
SERVERDATA = /gopher-data
```

The values of both variables, SERVERPORT and SERVERDATA, can be overridden at the command line. If you do not define them, however, you have to enter their values when you execute the service. To save keystrokes and lost time caused by simple mistakes, it is a good idea to define the defaults of these variables.

The other line that sets service options looks similar to the following:

```
SERVEROPTS = -DSETPROCTITLE -DCAPFILES #-DBIO -DDL
    -DLOADRESTRICT
```

The options following the equal sign (=) and before the pound sign (#) represent source code that is compiled into the Gopher service. All the options after the pound sign are ignored during Gopher's compilation.

The options you can use in this line follow:

Option	Description
–DADD_DATE_AND_TIME	Adds dates and time to Gopher titles
–DBIO	Use only if you use Don Gilbert's version of WAIS (wais8b5) to enable searching by symbols; not recommended for other usage
–DDL	Supports Tim Cook's dl database program
–DCAPFILES	Provides backward compatibility with the cap directory
–DLOADRESTRICT	Restricts user access based on the number of active users; also adds –lkvm in SERVERLIBS
–DSETPROCTITLE	Sets the name displayed by the ps command; for bsdish systems only

To use –DLOADRESTRICT, set the user access restriction in the conf.h file and uncomment the LOADLIBS line in the Makefile:

```
#LOADLIBS = -lkvm
```

To get Don Gilbert's version of WAIS, FTP to

```
FTP.bio.indiana.edu
```

To use the –DDL option, you must have the source code, getdesc.o and enddesc.o, in the directory specified by DLPATH. You also need to uncomment the DLOBJS line in the Makefile:

```
DLPATH = /home/mudhoney/lindner/src/describe
#DLOBJS = $(DLPATH)/getdesc.o $(DLPATH)/enddesc.o
```

You can get the source code for the program Describe, which creates the dl databases from

```
FTP.deakin.edu.au
```

where you get

```
pub/describe/describe-1.8.tar.Z
```

Configuring the Gopher Client

You also can set Gopher client options by using the following line:

```
CLIENTOPTS = #-DNOMAIL -DAUTOEXITONU
```

Just as with the SERVEROPTS variable, all options after the pound sign are ignored. The options available for client configuration follow:

Option	Description
–DNOMAIL	Prevents remote users from mailing documents (for use with the Gopher client)
–DAUTOEXITONU	Exits Gopher client using u (as well as q)

Note   The DREMOTEUSER option is no longer used.

Controlling Debugging

You might choose to include debugging source code when you first install your Gopher service to help track problems. After you have it working, however, you might like to reduce the size of the Gopher executable and slightly improve performance by eliminating the debugging source code.

To eliminate the debugging source code, comment out the following line in the Makefile:

```
DEBUGGING = -DDEBUGGING
```

Providing WAIS Indexes

If you want your Gopher service to be accessible by WAIS indexes, you must perform the following steps:

1. Download freeWAIS by ftping it from

   ```
   % FTP gopher.boombox.micro.umn.edu
   ```

   Retrieve the source in the following file:

   ```
   /pub/gopher/Unix/freeWAIS-0.4.tar.gz
   ```

2. Dearchive and decompress the WAIS file and edit the Makefile according to your system.

3. Change to the top WAIS directory and run make:

   ```
   % make
   ```

 Note   Alternatively, you can make just part of the source by executing one of these commands:

   ```
   % make lib
   ```

   ```
   % make ir
   ```

   ```
   % make bin
   ```

4. In the freeWAIS file, /ir/sersrch.c, comment out the following line:

   ```
   /* if (gLastAnd) printf("search_word: boolean 'and' scored/n:); */
   ```

5. Recompile freeWAIS by running make in the top directory of freeWAIS.

6. In the Makefile.config file, make sure the WAISTYPE variable is set correctly, as in the following code:

   ```
   WAISTYPE = #-DFREEWAIS_0_4
   ```

7. Link the freeWAIS and Gopher services by typing the following lines:

   ```
   % cd GopherSrc
   ```

   ```
   % ln -s WaisTop/include ./ir
   ```

   ```
   % ln -s WaisTop/src/client/ui .
   ```

   ```
   % ln -s WaisTop/bin .
   ```

in which GopherSrc is the directory of the Gopher source code—for example, /usr/local/etc/gopher1.14—and WaisTop is the directory of the freeWAIS source code—for example, /usr/local/etc/freeWAIS-0.4.

When you compile the Gopher service, these links automatically allow freeWAIS and Gopher to interact.

 Note Providing full-text indexing for NeXT computers requires a different procedure. For instructions, look in the INSTALL file.

Editing conf.h

The conf.h file contains configuration information for the service and the included Gopher client. Because the scope of this book is essentially the service, only the highlights of the Gopher client configuration options are discussed here.

Configuring the Service

The very end of the conf.h file contains the variables that relate to the Gopher service operation. Although the variables cover many topics, most relate to load and limitations of service execution.

The WAISMAXHITS variable defines the maximum number of returns a query to a WAIS index can generate, as in this example:

```
#define WAISMAXHITS 40
```

This code limits Gopher services from supplying more than 40 WAIS-generated matches to a query. Forty is a reasonable number to start with.

If you turned on the LOADRESTRICT definition earlier, the MAXLOAD variable defines the maximum load the Gopher service will bear before refusing to serve documents to users, as this code shows:

```
#define MAXLOAD 10.0
```

You can override this variable on the command line when you invoke the service.

Read the manpage for the signal() command on your system. Confirm that the return type is void. If it is not, you need to define the SIGRETTYPE variable to the correct type. The default type is void:

```
#define SIGRETTYPE void
```

The READTIMEOUT variable defines the time the service waits for a network read before timing out. The default is one minute:

```
#define READTIMEOUT (1 * 60)
```

The WRITETIMEOUT variable defines the time the service waits for a network write before timing out. The default is three minutes:

```
#define WRITETIMEOUT (3 * 60)
```

There is a problem with running Gopher under inetd: it can handle only a limited number of arguments. As you can see from the variables so far that can be overridden on the command line, the Gopher service potentially can use many command-line arguments. To handle this problem, gopherd builds a file of arguments, called gopherd.conf; its location is specified by the CONF_FILE variable, as shown in this code:

```
#if !defined(CONF_FILE)
#  define CONF_FILE      "/usr/local/etc/gopherd.conf"
#endif
```

Configuring the Client

You define the default language the Gopher service uses for system messages with the variable DEFAULT_LANG:

```
#define DEFAULT_LANG "En_US" /* English (US)
```

Gopher can use a variety of other languages, including the following:

```
/* #define DEFAULT_LANG "Da_DK" /* Danish */
/* #define DEFAULT_LANG "De_DE" /* German */
/* #define DEFAULT_LANG "En_GB" /* English (UK) */
/* #define DEFAULT_LANG "Es_ES" /* Spanish */
/* #define DEFAULT_LANG "Fr_FR" /* French */
/* #define DEFAULT_LANG "It_IT" /* Italian */
/* #define DEFAULT_LANG "Jp_JP" /* Japanese */
/* #define DEFAULT_LANG "No_NO" /* Norwegian */
/* #define DEFAULT_LANG "Sv_SE" /* Swedish */
```

object/VIews.c has more examples of foreign language definitions.

You can define two Gopher services that Gopher clients automatically contact when invoked by using the CLIENT1_HOST and CLIENT2_HOST variables:

```
#define CLIENT1_HOST "gopher.company.corp.com"
#define CLIENT2_HOST "gopher2.company.corp.com"
```

Which service of the two the Gopher client contacts is arbitrary. The idea is to have two servers running the Gopher service so they can load balance user requests. Load balancing is the process of distributing user requests equally across servers. When loads are balanced, system performance is maximized.

You also can set the Gopher client to look for a Gopher service on a different port number by setting the CLIENT1_PORT and CLIENT2_PORT variables:

```
#define CLIENT1_PORT 70
#define CLIENT2_PORT 70
```

If you only want one root machine, set CLIENT2_PORT to 0.

You change these port numbers only if you have put a special version of your Gopher service on a different port. For general access, keep your Gopher client requesting information on port 70.

International Options

If you are installing Gopher clients to be used by people who do not speak English, you should enable the –DGINTERNATIONAL option in the Makefile.config. The current offerings include help systems in German, Spanish, French, and Italian; and system messages in German, Spanish, Swedish, Italian, and piglatin(!).

To use these languages, you must perform the following steps:

1. Run make in the gopher2_1_3/gopher/locales directory to change the foreign language files into binary catalogs.

2. Install the message files in the location specified by NLSPATH. Customary locations include /usr/lib/locales, and /usr/lib/nls.

   If NLSPATH is not specified, the default path for the message files is defined by the DEF_NLSPATH variable in the nl_types header file.

 Note For more information on NSLPATH, read the man page for catopen().

3. Set the LANG or LC_MESSAGES environment variables to the appropriate message file. For example,

   ```
   LANG=Es
   ```

   or

   ```
   setenv LC_MESSAGES fr
   ```

If you have trouble making the messages work, the problem might be that the proper files are not in the /usr/lib/nls directory. In such a case, run

```
% make install
```

in which make creates a directory that contains all the message catalogs that a Gopher client checks if it cannot find message catalogs any other way.

Installing Programs for the Gopher Client

The Gopher client uses many external programs common to Unix systems. If you are providing a Gopher client, you should check the following list to make sure that your system has these programs:

◆ To run telnet 3270 connections, you need tn3270 or a version of telnet that understands tn3270.

◆ To enable the Gopher client to download files, your system must have kermit and zmodem. The corresponding binaries are kermit, sz, sb, and sx.

◆ To use documents in metamail, your system needs mm.tar.Z, which you get from thumper.bellcore.com.

◆ To display images, your system needs a generic graphics program—for example, xv or xloadimage.

Compiling the Gopher Service and Client

When you finish setting all the configuration variables, it is time to compile the source and install the image. You have several options, including whether you want to build just the service, just the client, or both.

To compile the client only, type

```
% make client
```

To compile the service only, type

```
% make server
```

To compile the client and the service, type

```
% make
```

Installing the Gopher Client and Service

After building the applications, you need to install them.

To install the client only, type

```
% cd gopher
% make install
```

To install the service only, type

```
% cd gopherd
% make install
```

To install everything, type

```
make install
```

The biggest problem that you might run into results from not having created all the directories defined in your configuration files.

The install command used in the build is the BSD version. If you have problems, or your system does not have the BSD version of install, you need to install the program manually, using the following procedure:

1. Move any old version of gopherd to another directory.

2. Copy (cp) gopherd to /usr/local/bin.

Whether or not you can run the automated install, you have to manually install the man page. Use the following code, for example:

```
# cd doc
# cp gopherd.conf.8 /usr/local/man/man8
```

Your service is ready.

Starting Your Gopher+ Service

You can start the Gopher+ service using or not using chroot() to limit users' access to your file system. Just like FTP, Gopher+ can restrict users to a subdirectory of your system using chroot(). The other option is to start the service with the –c option, which does not chroot() the user. The option does, however, make gopherd use secure versions of file-opening system calls.

Although the –c option works reasonably well and enables you to put symbolic links in the Gopher+ data directory, chroot() is still more secure.

To start the Gopher+ service using chroot(), type a line similar to the following:

```
% /usr/local/etc/gopherd  /home/gopher-data 70
```

in which `home/gopher-data` is the directory where the Gopher data resides.

To start the Gopher+ service without using chroot(), type a line similar to the following:

```
/usr/local/etc/gopherd -c /home/gopher-data 70
```

If you want to start the service automatically with the server, you can insert an entry into your rc.local file (or equivalent) similar to the following:

```
if [ -f /usr/local/etc/gopherd ]; then
 /usr/local/etc/gopherd /home/hostName/dataRoot 70
fi
```

Using Other Command-Line Options

The following options are available to you with the gopherd command:

Option	Function
–C	Disables directory caching; default is to cache them
–c	Runs without chroot() restrictions; default is to run with restrictions
–D	Enables debugging; default is off
–I	inetd invokes service; default is off
–L avgLoad	Sets maximum load average
–l logFileName	Creates log file where connections are recorded

Option	Function
–o fileName	Uses fileName as the configuration file instead of gopherd.conf
–u name	Sets name as the owner running gopherd
directory_for_data	Uses directory_for_data as the data directory for Gopher
port#	Uses port# as the port number for the service

For more information about the security benefits of having your service run under a subdirectory access-restricted by chroot(), see Chapter 10, "Managing an FTP Service."

To reduce response time, gopherd caches directories while fulfilling requests for them. When a second request for the directory is received, the service looks for a file named .cache in the directory. If the cached directory is less than the number of seconds specified by Cachetime in gopherd.conf, the cached directory is sent to the requester. If the directory is older (or if there is no .cache file), the cached version of the file is not used. The directory is fetched from the disk, sent to the requester, and cached for the sake of the next request.

You should enable debugging (–D) only while you are testing the service. You should turn off debugging when the service is online, because debugging hurts performance.

If you choose to run your service under inetd (and you probably should not), you must use the –I option so that gohperd knows not to run as a daemon, but as a service that fulfills one request and then terminates. It also is important to put this option first in the list of options; otherwise, the gopher client gets start-up messages inappropriately.

Log files specify the activity performed by the service. They list what topics were searched for, and they list the documents sent to Gopher clients, for example. Log files are valuable because they show you what terms users employ to find documents. You might consider adding aliases, for example, if people use the search criterion *plane* with no result when your documents use the word *airplane*. Log files are examined more closely in "Using Log Files," later in this chapter.

If you use the filename cwsyslog, gopherd sends the log information to syslog. It does not make much sense, however, to mix log information into other syslog information. Trying to see the large picture when everything is mixed together is difficult. Keep log data in its own file.

In order for the –L argument to work, gopherd must be compiled with the LOADRESTRICT option turned on. When the maximum load average is reached, the service stops sending data to clients; instead, it sends the message System Load Too High. This option supersedes the MAXLOAD variable defined in conf.h.

In Makefile.config, the file that is set equal to SERVERDIR is the default location of the configuration file, gopherd.conf. You can choose to use a different configuration file by following the –o option with a filename. If you are testing the service, perhaps you need an alternate configuration file. It is much easier to change from one configuration file to another at the command line rather than in a configuration file.

You always want to use the –u option to run gopherd as an unprivileged user. If clever hackers find a bug in gophered that they can exploit, you want them running around the file system as unprivileged users, not as root!

 Note   Running the service is different from starting the service. Determining who should be the owner of each action is confusing. The rule is that you want to run the service as a nonprivileged user, but you want to start the service as root so that chroot() can take effect. For more information about chroot(), see Chapter 10.

The directory_for_data option sets a new default directory for Gopher data; it supersedes the default defined in the configuration file.

There are not too many reasons why you would change the port number of the service from 70. If you are testing a new version of the service on another port number, you can start it with that port number by using the –U option. Make sure, however, that you also use the directory_for_data argument on the command line.

Starting gopherd with inetd

Up to this point, this chapter has assumed that you want to start gopherd in stand-alone mode. In this mode, gopherd runs constantly (as a daemon) on the server and forks off a copy of itself whenever a request for Gopher (on port 70) comes in. The good aspect of running gopherd in stand-alone mode is that start-up time for a new service is very quick. The downside is that running gopherd as a daemon consumes considerable CPU cycles. If you are running a dedicated server for the service, this is not a problem. If you are trying to run other programs, perhaps other services, as well from your server, you have to judge whether you can afford to run gopherd as a daemon. If it turns out that running gopherd in stand-alone mode consumes too much CPU time, at least you know that you can run the service using inetd. This option saves CPU time, assuming that the service is not accessed every other minute. If this assumption is true, restarting the service for every request probably consumes more CPU time than running it as a daemon. At that point, you need to make some decisions about buying more hardware or severely restricting access to the service by using MaxSessions and LOADRESTRICT, for example.

Running gopherd under inetd has the advantage of freeing up CPU time by shutting down the service between service requests. The *caveat*, as just mentioned, is that this advantage becomes a disadvantage if the service is accessed on a regular basis. This is because gopherd must reread all the configuration files as it starts up. With fast machines, this performance hit is minimized, but it is not eliminated.

Whether your service runs under inetd depends mainly on the popularity of your service. If your service is being accessed five times a day, you want it running under inetd in order to free up the CPU. If, on the other hand, the service is being accessed five times per minute, gopherd almost certainly should run in stand-alone mode.

To run gopherd under inetd, you must edit two files. The first file you must edit is /etc/services. To add a Gopher service, add to the file a line similar to the following:

```
gopher    70/tcp    #This is our gopher service (port 70)
```

This line says the Gopher service listens to requests on port 70 and it uses TCP. Everything after the pound sign (#) is a comment.

You also must edit the /etc/inetd.conf file by adding a line similar to the following:

```
gopher    stream    tcp    nowait    root    /usr/local/etc/gopherd    gopherd -I
-l logfile  -u restricted
```

Every field separated by tabs in this example is standard, except the last field, where the optional arguments are given that you want to use to start the service. Because you are starting the service under inetd, you must use the –I option and it must be the first argument in the list to prevent aberrant messages from reaching the Gopher client. In this example, gopherd uses a log file, named logfile, and it runs as user restricted. These users should have very limited permissions so that, in case gopherd has a bug and hackers gain access to the system through the bug, they will have only the permissions of restricted users.

This example shows that the service is started as root. This is necessary in order to restrict users to a subdirectory of the file system (–c was not used) defined by chroot(). Although gopherd starts up as root to take advantage of chroot(), it runs as user restricted. You therefore have the best of both worlds: users restricted to a chroot()'d subset of the file system and limited to the permission set of a restricted user.

/usr/local/etc is the standard location of gopherd. If you have placed it in a different directory, substitute the correct path to the service.

When you change a configuration file, remember to restart the service so the configuration files are reread and the changes can take effect. You use the hang-up signal to do this:

```
# kill -HUP pid
```

in which pid is the process ID of the inetd, which you can obtain by using the following commands:

```
# ps -ax ¦ grep inetd
 2463  ??  Is    0:00.31 inetd
29438  p0  RV    0:00.7  grep inetd (tcsh)
```

In this case, 2463 is the process ID of inetd.

Note   In BSD Unix systems, you can use

```
ps -acx ¦ grep inetd
```

to display the process.

Testing Your Service

Before you tell everyone that your service is working, it is a good idea to test it. The first way to test the service is by starting a Gopher+ client and connecting to the Gopher+ service.

After you connect to your service, press Enter. The service should respond by displaying the top directory of the Gopher resources.

Using telnet

In addition to using your Gopher+ client to test your service, you can use telnet. If your service is working correctly, your telnet session should look something like the following:

```
warp[8:21pm]-=> telnet gopher 70
Trying 128.101.95.29 ...
Connected to gopher.micro.umn.edu.
Escape character is '^]'.

0About Gopher /.about gopher.micro.umn.edu 150
7Search Micro Consultant asd joeboy.micro.umn.edu 156
7Search everywhere kdkdkd ashpool.micro.umn.edu 158
1Search parts of the gopher world /Search parts of the gopher world
gopher.micro.umn.edu 150
.
```

```
Connection closed by foreign host.
warp[8:40pm]-=>
```

Using gopherls

If you do not want to go through the hassle of running telnet, you can run gopherls, which is linked to gopherd. gopherls takes only one argument, but the argument is mandatory. The argument is the pathname to a directory. gopherls processes this directory as though it were a Gopher+ client request and displays the message that normally would be sent to the Gopher+ client.

```
# gopherls /usr/local/dataRoot
0About Gopher  0/about gopher.  micro.umn.edu 150
7Search  Micro Consultant asd    joeboy.micro.umn.edu 156
7Search  everywhere kdkdkd ashpool.  micro.umn.edu 158
1Search parts of the gopher world  /Search parts of the gopher world gopher.
micro.umn.edu 150
```

You can do a quick check of all your directories by using gopherls.

Publicizing Your Gopher Service

To get your Gopher service listed in Gopher menus, send mail to

`gopher@boombox.micro.umn.edu`

If you are in Europe, send mail to

`gopher@ebone.net`

Include the following information in your mail:

- ◆ Service's name (as it appears on the menu)

- ◆ Full host's name

- ◆ Port number (hopefully, 70)

- ◆ System administrator's name (use an alias) and e-mail address

- ◆ Short paragraph describing the contents of the service (include that you are running Gopher+ to distinguish your service from a Gopher service)

- ◆ Selector string (optional)

The *selector string* is a pathname where you want people to start in your data directory. Generally, you leave this option blank so that people start, by default, at the root of your data files. One exception is a server that runs services for multiple companies; each company wants people to start in their data files (not those of other companies).

Although none of these pieces of information takes great brain work to complete, you should be absolutely sure that what you submit is absolutely correct, final, and everlasting. You do not want to put the name of your current system administrator for the service in the form, for example, because that will change over time. After information goes out to thousands, if not millions, of people, it is hard (and can be damaging) to make corrections.

Using Log Files

After you get your service running, you will be interested in learning how (and how many) people are using your service. The log file contains connection information about each service request. Here is an excerpt from a log file.

```
Wed Apr 05 11:15:18 1995 19823 sgi.com : retrieved binary /Introduction
Wed Apr 05 11:16:23 1995 18738 192.34.234.33 : search /earnings
Wed Apr 05 11:18:22 1995 16736 sgi.com : retrieved Doc/First Quarter Earnings
Wed Apr 05 11:18:45 1995 18746 sgi.com : retrieved Doc/New Products Guide
Wed Apr 05 11:19:18 1995 11532 jan.sun.com : search /advances
```

Most of the fields in the display are transparent. The first five fields are the time stamp for the service request or reply. The next field is the process ID of the Gopher service working on the request or reply. The field after the process ID gives the IP address or host name of the host that originated the request or reply. The second-to-last field contains a reserved word, such as *retrieved* or *search*, that describes the kind of action the service took. The final fields describe the document type and the document searched for or retrieved by the service.

The following are other reserved words that can appear in log files:

Reserved Word	Action Performed
executed *script arguments*	Ran a script, named *script*, using *arguments*
retrieved binary *fileName*	The service returned a binary file (or image) named *fileName*
retrieved directory *dirName*	The service returned a directory named *dirName*
retrieved file *fileName*	The service returned a directory named *fileName*

Reserved Word	Action Performed
retrieved FTP:*FTPHost@fileDirName*	Service returned the file or directory, *fileDirName*, using an FTP gateway
retrieved maildir *mailFile*	Service returned an e-mail from *mailFile*
retrieved sound *fileName*	Service returned a sound file named *fileName*
Root Connection	Appears when a user connects as root to the service
search *dBASE* for *criteria*	Service searches the database, *dBASE*, for the search *criteria*

In addition to these reserved words, you might find one of the following error messages:

Error Message	Meaning
Client went away	Client dropped the connection to the service before the service could complete its reply.
System Load Too High	When a client tried to connect to the service, it exceeded the maximum average system load, and was refused connection.
Malformed hostdata file	The host data in an index was non-sensical.
Can't set UID!	System administrator used –U or –u to invoke the service, but the user could not be changed.
readline: Time out!	The service disconnected from the client because the client did not send data within the time specified by the conf.h variable, READTIMEOUT.
Possible Security Violation	Service detects possible breach of security.
Denied access for *hostName*	A host, named *hostName,* was refused service because of access permissions defined in gopherd.conf.

Getting the Big Picture

Log records can tell you many things. You can learn what search criteria people often use, you can learn which documents and directories are used and not used, and you can get an indication of the average load your service carries.

When log files get long, however, the big picture is often lost in the details. Many software packages are available on the Internet, some included with Gopher (but not Gopher+), that can give you a broader perspective of the log data. It is not within the scope of this book to describe these programs individually. As you might expect, each program provides some indication of all, or some subset of, the following:

◆ Service load by day of the week

◆ Peak number of service transactions

◆ Most popular directories

◆ List of hosts that have accessed the service

◆ List of all files requested

◆ Number of files requested

◆ List of all searches conducted

◆ Number of searches conducted

◆ List of all menus requested—the root menu or the subdirectories

◆ Total number of service requests and replies

◆ Number of text files retrieved

Table 14.1 lists the software that provides some of these functions.

TABLE 14.1
Gopher Log Interpreting Software

Software	Location	Description
gla	boombox.micro.umn.edu in pub/gopher/Unix/GopherTools	One of the better log analyzer scripts
GLASS	boombox.micro.umn.edu in pub/gopher/Unix/GopherTools	Produces 22 reports

Software	Location	Description
glog	boombox.micro.umn.edu in pub/gopher/Unix/GopherTools/ glog directory	Log analyzer that came with Gopher 1.*x*
Gophreport	feenix.metronet.com in /pub/perl/scripts/gopher/ tools	Reports Gopher usage based on days, time, files, hosts, errors
Logger	boombox.micro.umn.edu in pub/gopher/Unix/GopherTools	An older log analyzer

Updating Log Files

The longer a service runs, the longer the log file. At some point, you should archive the contents of the log file (and eventually remove the file). This is not exactly advanced system administration.

There is a script, however, that can help you automate your chores. Logger rotates files and keeps basic statistics about the service as inferred from the log file. You can use FTP to get Logger from

```
boombox.micro.umn.edu in pub/gopher/Unix/GopherTools
```

Constructing Your Menu System

Creating your directory and file structure is one of your most challenging jobs. It requires that you be familiar with the documents so that you can place them correctly in the file system and write abstracts for the documents.

This section describes the steps you take to add files and directories under your data root directory.

Creating Directories and Files

If you have ever laid your hands on a Unix workstation, you no doubt already know the (very) uncomplicated Unix commands it takes to copy files and create directories and files. Actually, that's the beauty of it: You do not have to learn the newest scripting language, Einsteinium, in order to create your Gopher menus and populate your database. The familiarity of the commands goes a long way toward reducing errors.

To create a Gopher menu (a directory), change to the directory in which you want to create the new directory and use mkdir:

```
% cd /usr/local
% mkdir hot_topics
```

Within your new directory, you need to create files or copy files. To copy a file, use the cp or rcp command:

```
% cd hot_topics
% rcp guest@warp:/usr/people/geckel/latest
```

Your last step is to create descriptive file and directory names, such as *Hot Topics*, *Latest Economic Figures*, and *Trends for 1995*. You use the mv command to rename the files:

```
% mv latest 'Hot Topics'
```

There is a limitation on the number of characters (80) you can use. Consequently, you have to be concise and descriptive when you create filenames. Remember, those who are using Gopher 1.*x* clients cannot access the abstract associated with the file (which Gopher+ clients receive after pressing the equal sign).

The menu items are the user's interface to your service; they are what the user sees first. You might have documents in your service that make you worthy of the next Nobel prize, but if they are named poorly, they might go unnoticed. Because the menu titles give users their first look at your service, your astuteness in naming the files and directories can directly influence the success of the service. So, avoid slapping on a half-baked filename, such as newDoc2.

Naming Files and Directories

Now that you are prepared to do your best to create descriptive filenames, you need to know the correct procedure. You cannot use mv, as in this example:

```
mv hippo  'Sounds of the Great African River Hippo'
```

Instead, you use a .cap directory. Suppose that you have three documents:

```
/usr/local/doc/hippo
/usr/local/doc/africa
/usr/local/doc/rivers/
```

Here's what you do:

```
% cd /usr/local/doc
```

```
% mkdir .cap
% cd .cap
% cat > hippo
Name=Sounds of the Great African River Hippo
Numb=2
^D

% cat > africa
Name=Animals in Africa
Numb=1
^D

% cat > rivers
Name=African Animals Living In Rivers
Numb=3
^D
```

Now review the procedure you just used.

1. You created a directory called .cap in the same directory as the documents you are naming.

2. You created files of the same name as the files you are naming.

3. You used the keywords Name and Numb to specify the name of the document as you want it to appear in menus, and the order in which it should be listed in menus. In this example, the Gopher menu would appear as the following:

```
1. Animals in Africa.
2. Sounds of the Great African River Hippo.
3. African Animals Living In Rivers/
```

Using .names Files

An alternative to using the .cap directory is using a .names file. The concept is the same, except that you put in one file what you create separately as three files in the .cap directory. For example, the equivalent of the preceding exercise follows:

```
% cd /usr/local/doc
% cat > .names
# You can add a comment here if you like

Path=./hippo
Name=Sounds of the Great African River Hippo
```

```
Numb=2

Path=./africa
Name=Animals in Africa
Numb=1

Path=./rivers
Name=African Animals Living In Rivers
Numb=3
Abstract=Beautiful pictures of animals living in and around major African
rivers and lakes with accompanying text about the wildlife.
```

As you can see in the last file, you can use other keywords to describe your files in greater detail. The Abstract keyword identifies the concise description of the file the users can see whenever they select a menu item and press the equal sign (=).

Another keyword is Ask, which you use to get user input. The Ask keyword, along with Gopher+ forms, is discussed in this chapter in the section, "Creating Forms."

The dot file does not have to be called .names, although this is the convention. Using .names files saves you the trouble of creating a .cap directory and a separate file for each file to be named.

The only reason you might not want to use .names files is that they are not compatible with Gopher 1.*x* clients.

Creating Links to Other Files and Directories

One of the great features of Gopher is that the source of the Gopher information is hidden from the user. One menu item on the service server can be followed by a menu item that exists on a different Gopher server, and followed by another menu item that links to an FTP service. To the user, everything transpires behind closed doors, and all that matters is the appropriateness of the returned file.

There are two ways to link one service to another. The first and simplest way is to create a file that is linked to another file on a (perhaps) remote server. By convention, all link files begin with periods; the convention is to name them .links files.

A link file contains five lines in the following format:

```
Name=
Type=
Port=
Path=
Host=
```

You also have the option of using the Numb field in your link files to specify the placement of the file in the list of files.

The Name field is the menu item that appears to users. The Type field contains a numerical description of the type of document to which the file is linked. The following are the possible values of the Type field:

Value	Type of Document
0	Text file
1	Directory
2	CSO name server
7	Full text index
8	telnet session
9	Binary file
h	HTML file
I	Image file
M	MIME file
s	Sound file

The Port field identifies the port of the (potentially) remote server to query. The Path field provides the path to the linked file on the remote server. The Host field identifies the (possibly) remote host by IP address or full host name with which you want to link.

.links files are similar to .names files; one difference is that the Path field starts with ./ in .names files, because the .names files always refer to a document in the directory in which the .names file is located.

Here is a simple example:

```
Name=New Product Offerings
Type=0
Port=70
Path=0/local/latest
Host=sgi.corp.com
```

You can retrieve this information for yourself so that you can prepare the .link files by using a Gopher client to find a file you want to link with, selecting it, and then pressing the equal sign. The Gopher service displays all the information needed for each of the fields in the .links files.

The other way to retrieve this information is by telneting into a service. When you do so, the remote server responds with the information in the following format:

```
objectType    Name    Path    HostName    Port#
```

All these fields must remain the same, except for the Name field, which you can change.

By using different values for the Type field, you can access different kinds of objects on servers. Here is a link to a directory:

```
Name=New Product Offerings
Type=1+
Port=70
Path=1/
Host=furnace.sgi.com
```

Notice that the convention is to mark anything in a Gopher+ service with a plus sign (+).

Using .cap Files

The other way of linking files is by using .cap files. Suppose, for example, that you have a sound file called Meow that you want to make available to people. Here is what you would do:

1. In the same directory as Meow, create a new directory called .cap.

2. Create a file in the .cap directory using the same filename as the sound filename, Meow.

The file should contain one or all five of the fields that identify the linked file—including Name, Type, Port, Path, and Host. You only need to put into the file under .cap the fields that are different. All other fields default to the information in the Meow file.

If Meow were in /usr/local/sounds, you would use these commands to make the link:

```
cd /usr/local/sounds
mkdir .cap
cat >Meow
Type=s
Name=Cat Sound
^D
```

In this case, the host supplies the three fields that are missing: Port, Path, and Host.

Linking with Other Services

Up to now, you have been linking to other Gopher services. It is just as easy to link with other services, such as telnet, FTP, WAIS, or a script.

Linking to telnet Services

You can use .link files to start telnet sessions, as in the following code:

```
Name=New Product Offerings
Type=8
Port=23
Path=guest
Host=@furnace.sgi.com
```

Note   To start a TN3270 link, set the Type field to T.

Linking to Other Services

To link to FTP, WAIS, or a script, you have to use the following format for the Path field:

```
Path=service_link:arguments
```

in which `service_link` is FTP, waissrc, or exec; and `arguments` is additional information needed by the remote service.

To link to an FTP service, use this format:

```
Name=Gopher menu title for FTP resource
Path=FTP:hostName@/pathname/[fileName]
Type=Remote resource type
Port=+
Host=+
```

in which `hostName` is the IP address or fully qualified domain name of the server where the FTP service is running. `fileName` is in brackets in the Path field definition because it is optional. The Path field can specify a directory or filename.

The plus signs in the Port and Host fields tell the remote FTP service to return results to this Gopher service. If you put the full host name of another Gopher into the Host field, the FTP service sends its reply to that host, so that host acts as a gateway to the FTP service and handles the client's request.

The default port number for an FTP service, 21, is always used.

Linking to WAIS Services

You can provide a link to a WAIS service to include its index in your service. To do so, use the following format:

```
Name=Menu title for WAIS resource
Path=waissrc:sourceFile
Type=7
Port=+
Host=+
```

in which `sourceFile` is the full pathname of the WAIS source (the src file). For more information about source files, see Chapter 11, "Setting Up a freeWAIS Service."

Using Links to Execute Scripts

All the other services so far return files that are static. Perhaps you want to generate some information on the fly and return it. You might want to extract some information from a database, for example. To offer dynamic information, you must use scripts. *Scripts* are programs that process the information you want your Gopher service to display.

To use a link to execute a script, format the .link file:

```
Name=Gopher menu title
Path=exec: "arguments" : scriptName
Type=type of script's output
Port=+
Host=+
```

in which `arguments` are arguments that you need to pass to the script, and `scriptName` is the full pathname, relative to Gopher's data directory, of the script executable. If the script does not require arguments, you still must include the argument's field by placing "" in it, as this example shows:

```
Path=exec:"":myScript
```

The Type field denotes the kind of reply that will be sent—for example, 0, which is text.

Searching Indexes

If you use a link to query an index, the client must specify the search criteria, and your .links file must specify the script as the Path item—not an index, as you would expect by setting Type=7 (index). A sample follows:

```
Name=Search Index for Search Criteria
Path=7/sbin/myScript
Type=7
Port=+
Host=+
```

You can query more than one index at a time by putting the host name, port number, and pathname to the index in a file that has the extension .mindex (multiple index). For example,

```
%cat > AirplaneSearch.mindex
furnace.sgi.com  70  7/indexes/airplane_index
oven.sun.com  70  7/indexes/flight_index
^D
```

Structuring Your File System

A great deal of effort often goes into the contents of your service files. They might be programs, images, or documents that your company has crafted at great expense and time. Too often, however, the people who toil so hard to create a product invest less energy in making it clear and presentable to others.

Your menu system is the user interface to the content in your files. Without a clear, concise, and well-thought-out hierarchy of files, filenames, file groupings, and directory names, navigating your service can prove more trouble than it is worth. Invest the time it takes to really look at the arrangement of directories, the groupings of files in the directories, and the names of files and directories.

You already have learned that file and directory names have to be descriptive—not shorthand afterthoughts, such as newDoc3. Other good rules for names include avoiding insults ("If you still don't understand, choose me."), being specific (avoid, for example, "civilization"), avoiding technical jargon when possible (not "Polling in Replicated Services"), and remaining simple (not "Restructuring Forecasted Gross Income Figures").

About the worst case of file structuring would be a service without subdirectories— everything in one directory. Less obvious offenders are nearly as bad. Consider this file structure:

```
Finances
      Fiscal Growth
            1st Quarter Growth
      2nd Quarter Growth
            Increasing Profit Margins
                  Reducing Expenditures
      3rd Quarter Growth
```

When you begin to structure a file system, it is sometimes hard to figure out what the future portends and how that should influence the file structure. Sometimes it is hard to figure out where to put new files. Are they different enough to warrant the creation of a new directory, or is there enough of a connection with other files in a current directory? You might find that, by mistake, you have parallel subdirectories in different parts of the file hierarchy. At some point, you might feel that the entire hierarchy is like a fortress of cards just waiting to fall down with the addition of one more file.

Reviewing the hierarchy of files is an important job that is hard to do well. Its importance often is obscured by the more technical tasks you are expected to perform. A program called *gophertree* helps you examine your file hierarchy. It lists only the directories in the system, for example, or it enables you to look at only a restricted part of the file hierarchy at one time.

You can obtain gophertree from boombox.micro.umn.edu in /pubs/gopher/Unix/ GopherTools.

Using Files Common to Other Services

You already might have a significant number of files outside the subdirectories restricted by chroot(). Some might be easy to move, but others might not be easy to move. Some files might be part of another service you are offering, such as FTP. You might want to avoid duplication of files by using symbolic links. Unfortunately, that does not work because the link points outside of the chroot()'d hierarchy. This leaves you with only one alternative: copy the files into the chroot()'d hierarchy.

Using FTP Files

If your company already has an FTP service, you can leverage the files for use with Gopher. Find out the root for the document files. Make that path equal to the root document path as specified in gopherd.conf.

If there are directories in the FTP file system that you do not want to access through Gopher, use the ignore keyword in gopherd.conf to prevent access to those directories. For more information about the ignore keyword, see the section earlier in this chapter, "Hiding Files Based on File Types."

Creating Forms

If you have ever wanted to get information from a user, you know that it can be tedious if you have to ask questions sequentially. Gopher+ enables you to present forms to users with multiple input points.

These forms also are called *ASK blocks*. You create forms in files that have the extension .ask. They contain keywords that define the contents of the line on which they reside. Here is a very short example:

```
Note:                   WriteIt!
Note:       Information Pamphlet Order Form
Note:
Note:
Ask: Topic:<tab>
Ask: Phone:<tab>
Ask: email: <tab>
Note:
Note:
Choose:Version:English<tab>Spanish<tab>
```

Note that the tabs that end each Ask line are not strictly necessary, but are backward compatible with older Gopher+ clients.

This form would display as shown in figure 14.1.

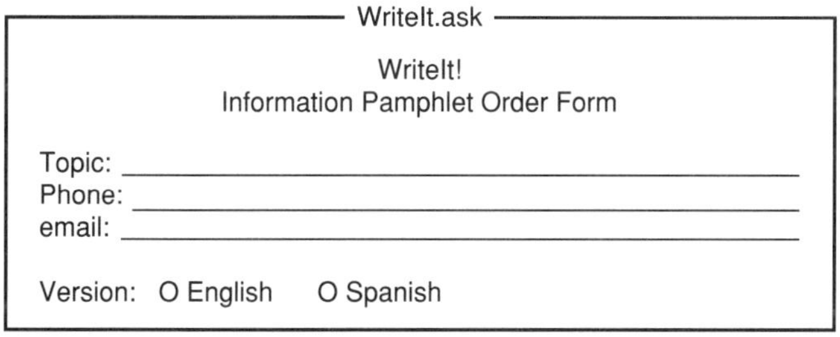

Figure 14.1

A Gopher form.

You can see that the keywords created places for user input.

The user-input keywords follow:

Keyword	Function
Ask	Presents question and provides space to fill in the answer
AskL	Presents question and provides multiple lines for the answer
Askp	Presents question and provides space to enter a password
Choose	Presents a question with a set of answers from which the user chooses; many clients display these fields as radio buttons
Note	Prints text on form
Select	Presents Approve/Disapprove question; many clients display check boxes on forms

You can add default values for any of these keywords by typing the default value:

```
Ask:Country:<tab>USA
```

in which USA is the default value for the Ask question.

The Select keyword works a little differently from the other keywords. Here is a short example:

```
Note: What colors do you want?
Select: Red?:1
Select: Blue?:0
Select: Green?:0
```

These lines create three check boxes under the question in the Note. The numbers following the colon, 0 or 1, specify whether the boxes are on or off by default. In this example, only the red color is on by default. Some Gopher+ clients, however, display to the user true and false or yes and no instead of 0 and 1.

Now that you have created a form, you must write the script to handle the input. For the preceding form, you could write the following PERL script:

```
#!/usr/sbin/forms/pampletOrder

# Retrieve user input
$Topic = <>;
$Phone = <>;
$email = <>;
$Version = <>;
```

```
# Strip out unwanted characters

$Topic =~ s/[^A-Za-z0-9. ]//g;
$Phone =~ s/[^A-Za-z0-9. ]//g;
$email =~ s/[^A-Za-z0-9. ]//g;
$Version =~ s/[^A-Za-z0-9. ]//g;

# Return information to client

print << "EOF"
```

The first four lines of the script read the user entries from standard input. The second four lines strip out unwanted characters to prevent any monkey business. The print statement returns the information to the Gopher client. Instead of returning the information to the client, you could save it in a file using a statement similar to the following:

```
open (OUTPUT, ">/forms/output/writeit.$$") || die "Can't     file to write in"
```

This script should be in a file that has the same root name as the .ask file—in this case, writeit.

To make all this work, you place the two files, writeit and writeit.ask, in the part of the Gopher service restricted by chroot() and make the script, writeit, executable by the same owner under which gopherd runs.

Finally, you should make a .names file for the script so that the menu title is more descriptive.

CHAPTER

15

Setting Up and Managing a ZDIST Service

When Thinking Machines created WAIS, they standardized their work on the Z39.50 protocol. Because the protocol was limited, however, Thinking Machines added a set of extensions to the protocol, which was renamed Z39.50-1988 (reflecting the year the extensions were added). This protocol, then, is what is used in WAIS.

While WAIS clients and servers gained popularity, work was done to enhance the Z39.50 protocol. The robust version of the protocol was named Z39.50-1992. This protocol has become nationally and internationally accepted as the new standard for networked information search and retrieval protocols. Unfortunately, the two protocols, Z39.50-1988 and Z39.50-1992, are not interoperable. For example, a WAIS client cannot communicate with a service based on the Z39.50-1992 protocol.

Note   CNIDR's goal is to make future versions of ZDIST backward-compatible with WAIS—but that could take years.

CNIDR, the organization that maintains freeWAIS, decided to switch to the 1992 protocol because of its enhanced features. In so doing, they had to write new service software because the incompatible protocols prevented the new service from using any of the freeWAIS code. Instead of naming the new service freeWAIS 1.0, they chose a new name, *ZDIST* (from the Z39.50 protocol name), to reflect its disassociation from the freeWAIS code.

 Note   As of this writing, ZDIST is in beta testing. Although you can download the service software, you might be better off to wait for the product to mature. To keep abreast of developments, explore the URL, http://cnidr.org/welcome.html.

ZDIST Distribution Software

The ZDIST service, by CNIDR, complies with ANSI/NISO Z39.50-1992, including the following software:

◆ ZDIST service (ZServer is a Unix server daemon)

◆ Unix client (ZClient doubles as an HTTP gateway)

◆ HTTP to Z39.50-1992 gateway

◆ E-MAIL to Z39.50-1992 gateway

◆ Search Application Programmer's Interface (SAPI)

ZServer

ZServer is a small, fast service that mounts database systems to provide ANSI/NISO Z39.50-1992 standardized access to those database systems. ZServer provides robust search and retrieval tools to "deep search" databases not offered by services based on other protocols.

You can run ZServer in standalone mode or under inetd. In both cases, you can limit the number of simultaneous sessions.

ZServer works on the most popular flavors of Unix.

Overview of the ZServer Installation

To install and configure ZServer, use the following procedure.

1. Download the software through CNIDR's WWW document, or ftp it directly using the same name:

   ```
   ftp://ftp.cnidr.org/pub/NIDR.tools/zdist/zdistX.X.tar.Z
   ```

Note As of this writing, the current beta version of the software, beta 1.1, is called zdist102b1-1.

2. Uncompress the software using the uncompress command, as follows:

   ```
   % uncompress zdistX.X.tar.Z
   ```

3. Dearchive the file with the tar command, as follows:

   ```
   % tar xvf zdistX.X.tar
   ```

4. Change to the zdist1.0 directory, as follows:

   ```
   % cd zdist1.0
   ```

5. Read the README file.

6. Edit the Makefile.

7. Type the following:

   ```
   % make build
   ```

8. Edit (or create) the service configuration file zserver.ini.

Configuring ZServer

After building ZServer, you should use your favorite editor to edit (or create) ZServer's configuration file, zserver.ini. (I'll give you a sample configuration file a bit later in this chapter.)

The zserver.ini file has two kinds of entries: directives and group names. Group names are enclosed in square brackets. The following list of directives belong in that group, and represent related functionality, for example:

```
[default]
ServerType=
MaxSessions=
Port=
```

In the preceding example, the Server Information Group called default contains three directives.

The configuration file has two groups:

◆ Server Information Group

◆ Database Information Group

You must have a database information group for every database listed in the DBList directive.

ZServer Configuration Directives

When you edit the configuration file, you must use the directives exactly as shown in the following table. When you give the directives values, you cannot leave a space between the equals sign and the value.

The following sections define the meaning of the directives.

ServerType

ServerType can have one of two values: INETD or STANDALONE. This variable controls how ZDIST is run on the server. If you choose INETD, INETD is responsible for starting the service whenever a service request comes to the server, as well as spawning a new service process for each concurrent service request. Each process exits after it services the request.

If you choose STANDALONE, ZDIST spawns a service process for each concurrent request. MaxSessions specifies the maximum number of concurrent requests that can be serviced. Generally, you should use STANDALONE for its superior efficiency to INETD. If, however, you debug the service, you should set the ServerType directive to INETD.

MaxSessions

The value of the MaxSessions variable represents the maximum number of concurrent sessions that ZDIST can service. The default value is 10. This value has no effect if ServerType is set to INETD.

Port

The port value specifies the port to which the server listens. The default value is 210. This value has no effect if ServerType is set to INETD.

TimeOut

The Timeout value specifies the number of seconds ZDIST should wait for a new request before exiting the session. The default value is 3600.

Trace

Trace can have two values: ON or OFF. This option turns on or off logging of debugging information to the file specified by TraceLog.

TraceLog

TraceLog specifies the file where you want to keep debugging information. The default filename is zserver_trace.log. This value only has meaning if the Trace directive is turned on.

AccessLog

AccessLog specifies the file in which you want to keep client access information. The default filename is zserver_access.log.

ServerPath

ServerPath specifies the pathname to zserver.ini. ZDIST occasionally rereads the configuration information and uses the value in this directive to find it. The default value is the current working directory.

DBList

Set DBList equal to a comma-separated list of all databases available on your server. Do not include any white spaces in the list. Make sure to update this list if you add new databases to your service.

Type

The Type directive can have two values: SCRIPT or NTSS, depending on the type of database. You must have a Type directive in each database group (and not in the default group). The default value is NTSS.

Location

The syntax of the Location directive depends on the value of the Type directive. If the Type value is NTSS, the Location directive should equal the path to the NTSS database. If the Type value is SCRIPT, the Location directive should equal the path to the shell script (or application) that conforms to the requirements of the SCRIPT search engine. You must include this directive in every database group.

Results

The Results directive has meaning only if you set the Type directive to SCRIPT. It defines the absolute pathname to a temporary file needed by the SCRIPT search engine.

Sample Configuration File

The following configuration file, zserver.ini, is the sample provided by CNIDR at the URL http://vinca.cnidr.org/software/zserver/zserver_ini.html.

```
This configuration file, zserver.ini, configures the server to operate as a
forking demon accepting no more than 50 simultaneous connections. The server
listens for client connections on port 2210 and writes debugging information to
the file /tmp/zserver_trace.log. Two databases are available for searching by
clients: MyNewServer and ManPages. Both of these databases are "indexed" by
the SCRIPT type search engine and each has its own Location (script) and
Results file location
(temporary file needed by the SCRIPT type search engine).
# This is the Server Information Group
[Default]
ServerType=STANDALONE
MaxSessions=50
Port=2210
Trace=ON
TraceLog=/tmp/zserver_trace.log
ServerPath=/usr/users/zdist1.02/bin
# Each name listed below should have a corresponding Database Information Group
DBList=MyNewServer,ManPages
# This is one of the two Database Information Groups
[MyNewServer]
Type=SCRIPT
Location=/usr/users/zdist1.02/bin/MyNewServer.sh
Results=/tmp/MyNewServer
```

```
# This is the second of the two Database Information Groups
[ManPages]
Type=SCRIPT
Location=/usr/users/zdist1.02/bin/ManPages.sh
Results=/tmp/ManPages
# This is a "special" diagnostic group. If you want the error messages
# changed, do so here.
[1.2.840.10003.3.1]
1=Permanent system error
2=Temporary system error
3=Unsupported search
4=Terms only exclusion (stop) words
5=Too many argument words
6=Too many boolean operators
7=Too many truncated words
8=Too many incomplete subfields
9=Truncated words too short
10=Invalid format for record number (search term)
11=Too many characters in search statement
12=Too many records retrieved
13=Present request out of range
14=System error in presenting records
15=Record no authorized to be sent intersystem
16=Record exceeds Preferred-message-size
17=Record exceeds Maximum-record-size
18=Result set not supported as a search term
19=Only single result set as search term supported
20=Only ANDing of a single result set as search term supported
21=Result set exists and replace indicator off
22=Result set naming not supported
23=Combination of specified databases not supported
24=Element set names not supported
25=Specified element set name not valid for specified database
26=Only a single element set name supported
27=Result set no longer exists - unilaterally deleted by target
28=Result set is in use
29=One of the specified databases is locked
30=Specified result set does not exist
31=Resources exhausted - no results available
32=Resources exhausted - unpredictable partial results available
33=Resources exhausted - valid subset of results available
100=Unspecified error
```

```
101=Access-control failure
102=Security challenge required but could not be issued - request terminated
103=Security challenge required but could not be issued - record not included
104=Security challenge failed - record not included
105=Terminated by negative continue response
106=No abstract syntaxes agreed to for this record
107=Query type not supported
108=Malformed query
109=Database unavailable
110=Operator unsupported
111=Too many databases specified
112=Too many result sets created
113=Unsupported attribute type
114=Unsupported Use attribute
115=Unsupported value for Use attribute
116=Use attribute required but not supplied
117=Unsupported Relation attribute
118=Unsupported Structure attribute
119=Unsupported Position attribute
120=Unsupported Truncation attribute
121=Unsupported Attribute Set
122=Unsupported Completeness attribute
123=Unsupported attribute combination
124=Unsupported coded value for term
125=Malformed search term
126=Illegal term value for attribute
127=Unparsable format for un-normalized value
128=Illegal result set name
129=Proximity search of sets not supported
130=Illegal result set in proximity search
131=Unsupported proximity relation
132=Unsupported proximity unit code
```

Currently Supported Search Engines

ZDIST currently supports two search engines: ISEARCH, an NTSS search engine, which is the default engine; and SCRIPT, which offers similar functionality to ISEARCH, but is more kludgy. Both engines are included in the software and written by CNIDR. SCRIPT tests the Search API. Patches are for bug fixes and enhanced functionality when you create a less-than-elegant application. ISEARCH supersedes SCRIPT.

For more information about ISEARCH, see the following URL:

```
http://vinca.cnidr.org/software/isearch/isearch.html.
```

For more information about SCRIPT, see the following URL:

```
http://vinca.cnidr.org/software/sapi/engines.html.
```

 Note If you want to use a custom search engine with the Search API, you must write a database driver that communicates between your system and the Search API. Although a Search API makes that task easier, the only documentation is the code itself, libsapi/sapi.c, in the sapi distribution.

Starting ZServer

You can start ZServer from the command line (if the Type directive is STANDALONE) or from inetd.

To start ZServer from the command line, use the following syntax, where *pathName* is the absolute pathname to zserver.ini, and *SIG* specifies a Server Information Group to use rather than [default]:

```
% zserver [-ipathName/zserver.ini[,SIG] \
    [-odirectiveName=value]]
```

Here are several examples:

To start ZServer with default values, type the following:

```
% zserver
```

To use a Server Information Group other than [default], type a command similar to the following, where *infoGroupName* is the name of the Server Information Group:

```
% zserver -i/pathName/zserver.ini,infoGroupName
```

To specify a non-default value for a directive, type a command similar to the following, where *directiveName* is the name of the directive and value is its value:

```
% zserver -i/pathName/zserver.ini -odirectiveName=value
```

If you want to start ZServer using inetd, add the following entry to your /etc/services file:

```
zserver 210/tcp # CNIDR ZServer
```

and add the following entry to /etc/inetd.conf:

```
zserver stream tcpnowait root \
    /home/zdistX.X/bin/zserver zserver -i/home zdistX.X
```

If you have troubles, make sure you have defined the path to zserver.ini correctly.

Testing ZServer

After you build and configure ZServer, CNIDR provides a test search page so that you can check the functionality of your installation. The test search page is at the URL, http://vinca.cnidr.org/software/zdist/zserver/servercheck.html.

Part III

Concerns

C H A P T E R

16

Client Overview

E ssentially, there are two choices for clients for a WWW based Intranet: NCSA's Mosaic or Netscape. The first half of this chapter looks at Mosaic, while the second looks at Netscape.

Mosaic System Requirements

Mosaic Alpha 7, as it is used on the Microsoft Windows platform, is how Mosaic is discussed here. Many of the procedures and navigational instructions shown here can be used for the Macintosh system; the installation instructions vary greatly, however, particularly the ones shown in this section. For specific installation procedures for the Macintosh, refer to the installation notes provided by NCSA at http:// www.uiuc.edu.

The latest version of Mosaic for Windows is a 32-bit application and can run on Windows 3.1 or later versions. Because Windows 3.1 is *not* a 32-bit operating system, you must either upgrade to Windows 3.11 (or a later version) or upgrade your current copy of Windows 3.1. Although upgrading to Windows 3.11 or Windows for Workgroups is not a bad idea, you can use a set of files provided by Microsoft to upgrade Windows 3.1 to run 32-bit applications, such as Mosaic. These files, known as WIN32s, version 1.20 (or WIN32s, version1.30, which became available at the time of this printing), are provided on many bulletin board systems (such as CompuServe), FTP and gopher sites, and through Microsoft.

 Note   The latest version of WIN32s (version1.30a—Called Win32s with OLE v1.30) helps to address the National Language Support problems encountered by previous versions of Windows and eliminates the COMPOBJ.DLL problems experienced by some users. If you use a language other than English (American) or have problems with COMPOBJ.DLL, you should upgrade to this version. If not, you can continue to use version 1.20.

You can obtain WIN32S.ZIP from the following sources:

Microsoft FTP server:

`ftp.microsoft.com\softlib\mslfiles\pw1118.exe`

NCSA FTP server:

`ftp.ncsa.uiuc.edu/Mosaic/Windows/Win31x/Win32s/ole32s13.exe`

Installing Mosaic

Like other Windows applications, Mosaic for Windows adheres to standard Windows conventions and installation procedures. Because the Mosaic file you receive probably will be compressed in a ZIP file, you need to unzip it by using PKUNZIP.

You can download a free copy of Mosaic (usually called WMOS20A6R1.ZIP or something similar) from several places. On the Internet, you can obtain it by means of FTP at the following locations:

◆ `ftp.ncsa.uiuc.edu/pcmosaic`

◆ `sunsit.unc.edu/pub/packages/infosystems/www/clients/mosaic/mosaic-ncsa/windows`

◆ `miriworld.its.unimelb.edu.au/pub/clients/pcmosaic`

◆ `ftp.luth.se/pub/infosystems/www/ncsa/windows`

◆ `ftp.sunet.se/pub/pc/mosaic`

If you have access to CompuServe, you can obtain Mosaic for Windows in the Internet New Users forum and Internet Resources forum. Check in several library sections for the latest version of the application. America Online might also have it posted someplace in its service.

Another great source is The National Center for Supercomputing Applications (NCSA), which created Mosaic. You can ask for a copy of the NCSA catalog, which offers manuals and other information, by e-mail at orders@ncsa.uiuc.edu, or from the following postal address:

NCSA Orders
152 Computing Applications Bldg.
605 East Springfield Ave.
Champaign, IL 61820-5518

Note You must make sure that you have a Winsock 1.1-compliant dynamic link library (DLL) on your system to run Mosaic. This DLL provides the compatibility between different TCP/IP applications and your TCP/IP protocol stack.

After Mosaic is placed on your hard drive, select **F**ile, **R**un from Program Manager. Next, fill in the **C**ommand Line field with the full path to where MOSAIC.EXE resides. If you have the Mosaic files in a subdirectory named \TEMP, for example, type **C:\TEMP\MOSAIC.EXE** in the **C**ommand Line field box. Click on OK to start the installation process. This process may take several minutes to complete.

Customizing Mosaic

Now that you have Mosaic installed on your hard drive, you are ready to start surfing the World Wide Web. Before you get too involved, however, you might want to customize Mosaic's appearance and the way it performs. Customization may reduce your initial headaches by speeding up the way Mosaic handles graphics and text.

The following configuration instructions are written on the assumption that you are comfortable editing and changing INI files. To change some of Mosaic's options, you need to change the MOSAIC.INI file. First, make a backup copy of MOSAIC.INI. This step is very important. You are going to edit several lines of the file and, if something goes wrong during the customization process, you might need to return to the original file. You will find the MOSAIC.INI file in the \WINDOWS directory on your system.

Next, open MOSAIC.INI in a text editor, such as Notepad (see fig. 16.1). The following sections describe individual components of the file and how to customize it for your particular setup. In some cases, given your experience with other Internet tools or services you have, you may decide not to change a setting. This is fine and should not cause you any problems. This discussion is intended to help you tweak Mosaic before you get online and lose track of time and responsibilities. (It happens, believe me.)

Figure 16.1

*MOSAIC.INI file
loaded into
Notepad for
editing.*

```
─                        Notepad - MOSAIC.INI                    ▼ ▲
File   Edit   Search   Help
[Main]                                                            ▲
E-mail="rtidrow@iquest.net"
Autoload Home Page=yes
Home Page=file:///c|\network\my_own1.htm
Help Page=http://www.ncsa.uiuc.edu/SDG/Software/WinMosaic/Docs/WMosTOC.html
FAQ Page=http://www.ncsa.uiuc.edu/SDG/Software/WinMosaic/FAQ.html
Bug list=http://www.ncsa.uiuc.edu/SDG/Software/WinMosaic/Bugs.html
Feature Page=http://www.ncsa.uiuc.edu/SDG/Software/WinMosaic/Features.html
Display Inline Images=yes
Dump memory blocks=no
Grey Background=yes
Fancy Rules=yes
Round List Bullets=yes
Current Hotlist=Home Pages
Anchor Underline=no
Anchor Cursor=yes
Show URLs=yes
Extended FTP=yes
Toolbar=yes
Status bar=yes
Title/URL bar=yes
Use 8-bit Sound=no

[Settings]
Anchor Color=0,0,255


[Main Window]                                                    ▼
←                                                                →
```

Setting Your E-Mail Address

The first line in the [Main] section is the E-mail= line, which enables you to correspond with the Mosaic developers if you send them a query. You will find this option
under the Mail to Developers option in Mosaic's Help menu. Change this line from
`user@site.domain` to your specific e-mail address. If, for example, your address is
`rtidrow@iquest.net`, then make the following change to the e-mail line:

`E-mail="rtidrow@iquest.net"`

Be sure to include the quotation marks ("") in the name.

Autoloading a Home Page

When you first start a Mosaic session, Mosaic (by default) loads a home page (see fig.
16.2). The Autoload Home Page= line is set to Yes (by default) in the MOSAIC.INI
file and logs you in to the Mosaic for Microsoft Windows Home Page at NCSA. This is
helpful for first-time users, but can get very tiresome after awhile. If you change the
Autoload Home Page= line to No, Mosaic does not load a home page when you start
up Mosaic. If you have a favorite starting point on the Web or if you have a local
HTML file on your hard drive, set this line to read that address or path.

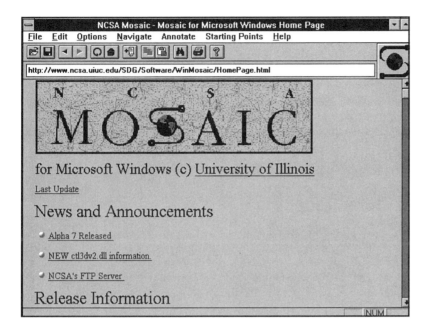

Figure 16.2

Autoloading a home page upon startup.

The line immediately after the Autoload Home Page= line tells Mosaic which URL address to use as the startup home page. Suppose, for example, that you visit the Microsoft Web site whenever you use Mosaic. You can make this site your first stop by making it your default home page every time you run Mosaic. To do this, type the following address in the Home Page= line:

```
Home Page=http://www.microsoft.com
```

To configure a default home page, substitute your favorite home page URL to the right of the equal sign (=) in the preceding line.

One thing you will soon discover when you use Mosaic (or any other Web browser for that matter) is that it is relatively slow when you are using a dial-up account and modem. To make your default home page appear quickly, save the home page to your hard drive and use that file as your default home page. The file must be saved as an HTML document (the file format used by the World Wide Web). If you have an HTML document named WWW.HTM on your hard drive in the subdirectory named \NETWORK\MOSAIC\, for example, type the following address in the Home Page= line:

```
file:///c¦\NETWORK\MOSAIC\WWW.HTM
```

Notice that HTML filenames have a three-character extension (.HTM) because of the character limitations imposed by DOS. Be sure to use the .HTM file extension for your local files and use the extension when you reference them.

Help, FAQ, and Bug Lines

The following lines in the MOSAIC.INI file reference the online Help pages maintained by NCSA and can remain the same. You can, however, change them if NCSA moves these documents in the future. If so, just change these lines to point to the new URLs.

```
Help Page=
FAQ Page=
Bug list
```

Displaying Inline Images

In addition to huge multimedia files, inline graphics on Web pages are the biggest hurdle for you to cross each time you access a site. Graphics greatly increase the time necessary to access a site, sometimes to such a degree that Mosaic seems to come to a halt. When you have a SLIP/PPP connection, you can set the Display Inline Images= line to No to tell Mosaic not to automatically download the graphics of each site. After you get to a site, you can view the graphics by clicking on the inline image icon with the right mouse button, and Mosaic will load the image for you.

The default for the Display Inline Images= line is Yes.

Dump Memory Blocks

Mosaic Alpha 7 (and later versions) do not include the Dump Memory Blocks= line. If you have an earlier version, keep the default setting of No.

Setting Background Color

The standard look of Mosaic is a gray background. To change Mosaic's standard gray background to a white background, modify the Grey Background=yes line, as follows:

```
Grey Background=no
```

Figures 16.3 and 16.4 contrast the two looks.

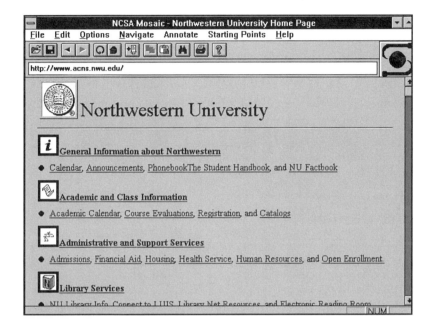

Figure 16.3

Mosaic with its standard gray background.

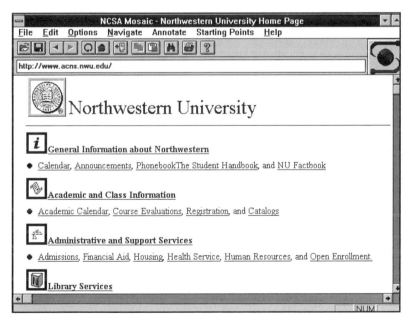

Figure 16.4

Mosaic with a white background.

Setting Page Layout Items

In the [Main] section of the .INI file, you can set two options that affect the way HTML documents appear onscreen. First, the Fancy Rules= line sets the type of rule (line) displayed. If you want the more decorative rule when a document is tagged with an <hr> coding, keep the default setting of Yes.

Secondly, you can change round bullets to flat lines by setting the Round List Bullets=Yes line to No. Round bullets are the dots (•) displayed in lists in many HTML documents. By substituting flat lines for the round bullets, you can greatly reduce the time needed to access a document.

Selecting the Default Hotlist

Mosaic enables you to save Web sites to a hotlist by means of the Hotlist menu option. This hotlist gives you a quick and easy way to return to sites you have visited and found interesting. You use the Current Hotlist= line to set the default hotlist name. When you first load Mosaic, the hotlist named "Home Pages" is the default. After you set up your own hotlist(s), remember to come back to this line and set it to your favorite hotlist to make that hotlist the current one.

Setting Anchor Preferences

Even if you have never been on the World Wide Web, you are probably familiar with anchors in Help files or other hypertext documents. *Anchors*, or *link anchors*, are the hyperlinks that link a word, phrase, graphic, or document to another document, phrase, word, or graphic. By default, these anchors are shown in blue, which is fine when you have a color monitor. Still, if you are using a monochrome monitor (or a laptop computer in a poorly lighted area), you might prefer to underline the anchor. To do so, set the Anchor Underline= line to Yes.

Another option you can change is the next line in the [Main] section. The Anchor Cursor= line tells Mosaic to change the mouse cursor from an arrow to a little hand when it is placed over a hyperlink entry. To invoke this function, make sure that this line is set to Anchor Cursor=yes. (To turn it off, set it to No.)

Displaying URLs

The Show URLs=yes line tells Mosaic to display the URL in the status bar when you move the cursor over an anchor. Set this line to No to turn off this feature. The default is Yes.

Setting FTP Options

The Extended FTP= line enables you to set Mosaic to show file icons and file sizes when you access a gopher or FTP site. To display these icons, set this option to Yes. When the line is set to No (the default setting is Yes), all that is displayed is a list of directories and files.

 Tip   You should keep the Extended FTP= line set to Yes so that you know the sizes of files before you access them. Large files, of course, take more time to access than smaller ones.

Setting Main Window Options

You can set three options that affect the way in which Mosaic's interface looks and displays information. The first of these options, the Toolbar= line, displays the toolbar at the top of the Mosaic window. When you set the Toolbar= line to Yes, it displays the toolbar. The No option shuts off the display. Unless you have a really good reason not to show the toolbar, you should keep this option set to Yes. The toolbar is very handy as you navigate the Web.

You can use another option to display the status bar in the lower left corner of the Mosaic window. This area displays transfer and file access information while you are accessing a site. Keep the Status bar= line set to Yes to keep the status bar displayed. (You can turn it off or on from the Options menu, as well.)

The third window option you can set is the Title/URL bar= line. This tells Mosaic to display the URL bar and Status Indicator (the rotating globe in the upper right corner of the window). Keep this line set to Yes to display these items. Keep this line set to No to turn them off.

Setting 8-Bit Sound

If you do not have a 16-bit sound card installed in your system, make sure that the Use 8-bit Sound= line is set to Yes. If you have a 16-bit sound card, such as a Sound Blaster 16, change this option to Yes.

 Note   Later in this chapter, in the [Viewers] section, you are shown how to configure multimedia devices so that you can use them with Mosaic.

Specifying Anchor Colors

The next section of MOSAIC.INI, [Settings], has a single line (Anchor Color=) that determines the color of the link anchor in the documents displayed. The default color is blue and its value is 0,0,255. To set the color to red, use the value 255,0,0; to set it to green, use the value 0,255,0; for other colors, experiment with these values until you find the color you like.

Determining Window Size and Position

The four lines that appear in the [Main Window] section of MOSAIC.INI tell Mosaic where the main window appears and how large it is. If you are comfortable with pixel heights and widths, adjust those numbers in this section. If not, return to the Mosaic main window and use your mouse to resize it. Then, from the **F**ile menu, choose Save P**r**eferences to save the current size and position of the Mosaic window.

 Tip Be sure to select the Save Preferences option after you resize and reposition your Mosaic window. Otherwise, the next time you start Mosaic, the window's size and location will be the same as they were before you changed them. You will wonder why your window keeps "jumping" back to its original location.

Setting E-Mail Titles

If you decide to send e-mail to the developers of Mosaic, use the [Mail] section of MOSAIC.INI to set the mail message's default title. When you load Mosaic, the default title (which appears in the Default Title= line) is "WinMosaic auto-mail feedback." You can change this to something more personal, such as "Help with Mosaic Wanted." Clearly, you can change the title when you compose the message. But if you know that this default title line exists, and what it says, you won't wonder why this title keeps appearing in your messages.

Configuring Newsgroup and Mail Settings

In the [Services] section, you can set the NNTP_Server= and SMTP_Server= lines to make sure that you can read USENET newsgroups and receive e-mail from the Mosaic developers (if you send them a message). The NNTP Server= line should be set to your service provider's Network News Transport Protocol (NNTP). The default setting in MOSAIC.INI is from the University of Illinois' `news.cso.uiuc.edu`. Set yours to your access provider's server. The syntax for the NNTP Server= line is usually "news.*site.domain,*"in which *site* is the name of your service (such as Iquest) and *domain* is the domain name (such as .net). Be sure to enclose the address in quotation marks. Ask your service provider for the site and domain names if you did not receive it when you obtained your account.

The SMTP_Server= line is the address of your local service's Simple Mail Transport Protocol (SMTP) server. The default setting for this line is NCSA's server, which is `ftp.ncsa.uiuc.edu`. Your provider's address may look something like `"smtp.iquest.net,"` or something similar. Be sure to enclose the address in quotation marks.

Configuring Multimedia Components

One of the most innovative features of the World Wide Web is the capability to transmit sound, graphics, and videos across great distances. Mosaic enables you to define which applications you want activated when you encounter one of these types of files during your navigations. The [Viewers] section in the MOSAIC.INI file lists the associations and directory paths to your multimedia applications. These applications (called Helper Applications) are external to Mosaic.

Table 16.1 shows the types of files Mosaic can recognize, and some of the available applications.

TABLE 16.1
Multimedia Applications and Mosaic

Media Types	File Extension	Application
Text	DOC, RTF, PS	Word for Windows
Sound	AU, WAV, MIDI	WHAM (must have sound card), WPlany (must have SPEAK.EXE loaded)
Graphic	JPG, GIF, TIF	LView, Photoshop
MPEG Movies	MPG, AVI, MOV	Movie Player (must have QuickTime for Windows)

Tip

If you need to acquire a copy of one or more of the applications in table 16.1, you can find some of them on CompuServe, America Online, or various FTP sites. Some of the listed applications are commercial applications and can only be purchased from registered software vendors.

Setting MIME Types

The [Viewers] section (see fig. 16.5) lists file types in the MIME format. MIME (Multipurpose Internet Mail Extensions) is a format used to attach sounds, images, and other files to e-mail. In the [Viewers] section of the MOSAIC.INI file, the lines TYPE0=, TYPE1=, and so on, indicate the MIME type Mosaic recognizes, (such as "audio/wav" for sound files, "image/gif" for graphics files, and "video/mpeg" for video files").

Figure 16.5

Multimedia settings in MOSAIC.INI.

```
Notepad - MOSAIC.INI
File  Edit  Search  Help
[Viewers]
TYPE0="audio/wav"
TYPE1="application/postscript"
TYPE2="image/gif"
TYPE3="image/jpeg"
TYPE4="video/mpeg"
TYPE5="video/quicktime"
TYPE6="video/msvideo"
TYPE7="application/x-rtf"
TYPE8="audio/x-midi"
TYPE9="application/zip"
rem TYPE9="audio/basic"
application/postscript="ghostview %ls"
image/gif="c:\winapps\lview\lview31 %ls"
image/jpeg="c:\winapps\lview\lview31 %ls"
video/mpeg="c:\winapps\mpegplay\mpegplay %ls"
video/quicktime="C:\WINAPPS\QTW\bin\player.exe %ls"
video/msvideo="mplayer %ls"
audio/wav="mplayer %ls"
audio/x-midi="mplayer %ls"
application/x-rtf="write %ls"
application/zip="C:\WINDOWS\APPS\ZIPMGR\ZM400.EXE %ls"
rem audio/basic="notepad %ls"
telnet="c:\network\qvt\tnstart.exe"

[Suffixes]
application/postscript=.ps,.eps,.ai,.ps
application/zip=.zip
```

Note You can add your own MIME type in the [Viewers] section by defining a new TYPE#, specifying a viewer, and, if necessary, adding a suffix list. (See the section called "Setting Media File Extension" later in this chapter for more details about a suffix list.)

For more information about MIME types, check out the following FTP site:

```
ftp://isi.edu/in-notes/media-types/media/types
```

Specifying Viewers

Immediately following the MIME sd lines is a section of lines (see fig. 16.6) in which you specify the viewer for each file type listed. Mosaic uses these INI lines to find which application to activate when a specific file type is downloaded. To ensure that

Mosaic can find and then activate the application you have associated with a given file type, you must edit these lines to reflect the path and executable name of the application.

```
━                        Notepad - MOSAIC.INI                   ▼ ‖
File   Edit   Search   Help
TYPE1="application/postscript"                                          ▲
TYPE2="image/gif"
TYPE3="image/jpeg"
TYPE4="video/mpeg"
TYPE5="video/quicktime"
TYPE6="video/msvideo"
TYPE7="application/x-rtf"
TYPE8="audio/x-midi"
TYPE9="application/zip"
rem TYPE9="audio/basic"
application/postscript="ghostview %ls"
image/gif="c:\winapps\lview\lview31 %ls"
image/jpeg="c:\winapps\lview\lview31 %ls"
video/mpeg="c:\winapps\mpegplay\mpegplay %ls"
video/quicktime="C:\WINAPPS\QTW\bin\player.exe %ls"
video/msvideo="mplayer %ls"
audio/wav="mplayer %ls"
audio/x-midi="mplayer %ls"
application/x-rtf="write %ls"
application/zip="C:\WINDOWS\APPS\ZIPMGR\ZM400.EXE %ls"
rem audio/basic="notepad %ls"
telnet="c:\network\qvt\tnstart.exe"

[Suffixes]
application/postscript=.ps,.eps,.ai,.ps
application/zip=.zip
text/html=
text/plain=                                                            ▼
◀ ▏                                                              ▶
```

Figure 16.6

These lines point to the application for the specific MIME viewer.

Suppose, for example, that you want to be able to view MPEG videos with Mosaic. To do so, you need to have on your hard drive an application, such as MPEGPLAY, that plays MPG files. To set up Mosaic to play MPEG videos, you must reference your MPEG application from the INI file. In the MOSAIC.INI file, find the following line:

```
video/mpeg="c:\winapps\mpegplay\mpegplay %ls"
```

This line simply tells you that Mosaic will play MPEG (.MPG) video files by accessing the MPEGPLAY application from this path. (The "%ls" extension simply replaces the normal .exe extension of a Windows application.)

If you happen to have the MPEGPLAY application (or another MPEG-compliant application) on your system but it does not reside in the c:\winapps\mpegplay directory, change the preceding line to reflect your specific path. If, for instance, you have your MPEGPLAY application in C:\MPEG\MPEGPLAY, your line would read as follows:

```
video/mpeg="c:\mpegplay\mpegplay %ls"
```

Be sure to keep the quotation marks in the line. Also, make sure you keep your backslashes and slashes going the right way. Remember, DOS systems use backslashes (\) in their names. (This can get very confusing when you start typing in HTTP addresses that use forward slashes.)

The last line in the [Viewers] section is a reference to the Telnet application on your system. Mosaic uses this line, `telnet="c:\trumpet\telw.exe"`, to connect to some servers. Be sure to update this line when you are configuring Mosaic. If, for example, you are using QVT WinNet as your telnet application and it is placed in your c:\network\qvt subdirectory, use the following syntax:

```
telnet="c:\network\qvt\tnstart.exe"
```

(Note that `tnstart.exe` is the executable file for QVN WinNet.)

Setting Media File Extensions

The preceding section showed you how to set your MIME TYPES and viewer applications. The next section in the MOSAIC.INI file, the [Suffixes] section, lists the various extensions for media files retrieved by FTP or from HTTP version 0.9 servers. When it encounters these files, Mosaic uses the information in the [Suffixes] section and the [Viewers] section to determine the name and path of the external viewer to launch.

Many World Wide Web servers, however, are HTTP/1.0. In these cases, the [Viewers] section lists all the information necessary for activating the external application.

Table 16.2 shows the default extensions for files in the [Suffix] section of MOSAIC.INI.

TABLE 16.2
File Extensions Listed in [Suffix]

Type of File	Extensions
application/postscript	.ps, .eps, .ai, .ps
application/x-rtf	.rtt, .wri
audio/wav	.wave, .wav, .WAV
audio/x-midi	.mid
image/gif	.gif
image/jpeg	.jpeg, .jpe, .jpg

Type of File	Extensions
image/x-tiff	.tiff, .tif
video/mpeg	.mpeg, .mpg
video/quicktime	.mov
video/msvideo	.avi

 Note When a file of a type listed in this section is written to your hard disk, it uses the last suffix in a particular line. If the viewer requires a specific extension, list that extension last. You might, for instance, use Paintshop Pro to view JPG files. Because these files sometimes are listed as JPEG or JPE, you need to make sure that .JPG is the last extension in the image/jpeg= line. This ensures that Paintshop Pro can read the image correctly.

To add other file types, list the type of file, add the equals sign (=), and list the extensions. The extensions must be separated by commas and always have a period before the extension, such as .jpg.

Specifying Annotation Directories

Mosaic enables you to add to Web documents text messages that do not edit the document, but are displayed whenever you view that document. You might, for instance, find an interesting document about space shuttle history. You can add some notes to this document by using the Annotate option in the Annotate menu. Then, when you view that document again, you can refer to those earlier annotations and add to them. Also, with Mosaic for Windows, you can share these annotations with others in a workgroup environment.

The [Annotations] section of MOSAIC.INI enables you to change the directory on your local drive (Directory= line) and your Group if on a network (Group Annotation Server= line). If you share the annotations across a network, the Group Annotation Server= line must include the machine name on the network and the port number. If you do not know your machine name and port number, you will need to ask your system administrator for them. If you do not plan to share annotations, keep the Group Annotation= line set to No.

You also can set the Default Title of the annotation in the Default Title= line.

Setting User Menus and Hotlists

The [User Menu*x*] and [HotList] sections of MOSAIC.INI refer to the menus and hotlists you set up while you are using Mosaic. You should not edit these sections in the INI file, because you may inadvertently damage these settings. These settings will be changed while you are actually using Mosaic while on the World Wide Web. Depending on the number of menus set up on your system; you may have several [User Menu*x*] sections, perhaps as many as five or six.

Caching Documents

The [Document Caching] section of the MOSAIC.INI file determines the number of documents Mosaic stores in memory. When you load a document, Mosaic retains the previous document (or as many as you indicate in the [Document Caching] section) in a memory cache, so that you can return to it quickly. The default is 2. If you have a large amount of memory (RAM), you might want to increase this number, perhaps to 6. If you find that your memory resources are being used quickly, decrease this number.

If you have very little memory (such as 4 MB) on your system, you might want to change the default number to 1 or even 0. By setting it to 0 (zero), you turn off caching. Remember to turn caching on if you upgrade your memory. You can turn caching back on by adding the number of documents that you want to cache, such as 1, 2, or so on.

Selecting Fonts

Do not edit the various [Font] sections in the MOSAIC.INI file. To change fonts, use the **C**hoose Font option from the **O**ptions menu while you are using Mosaic.

Configuring Proxy Information

Some MOSAIC.INI files have a section named [Proxy Information]. A *proxy gateway* enables Mosaic to pass on a network request to an outside agent through a *firewall*, which performs the request for Mosaic. The agent then returns the information to Mosaic. The network request is in the form of a URL. This type of gateway is set up so that Mosaic clients "sealed off" from the Internet can rely on agents to access the Internet for them. A user of a Mosaic software client using a proxy gateway still thinks he or she is on the Internet, even though he or she technically is not.

Proxy gateways currently are implemented on a per access method basis, such as FTP, gopher, wais, news, and http. Each URL access method can send its requests to a different proxy. The following sample INI section adds proxy support to Mosaic for Windows:

```
[Proxy Information]
http_proxy=http://aixtest.cc.ukans.edu:911/
ftp_proxy=http://aixtest.cc.ukans.edu:911/
wais_proxy=http://aixtest.cc.ukans.edu:911/
gopher_proxy= http://aixtest.cc.ukans.edu:911/
```

 Tip For more information about obtaining a Web server that supports proxy services, go to the following URLs:

```
http://info.cern.ch/hypertext/WWW/Daemon/Overview.html
http://www.ncsa.uiuc.edu/SDG/Software/WinMosaic/ProxyInfo.html
```

Using Netscape Clients

Netscape Communications' Netscape browser has become the premier Web browser on the World Wide Web frontier. By some estimates, Netscape has captured upwards of 70 percent of the market share of Web browsers. This chapter introduces you to some of Netscape's features and shows you how to customize the way it works and looks. This latter section also discusses some of the more advanced features of Netscape 1.1, such as security and mail handling.

Specifically, this section discusses the following:

◆ Sending e-mail in Netscape

◆ Using bookmarks

◆ Using the toolbar

◆ Using the status bar

◆ Using the current URL

◆ Using extended FTP

◆ Displaying inline images

◆ Using sound

◆ Choosing fonts

Understanding Netscape's Interface

Netscape's interface is similar in a lot of ways to the Mosaic interface. If you are comfortable with Mosaic, you should feel right at home with Netscape (see fig. 16.7). Netscape also offers new features, menus, and toolbar buttons that help you make the most out of your Web travels.

Figure 16.7

2.0 is the latest version, 1.1 is not for resale anymore.

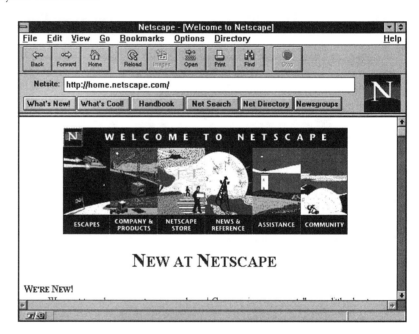

Viewing the Netscape Window

The primary area of Netscape is its main window, where you view Web documents and graphics. Figure 16.8 points out the major features of this window. See table 16.3 for descriptions of each of these features.

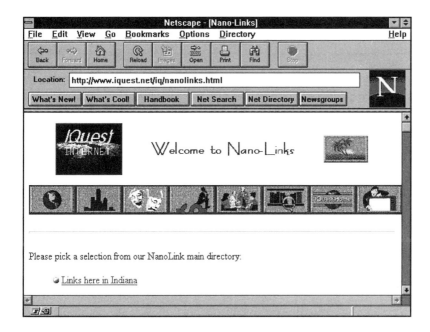

Figure 16.8

Netscape's main window, with major features highlighted.

TABLE 16.3
Netscape's Interface Features

Element	Description
Menus	Use the various menus to perform numerous tasks in Netscape, such as opening files, mailing messages, changing preferences, and finding help.
Toolbar buttons	Click on toolbar buttons to perform some of the most common tasks in Netscape, such as revisiting pages, reloading pages, printing, finding text strings, and stopping transfers in progress.
Window title	This is the main title of the Web document. The title appears in brackets ([]) next to the word "Netscape."
Title bar	This bar displays the current URL. You can type in a new URL and press Enter to move to another Internet site.

continues

TABLE 16.3, CONTINUED
TABLE 16.3, CONTINUED
Netscape's Interface Features

Element	Description
Directory buttons	Click on these buttons to bring up pages that help you navigate the Internet. You can find out what is new, see some cool sites, call up the Netscape Handbook (online documentation on the Netscape browser), search the Internet, choose sites from an Internet directory, and use newsgroups.
Status indicator	This is the Netscape company logo. During a transfer, animated meteors fly across the logo to indicate that the transfer is in progress. Click on this logo to stop a transfer and to return to the Netscape home page.
Colors and underlines	These features indicate hotlinks in a document. Underlining is used only on black-and-white monitors. After you select a hotlink, your selection is highlighted and changes colors to indicate that you have clicked on it recently. You can change this color by means of the Options menu.
Content area	This is the main document area in Netscape. Scroll bars on the right and bottom of the screen help you navigate through pages that may fill up more than your screen is capable of displaying.
Progress bar	One of the handiest features, the Progress bar indicates the size of the document Netscape is transferring and the percentage of the document that has been transferred.
Security indicator	This feature shows you if a document is secure or not. If the indicator displays a broken key, the document is not secure. If it displays a key with two teeth, the document is considered a high-grade encrypted document. If the indicator displays one tooth, the document is considered a medium-grade encrypted document. Netscape's security feature is discussed later in this chapter.

Using Netscape's Menus

Many of the features contained in Netscape's menus are similar to those in Mosaic or are self-explanatory. This section focuses on the menu options and some newer features of Netscape, followed by a lengthy discussion of bookmarks. See the "Using Bookmarks" section for information on using the Bookmarks menu.

Sending E-Mail in Netscape

One of the shortcomings of Web browsers has been the way they handle mail messages. With Netscape 1.1, you are given a much stronger environment to send mail and post newsgroup articles. In the File menu, the Mail Document option is available. By using this option, you can create a mail message and attach Web page attachments to it to send to someone. In the Send Mail/Post News dialog box (see fig. 16.9), you can address your mail message, specify the attachment URL (if you want to attach a page to your message), and write your mail message.

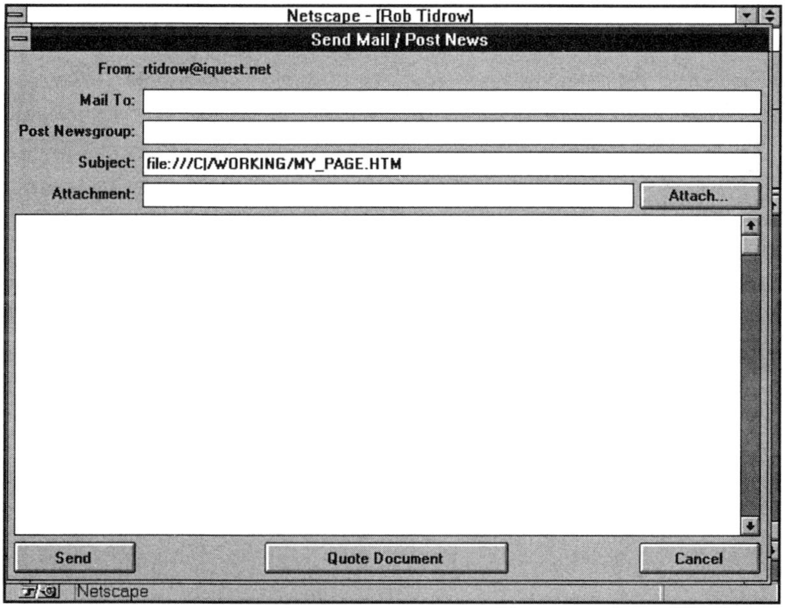

Figure 16.9

Use the Send Mail/Post News dialog box to create mail messages in Netscape.

The first time you use the Mail Document option, you must specify the name of your mail server (known as SMTP) and provide your e-mail address in the Mail dialog box (see fig. 16.10).

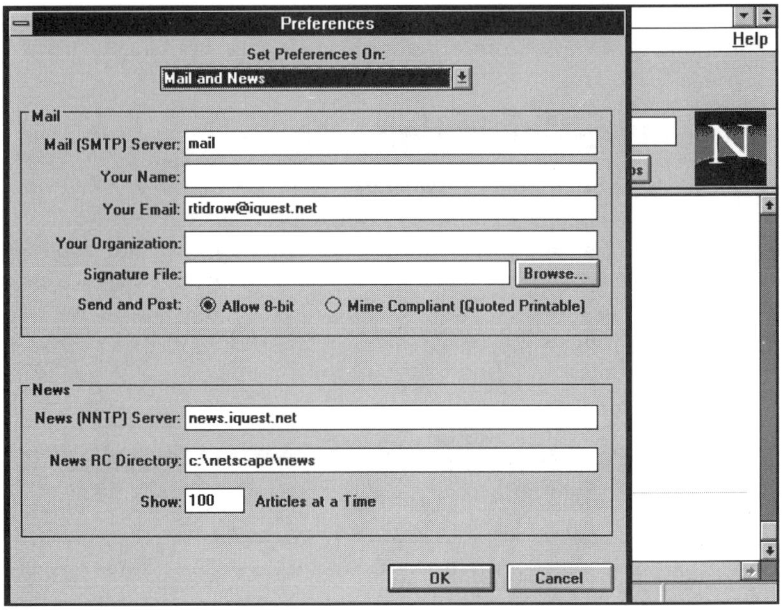

Figure 16.10

You must fill in the Mail dialog box before you send your first mail message with Netscape.

Using Bookmarks

Because information sources and methods of information retrieval vary, it's best to organize your resources by subject. Netscape not only serves as a World Wide Web browser, but it can also be used for searching other protocols such as FTP and Gopher. Thus, Netscape enables you to combine the most popular resources together for access when you need it. If you are looking for information on frogs, for example, you can include sites that have searchable databases by means of WWW, photographs by means of FTP, and research papers by means of gopher.

Different Web browsers have different ways of storing your favorite Internet sites. Netscape uses *bookmarks*. Bookmarks in Netscape are similar to bookmarks that you place in your favorite novel—they are simply references to Internet resources, such as Web pages, that you want to access quickly.

This section reviews how bookmarks work, and pays extra attention to how bookmarks can be subcategorized so that you can navigate the Internet in an organized manner.

After you access Netscape's Bookmarks feature in the **B**ookmarks menu, you will see two commands on the top of the menu, **A**dd Bookmark, and View **B**ookmarks (see fig. 16.11). When you pick Add Bookmark, Netscape adds your currently loaded document's URL into the list. The URL appears at the bottom of the menu the next time you look into it.

Figure 16.11

*Netscape's
Bookmarks menu
options: Add
Bookmark and
View Bookmark.*

When you choose the View **B**ookmarks function in Netscape, the Bookmark List
dialog box pops up with several options (see fig. 16.12). This dialog box serves as an
editor/navigator that lets you manage your favorite Internet resources. Here, you can
add your current document, jump to an Internet site that you have stored, or edit the
appearance and organization of your list.

Along the top of the Bookmark List dialog box are two buttons that relate to storing
and navigating the Internet. Add Bookmark adds the currently loaded document to
your bookmark list. In reality, the document's URL and not the actual document is
stored. This distinction is important because it enables you to store the *locations* of
documents, not the actual documents themselves. The next time you access this
document, you then are guaranteed that you are viewing the most recent version of
that document. Features like bookmarks are optimal for frequently changing information, such as news.

The other button at the top of the Bookmark List dialog box is the Go To button.
This button is dimmed until you click on one of the items in the Bookmark List, after
which you can click on the Go To button to download that document to your
browser.

Figure 16.12

*The Bookmark
List dialog box.*

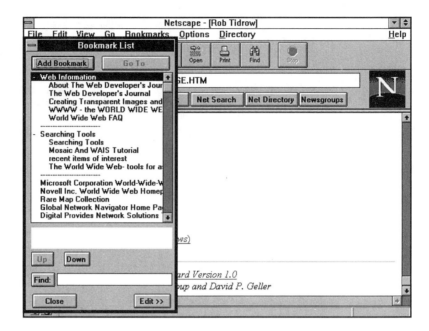

Note   Do not be surprised if you are denied access to a document that you have previously stored as a bookmark item. There are cases where Webmasters temporarily turn off their Web servers for general maintenance or other reasons. You also might have tried to access the document while it is being updated from another source. If you get a denied document error message, wait a couple of minutes and try again. If you cannot access a document for a couple of days, then you know its time to take the document's URL off your bookmark list.

Editing the Bookmark List

As you learned earlier, when you add a bookmark to a document to the Bookmark List, Netscape automatically places the new bookmark at the bottom of the Bookmark menu. This might be fine when you have only a few bookmarks saved, but it can become a little annoying when your list starts to grow. At this point, you may want to do some house cleaning on your list and organize your sites.

To do this, Netscape includes two buttons on the Bookmark List dialog box that helps you manage the placement of a bookmark. The Up and Down buttons (see fig. 16.13) enable you to move a selected bookmark up the list or down the list, depending on where you want it placed in the list.

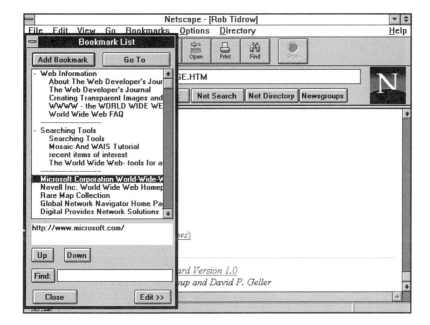

Figure 16.13

*Click on the Up
and Down
buttons to move
selected bookmarks
on the Bookmark
List.*

Another key feature of the Bookmark List dialog box is the Edit portion. You can expand the dialog box by clicking on the Edit button. This displays the complete Bookmark List dialog box (see fig. 16.14), in which you can add more organization and control over your Bookmark menu.

The View Bookmarks button loads a temporary document into Netscape with a listing of your site's hyperlinked text. Although there are other utilities on the Internet that can do this for you, with Netscape you can create a document and then save it as HTML format, or access the View Source option from the View menu (see fig. 16.15).

Exporting and importing bookmarks can also be done from this menu. If, for instance, you need to send people a list of URLs, the quickest and easiest way to accomplish this is to export the file and have them import it. As well as giving you a place to define a name and a URL for your document, the dialog box also has a field called Last Visited, where it notes the last time you looked at the document. Added on tells you when you added the URL to Netscape's Bookmark function, and includes an area where you can take notes on a document. This area is important to note, because Netscape does not have an annotate function.

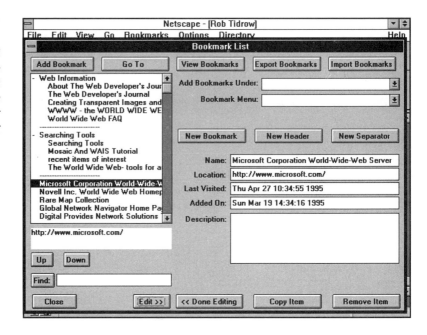

Figure 16.14

The expanded version of the Bookmark List gives you more control over your Bookmark dialog box.

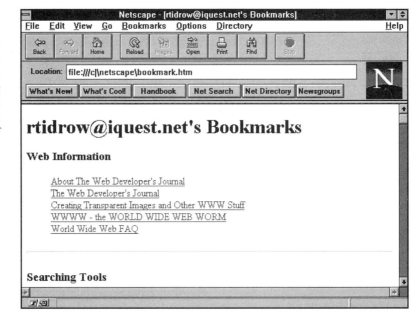

Figure 16.15

Clicking on the View Bookmarks button within the Bookmarks dialog box generates a file with a hyperlinked list of your stored URLs.

The buttons here are very simple in their purpose. The following explains the purpose of each button (see fig 16.14):

◆ **Two Arrows.** These buttons let you move the position of the Document name in the list of bookmarks.

◆ **Copy Item.** This button duplicates your selected page, where you can then edit the name or location to make changes.

◆ **Fewer Options.** This button makes the dialog box smaller, so you have more screen room to view pages while you are browsing.

◆ **Remove Item.** This button deletes your selected document from your Bookmark list.

◆ **New Bookmark.** This button adds documents to your bookmark list. This button brings up a dialog box where you can type in a document's URL and name.

◆ **New Header.** This button creates nested menus or submenus.

◆ **New Separator.** This button creates lines between sections within the Bookmark List menu. This feature is great for organizing URLs that are similar in topic.

The capability to organize the menu is what makes Netscape's Bookmark List menu's Bookmark function helpful. Netscape enables you to create a menu so you can organize your favorite URLs by topic. With the following steps, you can create your own submenus:

1. Select View **B**ookmarks from the Bookmarks menu.

2. Click on the New Header Button.

3. Enter the name of the nested menu as you would like it to appear in the menu itself.

4. Click once on the name of the header on the list to the left.

5. Click on the New Bookmark button.

6. Enter in the name and location of the document that you would like to appear in the nested menu.

7. Once you click on the Done Editing button, you can check to see if it worked!

In the future you can look forward to more advanced features that address the issue of storing and retrieving your favorite Web sites. Because the World Wide Web is, in reality, still in the beginning stages, there will be an explosion of sites as corporations, schools, and individuals realize that they have the power to publish on their own. You will need advanced features to sort, search, and store useful sites.

Using Netscape's Toolbar

The *toolbar* is the row of buttons along the top of the screen (see fig. 16.16). These buttons help you navigate between and store the documents you access while surfing the Net. With these buttons and a click of the mouse, you can apply the most popular menu commands. The toolbar buttons provide quick-and-easy access to documents while you browse.

Figure 16.16

Netscape's toolbar buttons.

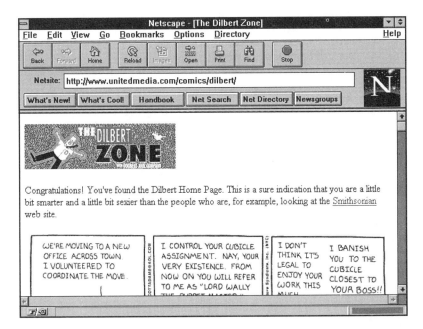

The following list describes the toolbar buttons (from left to right) and their functions:

- ◆ **Back.** With this button, you can view the previously viewed documents, one page at a time. Click on this button to load the page that precedes the current page.

- ◆ **Forward.** This button takes you one page forward if you have used the Page Backward button. Using this button does not load the next document from the World Wide Web, but only loads the next document ahead of the one in memory. Because the document is stored temporarily on your system, using the forward and backward buttons takes less time than retrieving the documents through the Net.

◆ **Home.** Click on this button to move immediately to your home page. Because you define home pages in your preferences, you can make it a default location loaded when you launch Netscape, such as your company's home page, where consistently changing information may warrant frequent access.

◆ **Reload.** Use this button to retrieve again a document and all its graphics from the file server. This feature is helpful for virtual documents and programming, where reviewing constantly changing files is necessary. Virtual documents, such as a weather report from a system or an order from an online mall, usually are created instantly by the World Wide Web server or by a database linked to the server. By clicking on the Reload button, you request the document as if it had never been received before. The process takes longer to use than the Page Forward and Page Backward buttons because it has to retrieve the document again through the Net.

The best use for this button, however, is to create your own HTML documents. Because most HTML editors are not WYSIWYG (what you see is what you get), they cannot display the document as Netscape can. By keeping Netscape loaded while you create your HTML documents in a text editor, you can preview the results of your editing. Whenever you make and save a change to the HTML document, click on the Reload button to see the results.

◆ **Open.** This button has the same effect as the File menu's Open URL function. It displays a dialog box that asks for a location. You can either type in a URL directly, or select one of the entries from your saved hotlist. The field on the left hand side contains the actual URL for the document. This is where you would enter one by hand if you type it in. The field at the upper right has the title of the document to which you are referring in your hotlist. Below the URL field, you can select the hotlist to which you want to refer.

◆ **Print.** This button prints the currently loaded page, including the graphics. Depending on your printer driver and settings, you may get the standard Netscape gray background on your prints.

◆ **Find.** Click on the Find button to do a text search in the currently loaded page. The Find button finds a string of text. This tool can be very useful for long documents, but it does not search linked documents. To search more than one document at a time, you have to go to sites that have a searchable database.

Note Saving a document is helpful for many reasons. You can refer to a saved document as often as you want. You also might want to set a document that is on your system locally for your home page. This way you will not have to wait for Netscape to retrieve the document before you can use Mosaic (or vice versa). With some programs, such as Netscape, you can interrupt a session by asking for another document, and then return to the Netscape session.

One of the best reasons for saving HTML documents is so that you can learn how to create your own HTML documents. After you save the document, you can switch to your word processor and study the commands used by the document's author. This is a good way to learn some of the complex HTML coding features.

Using Netscape's Directory Menu

To aid the user by providing a bunch of preset links, Netscape has included a menu called the directory menu. Inside this menu are Web documents that are helpful in the search for technical details on the Web or general Internet information. The following is a list of each of the functions listed in the menu and what they return:

◆ **What's New!** Brings you to a page on Netscape's Web server that lists new Web sites that the staff of Netscape Communications Co. feels are interesting.

◆ **What's Cool!** Selecting this option brings you to a page that lists sites that the staff of Netscape Communications Co. thinks are interesting and thorough.

◆ **Net Search.** Searching for specific information on the Internet can be a challenge—selecting this feature will present a list of databases that you can use to help you find what you are looking for.

◆ **Net Directory.** This will bring you to a document on Netscape's server that lists and links to other servers, which will help direct you to information that you are looking for.

◆ **Newsgroups.** This will log onto your Usenet News server and enable you to read current articles.

Figure 16.17

The results of clicking on the What's New? menu option.

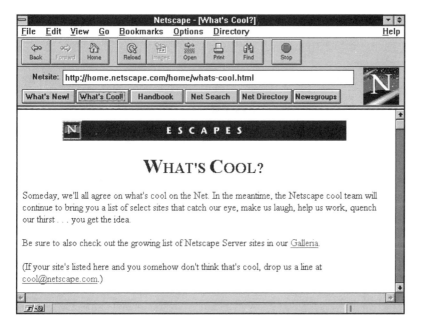

Figure 16.18

The results of clicking on the What's Cool? menu option.

Figure 16.19

The results of clicking on the Newsgroups menu option.

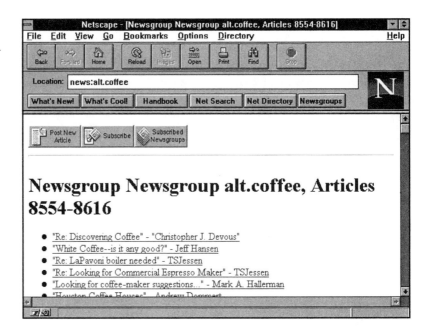

Figure 16.20

The results of clicking on the Internet Directory menu option.

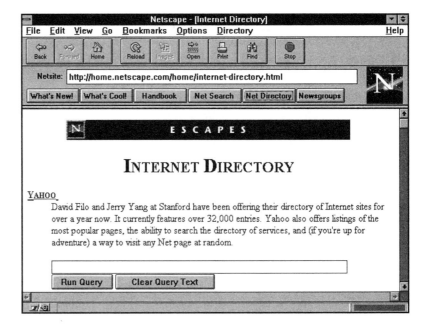

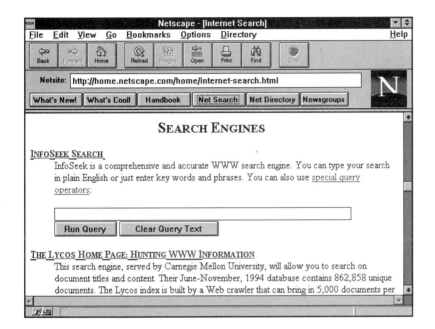

Figure 16.21

The results of clicking on the Internet Search menu option.

Using the Status Bar

Netscape's status bar displays the current status of a document—a handy feature, because retrieving a document can take a long time. When you move your pointer to the hypertext links in a loaded document, notice that the status bar (at the bottom of the window) displays the URL for the specific document or file linked by the text. Also, because the status bar displays whatever protocol was used to retrieve information, you can see not only the HTTP URL, but also whether the hypertext link is a gopher or FTP site.

The status bar also displays the steps being taken to acquire a document you have requested. Messages displayed include a request from a file server, a notice that the server is waiting for information, and a notice that it is receiving the information. Netscape will present a progress bar that displays the length of a download.

The status bar is for informational purposes only. You cannot do anything to or with the status bar—it just shows you what steps are being taken to retrieve a document.

Using the Current URL

A field just below the toolbar displays the URL for the currently loaded document. This field is mostly for your information, but you can edit the information (using the Cut, Copy, and Paste buttons) by clicking directly in this field. After you edit the information in the Current URL field and press Enter, Netscape tries to find the document whose URL you have entered. Although this shortcut is even faster than clicking on the Open URL button, you cannot use it to take information saved in your hotlist. To include that information, you have to remember the appropriate URL and enter it in here.

Just being able to see the location of a document is a big help. With the URL you can see not only the location of the file server that contains your document, but also the directories in which the document is located.

You can use Netscape just as easily in an FTP session. As the following section explains, by entering the FTP address you enable Netscape to display the directories and download the files for you.

Using Extended FTP

One of the benefits of using Netscape as a browsing tool is its adaptability. With this one program, you can access the World Wide Web, gopher, WAIS, and Newsgroups. Other forms of data and information use these protocols to give users unique services, such as whois, finger, and veronica.

This section focuses on how to use Netscape to retrieve files from other Internet sites, by using the file transfer protocol (FTP). In the most popular FTP, referred to as *anonymous FTP*, you access files and directories on other machines without actually having an account. Files are placed so that everyone can look at them, without compromising the security of a network. In Netscape, you can use FTP by entering a URL in the Current URL field, or by selecting Open URL from the File menu.

To use Netscape for the FTP, you must log in to the FTP server as user:anonymous. Be sure to put your name and e-mail in your preferences so that Netscape can answer the FTP server correctly. Sometimes FTP servers do not let you in if your e-mail address is not entered correctly.

When you are logged in to the file server, the list you see is similar to the list displayed in Netscape's gopher presentation. Next to the filenames is an icon that represents a directory or document. *Documents*, in this case, can mean either text files, graphics files, or executable programs. Although you are able to see executable programs, keep in mind that you are using FTP and are not able to launch a program without first downloading it. Because compressed files move more quickly through the Net than uncompressed files, you might have to decompress a file after you download it. See Chapter 8, "Managing a WWW Service," for more information about popular compression techniques and how to decompress files.

Most FTP servers give you an introduction and specific instructions for downloading files from the site you have logged on to. An introductory message might look something like this:

```
Message from FTP server:
230-Welcome to Vyne Communications' FTP server.
230-Our server is growing as fast as the rest of the I-way; Surf this way again
soon!
230-
230-We USED TO have the official release of Marvel's Generation X, but that
230-has now been taken offline. Please, even if you have come here for another
230-reason, send E-mail to joe@vyne.com asking for more Marvel images. We very
230-much would like to serve such files for you, but have yet to convince Marvel
230-that this is a good idea. Your support will help. Thanx.
230-
230-Comments, suggestions, constructive criticism:      joe@vyne.com
230-Complaints, whining, flames:                        /dev/null
230-
```

Netscape displays this message under a line that divides the list of files. At the top of the list of files, a notice alerts you to the message.

You use FTP in Netscape just as you use the Web. If you are interested in looking in a specific directory, just click on the hypertext name of that directory. When you do this, Netscape retrieves the contents of that file from the FTP server. When you click on the document name, Netscape starts downloading the file. You can monitor the downloading of the file by watching the status bar at the bottom of the window.

When Netscape downloads a file from the FTP server, it places the file in a specific directory. If you want this directory to be different from the one in which Netscape resides, you must change your temp directory in the preferences.

If you venture down a couple of layers in the directories, you might want to move back up (the equivalent of using the DOS CD command). To move up one directory, click on the hyperlinked text (called the Parent Directory) at the top of the list of FTP files.

You do not have to log out of the FTP server as you do with other FTP software. Simply quitting Netscape or opening a new document logs you out. If you need to, you can navigate back to the FTP session by using the Page Forward and Page Backward buttons at the top of the window.

Displaying Inline Images

Clicking on hypertext links and zooming from one location to another in seconds can be very exciting, especially because these documents can be located anywhere in the world. The images that people place in their documents make the experience entertaining. These images range from company logos to photographs of events and parties to pictures from NASA. A great way to keep people's interest is to use images in your documents. Just as the publishing industry continually improves graphics and illustrations in magazines to hold the interest of readers, the World Wide Web continues to change and improve its graphics.

The proper name for displaying an image within the Netscape document is called *inline images*. Netscape has an interesting way of displaying images. If the images are prepared a certain way, Netscape displays them first at low resolution, increasing the resolution as time passes. In this way, you can see the image quickly up front, and in more detail as you continue to download the images. Netscape can also download and display images simultaneously. Both of these features give the appearance of downloading the document faster.

To ensure that Netscape displays the images in the documents you browse through, pick Auto-Load Images in the Options menu. The next time you download a file, you will see the images.

Some people prefer to keep the Auto-Load Images option turned off, because viewing the document takes too long when the option is turned on. In this case, Netscape displays an icon at the location of each image, but does not retrieve the images. When you want to look at a specific image, all you have to do is click on the icon. Netscape then downloads only the image you click on.

Using Sound

Although Netscape can download images so that you can view them in a document, it cannot single-handedly download all multimedia formats and present them to you.

Netscape cannot play a sound file, for example, without some help. On the Internet, most of these files are in the Sun AU format—a UNIX format used mostly by Sun computers. Some files, however, are in Wav format for Windows, MPEG format for all platforms, or Quicktime format (for both Windows and the Mac).

Because Netscape cannot process these files, and because the file formats and technology change quickly, Netscape relies upon other software to do the work. In this way, the Netscape software remains a small and simple (and the developers can concentrate on HTML browsers and servers). Generally, a sound icon means that some audio exists to which you can listen.

To hear downloaded sounds, you must use your preferences to alert Netscape to the program you want to use. The preferences' Helper Applications include a list of file extensions; with a brief description of the file format they belong to. For each file format, you have to choose a player application and tell Netscape what directory the application is in.

When you click on the icon or hypertext link for the sound file, Netscape immediately begins to download the file, temporarily storing the data on the hard drive. After the file is downloaded, your program of choice automatically launches and plays the file.

Choosing Fonts

Generally, publishers of everything from magazines and books to CD-ROMs design the product carefully to make it attractive to potential buyers. This creative work in graphic design is a full-time job. Artists carefully work on the placement of photographs and type, using fonts, colors, illustrations, and headlines to create an attractive product.

With Netscape, the designer cannot control many conditions, such as the size of the window and the resolution of the screen. As a designer of the document, you may not even know whether the user is viewing the graphics. With this in mind, you have to work on the document in a way that enables the end user to have as much creative input into the look of your information as you do—viewers can choose their own fonts and type sizes.

Although this might seem a disadvantage to the designer of a document, it gives you, the viewer, greater control over what you see and how you see it. When someone creates an HTML document, that person is not concerned with the fonts a viewer is using. (As a matter of fact, the designer has no control over which fonts the viewer uses—the viewer controls the fonts.) The creator of a document is concerned only with the headlines and body text. Document creators can design the images in a document and can control which text is what size. Other options, such as which text is italicized, are in the creator's hands as well.

To change your font settings, open the Options menu and choose Preferences. Here, you can pick settings for your fonts. The styles are organized in the same manner as that in which the HTML code is written. You can go through the different logical styles and pick a font for each of them.

Netscape is a powerful browsing tool with which you can tour the world. The controls discussed in this chapter are helpful in easing your search and assist you in remembering the sites you liked the best. The controls also help you make documents look the way you want them to look.

Network Security

A secure network does not exist; nor does a secure computer. The only secure computer is one that is unplugged, locked in a secure vault that only one person knows the combination to, and that person died last year. When you move beyond that scenario, you must expect lapses in security.

The question is how much "insecurity"—for lack of a better term—are you willing to accept? The next question is to what do you want to apply security? Are you trying to keep people from using your CPU processor? Are you trying to keep them from seeing your data? Are you trying to keep them from ruining your hardware? What, exactly, are you attempting to keep safe?

The Unix operating system inherently contains a few loopholes and inconsistencies that can be exploited by a wily hacker to his or her benefit. Originally, Unix was not written with security in mind, but rather ease of use. In fact, many vendor versions of Unix shipped with known security holes, and it was the responsibility of the system administrator to close those holes. Were it not for events like the Robert Morris Internet Worm of 1988, many of those holes would still exist.

Although Unix sounds less than trustworthy, compare Unix to a DOS-based operating system, which has no security whatsoever. Considered in that light, Unix turns out to be one of the most secure operating systems still considered usable.

What happens when you connect a secure computer to a network, though? Suddenly individuals are allowed to access data and perform operations without the necessity of sitting at the keyboard. A network provides so many advantages over a standalone computer, that standalones are virtually dinosaurs of the past. At the same time, however, the benefits bring disadvantages. Those disadvantages are risks—you are allowing someone into your system and trusting that they will respect your system and its data.

This chapter looks at ways of reducing the risks to which you expose your system. Understand, however, that no system is entirely foolproof. The first step in risk reduction is to comprehend the different levels of security that can be applied to operating systems.

Understanding Security Levels

The Trusted Computing Standards Evaluation Criteria (also known as the Orange Book), established by the United States Department of Defense, concludes that one cannot simply say that a computer is secure or not secure. Instead, it says that different levels of security can be assigned to an operating system. All these levels are based upon the *trust* you have in the operating system. A highly trusted system prevents intruders from entering the system, whereas a less trusted system has more possibilities of an intruder coming in unnoticed.

Four different levels of security are represented by letters ranging from A to D. Within each level of security, a number can be used to subdivide the level further, as in A1, A2, and so on. DOS is representative of a D1-level operating system. DOS has no security whatsoever; whoever is sitting at the keyboard has complete access to everything on the system. The concept of file ownership and permissions is virtually nonexistent in DOS—all the files are owned by the current user.

At the other end of the spectrum, an A1 level is virtually the machine locked in the vault without power or users. Everything else falls somewhere in-between.

C-level operating systems have more security than D-level ones, and have a means by which a user is identified before he or she is allowed to access and manipulate files. Standard Unix, without any features other than logins, passwords, and file ownership concepts, represents C1 security. C2 is a step higher than C1 and includes the capability to keep users from executing commands if they lack certain criteria, as well as the capability to audit every action that takes place. Many Unix systems today, notably SCO Unix, allow for these additional facilities and are C2-certified.

B-level operating systems must offer further security restraints—including an inability for the owner of a file to change the permissions of it. Very few operating systems, and certainly not those readily available in the commercial market, meet any of the B level-requirements.

Deciding How Much Security to Implement

Although some experts issue the blanket statement that you can never have enough security and that the best thing you can do is implement more, more, more security, these generalities could not be further from the truth. Security, inherently, makes it harder to enter a system by providing additional locks that users must pass. Unfortunately, legitimate users must pass those locks as well. Every security measure installed creates more work for someone. In the instance of applying additional passwords, additional work is required by all users to further identify themselves before being allowed to do the transactions they want to do. With auditing, which may be invisible to the end user, the system administrators must assume additional tasks; they must define rights, maintain log files, and audit them on a regular basis.

Figure 17.1 shows a crude representation of the security spectrum. At one end is no security whatsoever; the system is easy to use by virtue of the fact that no constraints are placed on users or administrators.

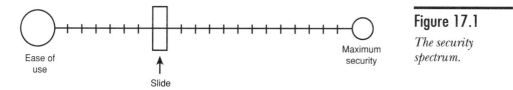

Ease of use

Slide

Maximum security

Figure 17.1

The security spectrum.

At the other end of the spectrum is maximum security—again referring to the unplugged machine locked in a vault. At this end, the system is as secure as it can be, but so difficult to use that no one wants to. The slide in the middle is moveable so that it can be custom-tailored to each site.

Because absolutes rarely exist in life and little can be shown with a straight line, figure 17.2 presents the same information in a more realistic manner. The left side of the graph tracks the number of computer problems relating to security measures (including both user and administrator problems), whereas the bottom represents the amount of security implemented. When no security is implemented, no problems occur. As soon as security is implemented, the number of problems begins to increase. The term "problems" is used to represent legitimate complaints as well as additional workload.

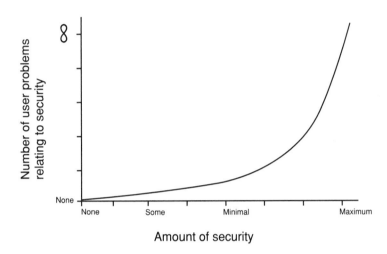

In figure 17.2, notice that the line does not grow in a linear fashion; this is known instead as an *indifference curve*. As a small amount of security is implemented, only a few problems occur. It is, in fact, possible to implement more security without affecting the number of problems too significantly. When the security measures begin to tighten significantly, the number of problems begins to increase at a rapid pace.

Just looking at this chart, however, is not enough to formulate an answer as to how much security to implement. For one thing, you need to define what you are trying to secure. This ties in to the earlier question of what you are trying to protect. Is the cost of protecting that entity worth doing so? For example, it can be costly to prevent someone from deleting the operating system from a machine. Is it worth it? Most operating systems can be reinstalled within a short period of time—a day at the very most. After you buy an operating system and install it, no changes are made to it beyond that, so you can always go back and restore it to the way it was when you installed it.

What about your hard drive? Can you protect it from someone driving a tank through the front door and blasting it with artillery shells? The answer is yes, you can, but is it worth the cost of constructing a bunker? Probably not. Most hard drives can be formatted, and reconstructed—again within a day usually.

What you cannot recover, and what your biggest investment is in, is your data. You can run to the computer store and buy an operating system. You can run there and buy a hard drive. But you cannot run to the store and buy a copy of your data that has been in the process of being defined since the day you opened your doors for business. That is what you should devote your time and talents to protecting (and backing up).

With regard to that data, the next item that needs to be investigated is the possibility of a system intrusion that could affect that data. Figure 17.3 shows a simple graph charting the potential/possibility for intrusion against the amount of security implemented. This example is for a small business and not indicative of a giant firm. With no security whatsoever, the potential for intrusion is unlimited. Implementing some security measures reduces this risk significantly, whereas implementing maximum security all but eliminates it.

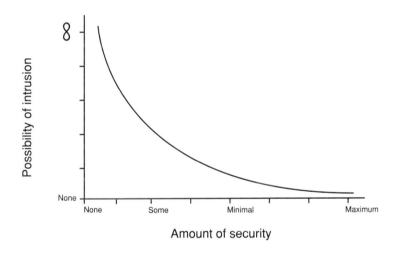

Figure 17.3

Weighing the amount of security against the possibility of intrusion.

The actual representation of the graph shown in figure 17.3 is different for every organization. It depends upon the number of users accessing the system, the value of the data (the more valuable, the more incentive to try and break in), and how access is allowed (must users log in here, or are they granted access to everything on the system by virtue of logging into another host).

Figures 17.2 and 17.3 are different for every organization, and one of the key jobs of management and administration is to define what each graph looks like for their organization. After those two items (potenial for intrusion and number of problems created) have been defined, they can be weighed against each other, as in figure 17.4, to find the equilibrium point at which they meet.

In figure 17.4, an equilibrium point is found by weighing the possibility of intrusion against the number of user problems inherent in implementing security measures. That equilibrium point denotes the point at which the company works the most effectively. The potential for intrusion is curtailed somewhat by the implementation of security measures, yet users are inconvenienced only slightly.

The amount of inconvenience the users tolerate is offset by the gains that come from reducing the possibility for system intrusion. Understanding where the equilibrium lies is essential in planning what measures to take. If the implemented measures fall on either side of the equilibrium, as shown in figure 17.5, then full realization is not obtained.

Figure 17.4

Finding the equilibrium point.

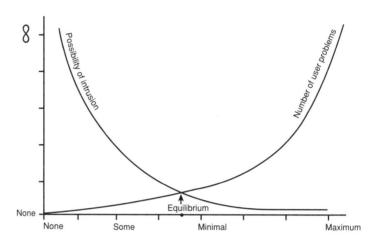

Figure 17.5

Points of non-equilibrium.

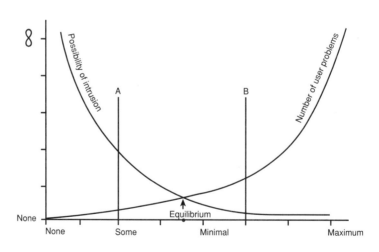

Within figure 17.5, point A represents a conservative attempt at security. The users are not inconvenienced significantly and, at the same time, the potential for system intrusion is still great. Not enough preventive measures have been taken, and intruders can more easily access this system than should be the case. The flip side of this is reflected in point B. Here, security measures have been liberally applied. The possibility of system intrusion is significantly reduced, yet users are required to go through more steps than they should—possibly entering multiple passwords and being forced to log out exactly at 5:00 p.m. The thing to note is that with implementation falling to either side of the equilibrium point, a loss in potential is generated. Falling on the A side, you lose the potential to provide adequate security to protect your system. Falling on the B side, you lose the potential to get more productivity from users by requiring them to deal with more security measures than they should.

One last item of note regarding the amount of security to implement is that after you define your equilibrium point, you should always be cognizant to factors that can cause it to change. Firing a number of programmer/analysts can create an outside body of disgruntled ex-employees who would like to break into your system. Possessing knowledge about the way your system is configured and works, they have enhanced skills that would allow them to break into your system, and the entire possibility of intrusion shifts to the right, as depicted in figure 17.6.

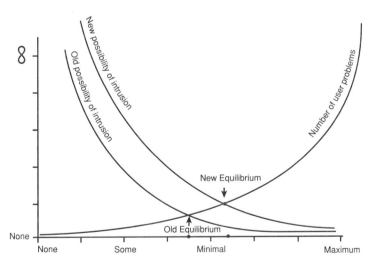

Amount of security

Figure 17.6

A shift in the possibility of intrusion changes the equilibrium point.

The shifting in the indifference curve depicted in figure 17.6 causes the equilibrium point also to shift to the right. More security measures should be implemented to counter the shift. The security measures can be installed locally and across the network—depending upon your actual scenario.

Local Security

Before concerning yourself with the security of a host on a network, it is important to look at how secure the host is as a standalone. For much of this discussion, the Unix operating system is used as an example. The reasons for this are that Unix can represent a C2-level operating system, and that the files in question are indicative of those found on other operating systems. Finally, TCP/IP is currently running on more Unix hosts than on any other operating system (not to mention the fact that no local security exists on many other operating systems).

Viruses

Computer viruses are really operating system viruses. They are written to take advantage of the way an operating system works—and here an important distinction must be made: not *any* operating system, but rather *an* operating system. No viruses exist that can work on any computer regardless of the operating system running. The majority of known viruses are written for DOS—an incidental that makes sense given the way the operating system is written: little security, simple file allocation table, and so on. No known viruses exist in Unix, and with the exception of the Internet Worm, most of the problems inherent in Unix fall into the category of loopholes, or poor system administration.

The passwd File

When users log in to a machine, they must supply the following two things:

◆ A user name, or login id

◆ A password

The name appears while it is being typed, for it is assumed to be common knowledge. Whenever another user wants to address this user, such as with the write or mail commands, they must refer to them by their login id. The password, on the other hand, does not appear when it is typed. It is not (supposed to be) common knowledge, and should be changed on a fairly regular basis.

When both these entities are given to the operating system, it compares them with the /etc/passwd file to see if the user has successfully completed the login requirements. If user "hannah" logs in with the password "firewall," the login routine looks through the passwd file to find a matching entry. A sample of this file follows:

```
root:kjsd:0:1::/:/bin/sh
hannah:eadkad:100:9:Hannah Elaine:/usr/acct/hannah:/bin/ksh
```

```
karens::101:9:Karen Scott:/usr/acct/karend:/bin/ksh
kristind:djfkjdkfjdk:102:1:Kristin Dulaney:/usr/acct/kristind:/bin/csh
```

This is a colon-delimited file, wherein the first field represents the login id. The second field is the password of the user in an encrypted format—thus "firewall" does indeed match "eadkad" on this system. The encryption is accomplished using hashing routines that add "salt" (extra characters) to an entry before encrypting it. In so doing, it makes it virtually impossible to decipher a password entry from viewing the encrypted listing. The word "firewall" can be encrypted many different ways.

Note   Because one word can be encrypted many ways, the user can use the same password on multiple systems without this fact being readily apparent.

The third field is the *user id number* (uid) that the system uses to actually keep track of the user. The fourth field represents the *group id number* (gid), identifying what other group of users this user is associated with. The fifth field is free text that is useful only to the administrator in trying to identify the listing. The sixth field denotes the home directory of the user, whereas the last field is the shell (command interpreter) they use by default.

It is important to note that not every field need have a value. The fifth field for the root user is blank, meaning that no verbose description of the administrative user exists. More frightening, however, is the blank second field on the karens user. Without an encrypted password here, anyone can log in as karens (login ids are common knowledge), and they will not be prompted for a password. That intruder would appear to the system as karens and be able to change, delete, or modify any files owned by karens, or the group she belongs to (assuming appropriate permissions). There should never be any entry in the passwd file, on a secure system, for which an assigned, encrypted password does not exist.

The /etc/shadow File

On newer Unix systems, the /etc/passwd file contains only an "x" in the second field for every user. If this is so, it indicates that another file is used in conjunction with passwd—the /etc/shadow file. The passwd file, although not writable, must be readable by every user by the sheer nature of it. This means that every user who can successfully log into the system can view the file. To add an additional level of security, /etc/shadow holds the encrypted passwords, and is readable only by the system administrator.

The /etc/group File

The /etc/group file contains information about members of computing groups. Users can be placed in groups when they need to share information. For example, if a spreadsheet is on the system, the chief accountant may own it, but the entire accounting department may need to view it. By establishing an accounting group, this permission can be applied to all members of that group.

The fourth field of /etc/passwd contains the group number that users belong to. Looking at the earlier example, one security breach is worth noting:

```
root:kjsd:0:1::/:/bin/sh
hannah:eadkad:100:9:Hannah Elaine:/usr/acct/hannah:/bin/ksh
karens::101:9:Karen Scott:/usr/acct/karend:/bin/ksh
kristind:djfkjdkfjdk:102:1:Kristin Dulaney:/usr/acct/kristind:/bin/csh
```

The user kristind belongs to group 1. If you look at the first entry, you can see that group 1 is also the group to which root belongs. No user should belong to the same group as the system administrator/root user.

By the same token—and far more critical—it is imperative that no two users have the same user id. Take the following example:

```
root:kjsd:0:1::/:/bin/sh
hannah:eadkad:100:9:Hannah Elaine:/usr/acct/hannah:/bin/ksh
karens::0:9:Karen Scott:/usr/acct/karend:/bin/ksh
kristind:djfkjdkfjdk:102:1:Kristin Dulaney:/usr/acct/kristind:/bin/csh
```

The first thing wrong is that any user can log in as karens without having to supply a password. The second thing is that karens shares the same uid number as the root user. When a user requests an operation—such as creating files, deleting them, and so on—the system checks to see if they have the appropriate permissions to do so. It checks them with their uid number, and the file is read sequentially. Thus, even though karens is not the root user—does not have the same home directory, does not use the same shell, and so on—she essentially has all rights to the system and can do whatever she wants to without restriction. For all practical purposes, she is the root user.

Although root represents a special user, the concept holds true for any duplicated uid. The second user in the list has the permissions of the first user, even though they are not the same person.

Things to Watch For

With regard to local security, the items you should check for mainly include the /etc/passwd file. Check for the following items:

◆ Every user has a password

◆ Every user has a unique user id number

◆ Users are assigned to the appropriate groups

Other common-sense measures can also be implemented. For example, if the machine hardware you are using allows for a bootup password (contained within the CMOS), then implement that; if you can remove the keyboard from a server that no one uses as a console, then do so; and so on. It is very important to step away from the administrator's role every now and then and view your system as if you were an intruder. Ask yourself how you would get in, what the weak links are, and what you would target. Armed with that train of thought, step back into the administrator's role and look for ways to circumvent those attacks.

TCP/IP Concerns

The TCP/IP protocol represents a security risk simply because it enables remote users to access files and data on machines other than their own. Aside from that, it offers a number of features designed to make using the protocol easier for users. Unfortunately, some of these (such as the .rhost concept) open additional security loopholes. This section looks at those issues and makes recommendations that can save you grief down the road.

Host Equivalency

TCP/IP enables you to create a file on each host system, /etc/hosts.equiv, that defines a list of special hosts. Although intended to be a time-saving device, it creates something of a security risk. The purpose behind it is to enable a user from one system to log into another without requiring them to supply a password. The file says that they are equivalent on this system to the user by the same name on the originating system. A sample file on a host named scott is as follows:

```
lloyd
tim
rob
cheri
drew
matthew
```

The names listed in the file represent the names of host computers other than this one. The hosts.equiv file is telling the operating system that if user karens, who is currently logged in on the lloyd machine attempts to remotely log into this system, then let her in without requiring a password. You are trusting her because she has successfully logged in on host lloyd, and you have an equivalent user on this system.

The security risks here should be readily apparent. If an intruder can successfully break into one system, you are giving them carte blanche to visit your other hosts. The root user cannot be placed into the hosts.equiv file, but that is only of little consolation. Because karens's files are valid on one system, you are trusting that an intruder will not log in as karens on another system.

The /etc/hosts.equiv file is also saying that *every* user on the other host is a trusted user and allowed to log into this host without regard. All that must exist for a user to log in this way is an /etc/passwd entry by the same user name the user is currently using. Imagine the ramifications if this host had a user named Hanna Harrison, and she used the login id of hannah, and the lloyd host had a user named Hannah Alden, who also used a login id of hannah. Even though they are not the same person, and should not be viewing the same files, Hannah Alden has full access to all of Hanna Harrison's files.

To further hammer the point home, suppose that the host computer tim has a user rlawson. No such user exists on our example host, but rlawson, by virtue of the fact that he is coming from an equivalent host, can log in here as any user whose login id he can guess. If he knows that Hannah works on this computer and he always sends mail to her as hannah, then all he need do is issue the following command:

```
rlogin scott -l hannah
```

And once again, because he is coming from a trusted host, he is allowed on this system as hannah without ever needing to supply a password.

It is highly recommended that you not employ /etc/hosts.equiv files if security is of any concern to you.

User Equivalence

Just slightly better than trusting an entire host, is trusting individual users—a process done through .rhosts files. .rhosts files have one good thing going for them right off the bat: by beginning with a period they are "invisible" to all directory listings not using the -a option.

Multiple .rhosts files can exist, and they must reside in the home directory of the user in question. Within the file is a list of the hosts from which the user can log in without needing to supply a password. For example, look at kristind's /etc/passwd entry from earlier:

```
kristind:djfkjdkfjdk:102:1:Kristin Dulaney:/usr/acct/kristind:/bin/csh
```

The sixth field shows her home directory as /usr/acct/kristind. Going to that directory, she can create a .rhosts file with the following information:

```
lloyd
tim
rob
cheri
drew
matthew
```

Now, if she is logged into another system—the matthew host, for example—she can log into this machine without needing to give a password. A quickly visible drawback in the scheme, however, is the rlawson character previously discussed. He can still log in to this system from any of the hosts listed, using the -l option to rlogin to become kristind, and he can get in without needing to know her password.

To circumvent this scenario, a second field can be added to the .rhosts file, denoting how the user must be known on the first machine before they can log in on this system:

```
lloyd kristind
tim kristind
tim emmett
rob kdulaney
cheri kristind
drew kristind
matthew
```

Now, if a user is logging in as kristind on this host, he or she must be known by that name on hosts lloyd, cheri, or drew. If users are coming from the host rob, then they must be known as kdulaney—this is an excellent means of executing remote logins when the user id for the same person is not the same on two different machines. Coming from the host tim, two possibilities present themselves. First, kristind can remotely log in on this system without the need for giving a valid password, and if emmett is trying to come over to this system as her with the following:

```
rlogin scott -l kristind
```

then he is allowed to do so. In other words, he is emmett where he was, he is now kristind here, and will be emmett once more when he exits this host. This procedure provides a means of allowing a support person to access the system when necessary. From the last host listed, matthew, any user can login as kristind without needing to provide a password.

Drawbacks to .rhosts are numerous. The first is if the second field is not used—as with the matthew host in the previous example—and left blank, any user from any host can come over to this system as that user. The second drawback is if multiple users have the same login id on different hosts. The third is that a .rhosts file can exist in the root (/) directory—giving root authority to any user who logs in with the following:

```
rlogin scott -l root
```

Additional Security Steps

You can take a number of security steps above and beyond those required. The more you implement, the more secure you can feel your data is. The more you implement, however—rest assured—the more your users will complain. A painless security does not exist, and all require additional steps that can be viewed as inconveniences by your clientele. You must assess risks and weigh for yourself how much security you consider to be sufficient for your implementation.

Utilize Subnets

Using subnets, you can divide your large network into smaller portions and assign a system administrator to each portion. When viewing the network as a whole (depending upon the size of the system), it can often appear overwhelming; and security is only one aspect for which this holds true. When broken into manageable components, however, each task is smaller and more controllable.

Taken as a whole, the concept of security can never be implemented by one person. Broken into subnets, though, each administrator is responsible for a limited number of local users and hosts, and security stands a better chance of being properly implemented.

Dialup Passwords

If your host is connected to the outside world through modems, consider adding another password before allowing access to the operating system. *Dialup passwords* (implemented with the dpasswd utility) are encrypted the same as other passwords, but reside in a separate file. Additionally, they can be assigned to specific ports, and only used if a user attempts to log in with a given id.

During the login process, the user who is calling in and not connected directly gives his or her login id, followed by a password, and then the dialup password that is the same for everyone on the host. If all three are correct, the user is allowed in. If any of the three are incorrect, the user is asked to log in again; he or she has no indication of which item was incorrect, making it more difficult for intruders to gain access. Because the intruders you are concerned about are not sitting at the terminal most of the time, dialup passwords make great sense.

/etc/dpasswd is the executable file used to manage dialups, and the options that can be used include the following (at least one is required each time you use it):

◆ **a {list}.** The list of terminals given is added to /etc/dialups; thus, when a user logs in from one of the terminals and has a shell defined in /etc/d_passwd, the user has to give the dialup password. Entries in the list have to be separated by spaces or commas and enclosed in quotes.

◆ **d {list}.** The given list of terminals is removed from /etc/dialups. This eliminates the need for the user to supply a dialup password when logging in.

◆ **r {list}.** This option changes the login shell to /bin/sh for every user listed in the list.

◆ **s {shell}.** This option updates an entry in the /etc/d_passwd file or adds a new one.

◆ **u {list}.** This option causes a new shell to be created for the names in the list. The list of user names must be separated by spaces and enclosed in quotation marks. Entries are made in the /etc/d_passwd file for the shell, and the password works for all users unless otherwise specified.

◆ **x {shell}.** This option removes the shell and its password from the /etc/d_passwd file.

The file created in all instances (regardless of which option you use) is /etc/dialups. It is nothing more than an ASCII file with each terminal line entry contained on a single line. When a user logs in on one of the listed devices and the user's shell matches an entry in the /etc/d_passwd file, the user is prompted for a dialup password before being allowed to complete the login.

The following example creates a dialup password on device ttya for those using the standard shell:

```
# dpasswd -a ttya
#
# dpasswd -s /bin/sh
New password:    {4Rinfo}
Re-enter new password:    {4Rinfo}
#
```

Now, when a user attempts to login from /dev/ttya, the routine becomes the following:

```
login: jenna
Password:  <------ the password for user jenna must be satisfied
Dialup Password: <----- password for ttya device
```

The dialup password is active only for that device. If the user attempts to log in from a different device, the second password is not asked for. If a user fails the user password, he or she must try again. The dialup password is asked for only after all else has been satisfied.

The two new files created by this utility are in the /etc directory, as shown by the following:

```
# cd /etc
#

# ls -l d_passwd dialups
-r--r--r--  1 root     rootgrp      23 Feb  7  1992 d_passwd
-r--r--r--  1 root     rootgrp      10 Feb  7  1992 dialups
#

# file d_passwd dialups
d_passwd:      ascii text
dialups:       ascii text
#
# cat dialups
/dev/ttya
#

# cat d_passwd
/bin/sh:sWdYehOXZSGb.:
```

/bin/sh is the name of the shell that must be associated with the user, whereas *sWdYehOXZSGb.* represents the encrypted password.

If your system supports dialup passwords, it is strongly suggested that you use them. This is particularly important on modem connections where hackers can play with less detection. It provides one more firewall toward keeping them out.

Password Aging

Users should not be able to use the same password for their entire life. The more frequently you change passwords, the more frequently you thwart those who may be trying to guess one and become an intruder. Theoretically, you could change passwords every day, but that would start a mutiny among users.

A good recommendation is to change passwords every 30 to 60 days, coupled with the requirement that users use unique passwords for eight times. Be sure you stress to your users the importance of using good passwords, and keeping them to themselves (not scribbling them on post-it notes attached to the monitor).

As an administrator, you should take great pains to disable the accounts of inactive users. These represent open doors for anyone wanting to hack into a system. When a user leaves the organization, remove his or her entry from /etc/passwd, or disable it. The easiest manner in which to disable it is to place a "z" as the only entry in the second field of the listing. Should the user return to the company, you can then remove the "z" and use the passwd command to give them a new password.

Use Firewalls

When apartment complexes are built, brick walls are constructed between townhouses. If a fire occurs at the complex, the walls keep the fire from spreading to adjoining townhouses—hence these walls are called *firewalls*.

When you connect your host to the outside world, you can get much information that you otherwise could not get. Unfortunately, you also leave a means by which the outside world can get into your system and access things they maybe should not. A computer firewall is a router through which your outgoing requests are transmitted, and through which incoming requests are filtered. In other words, you are allowing intruders to break into your router and not into your system—putting a firewall between you and the outside world.

A firewall router is fairly common for many sites connected to the Internet. An existing router can be converted to perform such functions if it can support the more complex filtering configuration. If it cannot, you can choose to build your own from scratch or turn to third-party solutions. One such example is the FireWall-1 product from CheckPoint Software Technologies Ltd.

In September 1994, SunSoft Inc., a division of Sun Microsystems Inc. announced the addition of the FireWall-1 product to their Internet Product Family of products. Coupling FireWall-1 with SunSoft's Internet Gateway software, you can easily turn a Solaris server into a very secure Internet server solution that provides full Internet access for your users, while preventing unauthorized access to and from your networks.

This book does not have the size or scope to detail the method by which you can build your own firewall, but it is highly recommended you read *Internet Firewalls and Computer Security* (New Riders Publishing).

Other Security Options

If you are using a bridge in your network, investigate its filtering capabilities. With some bridges, for example, you can configure a hardware address filter table. Depending on the vendor, the address filter can be applied to either incoming or outgoing addresses. Under this configuration, all frames matching the addresses listed in the filter table are discarded by the bridge. However, this is somewhat labor-intensive to maintain.

For example, if you want to ensure that no one outside of this segment can access one of your servers, put its hardware address in the filtering table. However, if you change the network card in the server, you need to update the filter table.

If you want to limit certain workstations from accessing resources outside their local segments, you can put their hardware addresses in the filter table. Again, if the hardware is changed, remember to update the filter table.

Some more advanced bridges can filter frames by protocols (very much like a router in this sense). All frames carrying that particular protocol are blocked by the bridge. This is one way of localizing certain protocols to a segment, which is a cheaper alternative than using a router.

If you are using routers, you can selectively block protocols or only certain protocols within a protocol suite. For example, if you do not want any RIP traffic on your TCP/IP network, you can block that using the router, and let the rest of the TCP/IP traffic through.

In some cases, for security reasons, you may only allow e-mail to come into your network, but not other TCP/IP services such as FTP (File Transfer Protocol) or Telnet (Terminal Emulation). Using routers, you can selectively filter out those kinds of traffic. You can even set up the filter table such that FTP and Telnet traffic can *go out* of the network, but not come in. You have thus allowed your users to access outside resources, but at the same time shielded yours from others, which effectively turns your router into a firewall (discussed in the preceding section).

Data Encryption

One possibility that should never be overlooked is the encryption and deencryption of data before it is sent over the network. In Sweden, all data communications must be encrypted (per government edict), and a thriving market in encryption modems exists. The United States would do well to consider similar measures.

Numerous utilities are available that enable you to encrypt messages. Within standard Unix, the crypt command enables you to apply to file contents the same hashing routine that you use to encrypt passwords. When received at the other side, they can be unencrypted for viewing.

File encryption and e-mail can be combined into a lethal combination using the following three commands:

- ◆ enroll
- ◆ xsend
- ◆ xget

enroll is used to add a user to the secure mail system. After entering the command, you are required to supply a *key*. The key is a character that is used to determine your encryption/decryption—for example, the letter "a."

You can use xsend in place of regular mail or mailx to send a message, if you want to secure it. This places the utility into input mode, and all other operations are identical to the way they work with the other mail routines. Secured mail can only be sent to one user, however, and you cannot specify more than one name on the command line.

When you login, the message you have mail appears. When you then attempt to view your mail, you are informed that an encrypted message has been sent and the user who sent it (as well as date and time). To read the message, you must use xget.

xget prompts you for the key, and you must enter the same key as was entered during the enroll. If you give the proper key, the message is displayed, and the same options are available as for reading any mail message. If you give the wrong key, the message is still displayed, but it is all control characters and totally unreadable.

NFS provides a security risk just by the definition of its operation. To compensate for this, you can increase its security slightly by invoking the "secure" option.

Encryption is involved and a public key is assigned to the file system mounted securely. A *public key* is a piece of common knowledge—such as the time—that is encrypted. The client encrypts the public key and sends it to the server with every request. The server decrypts it and compares the value to what it believes it should be. If they match, transactions continue to take place. If they do not match, the client is not allowed access to the host file system.

The root user can create keys to be used in the encryption with the newkey command, or regular users can create keys using the chkey command. When you attempt to remotely log in to the system, the keylogin utility is used to verify the encryption. After you are in, any commands you give are unencrypted by keyserv until you issue a keylogout command.

Log Files

One of the most important things you can do is monitor the transactions that take place in your log files. No one should ever implement auditing on a system just to watch log files grow and their hard drives shrink. Entries are written to log files for a reason, and it is important to monitor them.

The last command shows the contents of /etc/wtmp. This file contains information about who logged in as well as the time, when they logged out, and the total amount of time they were on the system. If you suspect someone is using your system on off-hours, this should be one of the first places to check.

Commands can be placed into queues and executed at later times with the cron and at commands. Each of these commands writes to a cron log file, detailing the name of the person requesting the job, the job, and the time executed. A cursory glance through this file on a regular basis can be of great benefit, as can a glance to see what jobs are currently spooled up to execute at dates in the future. You must have root permissions and a good knowledge of Unix to examine these files. *Inside UNIX* (New Riders Publishing) provides you with the knowledge you need to examine these files.

One file that should NEVER be overlooked is sulog. Any user can become any other user with the su command, providing that they know the password of the user they want to become. The sulog file records each time a user does this. Not only that, but it also reports every unsuccessful attempt. Keep a very close eye on this file because it can provide you with information about users trying to crack passwords far sooner than they are able to do so.

Glossary

anchor a hypertext link in the form of text or a graphic that, when clicked upon, takes you to the linked file

annotation a Mosaic feature that enables you to add a comment to a viewed document

anonymous FTP enables you to download (and sometimes upload) files without needing to use a password

Archie a search engine that finds filenames on anonymous FTP services

ARPAnet the first network of computers funded by the US Department of Defense Advanced Projects Agency

au extension for audio files

backbone generally very high-speed, T3 telephone lines that connect remote ends of networks and networks to one another; only service providers are connected to the Internet in this way

browser a graphical software interface that enables you to look at information on the WWW

CERN home of WWW

checksumming   a service performed by UDP that checks to see if packets were changed during transmission

client   an application that makes a request of a service on a (sometimes) remote computer; the request can be, for example, a function call

database   an organization of data into one or more tables of related data that is used to answer questions

dialup   a connection to the Internet through a modem and telephone line that allows (only) e-mail and running processes on a remote computer

direct connection   a connection to the Internet through a dedicated line, such as ISDN

Directory of Servers   a service that describes what is available on servers throughout the world

Doc-ID   in WAIS, an ID that identifies a specific document in a database

Eudora   the most widely used e-mail system

FAQ   acronym for Frequently Asked Question; often a question and answer approach to common problems

FTP   acronym for File Transfer Protocol; a popular mechanism for transferring files over the Internet

gif   an image format (Graphics Interchange Format)

gopher   provides menu descriptions of files on Internet servers; used primarily to find Internet information

Gopherspace   connected Gopher services

home page   a document that serves as the entryway for all the information contained in a company's WWW service

host   a server connected to the Internet

HTML   acronym for Hypertext Markup Language; the protocol used to define various text styles in a hypertext document, including emphasis and bulleted lists

html   the extension for HTML files

HTTP   acronym for Hypertext Transfer Protocol; the protocol used by WWW services

hypertext   a highlighted word that, when clicked on, opens another document

index files files created by waisindex that make up the WAIS source database

ISDN a dedicated telephone line connection that transmits digital data at the rate of 56 Kbps

JPEG a compression standard (Joint Photographic Expert Group)

leased connection a connection to the Internet through a local phone company that allows your company to set up, for example, FTP, WWW, and Gopher services on the Internet at a permanent address

local area network (LAN) a group of computers linked by hardware and protocols such as Ethernet or Token-Ring

login the process of entering your user ID and password at a prompt to gain access to a service

MIME a protocol that describes the format of Internet messages (Multipurpose Internet Mail Extension)

Mosaic a graphical interface for the World Wide Web that employs hypertext, images, video clips, and sound

news reader enables you to read about one of the thousands of special interest groups on the Internet

proxy a connection through a modem and telephone line to the Internet that enables you to use full-screen programs, such as Mosaic and Netscape, to browse the Internet

relevance feedback in WAIS, a score, between 0 and 1,000, that represents how closely a document satisfies search criteria

server a computer that runs services

service an application that processes requests by client applications, for example, storing data, or executing an algorithm

SGML acronym for Standard Generalized Markup Language; a language that describes the structure of a document

source in WAIS, describes a database and how to reach it

T1 a dedicated telephone line connection that transfers data at the rate of 1.4 Mbps

T3 a dedicated telephone line that transfers data at the rate of 45 Mbps

tags   annotations used by HTML, such as <H2>, </H2>

TCP/IP   acronym for Transmission Control Protocol/Internet Protocol; a communications protocol that allows computers of any make to communicate when running TCP/IP software

telenet   enables you to log on to a computer over telephone lines (not through an Internet service provider)

tiff   a graphics format (Tag Image File Format)

URL   acronym for Universal Resource Location; a means of specifying the location of information on the Internet for WWW clients

Usenet   an online news and bulletin board system accommodating over 7,000 interest groups

Veronica   a tool that helps you find files on Gopher servers

viewer applications   software that gives you access to the images, video, and sounds stored on Internet servers

WAIS   acronym for Wide Area Information Server; a tool that helps you search for documents using keywords or selections of text as search criteria

WAIS client   an application that formats user-defined search criteria to be used by waisserver; the goal is to find matches between search criteria and data files (of all types)

WAIS sources   databases created by waisindex that include, for example, a table of all unique words contained in a document

waisindex   a mechanism that extracts data from raw data files (of most types) to put into databases, called WAIS sources, which allow waisserver to match search criteria to data files quickly

waisserver   a mechanism that compares search criteria, supplied by a WAIS client, to WAIS sources

Web   short for World Wide Web (WWW)

wide area networks (WAN)   connecting computers over long distances using high-speed dedicated telephone lines or microwave transmissions

World Wide Web (WWW)   a hypertext-based, multimedia system that enables you to browse and access information on the Internet

xbm   a graphics format (X bitmapped)

Index

V

variables
environment, gateway scripts, 206-208
library variables (freeWAIS), 281
SERVERPORT, 337
WU version (ftp), 241-243
verification, passwords formats, 260
Veronica, 313, 442
viewers, 442
viewext (Gopher), 328
definitions, 329-330
viewing bookmarks, 403
VINES, 53
virtual circuits, 29
viruses, 426

W

WAIS (Wide Area Information Server), 442
accessing with WWW browsers, 212-214
clients, 442
Gopher, 340-341
history of, 273-274
linking Gopher to, 362
reasons for creating, 273
relevance feedback, 441
sources, 441-442
Thinking Machines, 369
WAIS source, 296
wais-sources directory, 279
wais-test directory, 279
WAIS-to-WWW gateways, 213
waisindex, 296-298, 442
command-line options, 296-297
data file types, 302-304

data files
indexing multiple files, 305
searching with WWW browsers, 305-308
excluding files from index, 308
index files, 298-305
Dictionary, 299
Document, 298-299
Filename, 299
Headline, 299
Inverted, 298
Source Description, 299-300
Status, 300
searches
relevance ranking, 300-301
synonyms, 306
sending messages to log files, 308
source files, 306-308
stopwords, 301
see also freeWAIS
waisserver, 442
clients, restricting by domain, 293-294
logging levels, 298
user IDs, changing, 292
WAN (wide area network), 32, 442
What's Cool? menu (Netscape), 410
What's New? menu (Netscape), 410
wide area network, *see* WAN
wild cards
access restrictions, 258
freeWAIS searches, 283
windows
Mosaic
customizing, 389
placement, 390
Netscape, 398-401
titles, 399

X

Check Us Out Online!

CNE Endeavor

New Riders has emerged as a premier publisher of computer books for the professional computer user. Focusing on CAD/graphics/multimedia, communications/internetworking, and networking/operating systems, New Riders continues to provide expert advice on high-end topics and software.

Check out the online version of *New Riders' Official World Wide Web Yellow Pages, 1996 Edition* for the most engaging, entertaining, and informative sites on the Web! You can even add your own site!

*Hind Fire
Copyright 1995 - John Brooks*

Brave our site for the finest collection of CAD and 3D imagery produced today. Professionals from all over the world contribute to our gallery, which features new designs every month.

From Novell to Microsoft, New Riders publishes the training guides you need to attain your certification. Visit our site and try your hand at the CNE Endeavor, a test engine created by VFX Technologies, Inc. that enables you to measure what you know—and what you don't!

SEARCH THE BOOKSTORE

http://www.mcp.com/newriders

WANT MORE INFORMATION?

CHECK OUT THESE RELATED TOPICS OR SEE YOUR LOCAL BOOKSTORE

CAD and 3D Studio

As the number one CAD publisher in the world, and as a Registered Publisher of Autodesk, New Riders Publishing provides unequaled content on this complex topic. Industry-leading products include AutoCAD and 3D Studio.

Networking

As the leading Novell NetWare publisher, New Riders Publishing delivers cutting-edge products for network professionals. We publish books for all levels of users, from those wanting to gain NetWare Certification, to those administering or installing a network. Leading books in this category include *Inside NetWare 3.12*, *CNE Training Guide: Managing NetWare Systems*, *Inside TCP/IP*, and *NetWare: The Professional Reference*.

Graphics

New Riders provides readers with the most comprehensive product tutorials and references available for the graphics market. Best-sellers include *Inside CorelDRAW! 5*, *Inside Photoshop 3*, and *Adobe Photoshop NOW!*

Internet and Communications

As one of the fastest growing publishers in the communications market, New Riders provides unparalleled information and detail on this ever-changing topic area. We publish international best-sellers such as *New Riders' Official Internet Yellow Pages, 2nd Edition*, a directory of over 10,000 listings of Internet sites and resources from around the world, and *Riding the Internet Highway, Deluxe Edition*.

Operating Systems

Expanding off our expertise in technical markets, and driven by the needs of the computing and business professional, New Riders offers comprehensive references for experienced and advanced users of today's most popular operating systems, including *Understanding Windows 95*, *Inside Unix*, *Inside Windows 3.11 Platinum Edition*, *Inside OS/2 Warp Version 3*, and *Inside MS-DOS 6.22*.

Other Markets

Professionals looking to increase productivity and maximize the potential of their software and hardware should spend time discovering our line of products for Word, Excel, and Lotus 1-2-3. These titles include *Inside Word 6 for Windows*, *Inside Excel 5 for Windows*, *Inside 1-2-3 Release 5*, and *Inside WordPerfect for Windows*.

New Riders Publishing   201 West 103rd Street ◆ Indianapolis, Indiana 46290 USA

REGISTRATION CARD

Intranet Working

Name _____ Title _____

Company _____ Type of business _____

Address _____

City/State/ZIP _____

Have you used these types of books before? ☐ yes ☐ no

If yes, which ones? _____

_____

How many computer books do you purchase each year? ☐ 1–5 ☐ 6 or more

How did you learn about this book? _____

Where did you purchase this book? _____

Which applications do you currently use? _____

_____

Which computer magazines do you subscribe to? _____

_____

What trade shows do you attend? _____

_____

Comments: _____

_____

_____

Would you like to be placed on our preferred mailing list? ☐ yes ☐ no

☐ **I would like to see my name in print!** You may use my name and quote me in future New Riders products and promotions. My daytime phone number is: _____

New Riders Publishing 201 West 103rd Street ◆ Indianapolis, Indiana 46290 USA

Fax to 317-581-4670

Fold Here

- -